D1054996

Fodor's

PHILADELPHIA & THE PENNSYLVANIA DUTCH COUNTRY

16th Edition

Where to Stay and Eat
for All Budgets

Must-See Sights
and Local Secrets

Ratings You Can Trust

Fodor's Travel Publications   New York, Toronto, London, Sydney, Auckland
www.fodors.com

FODOR'S PHILADELPHIA & THE PENNSYLVANIA DUTCH COUNTRY
Editor: Salwa C. Jabado

Writers: Robert DiGiacomo, Andrea Lehman, Piers Marchant, Josh McIlvain, Caroline Tiger, Bernard Vaughan

Production Editor: Astrid deRidder
Maps & Illustrations: David Lindroth, *cartographer;* Bob Blake, Rebecca Baer, *map editors;* William Wu, *information graphics*
Design: Fabrizio La Rocca, *creative director;* Guido Caroti, Siobhan O'Hare, *art directors;* Tina Malaney, Chie Ushio, Ann McBride, Jessica Walsh, *designers;* Melanie Marin, *senior picture editor*
Cover Photo: Independence Hall, Philadelphia: Kord.com/age fotostock
Production Manager: Amanda Bullock

SPECIAL SALES

This book is available at special discounts for bulk purchases for sales promotions or premiums. Special editions, including personalized covers, excerpts of existing books, and corporate imprints, can be created in large quantities for special needs. For more information, write to Special Markets/Premium Sales, 1745 Broadway, MD 6-2, New York, New York 10019, or e-mail specialmarkets@randomhouse.com.

AN IMPORTANT TIP & AN INVITATION

Although all prices, opening times, and other details in this book are based on information supplied to us at press time, changes occur all the time in the travel world, and Fodor's cannot accept responsibility for facts that become outdated or for inadvertent errors or omissions. So **always confirm information when it matters,** especially if you're making a detour to visit a specific place. Your experiences—positive and negative—matter to us. If we have missed or misstated something, **please write to us.** We follow up on all suggestions. Contact the Philadelphia & the Pennsylvania Dutch Country editor at editors@fodors.com or c/o Fodor's at 1745 Broadway, New York, NY 10019.

PRINTED IN THE UNITED STATES OF AMERICA

10 9 8 7 6 5 4 3 2 1

Be a Fodor's Correspondent

Your opinion matters. It matters to us. It matters to your fellow Fodor's travelers, too. And we'd like to hear it. In fact, we need to hear it.

When you share your experiences and opinions, you become an active member of the Fodor's community. That means we'll not only use your feedback to make our books better, but we'll publish your names and comments whenever possible. Throughout our guides, look for "Word of Mouth," excerpts of your unvarnished feedback.

Here's how you can help improve Fodor's for all of us.

Tell us when we're right. We rely on local writers to give you an insider's perspective. But our writers and staff editors—who are the best in the business—depend on you. Your positive feedback is a vote to renew our recommendations for the next edition.

Tell us when we're wrong. We're proud that we update most of our guides every year. But we're not perfect. Things change. Hotels cut services. Museums change hours. Charming cafés lose charm. If our writer didn't quite capture the essence of a place, tell us how you'd do it differently. If any of our descriptions are inaccurate or inadequate, we'll incorporate your changes in the next edition and will correct factual errors at fodors.com immediately.

Tell us what to include. You probably have had fantastic travel experiences that aren't yet in Fodor's. Why not share them with a community of like-minded travelers? Maybe you chanced upon a beach or bistro or B&B that you don't want to keep to yourself. Tell us why we should include it. And share your discoveries and experiences with everyone directly at fodors.com. Your input may lead us to add a new listing or highlight a place we cover with a "Highly Recommended" star or with our highest rating, "Fodor's Choice."

Give us your opinion instantly at our feedback center at www.fodors.com/feedback. You may also e-mail editors@fodors.com with the subject line "Philadelphia & the Pennsylvania Dutch Country Editor." Or send your nominations, comments, and complaints by mail to Philadelphia & the Pennsylvania Dutch Country Editor, Fodor's, 1745 Broadway, New York, NY 10019.

You and travelers like you are the heart of the Fodor's community. Make our community richer by sharing your experiences. Be a Fodor's correspondent.

Happy Traveling!

Tim Jarrell, Publisher

CONTENTS

CENTRAL 3rd FL

MAPS

ABOUT THIS BOOK

Our Ratings

Sometimes you find terrific travel experiences and sometimes they just find you. But usually the burden is on you to select the right combination of experiences. That's where our ratings come in.

As travelers we've all discovered a place so wonderful that its worthiness is obvious. And sometimes that place is so experiential that superlatives don't do it justice: you just have to be there to know. These sights, properties, and experiences get our highest rating, **Fodor's Choice,** indicated by orange stars throughout this book.

Black stars highlight sights and properties we deem **Highly Recommended,** places that our writers, editors, and readers praise again and again for consistency and excellence.

By default, there's another category: any place we include in this book is by definition worth your time, unless we say otherwise. And we will.

Disagree with any of our choices? Care to nominate a place or suggest that we rate one more highly? Visit our feedback center at www. fodors.com/feedback.

Budget Well

Hotel and restaurant price categories from ¢ to $$$$ are defined in the opening pages of each chapter. For attractions, we always give standard adult admission fees; reductions are usually available for children, students, and senior citizens. Want to pay with plastic? **AE, D, DC, MC, V** following restaurant and hotel listings indicate whether American Express, Discover, Diners Club, MasterCard, and Visa are accepted.

Restaurants

Unless we state otherwise, restaurants are open for lunch and dinner daily. We mention dress only when there's a specific requirement and reservations only when they're essential or not accepted—it's always best to book ahead.

Hotels

Hotels have private bath, phone, TV, and air-conditioning and operate on the European Plan (aka EP, meaning without meals), unless we specify that they use the Continental Plan (CP, with a continental breakfast), Breakfast Plan (BP, with a full breakfast), or Modified American Plan (MAP, with breakfast and dinner), or are all-inclusive (AI, including all meals and most activities).

We always list facilities but not whether you'll be charged an extra fee to use them, so when pricing accommodations, find out what's included.

Many Listings
★ Fodor's Choice
★ Highly recommended
⊠ Physical address
✛ Directions or Map coordinates
⬡ Mailing address
☎ Telephone
🖷 Fax
⊕ On the Web
✐ E-mail
🎟 Admission fee
☉ Open/closed times
Ⓜ Metro stations
⊟ Credit cards

Hotels & Restaurants
🏨 Hotel
🛏 Number of rooms
⚲ Facilities
†○† Meal plans
✗ Restaurant
⚲ Reservations
🏛 Dress code
⚲ Smoking
🍷 BYOB

Outdoors
🏌 Golf
⛺ Camping

Other
☺ Family-friendly
⇨ See also
⊠ Branch address
☞ Take note

Experience Philadelphia

WHAT'S WHERE

1 Historic Area and Old City. As the birthplace of the country, "America's most historic square mile" was the setting for the nation's march to independence. *Everything* here is a highlight, most notably Independence Hall and the Liberty Bell. Old City, north of the Historic Area, is associated with three historic monuments: the Betsy Ross House, Christ Church, and Elfreth's Alley.

2 Society Hill and Penn's Landing. Well-preserved Society Hill, south of the Historic Area, represents Philadelphia as it has been for more than 200 years, with cobblestone streets and hidden courtyards. Once home to sailing ships, Penn's Landing along the Delaware River has become a 37-acre riverside park.

3 Queen Village, Bella Vista, and South Philadelphia. The revitalized Queen Village contains some of the most charming streets in the city. South Philadelphia gave the world Rocky Balboa and the five-block Italian Market. Bella Vista, the residential nabe around the market, is more hipsters and yuppies than old Italian families.

4 Center City. Philadelphia has many pasts, but if you're interested in its present and future, head for Center City.

This is Philly's business district, anchored by skyscrapers and City Hall. The Pennsylvania Academy of Fine Arts and Reading Terminal are also here.

5 Rittenhouse Square. The prettiest of Philadelphia's public squares, Rittenhouse is the heart of upper-crust Philly. Many treasures are found here, including the Curtis Institute of Music and the Rosenbach Museum and Library.

6 Benjamin Franklin Parkway. From City Hall the parkway stretches northwest to a Greco-Roman temple on a hill—the Philadelphia Museum of Art. Along the way are many of the city's finest cultural institutions: the Academy of Natural Sciences, the Franklin Institute, and the Rodin Museum.

7 Fairmount Park. The largest landscaped city park in the world at 8,500 acres, Fairmount beckons with a wide range of pleasure. You can jog, walk, bike, or row, as well as visit the Please Touch Museum and the Philadelphia Zoo.

8 University City. Two of Philadelphia's larger institutions, the University of Pennsylvania and Drexel University, are in an area dubbed University City in

GERMANTOWN
AND CHESTNUT HILL [10] ↑ TO
TEMPLE UNIVERSITY

Ridge Ave.
yard St.

Poplar St.

NORTHERN
LIBERTIES

Wildey St.

Ⓜ FAIRMOUNT

North St.

Fairmount Ave.

Brown St.

95

Wallace St.

SPRING GARDEN
Ⓜ

SPRING GARDEN
Garden St.

Clay St.

Green St.

Spring Garden St.

Buttonwood St.

Ⓜ CHINATOWN

Buttonwood St.

Willow St.

Callowhill St.

Ridge Ave.

Callowhill St.

Ⓜ RACE-VINE

Ben
Franklin
Br.

Vine St.

Vine St.

30

30 676

Race St.

CHINATOWN

Franklin
Square

Delaware River

demy
Natural
nces

PARKWAY

Pennsylvania
Convention Center
and Reading
Terminal Market

Race St.

OLD CITY

Suburban JFK
Station Plaza

U.S. Mint

Arch St.

ket-Frankford Subway

Market East
Station
Filbert St.

Independence
National
Historical Park

[1] PENN'S
LANDING

19TH
dlow St.

Ⓜ
15TH AND
MARKET

Ⓜ City Hall
Ⓜ
13TH 11TH

Ⓜ
8TH AND
MARKET

Ⓜ
MARKET ST.

HISTORIC AREA

PENN'S
LANDING

nut St.
n St.

CENTER CITY

CITY HALL

Chestnut St.
Sansom St.

Independence
Hall
Independence
Square

Ferry
Dock

Walnut St.

[4]

Walnut St.

Locust St.

[2]

nhouse
quare

Ⓜ
Locust St. WALNUT-LOCUST

Locust St.

Washington
Square

Spruce St.

Spruce St.

TO →
CAMDEN, NJ

Pine St.

LOMBARD-SOUTH Ⓜ

Lombard St.

Bainbridge St.

South St.

95

Bainbridge St.

Fitzwater St.

SOUTH PHILADELPHIA
AND QUEEN VILLAGE

TO
WALT WHITMAN
BRIDGE
↓

Webster St.

Catharine St.

Fitzwater St.

Christian St.

[3]

Catharine St.
Queen St.

Carpenter St.

Washington Ave.

TO
SPORTS
STADIUMS
↓

Wharton St.

Rte. 611

inson St.

Dickinson St.

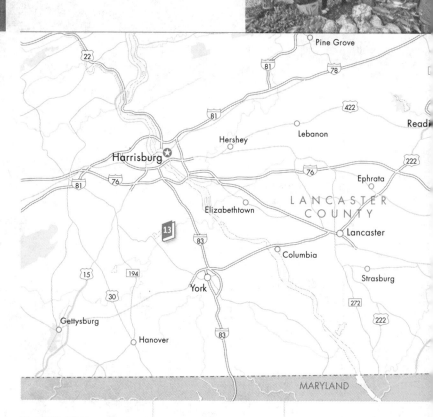

West Philadelphia. Take Locust Walk to explore U Penn's Ivy League campus. Here, too, is the University Museum, containing one of the world's finest archaeology and anthropology collections.

9 Manayunk. This old mill town, wedged between the Schuylkill River and some very steep hills 7 mi northwest of Center City, was once crucial to Philadelphia's industrial fortune. Today it's bringing in dollars with its restaurants and boutiques.

10 Germantown and Chestnut Hill. Germantown, 6 mi north of Center City, was once where affluent Philadelphians built grand country homes to escape the city's summer heat. They didn't escape the British, however, who occupied the town during the Battle of Germantown. Today Germantown has several historic houses open for tours. Germantown Avenue culminates in charming Chestnut Hill.

11 Brandywine Valley and Valley Forge. Brandywine Valley is Andrew Wyeth Country, with stone or clapboard farmhouses, forests, and meadows that were often the subject of paintings by the Pennsylvania artist. Its heart, Chadds Ford, is near the splendid homes and estates of the du Ponts: Winterthur,

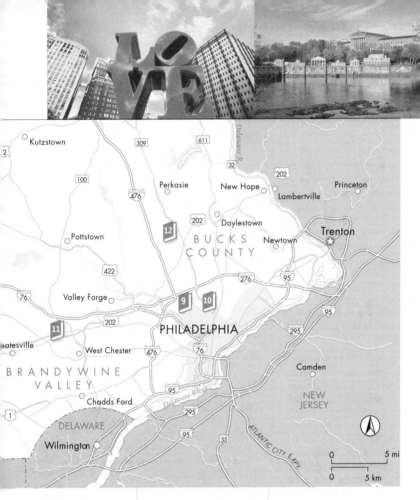

Nemours, and Longwood Gardens. Nearby, the Valley Forge area offers contrasting sites: George Washington's heroic 1777–78 encampment and the massive King of Prussia Mall.

12 Bucks County. Long a vacation spot for New Yorkers and Philadelphians, Bucks County is a daytripper's delight. New Hope and Lahaska offer delightful shopping and antiquing; Doylestown has Fonthill Museum; and the Delaware Canal towpath runs through countryside that conjures up England's Cotswolds.

13 Lancaster County, Hershey, and Gettysburg. Around the hub of Lancaster, about an hour away, you can tour farmers' markets and replicas of Amish villages, or twist your own pretzel at the oldest pretzel bakery in the country. Take the kids west to Hershey for chocolate-themed fun.

About 55 mi from Lancaster is Gettysburg, where the greatest artillery battle on this continent was fought in July 1863—and later immortalized through the words of Lincoln's Gettysburg Address.

PHILADELPHIA PLANNER

Our Streets

If you ever feel lost, you can calibrate yourself by gauging where you stand in comparison to the two main thoroughfares that intersect at the city's center: Broad (or 14th) Street (the city's spinal column, which runs north–south), and Market Street (which runs east–west). Where Broad and Market meet, neatly dividing the city center into four segments, you'll find City Hall, Philadelphia's center of gravity.

Within Center City, the numbered streets start on the eastern side, from the Delaware River beginning with Front Street (consider it "1st Street") all the way west to 25th Street on the banks of the Schuylkill (pronounced "SKOO-kull") River. In between Market street to the north and Lombard street to the south, most of the east–west streets have tree names (from north to south, Chestnut, Walnut, Locust, Spruce, and Pine).

Center City has four roughly equal-size city squares, one in each quadrangle. In the northwest quadrangle there's Logan Square; in the southwest is Rittenhouse; in the northeast there's Franklin Square; and in the southeast is Washington Square. Running along the banks of the Delaware River is Columbus Boulevard/Delaware Avenue.

Getting Around Center City and the Historic Area

CAR TRAVEL

Laid out in a grid pattern by its founder William Penn, you would think that Center City would be relatively easy to navigate by car. Despite its regularity, many streets are one-way, and the main thoroughfares are often congested with traffic. Furthermore, parking can be tough. A spot at a parking meter, if you're lucky enough to find one, costs $1 to $2 per hour. Parking garages are plentiful but can charge up to $1.50 per 15 minutes and up to $20 or more per day. Police officers are vigilant about ticketing. Your best bet is to walk and to supplement walking with public transportation and taxis as needed.

PUBLIC TRANSPORTATION

Philadelphia's **SEPTA buses** provide good coverage of Old City and the Historic Area, Center City, and farther west to University City. A bus ride costs $2 in cash with exact change. Find fares, maps, and schedules at the Independence Visitor Center and online at ⊕ *www.septa.org*. From May through October, purple **Phlash trolleys** follow a Center City route to 27 downtown sights; you can buy a hop-on, hop-off all-day pass for $5 (or $10 for a family) at the Independence Visitor Center or when you board the trolley.

The **SEPTA subway** trains come regularly, but the underground stations are rather dank, and the two lines are limited. One runs east–west along Market Street, the other north–South along Broad Street, and stations are few and far between.

TAXI TRAVEL

If you're tired of pounding the pavement, taxis are plentiful in Center City, especially along Broad, Market, Walnut, and Chestnut streets and near any major hotels and train stations. They're hailed streetside. Fares rise according to distance—$2.70 plus 23¢ for each one-tenth of a mile—and you can now pay using credit cards. The standard tip for cabdrivers is about 15% of the fare.

Philadelphia Online Resources

ARTS AND ENTERTAINMENT

Uwishunu blog (⊕ *www.uwishunu.com*) is an edgier extension of the more comprehensive **Go Phila** (⊕ *www.gophila.com*) visitor site. Uwishunu bills itself as a guide to seeing Philly like a local. Written by a diverse cast of locals with different interests, it lives up to its local point of view. Go Phila is a comprehensive guide to events throughout the year; it also includes new entries in Philly dining, attractions, and shopping.

For events listings and more local blogging, visit **Philadelphia Magazine's** Web site (⊕ *www.phillymag.com*), where staffers hold forth on everything from street style to restaurants to shopping. The **City Paper** (⊕ *www.citypaper.net*) has an arts and entertainment blog as well as updated movie, music, and arts listings each week.

FOOD

Like any city with a vibrant restaurant scene, Philly has its share of food blogs. Well, Philly might actually have more than its fair share, which just shows you how important food is to Philadelphians. **Foobooz** (⊕ *foobooz.com*) mixes news of restaurant openings and closings with food industry gossip and restaurant reviews. It also acts as a clearinghouse for other online reviews. **Unbreaded** (⊕ *unbreaded.com*), written by sandwich enthusiasts, tracks the city's best meals between bread slices, very important for a city whose identity is so closely tied to the cheesesteak sandwich. **Fries with that Shake** (⊕ *frieswiththatshake.net*) is written by two opinionated young women who manage to visit an impressive number of Philadelphia restaurants. The *City Paper's* **Meal Ticket** blog (⊕ *mealticket.blogs.citypaper.net/blogs/mu*) is also a fun resource. For those who pride themselves on being in the know about the restaurant scene, check out "Table Talk" by Michael Klein at the **Philadelphia Inquirer** (⊕ *www.philly.com/inquirer*).

Safety

Philadelphia got a bad rap for a high crime rate earlier this decade, but since Mayor Michael Nutter was elected in 2007 overall violent crime has dropped significantly. And it's worth noting that the majority of these crimes occur outside of Center City—specifically a few downtrodden pockets of West, North, and Southwest Philadelphia. As in any major city, visitors should always exercise caution and be aware of their surroundings.

When to Go

Any time is right to enjoy the area's attractions, and a variety of popular annual events take place throughout the year. To avoid the largest crowds and be assured that all seasonal attractions are open, visit in May–June or September–October. If you don't mind waiting in longer lines to see popular attractions, visit around July 4, when the city comes alive with fireworks, parades, and festivals. The top draw is the **Welcome America!** festival, whose climax on the Benjamin Franklin Parkway usually boasts a blockbuster musician or two. There are special activities in the Historic Area all summer long. Concert and theater seasons run from October through the beginning of June—but the World Champion Phillies play from summer through the fall. You may find some better lodging deals—and a beautiful snowfall—in winter, if you don't mind bundling up. In spring the city's cherry blossoms bloom, rivaling those of Washington, D.C.'s Tidal Basin.

Like other northeastern American cities, Philadelphia can be hot and humid in summer and cold in winter (winter snowfall averages 21 inches).

PHILADELPHIA'S TOP ATTRACTIONS

Liberty Bell

(A) One of the country's most powerful symbols of freedom, the bell, replete with famous crack, now sits in its own dedicated center, still hanging from its original yoke. Despite the dispute among historians about its most famous ringing—for the first public reading of the Declaration—the bell remains a historic mainstay.

Philadelphia Museum of Art

(B) Ascend the very steps Rocky triumphantly galloped, and check out the Museum of Art's outstanding permanent collection, including masterworks by Renoir, Van Gogh, Cézanne, and local boy Thomas Eakins, in addition to excellent ongoing exhibits. It's also host to one of the best views of the city.

Independence Hall

(C) This relatively unimposing brick building on Chestnut Street is where both the Declaration and Constitution were composed, argued about, and eventually signed. From such humble beginnings do mighty nations eventually arise. Just behind it is a small park, perfect for walking around and mulling the fate of a new nation.

Reading Terminal Market

(D) A massive, enclosed market in a former train shed, Reading Terminal houses more than 80 different vendors, ranging from fresh produce to seafood to killer cupcakes. The Amish community is also well represented with several outlets, including a sit-down diner that offers pancakes the size of a tractor tire complete with their own stick of (home-churned) butter.

Betsy Ross House

(E) Whether Betsy Ross ever actually lived in this house in the Old City and whether or not she actually sewed the first Stars and Stripes flag is up for debate, but the house is fun to visit. Built in 1760, it's a great example of a Colonial house, and

Betsy
Ross
House

the rooms overflow with interesting arti-facts including Betsy's reading glasses and family Bible.

The Franklin Institute

(F) This science museum founded in 1824 to honor Philly's most famous sci-entist and inventor, Benjamin Franklin, houses multiple wondrous exhibits. Walk through the world's largest model of a human heart; sit in the cockpit of a T-33 jet trainer; or catch a show in the state-of-the-art planetarium or IMAX Theater.

Rittenhouse Square

(G) Philadelphia's most elegant square often draws comparisons to its Parisian counterparts, and it's true it was designed by a Frenchman, Paul Cret. One of William Penn's five original squares, it has gone from a grazing ground for cows and sheep to ground zero for the city's grandest town homes to today's incar-nation, a hybrid of preserved manses,

swank apartment buildings, and lively sidewalk cafés.

Fairmount Park

(H) The world's largest landscaped park is often impossible even for natives to fully conquer, but visitors should seek out at least a taste of its varied offerings. Pick one attraction: stately Boathouse Row; Belmont Plateau, with a historic house and a killer view of the skyline; the his-toric Fairmount Waterworks along the Schuylkill River; or the Japanese House—a must when the cherry blos-soms are in bloom.

Landis Valley Museum

(I) To experience Lancaster County's pre-commercialized past, head to the Landis Valley Museum. The open-air museum is an immersion in Pennsylvania German rural life and folk culture that sprawls over 15 buildings, including a farmstead and a country store.

TOP EXPERIENCES

Let History Entertain You

Exciting, outside-the-textbook presentations of our nation's history abound in Philadelphia, and can be a great way to get kids and history-phobes to enjoy learning about the past. The **National Constitution Center** presents a fun, multimedia experience that explains the evolution and importance of the Constitution. See the show *Freedom Rising,* performed by an actor against a backdrop of music, video, lighting effects, and dramatic voiceovers. Then mingle with the Founding Fathers in **Signers' Hall;** the life-size bronze statues of the Constitution's signers show how George Washington literally towered over his peers. Visit the **Once Upon a Nation** storytellers' benches to hear history from the mouths of those who experienced it. At night, check out the **Lights of Liberty Show,** which tells the story of the American Revolution via laser-light images up to 50 feet high projected onto the buildings of Independence Park with narration by Charlton Heston, Whoopie Goldberg, and Walter Cronkite.

Get a Chill

At the **Mütter Museum,** a macabre collection of medical abnormalities, like conjoined twins, celebrity body parts, and a massive human colon, are on display. The **Eastern State Penitentiary,** the first prison to try placing inmates in their own individual cells, was once home to Al Capone and Willie Sutton. Today it's a bone-chilling museum that often doubles as a venue for art installations and exhibits. Centuries-old **Laurel Hill Cemetery** has a beautiful view of the city and river, and is the final resting place of many of Philadelphia's fascinating early residents.

Visit an Offbeat Museum or Two

There's still time to see the **Barnes Foundation**—a collection of impressionist and postimpressionist art gathered by eccentric Albert C. Barnes—in situ at its original location on the Main Line. Paintings by such luminaries as Picasso, Matisse, and Cézanne hang alongside African sculpture and pieces of American ironwork. The whole shebang will soon move to Center City just a stone's throw from the elegant and often overlooked Rodin Museum. The small galleries and lovely garden of the **Rodin Museum** display the best collection of the sculptor's work outside of Paris. On the other side of the city, the **Mummer Museum** explores the history and significance of that quirky tradition that has beefy Italian men dressing up like drag queens and parading down Broad Street every New Year's Day.

Neighborhood Hop

Like most old cities on the East Coast, Philly is meant to be walked. **Center City** is tiny—about 2½ mi by 2 mi, from river to river and from South Street to Fairmont Avenue. Try walking from the Schuylkill to the Delaware in a day, swerving from neighborhood to neighborhood. You can hit **Rittenhouse Square, Washington Square, Society Hill, Old City,** and **Queen Village** (also called Southwark). Let yourself get lost among the tiniest streets. Hunt for hidden alleyways, courtyards, and gardens.

Weigh In on the Cheesesteak Face-off

Different flavor-of-the-month restaurants will always claim to have come up with the tastiest new cheesesteak in town, but the original face-off is ongoing at 9th and Passyunk in South Philadelphia, where **Pat's** and **Geno's** occupy separate corners. Pat's invented the cheesesteak. Geno's says it perfected the iconic Philly sandwich.

While both serve up equally heaping portions of sliced rib-eye steak, grilled onions, and melted cheese on freshly baked bread, the lines of regulars out front have strong opinions about which is best.

Tour This Old House

Philadelphia's house museums tend to get lost in the shuffle, but there's no better way to soak up history than to see how people really lived. In Society Hill, check out **Powell House,** a 1765 Georgian Mansion, and **Physick House,** a Federal-style home built in 1768 and named after Dr. Physick, the doctor who invented carbonated soda. **Elfreth's Alley** in Old City is the longest-continually-residential street in America; one home has been turned into a museum, but if you're lucky you might catch one of the twice-yearly tours when residents open their homes to the public. Germantown, 6 mi north of Center City, has some real jewels in **Cliveden, Upsala,** the **Deshler-Morris House,** and the **Ebenezer Maxwell Mansion.** The town's history as an upscale retreat-turned-Revolutionary battleground makes for a rich, multilayered past. ■TIP→ A reenactment of the Battle of Germantown happens here the first Saturday of October.

Enter a Secret Garden

Philadelphia's positively bursting with hidden gardens if you know where to find them: **Bartram's Garden,** home to John Bartram, the country's first botanist, is a short drive south of the city and has an extensive Colonial garden that slopes up from a riverbank. In **Fairmount Park,** the **Japanese House** boasts hundreds of cherry trees that bloom in spring and a traditional Japanese-style garden that's pleasing year-round. The 166-acre **Morris Arboretum** just outside the city has romantic winding paths, a fernery, a rose garden, and meadows. The **Magic Garden** on South Street is a garden of another kind—a still-growing garden of mosaics using mostly found objects. And in Society Hill and the historic area, small pocket gardens abound, like the tidy formal variety at 4th and Walnut, adjacent to Dolly Madison's former home.

See the City through its Murals

With more than 2,800 murals spread throughout the city, Philadelphia beats out every other metropolis in number of murals per capita. This is thanks to the **Mural Arts Program,** which began as an anti-graffiti endeavor in the 1980s and evolved into a program that matches professional artists with residents to revitalize neighborhoods, beat blight, and provide an opportunity for young people to explore this means of self-expression. You can take a two-hour guided tour of the murals in an open-air trolley—a different section of the city is featured each week. ■TIP→ Go to ⊕ *muralarts.org* **for information and to buy tour tickets.**

Eat at a BYOB

The Pennsylvania Liquor Control Board's complicated laws and fees, which make procuring a liquor license an expensive prospect, have spawned more than 200 BYOB (bring-your-own-bottle) restaurants. Natives know that the BYOBs, where the food and atmosphere are more flavorful and the bill is easier to digest, are hidden jewels. Some favorites include **Pumpkin, Dmitri's, Lolita** (bring your own tequila for homemade margaritas), and **Modo Mio.** ■TIP→ **In Philadelphia wine is sold only at state-owned Pennsylvania Wine & Spirit Stores.**

GREAT ITINERARIES

PHILADELPHIA IN 6 DAYS

In a city with as many richly stocked museums and matchless marvels as Philadelphia, you risk seeing half of everything or all of nothing. So use the efficient itineraries below to keep you on track as you explore both the famous sights and those off the beaten path.

Day 1

Begin your first day with an exploration of the city's Historic Area. Sign up at the **Independence National Historical Park Visitor Center** for a walking tour hosted by a National Park Service guide; try a go-at-your-own-pace tour offered by Audio Walk and Tour; or take a walk on your own. For lunch, proceed to the **Reading Terminal Market,** where you can sample the real Philadelphia "cuisine"—cheesesteaks, soft pretzels, and Bassett's ice cream—or something else from the dozens of food stalls. After lunch, walk nine blocks east on Arch Street (or take a bus on Market Street) to Old City; **Christ Church,** the **Betsy Ross House,** and **Elfreth's Alley** are all in close proximity. The galleries and cafés in the area may tempt you to take a short break from your pursuit of history. In the late afternoon, head back to **Independence Hall** for a horse-drawn carriage ride. Have dinner in Old City; then catch the **Lights of Liberty** walking sound-and-light show.

Day 2

Spend the morning of Day 2 exploring the **Philadelphia Museum of Art** on Benjamin Franklin Parkway, followed by lunch in the museum's lovely dining room. Afterward, depending on your interests and the day of the week, you could head to Merion by bus or car to see the world-renowned collection of impressionist paintings at the **Barnes Foundation** (open Friday–Sunday). Or you could walk to **Eastern State Penitentiary Historic Site** for a tour of a former prison or to the **Franklin Institute.**

Day 3

Start Day 3 in Center City with a ride to the top of **City Hall** for a pigeon's-eye view of the city. Next, head across the street to the **Masonic Temple** for a surreal tour through time—and architectural history—led by a Mason. Art lovers may prefer a visit to the **Pennsylvania Academy of the Fine Arts,** two blocks north of City Hall at Broad and Cherry streets. Eat lunch at the **Reading Terminal Market.**

If you want to stay inside, head to Rittenhouse Square's **Rosenbach Museum and Library,** which has a diverse collection ranging from the original manuscript of James Joyce's *Ulysses* to the works of beloved children's author Maurice Sendak. If you prefer being outdoors, visit Penn's Landing, where you can check out the **Independence Seaport Museum** and/or take the ferry across the river to the **Adventure Aquarium** and **Camden Children's Garden.** At sunset, have a drink on the deck of the *Moshulu.*

Day 4

Begin Day 4 by exploring either Society Hill or the Rittenhouse Square area. Then take a bus west on Walnut Street to the **University Museum of Archaeology and Anthropology,** in University City. You can have lunch at the museum or on campus. In the afternoon, return to Center City to the corner of 16th Street and John F. Kennedy Boulevard, to pick up the Philadelphia Trolley Works' narrated tour of **Fairmount Park;** or if you have children along, visit the **Philadelphia Zoo.** Afterward, drive or catch the SEPTA R6 train to Manayunk, where you can have dinner in one of the restaurants lining

Main Street; many stores here are open late, too.

Day 5

On Day 5, head out of the city by car to **Valley Forge National Historical Park,** where you can hike or picnic after you've taken the self-guided auto tour of General Washington's winter encampment. If you like to shop, spend the afternoon at the nearby **King of Prussia Mall.** Or drive back toward the city to take in the **Barnes Foundation,** the **Eastern State Penitentiary,** or the **Franklin Institute**—whichever ones you didn't see on Day 2.

Another option for Day 5 is to stay in the city and explore Queen Village in Southwark and South Philadelphia. Follow up a visit to the **Mummers Museum** with a strut along 9th Street, site of the outdoor **Italian Market.** You can pick up the makings for a great picnic, or duck into one of the restaurants here for lunch. In the afternoon, visit the museums you missed on Day 2. Check the local papers for an evening activity—perhaps a sporting event at the South Philadelphia stadiums, a show in Center City, or live music at a jazz club.

Day 6

Get out of the city again with a day trip by car to the Brandywine Valley. Your first stop will be the **Brandywine River Museum** in Chadds Ford, which showcases the art of Andrew Wyeth and his family, as well as works by other area painters and illustrators. Next, head south to **Winterthur** and feast your eyes on Henry Francis du Pont's extraordinary collection of American decorative art in an equally extraordinary mansion. Spend the balance of your day strolling through **Longwood Gardens** in Kennett Square, which is in bloom even in winter. If it's a Tuesday, Thursday, or

Saturday in summer, stay for dinner and the fountain light show.

IF YOU HAVE MORE TIME

More time means you'll be able to delve even deeper into Philly's other—and outer—neighborhoods. Check out Chinatown in Center City, take a drive through Germantown and Chestnut Hill (stopping at **Cliveden**), or devote a full day to shopping in trendy Manayunk. If the weather's nice, you can drive to the northwestern tip of **Fairmount Park** and check out the **Wissahickon**—a local favorite for all sorts of activities, from strolling to cycling.

You can also break up your city exploring with longer side trips to Bucks County or Lancaster County. Both have an abundance of charming bed-and-breakfasts that make for perfect overnight or weekend stays.

IF YOU HAVE 2 DAYS

You could easily spend two weeks exploring Philadelphia, but if you have only a few days, you can still get a good taste of what the city has to offer. You'll want to get the tour of the historic sights out of the way on Day 1. Either follow the itinerary above, or forgo the **Lights of Liberty** show and check out Old City's bars and clubs instead. Then spend a leisurely day exploring either the **Philadelphia Museum of Art** or the **Barnes Foundation.** Wrap up Day 2 with a stroll around **Rittenhouse Square** or through **Fairmount Park.**

LIKE A LOCAL

Skip the sightseeing and make like a Philadelphian for a day. These locals-only experiences will help you fully embrace the city of brotherly love.

Shop the Farmers' Markets

At the year-round **Italian Market,** which lines 9th Street between Bainbridge and Washington, vendors have offered everything from fresh sausage to homemade ricotta since the early 1900s. You can also find a growing number of South American and Asian stores here. **Reading Terminal** is another place to find fresh, local foodstuffs even through the winter months. Check out ⊕ *www.thefoodtrust. org* to find out the schedule of farmers' markets. At **Head House Square,** in Society Hill, farmers, artisanal cheese and fudge makers, flower growers, and bread bakers from Lancaster County to South Jersey sell to a packed crowd of locals on Saturdays and Sundays.

Take a Bike Ride

The ever-expanding **Schuylkill River Bike Path** provides a direct 12-mi route from Center City to Valley Forge, through Manayunk and Conshocken. Rent a bike at **Trophy Bikes,** situated close to the entrance to the bike path, and start cycling past the Art Museum and Waterworks. In Manayunk, stop and have lunch alfresco at casual, scrumptious **Le Bus** (✉ *4266 Main St., Manayunk* ☎ *215/487–2663*).

Hang at the Piazza

Brand new **Piazza at Schmidt's,** a local developer's one-acre interpretation of Rome's Piazza Navona in hip Northern Liberties, features a slew of independent restaurants and boutiques. The landlord's no-chain-stores policy has resulted in a truly unique retail and dining atmosphere.

Play Quizzo

If it's after dark, there's probably a **Quizzo** (team trivia) game in progress in at least one bar in the city. The topics at different Quizzos can be anything under the sun—'80s sitcoms, classic literature, sci-fi films—and prizes usually involve free beer. **Fergie's Pub** (✉ *1214 Sansom St., Center City* ☎ *215/928–8118*) is one of the best places for Quizzo in the city—if you can take extra-fierce competition.

Buy (and See) Art on the Cheap

Each June, the **Art for the Cash Poor** (⊕ *www. inliquid.com*) festival takes over a block in the Old City; no piece is priced over $150. The **Art Star Craft Bazaar** (⊕ *www.artstarcraftbazaar.com*) is a newer annual festival that takes place at Penn's Landing the last weekend in May. It is organized by Art Star Gallery and Boutique, a shop in Northern Liberties founded by two local art-school grads. The citywide weeklong **Fringe Festival** (⊕ *www.pafringe.com*), held every September, is an affordable way to take in more ephemeral, experimental art.

Linger Over Brunch

It's not surprising that food-obsessed Philadelphians are big on brunch. At **Sabrina's Café** (✉ *910 Christian St., South Philadelphia* ☎ *215/574–1599*), the Barking Chihuahua Breakfast and unusually thick slices of French toast account for the giant crowd waiting outside every Sunday. **Morning Glory Diner** (✉ *735 S. 10th St., South Philadelphia* ☎ *215/413–3999*) dishes out giant frittatas and omelets with homemade biscuits and stewed apples. The Aussie owners at **Ants Pants Café** (✉ *2212 South St., Center City West* ☎ *215/875–8002*), influence the food—you can order a Brekkie Platter and a flat white—and the laid-back ambience.

THE PENNSYLVANIA DUTCH

The country's largest and oldest settlement of Plain people—more than 85,000 people in more than 41 Amish, Mennonite, and Brethren sects—makes Lancaster County their home. Collectively, the sects are known as the Pennsylvania Dutch. Despite their name, they aren't Dutch at all, but descendants of German and Swiss immigrants who came to the Lancaster area to escape religious persecution. Because of a misunderstanding of the word *Deutsch,* meaning "German," they became known as the "Dutch."

The Mennonite movement, named after its leader, Dutch Catholic priest Menno Simons, began in Switzerland in the early 16th century, the time of the Reformation. This radical religious group advocated nonviolence, separation of church and state, adult baptism, and individual freedom in choosing a religion. In 1710 eight families led by Mennonite bishop Hans Herr accepted William Penn's invitation to settle in Lancaster County. In 1693 Swiss Mennonite bishop Jacob Amman, whose stricter interpretation of church tenets had attracted a following, broke off from the movement and formed his own group, the Amish. Like the Mennonites, the Amish came to live in Lancaster County.

Lancaster County has the second-largest Amish community in the country, with an estimated 22,000 Old Order Amish. That the number of Amish has doubled in the past two decades suggests that theirs is still a viable lifestyle. The eight Amish, 24 Mennonite, and nine Brethren groups differ in their interpretations of the Bible, their use of technology, the value they place on education, their use of English, and their degrees of interaction with outsiders. Brethren and Mennonite groups use modern conveniences more than Old Order Mennonites and Amish sects do, particularly the Old Order Amish, who shun technology.

The Amish religion and way of life stress separation from the world, caring for others of the faith, and self-sufficiency. The Amish, who reject compulsory school attendance and military registration, do pay taxes but they don't pay social security nor do they accept social-security benefits or purchase life or property insurance. Old Order Amish send their children to one-room schoolhouses with eight grades to a room. They avoid public schools to prevent the exposure of their children to the influence of "outsiders." Though Amish students study many of the traditional subjects, they learn less about science and technology. The Supreme Court has ruled that Amish children need not attend school beyond the eighth grade, after which students learn agriculture, building trades, and domestic skills at home.

Dress and grooming symbolize each person's role in Amish society. Men must begin to grow a beard upon marriage, and they wear several different styles of hats to distinguish their age, status, and their religious district. Amish women wear full-length dresses, capes, and aprons. Those who are baptized wear white organdy caps and don't cut their hair.

It's impossible to miss the Amish if you're traveling in Lancaster County. They, and their horses and buggies, are everywhere, even on the major routes. The Amish often sell quilts and other crafts from their homes. Any Lancaster County visitor center will be able to give you a map that marks the locations of some of the larger of these retail operations.

FREE IN PHILLY

Many of Philadelphia's most historic and best-known attractions are free—or suggest a small donation for admission—every day. This lengthy list includes **Independence Hall**, the **Liberty Bell, Carpenter's Hall, Franklin Court**, and the other buildings and sites of **Independence National Historic Park**. But thanks in part to a lively student population and arts scene, there are plenty of other free and cheap activities to discover in the city.

Music and Theater

Check the **Curtis Institute of Music**'s (⊕ *www.curtis.edu*) calendar to catch one of their frequent free concerts by a rising star. The **Philadelphia Orchestra** (⊕ *www.philorch.org*) also gives free neighborhood concerts. Visit the **Macy's** across from City Hall; the former Wanamaker's boasts the largest pipe organ in the world, and there are daily free concerts. The Christmas show around the holidays is a definite fan favorite. Check out a dress rehearsal at the **Arden Theater**—they are open to the public and tickets are "pay what you can." Local independent radio station WXPN offers free concerts every Friday at noon at their homebase, **World Café Live** (⊕ *www.xpn.org*)

Outdoor Fun and Festivals

Take your pick of activities in **Fairmount Park**: hike the trails of the **Wissahickon** (⊕ *www.fow.org*), bring a picnic to **Belmont Plateau** and enjoy the view; or meander around the **Horticultural Center**, trying to find all the pieces of public art. All summer long, multicultural festivals at **Penn's Landing** feature live music and dance instruction.

Architecture, Art, and Literature

Take a tour of **City Hall**. Visit Chinatown's **Friendship Gate**, the four-story gift to Philadelphia from its sister city in China, Tianjin. See Maurice Sendak's original illustrations and James Joyce's *Ulysses* manuscript among other treasures at the **Rosenbach Museum and Library**. Visit the lobby of the **Curtis Center** to gawk at the giant *Dream Garden* by Maxfield Parrish. Tour the **Masonic Temple**, a masterpiece inside and out, that's also historically significant as the birthplace of freemasonry in America. Visit the **Galleries at the Moore College of Art & Design**, the first and only women's visual arts college in the U.S.

It's always fun to stroll the galleries in Old City, but it's especially fun on **"First Fridays"**—the first Friday of every month is celebrated with wine receptions, and galleries keeping later hours. Visit the **African American Museum** (free from 5 to 7). The first Sunday of each month is "pay what you wish" all day at the **Philadelphia Museum of Art**. The **Institute of Contemporary Art** at the University of Pennsylvania is free all the time. You can check out contemporary art at any time by taking a free tour of the city's many vibrant **murals** (⊕ *www.muralarts.org*).

History Tours

Take yourself on a walk by downloading and printing the self-guided **Constitutional Walking Tour** of more than 30 sites around historic Philadelphia from ⊕ *www.theconstitutional.com*. Take cell-phone tours of **Elfreth's Alley** (☎ *585/627–4152*) and of **Valley Forge National Historical Park** (☎ *484/396–1018*). In the summer, look for the storytellers with **Once Upon a Nation** who set up camp at 13 benches throughout Philadelphia's historic area. Hop from bench to bench for a free, interactive tour, during which stories of colonial Philadelphia are related by actors in character.

PHILADELPHIA WITH KIDS

Philadelphia has fantastic activities and sights for tots. Best of all, these stops appeal to adults as well.

Historic Area

The **Betsy Ross House** has an audio tour and scavenger hunt designed for kids, and the underground museum at **Franklin Court** is fun to explore. The **National Constitution Center**'s interactive exhibits are way better than learning from a history book. Your kids might enjoy being "sworn in" as a Supreme Court Justice. If you prefer a sightseeing tour, the amphibious **Duck Tour,** which leaves opposite the Liberty Bell, does the historic-Philadelphia circuit. Nearby **Franklin Square** is the prefect place to take a break from all the learning. It boasts a carousel, miniature-golf course, and an excellent burger stand that also serves up Cake Shakes (milkshakes made with Butterscotch Krimpet Tastykakes). At night, kids love the **Lights of Liberty** show, or for something spookier, check out one of the **Ghost Tours** offered around the Historic Area.

Fairmount Park

The **Please Touch Museum** is essentially a giant playground for kids. In its new location in majestic Memorial Hall—one of the few remnants from the 1876 Centennial Exhibition—the museum is bigger (38,000 square feet of exhibits) and better than before. Kids are encouraged to dress up for tea with Alice and the Mad Hatter; to drive a SEPTA bus; and to play a tune on the giant floor-piano that was featured in the Tom Hanks movie *Big*. Nearby **Philadelphia Zoo** is another great spot, with a petting zoo, tree house, and a ride in the Zooballoon (a hot-air balloon). The sprawling indoor–outdoor **Smith Memorial Playground and Playhouse** nearby has a giant wooden slide and a mansion-like playhouse.

Benjamin Franklin Parkway

At the **Franklin Institute**, kids can't resist walking through the giant heart and seeing their hair go spazzy in the static-electricity exhibit. The nearby **Academy of Natural Sciences** has great, kid-friendly exhibits about dinosaurs and architectural digs. If you want to top off all the sciencey adventures with a treat, stop in at the **Four Seasons** for a once-in-a-lifetime tea party.

Penn's Landing

At **Penn's Landing** kids can climb in the bunks used in steerage or hop in a scull and row along the Schuylkill at the **Independence Seaport Museum.** Next take the **RiverLink Ferry** across the river to the Camden Waterfront to explore the **Adventure Aquarium.** The **Shark Realm,** an enormous tank filled with sharks, stingrays, and sawfish, is the central attraction here. The **Camden Children's Garden** is an interactive horticultural garden with exhibits that allow you to taste, smell, and touch different elements.

Around Town

There's something for everyone in the family at **Reading Terminal Market.** Kids will like watching the workers at Fisher's Soft Pretzels wind the dough into pretzel shapes. They can also feed pennies to Philbert, the bronze pig at the market's center (the money goes to feed the hungry). For a fancier meal option, the **City Tavern** is a great way into history, and it has a good kids' menu. If you're in the mood for a ball game, **Citizen's Bank Park,** home to the world-champion Phillies, is one of the most kid-friendly major league-ball parks. The **Phanatic Fun Zone** is a huge play area, and kids enjoy dollar dogs and sodas all game long.

A GUT-BUSTING WALK THROUGH SOUTH PHILLY

The Italian Market in South Philadelphia is a local treasure. Generations of Italian families and newcomers shop at this bustling indoor–outdoor market for homemade pasta, produce, cheeses, and olive oil. Wander through the heart of the Italian Market and sample its mouth-watering delicacies.

Italian Market

The **Italian Market** is a stretch of 9th Street in an area settled by Italian immigrants in the late 1800s. Today, the market is a scene of controlled chaos, with vendors peddling fish, produce, meat, cheese, pasta, pastries, spices, espresso, and more. More recently, Mexican, Vietnamese, and other South Asian flavors have joined the party.

Begin your walk at **Fante's Kitchen Wares Shop,** a 103-year-old kitchenware store. Fante's is a cook's paradise, with everything from pastry bags to pasta makers stacked floor to ceiling. Turn left out of Fante's and continue north on 9th Street to **DiBruno Bros.** This is the original DiBruno Bros., dating back to 1939; the enormous Rittenhouse location opened in 2004. The shop is long, narrow, and packed with cheeses, prosciutto, and olives. The staff is all-knowing and very generous with samples. Continue walking north on 9th Street, past the **mural of Frank Rizzo,** the legendary former police commissioner and mayor, at 9th and Montrose. Stop in at **Anthony's Italian Coffee House** for some killer espresso. At Christian Street, turn left and walk two blocks west to **Isgro Pastries** for what some claim are the best cannolis in the city. (Anthony's and Termini Bros. are also good.) Backtrack down Christian Street to the corner of 7th, where the unassuming **John's Water Ice** is open seasonally. This is a purist's

Italian ice—there are only four flavors (chocolate, cherry, pineapple, and lemon) and each tastes exactly as it should.

Bella Vista

Turn left to walk north on 7th Street, through the residential neighborhood of Bella Vista. This is where Italian South Philly meets funky South Street, and it harbors some elements of each. Among the row homes and BYOBs are vintage stores and coffee shops. Take a left on Bainbridge and walk two blocks to **Chapterhouse Café,** a great place to nurse a coffee and people-watch. For vintage clothing, check out **Vintage Connection** across the street and **Decades Vintage** a few blocks east on Bainbridge. **Antiquarian's Delight,** in a converted synagogue on 6th between South and Bainbridge streets, is a co-op filled with vendors selling clothes, accessories, housewares, and furniture.

From 6th and Bainbridge, walk east toward 4th Street. **Famous 4th Street Delicatessen** is the place to order a brisket sandwich that'll make your plate groan. Famous is really famous, though, for its amazing chocolate-chip cookies. And **Southwark** across the street has a reputation for serving the city's best cocktails.

Not that you're likely to have room for it, but you're only two blocks away from the third-most-famous cheesesteak in Philly, **Jim's Steaks.** Maybe you can take one to go?

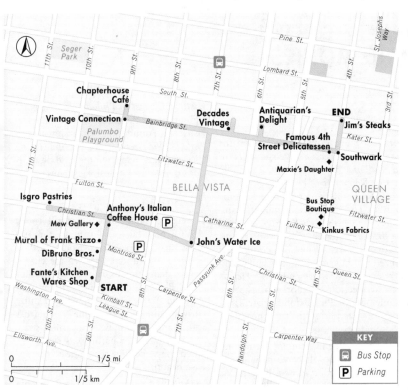

Where to Start:	Fante's at 1006 S. 9th and Carpenter streets
Getting Here	Walk or take SEPTA bus 47 to the 8th Street and Washington Avenue stop and then northwest to the start. Free municipal lots are located on the 800 block of Christian Street and the 1000 block of 8th Street.
Length:	2 mi (about three hours)
Where to Stop:	**Jim's** at 400 South Street. Head back up town on bus 47 at 7th and Lombard streets.
Best Time to Go:	When your stomach is growling.
Worst Time to Go:	Sunday afternoon or anytime Monday, when the Italian Market is closed.
Even more shopping:	**Bus Stop Boutique** (750 S. 4th St.) sells fashion-forward women's shoes by international designers. **Mew Gallery** (906 Christian St.) is a collective for local artists and designers—find original art and handmade clothing, jewelry, and funky housewares.
Historic Tip:	South 4th Street is Fabric Row, which was lined with pushcarts in the early 1900s selling calico, notions, and trimming. Some of the old fabric stores, like **Kinkus Fabrics** (754 S. 4th St.) and **Maxie's Daughter** (724 S. 4th St.), remain.

PHILLY BOOKS AND MOVIES

BOOKS

Fiction

Journalist Steve Lopez (best known for *The Soloist*) set his hard-edged novel *Third and Indiana*, in the less-than-friendly parts of Kensington. Philly native Solomon Jones's collection of stories *Keeping Up With The Jones* details modern family life, while his novels *Pipe Dreams* and *The Bridge* deal with violence and drugs. Jonathan Franzen's *The Corrections* is set in the very non-gritty Chestnut Hill neighborhood. *Philly Fiction* and *Philly Fiction 2*, two collections of short stories set in Philadelphia by Philadelphia writers, are good introductions to the city's neighborhoods and people.

On the chick-lit end, Jennifer Weiner has set most of her novels here, including *In Her Shoes* and *Good in Bed*. Elise Juska, another local novelist, uses Philly throughout *Getting Over Jack Wagner*.

History

Frank Rizzo: The Last Big Man in Big City America by S. A. Paolantonio, about the city's revered and despised former mayor, and Buzz Bissinger's *A Prayer for the City* about then-Mayor Ed Rendell in the 1990s, are two great introductions to the joys of Philadelphia politicking. For some history overload, try *Philadelphia: A 300-Year History*, with essays edited by Russell F. Weigley. Catherine Drinker Bowen's *Miracle at Philadelphia* tells the story of the Constitution. *Up South: Civil Rights and Black Power in Philadelphia*, by Matthew J. Countryman, examines the postwar period in the civil rights movement.

Architecture

Two books that feature the stunning architectural photographs of Tom Crane, *Historic Sacred Places of Philadelphia* and *Historic Houses of Philadelphia*, provide a glimpse into the many historic places to visit. The Foundation for Architecture's *Philadelphia Architecture: A Guide to the City* contains maps, photos, and descriptions of almost 400 historical sites.

MOVIES

The classic Philadelphia film is still *Rocky* (1976), and fans still run up the Art Museum steps every day. *Rocky Balboa* (2006) is like a love letter to the city, it has so many great city scenes. Another iconic Philly film moment is the murder scene in *Witness* (1985), when Danny Glover knifes a man in the 30th Street Station men's room. Be forewarned, some 25 years later, the bathrooms look very much the same, but the station is otherwise beautiful.

In the past forty years most Philadelphia films have emphasized the city's majestic grittiness. A lot of that grittiness no longer exists in Center City and surrounding neighborhoods (see the Rittenhouse Square in *Trading Places* [1983] vs. what it looks like today). Recent films like *In Her Shoes* (2005) and *Baby Mama* (2008) show the cleaned-up city, with more films like them on the way.

M. Night Shyamalan's *The Sixth Sense* (1999) has terrific shots of Philly, especially its statues. Terry Gilliam's *12 Monkeys* (1995) places elephants in front of City Hall and uses the Eastern State Penitentiary, the former prison home of criminals like Al Capone, as an insane asylum (visit and you'll know why). *National Treasure* (2004) has Nicholas Cage stepping all over Independence Hall.

Exploring Philadelphia

By Robert
DiGiacomo

"On the whole, I'd rather be in Philadelphia." W.C. Fields may have been joking when he wrote his epitaph, but if he were here today, he would eat his words. They no longer roll up the sidewalks at night in Philadelphia. A construction boom, a restaurant renaissance, and cultural revival have helped transform the city. For more than 15 years there has been an optimistic mood, aggressive civic leadership, and national recognition of what the locals have long known: Philadelphia is a vibrant place to live—a city with an impressive past and a fascinating future.

Philadelphia is a place of contrasts: Grace Kelly and Rocky Balboa; Le Bec-Fin—one of the nations finest French haute-cuisine restaurants—and the fast-food heaven of Jim's Steaks; Independence Hall and the modest Mario Lanza Museum; 18th-century national icons with 21st-century–style skyscrapers soaring above them. The world-renowned Philadelphia Orchestra performs in a stunning concert hall—the focal point of efforts to transform Broad Street into a multicultural Avenue of the Arts. Along the same street, 25,000 Mummers dressed in outrageous sequins and feathers historically have plucked their banjos and strutted their stuff to the strains of "Oh, Dem Golden Slippers" on New Year's Day. City residents include descendants of the staid Quaker Founding Fathers, the self-possessed socialites of the Main Line (remember Katharine Hepburn and Cary Grant in *The Philadelphia Story*?), and the unrestrained sports fans, who are as vocal as they are loyal.

Historically speaking, Philadelphia is a city of superlatives: the world's largest municipal park; the best collection of public art in the United States; the widest variety of urban architecture in America; and according to some experts, the greatest concentration of institutions of higher learning in the country.

A CITY OF NEIGHBORHOODS

Philadelphia is known as a city of neighborhoods (109 by one count). Shoppers haggle over the price of tomatoes in South Philly's Italian Market; families picnic in the parks of Germantown; street vendors hawk soft pretzels in Logan Circle; and all over town kids play street games such as stickball, stoopball, wireball, and chink. It's a city of neighborhood loyalty: ask a native where he's from and he'll tell you: Fairmount, Fishtown, or Frankford, rather than Philadelphia. The city's population is less transient than that of other large cities; people who are born here generally remain, and many who leave home to study or work eventually return. Although the population is nearly 1.5 million, its residents are intricately connected; on any given day, a Philadelphian is likely to encounter someone with whom he grew up. The "it's-a-small-world" syndrome makes people feel like they belong.

THE PHILADELPHIA STORY

William Penn founded the city in 1682, and chose to name it Philadelphia—Greek for "brotherly love"—after an ancient Syrian city, site of one of the earliest and most venerated Christian churches. Penn's Quakers settled on a tract of land he described as his "greene countrie towne." After the Quakers, the next waves of immigrants to arrive were Anglicans and Presbyterians (who had a running conflict with the "stiff Quakers" and their distaste for music and dancing). The new residents forged traditions that remain strong in parts of Philadelphia today: united families, comfortable houses, handsome furniture, and good education. From these early years came the attitude Mark Twain summed up as: "In Boston, they ask: 'What does he know?' In New York, 'How much does he make?' In Philadelphia, 'Who were his parents?' "

The city became the queen of the English-speaking New World from the late 1600s to the early 1800s. In the latter half of the 1700s Philadelphia was the largest city in the colonies, a great and glorious place. So when the delegates from the colonies wanted to meet in a centrally located, thriving city, they chose Philadelphia. They convened the First Continental Congress in 1774 at Carpenters' Hall. The rest, as they say, is history. It is here that the Declaration of Independence was written and adopted, the Constitution was framed, the capital of the United States was established, the Liberty Bell was rung, the nation's flag was sewn by Betsy Ross (though scholars debate this), and George Washington served most of his presidency.

GETTING YOUR BEARINGS

Today you can find Philadelphia's compact 5-square-mi downtown (William Penn's original city) between the Delaware and the Schuylkill (pronounced *skoo*-kull) rivers. Thanks to Penn's grid system of streets—laid out in 1681—the downtown area is a breeze to navigate. The traditional heart of the city is Broad and Market streets (Penn's Center Square), where City Hall now stands. Market Street divides the city north and south; 130 South 15th Street, for example, is in the second block south of Market Street. North–south streets are numbered, starting with Front (1st) Street, at the Delaware River, and increasing to the west. Broad Street is the equivalent of 14th Street. The diagonal Benjamin Franklin Parkway breaks the rigid grid pattern by leading from City Hall out of Center City into Fairmount Park, which straddles the Schuylkill River and Wissahickon Creek for 10 mi.

Although Philadelphia is the sixth-largest city in the nation (nearly 1.5 million people live in the city, 6.2 million in the metropolitan area), it maintains a small-town feel. It's a cosmopolitan, exciting, but not overwhelming, city, a town that's easy to explore on foot yet big enough to keep surprising even those most familiar with it.

HISTORIC AREA

Fodor's Choice
★

Any visit to Philadelphia, whether you have one day or several, should begin in the city area that comprises **Independence National Historical Park.** Philadelphia was the birthplace of the United States, the home of the country's first government, and nowhere is the spirit of those miraculous early days—the boldness of conceiving a brand-new nation—more palpable than along the cobbled streets of the city's most historic district.

In the late 1940s, before civic-minded citizens banded together to save the area and before the National Park Service stepped in, the Independence Hall neighborhood was crowded with factories and run-down warehouses. Then the city, state, and federal government took interest. Some buildings were restored, and others were reconstructed on their original sites; several attractions were built for the 1976 Bicentennial celebration. In recent years a flurry of construction has again transformed the area, with several notable buildings—including an expanded visitor center, a more attractive home for the Liberty Bell, and a national museum to celebrate the U.S. Constitution. Today the park covers 42 acres and holds close to 40 buildings. Urban renewal in Independence Mall plaza and in Washington Square East (Society Hill) have ensured that Independence Hall will never again keep unsightly company. The city's most historic area is now also one of its loveliest.

PLANNING YOUR TIME

If you've put on your walking shoes and are good at negotiating the cobblestones, you can wander through this compact area in about two hours. But the city's atmospheric historic district warrants a slower pace.

TOP ATTRACTIONS

❸ **Franklin Court.** This highly interactive and informative museum built on
☾ the site that was Benjamin Franklin's first permanent home in Philadelphia has seen better days, and is scheduled to close for a complete overhaul in the fall of 2010 and reopen in 2012. The new exhibits will offer a highly interactive celebration of this Renaissance man: scientist and inventor (of bifocals and the lightning rod), philosopher and writer, savvy politician, and successful businessman. Franklin, publisher of *Poor Richard's Almanac,* helped draft the Declaration of Independence and negotiate the peace with Great Britain. He also helped found Pennsylvania Hospital, the University of Pennsylvania, the Philadelphia Contributionship, and the American Philosophical Society.

In the courtyard adjacent to the museum, architect Robert Venturi erected a steel skeleton of Franklin's former home. You can peek through "windows" into cutaways to see wall foundations, outdoor privy wells, and other parts of his home that were uncovered during excavations. At the Market Street side are several houses, now exhibition halls, that Franklin had rented in addition to his main home. In one, you can see how Franklin fireproofed the building: his interest in fireproofing led him to experiment with kite flying and lightning. Here, too, you can find a restoration of a Colonial-era print shop and a post office. Don't forget to get a letter hand-stamped with a "B. FREE FRANKLIN" cancellation. These buildings will remain open during the museum's reconstruction.

GREAT EXPERIENCES IN HISTORIC AREA

Independence Hall: The United States literally got its start in this modest redbrick building, where the Declaration of Independence was signed and the U.S. Constitution was adopted.

Liberty Bell: Yes, the bell really does have a giant crack, but more importantly, it still resonates as a symbol of the right of all Americans to be free.

National Constitution Center: Check out the museum's clever interactive displays demonstrating to young and old alike the relevance of our nation's founding document.

The Curtis Center: Don't miss the building's stunning glass mosaic mural, *The Dream Garden*, which was crafted by the Louis C. Tiffany Studios from a painting by Maxfield Parrish.

Franklin Square: If you're traveling with kids, avoid history overload with a stop at this public park, which has playground equipment, a food stand, a carousel, and a miniature golf course.

✉ *314–322 Market St., or enter from Chestnut St. walkway, Historic Area* ☎ *215/965–2305* ⊕ *www.nps.gov* 🖂 *Free* ☉ *Hrs vary.*

❹ Independence Hall. The birthplace of the United States, this redbrick
★ building with its clock tower and steeple is one of the nation's greatest icons. America's most historic building was constructed in 1732–56 as the Pennsylvania State House. What happened here between 1775 and 1787 changed the course of American history—and the name of the building to Independence Hall. The delegates to the Second Continental Congress met in the hall's Assembly Room in May 1776, united in anger over the blood that had been shed when British troops fired on citizens in Concord, Massachusetts. In this same room George Washington was appointed commander in chief of the Continental Army, Thomas Jefferson's eloquent Declaration of Independence was signed, and later the Constitution of the United States was adopted. Here the first foreign minister to visit the United States was welcomed; the news of Cornwallis's defeat was announced, signaling the end of the Revolutionary War; and, later, John Adams and Abraham Lincoln lay in state. The memories this building holds linger in the collection of polished muskets, the silver inkstand used by delegates to sign the Declaration of Independence, and the "Rising Sun" chair in which George Washington sat. (After the Constitution was adopted, Benjamin Franklin said about the sun carving on the chair, "I have the happiness to know that it is a rising and not a setting sun.")

In the **East Wing**—attached to Independence Hall by a short colonnade—you can embark on free tours that start every 15 to 20 minutes and last 35 minutes. Admission is first-come, first-served; you may have to wait in line. The **West Wing** of Independence Hall contains an exhibit of the national historical park's collection of our nation's founding documents: the final draft of the Constitution, a working copy of the Articles of Confederation, and the first printing of the Declaration of Independence.

Historic Area and Old City

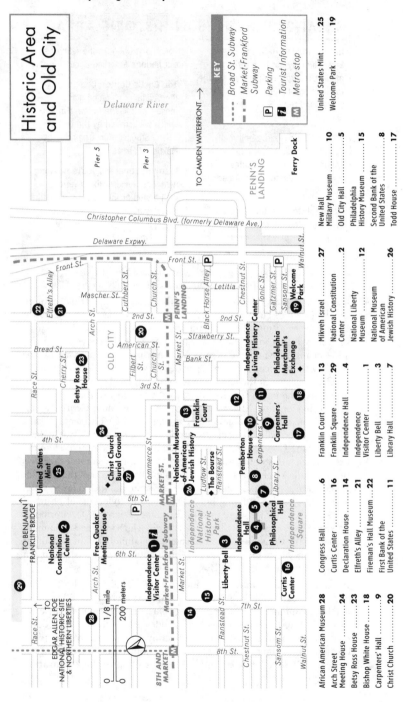

KEY

- - - - Broad St. Subway
— — Market-Frankford Subway
P Parking
i Tourist Information
M Metro stop

Delaware River

Pier 5

Pier 3

TO CAMDEN WATERFRONT →

PENN'S LANDING

Ferry Dock

Christopher Columbus Blvd. (formerly Delaware Ave.)

Delaware Expwy.

Front St.

Elfreth's Alley

Mascher St.

Cuthbert St.

Arch St.

Church St.

2nd St.

American St.

Strawberry St.

Bank St.

Bread St.

Filbert St.

Cherry St.

Race St.

Betsy Ross House

OLD CITY

3rd St.

4th St.

Christ Church Burial Ground

Commerce St.

National Museum of American Jewish History

The Bourse

Pemberton House

Library St.

Franklin Court

Carpenters' Court

Carpenters' Hall

Independence Living History Center

Philadelphia Merchant's Exchange

Letitia

Ionic St.

Gatzmer St.

Sansom St.

Welcome Park

Chestnut St.

2nd St.

Black Horse Alley

Walnut St.

United States Mint

TO BENJAMIN FRANKLIN BRIDGE

National Constitution Center

Free Quaker Meeting House

Independence Visitor Center

Liberty Bell

Independence Hall

Philosophical Hall

Independence Square

Independence National Historic Park

Ludlow St.

Ranstead St.

5th St.

MARKET ST.

Market St.

Curtis Center

6th St.

Arch St.

First Bank of the United States

TO EDGAR ALLEN POE NATIONAL HISTORIC SITE & NORTHERN LIBERTIES

Race St.

1/8 mile
200 meters

Ranstead St.

Chestnut St.

Sansom St.

Walnut St.

7th St.

8th St.

8TH AND MARKET

In front of Independence Hall, next to the statue of George Washington, note the plaques marking the spots where Abraham Lincoln stood on February 22, 1861, and where John F. Kennedy delivered an address on July 4, 1962. With Independence Hall in front of you and the Liberty Bell behind you, this is a place to stand for a moment and soak up a sense of history. ■ **TIP→ From March through December and on major holidays, free, timed tickets from the visitor center are required for entry. Tickets also can be reserved by calling** ☎ *800/967–2283* **or by logging on to** ⊕ *www.recreation.gov.* ✉ *500 Chestnut St. between 5th and 6th Sts., Historic Area* ☎ *215/965–2305* ⊕ *www.nps.gov/inde* ✇ *Free* ✆ *Daily 9–5.*

❶ **Independence Visitor Center.** This is the city's official visitor center as well as the gateway to Independence National Historical Park. Here, you'll find a fully staffed concierge and trip-planning desk, which provides information on the Park, the Philadelphia Museum of Art, the Philadelphia Zoo, and other attractions, as well as a reservation and ticketing service. Before you set off on a walking tour, acquaint yourself with Colonial American history by watching the Founding Fathers come to life in the 30-minute movie *Independence,* one of the films being shown in the center's three theaters. There are also a coffee bar with a sandwiches, salads, and desserts, and an excellent bookstore, where you can stock up on books, videos, brochures, prints, wall hangings, and souvenirs about historic figures and events. An atrium connects the visitor center to a renovated underground parking area. The outdoor café Independence Al Fresco, on the east side of the visitor center, is open May through September.

To see two of the city's famous historic homes—the Bishop White and Todd houses—you'll need to stop at the information desk to get a free, timed ticket, and reserve a spot on one of the tours, each of which takes about 30 minutes. ✉ *6th and Market Sts., Historic Area* ☎ *215/965–7676 or 800/537–7676* ⊕ *www.independencevisitorcenter.com* ✆ *Sept.–Mar., daily 8:30–5; Apr.–May, daily 8:30–6; June–Aug., daily 8:30–7.*

❸ **Liberty Bell.** The bell fulfilled the biblical words of its inscription when
★ it rang to "proclaim liberty throughout all the land unto all the inhabitants thereof," beckoning Philadelphians to the State House yard to hear the first reading of the Declaration of Independence. Ordered in 1751 and originally cast in England, the bell cracked during testing and was recast in Philadelphia by Pass and Stow two years later. To keep it from falling into British hands during the Revolution—they would have melted it down for ammunition—the bell was spirited away by horse and wagon to Allentown, 60 mi to the north. The bell is the subject of much legend; one story says it cracked when tolled at the funeral of Chief Justice John Marshall in 1835. Actually, the bell cracked slowly over a period of years. It was repaired but cracked again in 1846 and was then forever silenced. It was called the State House Bell until the 1830s, when a group of abolitionists adopted it as a symbol of freedom and renamed it the Liberty Bell.

After more than 200 years inside Independence Hall, the bell was moved to a glass-enclosed pavilion for the 1976 Bicentennial, which for many

CLOSE UP

Visiting Independence National Historical Park

Your first stop should be the Independence Visitor Center, where you can buy tickets for tours and pick up maps and brochures. From here you can easily explore the park on your own; in each building a park ranger can answer all your questions. In summer more than a dozen storytellers wander through the park, perching on benches to tell tales of the times. At Harmony Lane, 4th and Walnut streets, there's a Colonial street scene, with games such as hoops and scotch hoppers (known today as hopscotch) and activities such as butter churning. Special paid guided tours are also available through the Independence Visitor Center.

Hours and Fees: The Independence Visitor Center is open daily 8:30 to 5, and Independence Hall and the Liberty Bell Pavilion are open daily year-round from 9 to 5. In summer the closing times are often later. Other park buildings are also open daily, although their hours may vary from season to season. Call ☎ *800/537-7676*, the 24-hour hotline, for current hours plus a schedule of park programs; or visit ⊕ *www.nps.gov/inde*. Except as noted, all attractions run by the park are free.

When to Go: The best time to visit America's birthplace is on America's birthday; just expect big crowds. The city throws the weeklong Sunoco Welcome America! party. From June 27 to July 4 there are more than 50 free events, including parades (the Mummers and an illuminated boat procession), outdoor concerts, historical reenactments, and eye-popping fireworks. The rest of the summer is filled with plays, musicals, and parades. For information on the entertainment schedule, call **Historic**

Philadelphia Inc. (☎ *215/629–4026* ⊕ *www.onceuponanation.org*).

Lights of Liberty: A nighttime multimedia extravaganza, this walkable sound-and-light show is scheduled to unveil a new $10 million version using all-digital technology in spring 2010. The one-hour show, which dramatizes the events that led up to the American Revolution, culminates at Independence Hall on July 8, 1776, with the first public reading of the Declaration of Independence. You wear wireless headsets and view high-definition five-story projections on the area's historic buildings. The walking distance is a half-mile, and the route is wheelchair accessible. The new version will also include an indoor edition for inclement weather. ⊠ *PECO Energy Liberty Center, 6th and Chestnut sts., Historic Area* ☎ *215/542–3789 or 877/462–1776* ⊕ *www.lightsofliberty.org* 🎟 *$19.50* ☉ *Apr.–Oct., daily from just after dark.*

How Long to Stay: Budget a full day here. An early start lets you reserve timed tickets for a tour of the Todd and Bishop White houses and adjust your schedule to catch some of the special events on the visitor center's daily schedule. Allow about 40 minutes for the Independence Hall tour and another hour each at Franklin Court and the Todd and Bishop White houses. Allow 30 minutes each at Declaration House and the visitor center, where it's a good idea to see the film *Independence* before you set out. You might want to dine in the area and then catch the Lights of Liberty show.

seemed an incongruous setting for such a historic object. In mid-2003 the bell once again moved to another glass-enclosed pavilion with red-brick accents. This time, great care was taken to improve access to the bell and the view of its former home at Independence Hall, which is seen against the backdrop of the sky—rather than 20th-century buildings. The Liberty Bell complex houses a bell chamber, an interpretive exhibit area with historic displays and memorabilia, and a covered area for waiting in line.

During construction for the bell's current home, the foundation and other archaeological remains of The President's House, the home of the nation's chief executives before the capital shifted to Washington, D.C., were discovered, as well as evidence of slaves owned by President George Washington who lived there during his time in office. A temporary exhibit about the discovery is scheduled to be replaced on July 4, 2010, with a permanent installation that will include a series of video panels focusing on the stories of the nine enslaved African-Americans, as well as glass panels through which you can view the remains of the structure's foundation. ⊠ *6th and Chestnut Sts., Historic Area* ☎ *215/965–2305* ⊕ *www.nps.gov/inde/liberty-bell-center. htm* ⊠ *Free* ☉ *Daily 9–5.*

NEED A BREAK? Enter the **Bourse** (⊠ *5th St. across from Liberty Bell Pavilion, Historic Area* ☎ *215/625–0300* ⊕ *www.bourse-pa.com*) and you're in another century. The skylighted Great Hall, with its Corinthian columns, marble, wrought-iron stairways, and Victorian gingerbread details, has been magnificently restored. Built in 1895 as a stock exchange, it now houses shops and a food court, where you can grab a cup of cappuccino or a Philly cheesesteak.

WORTH NOTING

18 Bishop White House. Built in 1786, this restored upper-class house embodies Colonial and Federal elegance. It was the home of Bishop William White (1748–1836), rector of Christ Church, first Episcopal bishop of Pennsylvania, and spiritual leader of Philadelphia for 60 years. White, a founder of the Episcopal Church after the break with England, was chaplain to the Continental Congress and entertained many of the country's first families, including Washington and Franklin. The second-floor study contains much of the bishop's own library. Unlike most houses of the period, the bishop's house had an early form of flush toilet. The house tour is not recommended for small children. Get free tickets at the visitor center for one-hour tours that include the Todd House. ⊠ *309 Walnut St., Historic Area* ☎ *215/965–2305* ⊕ *www.nps.gov/ inde/bishop-white-house.htm* ⊠ *Free* ☉ *Hrs vary.*

9 Carpenters' Hall. This handsome, patterned red-and-black brick building dating from 1770 was the headquarters of the Carpenters' Company, a guild founded to support carpenters, who were both builders and architects in this era, and to aid their families. In September 1774 the First Continental Congress convened here and addressed a declaration of rights and grievances to King George III. Today re-creations of Colonial settings include original Windsor chairs and candle sconces and displays of 18th-century carpentry tools. The Carpenters' Company

PARKING STRATEGIES

Narrow, 18th-century streets have resulted in a 21st-century challenge: parking.

Your best option for the Historic District and Center City—especially if you plan to park once and walk or take public transit—is to use a garage.

The Philadelphia Parking Author-ity (☎ 215/683–9600 ⊕ www.phila-park.org) operates several garages in key locations, including 5th and Market streets (near Independence Mall), and offers some of the city's most competitive rates.

Central Parking System (☎ 215/567–1558 ⊕ www.parking.com) has many garages around Independence Hall and Center City. **Parkway Corporation** (☎ 215/575–4000 ⊕ www.parkwaycorp.com) has 48 parking garages in the Philadelphia area. Hotel packages offered through **Greater Philadelphia Tourism Marketing Corp.** (⊕ www.gophila.com) often include free parking.

If you plan to move your car over the course of a day, or if you enjoy the thrill of the hunt, try for on-street parking. Meters and restrictions in many—but not all—parts of Center City are Monday through Saturday only.

Meters typically cost $2 per hour, payable in change or by using a **Smart Card.** Available in $10, $20, or $50 denominations, Smart Cards are sold through the Parking Authority Web site, or by calling ☎ 215/222–9100.

While most meters restrict parking to two hours, there are longer-term (at least four hours) metered spaces in the Historic District on Front Street, between Market and Dock streets, and on the Benjamin Franklin Parkway between 20th and 26th streets.

Let the street parker beware: meter attendants track spaces regularly during posted hours. Never leave your car unattended in a no-parking or tow away zone.

still owns and operates the building. ⊠ *320 Chestnut St., Historic Area* ☎ *215/925–0167* ⊕ *www.nps.gov/inde* ☑ *Free* ☉ *Jan. and Feb., Wed.–Sun. 10–4; Mar.–Dec., Tues.–Sun. 10–4.*

⑥ Congress Hall. Formerly the Philadelphia County Courthouse, Congress Hall was the meeting place of the U.S. Congress from 1790 to 1800—one of the most important decades in our nation's history. Here the Bill of Rights was added to the Constitution; Alexander Hamilton's proposals for a mint and a national bank were enacted; and Vermont, Kentucky, and Tennessee became the first new states after the original colonies. On the first floor you can find the House of Representatives, where President John Adams was inaugurated in 1797. On the second floor is the Senate chamber, where in 1793 George Washington was inaugurated for his second term. Both chambers have been authentically restored. ⊠ *520 Chestnut St., at 6th St., Historic Area* ☎ *215/965–2305* ⊕ *www.nps.gov/inde* ☑ *Free* ☉ *Daily 9–5.*

⑯ Curtis Center. The lobby of the Curtis Publishing Company building has a great treasure: a 15- by 50-foot glass mosaic mural, *The Dream Garden,* based on a Maxfield Parrish painting. It was executed by the Louis

C. Tiffany Studios in 1916. The work's 260 colors and 100,000 pieces of opalescent hand-fired glass laced with gold leaf make it perhaps the finest Tiffany mural in the world. The mural has also been designated a "historic object" by the Philadelphia Historical Commission after its owner, the estate of a local art patron, put it up for sale for $9 million in 1998; the designation, the first in the city's history, stopped the sale and the mural remains in public view. ⊠ *6th and Walnut Sts., Historic Area* ☎ *215/627–7280* ⌸ *Free* ☉ *Weekdays 9–5.*

⑭ Declaration House. In a second-floor room that he had rented from bricklayer Jacob Graff, Thomas Jefferson (1743–1826) drafted the Declaration of Independence in June 1776. The home was reconstructed for the Bicentennial celebration; the bedroom and parlor in which Jefferson lived that summer were re-created with period furnishings. The first floor has a Jefferson exhibition and a seven-minute film, *The Extraordinary Creation.* The display on the Declaration of Independence shows some of the changes Jefferson made while writing it. You can see Jefferson's original version—which would have abolished slavery had the passage not been stricken by the committee that included Benjamin Franklin and John Adams. ⊠ *701 Market St., at 7th St., Historic Area* ☎ *215/965–2305* ⊕ *www.nps.gov/inde/declaration-house.html* ⌸ *Free* ☉ *Hrs vary.*

⑪ First Bank of the United States. A fine example of Federal architecture, the oldest bank building in the country was headquarters of the government's bank from 1797 to 1811. Designed by Samuel Blodget Jr. and erected in 1795–97, the bank was an imposing structure in its day, exemplifying strength, dignity, and security. Head first to the right, to the north side of the structure, to find a wrought-iron gateway topped by an eagle. Pass through it into the courtyard, and you magically step out of modern-day Philadelphia and into Colonial America. Before you do so, check out the bank's pediment. Executed in 1797 by Clodius F. Legrand and Sons, its cornucopia, oak branch, and American eagle are carved from mahogany—a late-18th-century masterpiece that has withstood acid rain better than the bank's marble pillars. ⊠ *120 S. 3rd St., Historic Area* ☉ *Interior closed to public.*

㉙ Franklin Square. One of five squares William Penn placed in his original design, this park is now a family-friendly destination. There are two modern playgrounds (for younger and older kids) open year-round. From April through October the square also features a carousel, a food stand with burgers, salads, shakes, and gelato operated by famed local restaurateur Stephen Starr, and an 18-hole miniature-golf course, whose holes boast scale models of Independence Hall, the Philadelphia Museum of Art, Ben Franklin Bridge, and other local landmarks. ⊠ *6th and Race Sts., Historic Area* ☎ *215/629–4026* ⊕ *www.historicphiladelphia.org* ⌸ *Free* ☉ *Daily dawn–dusk.*

Independence Living History Center. The park's former visitor center now houses the ongoing archaeological work on the more than 1 million artifacts unearthed during the construction of the National Constitution Center. You can watch archaeologists at work and ask them questions. In summer the center also offers screenings of the movie musical *1776.*

✉ *3rd and Chestnut Sts., Historic Area* ☎ *215/629–4026* ⊕ *www.nps. gov/inde/ilhc.htm* ✉ *Free* ⊘ *Daily 9–5.*

Independence Square. On July 8, 1776, the Declaration of Independence was first read in public here. Although the square is not as imposing today, it still has great dignity. You can imagine the impact the reading had on the colonists. ✉ *Bounded by Walnut and Chestnut Sts. and 5th and 6th Sts., Historic Area.*

❼ Library Hall. This 20th-century building is a reconstruction of Franklin's Library Company of Philadelphia, the first public library in the colonies. The American Philosophical Society, one of the country's leading institutions for the study of science, has its library here. The vaults contain such treasures as a copy of the Declaration of Independence handwritten by Thomas Jefferson, William Penn's 1701 Charter of Privileges, and journals from the Lewis and Clark expedition of 1803–06. The library's collection also includes first editions of Newton's *Principia Mathematica,* Franklin's *Experiments and Observations,* and Darwin's *On the Origin of Species.* ✉ *105 S. 5th St., Historic Area* ☎ *215/440–3400* ⊕ *www.amphilsoc.org/about/libhall.htm* ✉ *Free* ⊘ *Weekdays 9–4:45.*

❷ National Constitution Center. This 160,000-square-foot museum brings the U.S. Constitution alive through a series of highly interactive exhibits tracing the development and adoption of the nation's landmark guiding document. The heart of the sprawling museum, "The Story of We the People," takes you from the American Revolution through the Constitution's ratification to major events in the nation's constitutional history, including present-day events like the inauguration of President Barack Obama, Hurricane Katrina, and the recent economic crisis. Later, you can play the role of a Supreme Court justice deciding an important case, and walk among the framers in Signers Hall, where you can decide whether to add your signature to the list of Founding Fathers. The facility has 100-plus exhibits, plays host to many events with major historians, authors, and political figures, and also houses the Annenberg Center for Education and Outreach, a hub for constitutional education efforts. ✉ *525 Arch St., Historic Area* ☎ *215/409–6600* ⊕ *www.constitutioncenter.org* ✉ *$9* ⊘ *Weekdays 9:30–5, Sat. 9:30–6, Sun. noon–5.*

⓬ National Liberty Museum. Using interactive exhibits, video, and works of art, the museum aims to combat bigotry in the United States by putting a spotlight on the nation's rich traditions of freedom and diversity. Galleries celebrate outstanding Americans, including 19 Nobel Peace Prize winners, and heroes from around the world. The museum's collection of glass art is symbolic of the fragility of peace; its highlight is Dale Chihuly's 20-foot-tall red glass sculpture *Flame of Liberty.* Sandy Skoglund's colorful Jelly Bean People is a reminder that many of our differences are only skin deep. ✉ *321 Chestnut St., Historic Area* ☎ *215/925–2800* ⊕ *www.libertymuseum.org* ✉ *$7* ⊘ *Sept.–May, Tues.–Sun. 10–5; June–Aug., daily 10–5.*

⓾ New Hall Military Museum. The original of this reconstructed 1790 building briefly served as headquarters for the U.S. Department of War. On display are Revolutionary War uniforms, medals, and authentic weapons, including powder horns, swords, and a 1763 flintlock musket. Dioramas depict highlights of the Revolutionary War. The building also houses a Marine Corps memorial. ⊠ *320 Chestnut St., east of 4th St., Historic Area* ☎ *215/965–2305* ⊕ *www.nps.gov/inde/new-hall.htm* ▣ *Free* ☉ *Hrs vary.*

❺ **Old City Hall.** Independence Hall is flanked by Congress Hall to the west and Old City Hall to the east: three distinctive Federal-style buildings erected to house the city's growing government. But when Philadelphia became the nation's capital in 1790, the just-completed city hall was lent to the federal government. It housed the U.S. Supreme Court from 1791 to 1800; John Jay was the Chief Justice. Later, the boxlike building with a peaked roof and cupola was used as the city hall. Today an exhibit presents information about the early days of the federal judiciary. ⊠ *5th and Chestnut Sts., Historic Area* ☎ *215/965–2305* ⊕ *www. nps.gov/inde/old-city-hall.html* ▣ *Free* ☉ *Daily 9–5.*

⓯ **Philadelphia History Museum.** Formerly known as the Atwater Kent Museum, this facility chronicling the city's history is scheduled to reopen in September 2010 following an extensive renovation. Philadelphia's official history museum tells the city's story, beginning with its founding more than 300 years ago. Started in 1938 by A. Atwater Kent, a wealthy inventor, radio magnate, and manufacturer, the museum contains more than 100,000 objects—everything from textiles to toys—that illustrate what everyday life was like for generations of Philadelphians. New exhibits will include the interactive "Experience Philadelphia!"—which boasts a large walkable map of the city—as well as galleries exploring contemporary urban themes, the city's sports history, and its arts and cultural contributions. It occupies an elegant 1826 Greek Revival building designed by John Haviland, who was also the architect of the Eastern State Penitentiary. Among the museum's holdings are a 17th-century wampum belt given to William Penn by the Lenape people, and a sizable collection of works by Norman Rockwell, the best-known American illustrator of the 20th century, including the artist's 332 covers for the *Saturday Evening Post.* ⊠ *15 S. 7th St., Historic Area* ☎ *215/685–4830* ⊕ *www.philadelphiahistory.org* ☉ *Wed.–Sun. 1–5.*

Philadelphia Merchant's Exchange. Designed by the well-known Philadelphia architect William Strickland and built in 1832, this impressive Greek Revival structure served as the city's commercial center for 50 years. It was both the stock exchange and a place where merchants met to trade goods. In the tower a watchman scanned the Delaware River and notified merchants of arriving ships. The exchange stands behind Dock Street, a cobblestone thoroughfare closed to traffic. The building houses a small exhibit on its history and park offices. ⊠ *313 Walnut St., at 3rd St., Historic Area* ☎ *215/965–2305* ▣ *Free* ☉ *Weekdays 8:30–4:30.*

Philosophical Hall. This is the headquarters of the American Philosophical Society, founded by Benjamin Franklin in 1743 to promote "useful knowledge." The members of the oldest learned society in America have included Washington, Jefferson, Lafayette, Emerson, Darwin, Edison, Churchill, and Einstein. Erected between 1785 and 1789 in what has been called a "restrained Federal style" (designed to complement, not outshine, adjacent Independence Hall), Philosophical Hall is brick with marble trim and has a handsome arched entrance. The society's library is across the street in Library Hall. ⊠ *104 S. 5th St., Historic Area* 📞 *215/440–3400* ⊕ *www.amphilsoc.org* 🎟 *$1* ⊙ *Oct.–Feb., Fri.–Sun. 10–4; Mar.–Sept., Thurs.–Sun. 10–4.; May–Aug., Wed. 5–8.*

❽ Second Bank of the United States. When Second Bank President Nicholas Biddle held a design competition for a new building, he required all architects to use the Greek style; William Strickland, one of the foremost architects of the 19th century, won. Built in 1824, the bank, with its Doric columns, was based on the design of the Parthenon and helped establish the popularity of Greek Revival architecture in the United States. The interior hall, though, was Roman, with a dramatic barrel-vault ceiling. Housed here are portraits of prominent Colonial Americans by noted artists such as Charles Willson Peale, William Rush, and Gilbert Stuart. Don't miss Peale's portraits of Jefferson and Lewis and Clark: The former is the only one that shows the third president with red hair, and the latter is the only known portrait of the famous explorers. The permanent exhibition, "The People of Independence," has a life-size wooden statue of George Washington by William Rush; a mural of Philadelphia in the 1830s by John A. Woodside Jr.; and the only known likeness of William Floyd, a lesser-known signer of the Declaration of Independence. ⊠ *420 Chestnut St., Historic Area* 📞 *215/965–2305* ⊕ *www.nps.gov/inde/second-bank.html* 🎟 *Free* ⊙ *Hrs vary.*

⑰ Todd House. Built in 1775 by John Dilworth, Todd House has been restored to its 1790s appearance, when its best-known resident, Dolley Payne Todd (1768–1849), lived here. She lost her husband, the Quaker lawyer John Todd, to the yellow fever epidemic of 1793. Dolley later married James Madison, who became the fourth president. Her time as a hostess in the White House was quite a contrast to her years in this simple home. There's an 18th-century garden next to Todd House. Get free tickets at the visitor center for one-hour tours that include the Bishop White House. ⊠ *4th and Walnut Sts., Historic Area* 📞 *215/965–2305* ⊕ *www.nps.gov/inde/todd-house.html* 🎟 *Free* ⊙ *Hrs vary.*

⑲ Welcome Park. A scale model of the Penn statue that tops City Hall sits on a 60-foot-long map of Penn's Philadelphia, carved in the pavement of Welcome Park. (The *Welcome* was the ship that transported Penn to America.) The wall surrounding the park displays a time line of William Penn's life, with information about his philosophy and quotations from his writings. The park was the site of the slate-roof house where Penn lived briefly and where he granted the Charter of Privileges in 1701. Written by Penn, the Charter of Privileges served as Pennsylvania's constitutional framework until 1776; the Liberty Bell was commissioned to commemorate the charter's 50th anniversary. The City Tavern, across the street, marks the site where George Washington once dined. It's still open for historically accurate lunches and dinners. ⊠ *2nd St. just north of Walnut St., Historic Area.*

OLD CITY

In Colonial days the rich folks in residential Society Hill whispered of those who lived "north of Market," for this area, between Front and 5th streets and Chestnut and Vine streets, was the city's commercial district for industry and wholesale distributors, filled with wharves and warehouses and taverns. It also held the modest homes of craftsmen and artisans. Old City (as it became known some 40 years ago, to distinguish it from the national park area around Independence Hall) is aptly named: it's one of the city's oldest and most historic neighborhoods, home to Elfreth's Alley; the Betsy Ross House; and Christ Church, where George Washington and John Adams came (across the tracks!) to worship at services. There's evidence of the Quaker presence here, too, in the Arch Street Meeting House.

Today Old City is one of Philadelphia's trendiest neighborhoods, a local version of New York's SoHo. Many cast-iron building facades remain, though the old warehouses, with telltale names such as the Sugar Refinery and the Hoopskirt Factory, now house well-lighted loft apartments popular with artists and architects. There are small theaters—the Painted Bride, the Arden Theatre Company—and numerous art galleries and boutiques. The Old City Arts Association hosts a festive, popular event the first Friday of each month—known, appropriately enough, as First Friday—when the galleries throw open their doors during evening hours.

PLANNING YOUR TIME

If possible, set aside four or five hours on a Sunday for your visit to Old City. You could attend the 9 AM service at Christ Church, as George and Martha Washington did, and then join the 10:30 Quaker meeting at the Arch Street Friends Meeting House, where William Penn worshipped. Try to avoid scheduling a Monday visit from November through February, when two of the top sights—the Betsy Ross House and Elfreth's Alley—are closed. If you detour to the Poe House, allow another two hours.

TOP ATTRACTIONS

23 **Betsy Ross House.** It's easy to find this little brick house with the gabled roof: just look for the 13-star flag displayed from its second-floor window. Whether Betsy Ross, also known as Elizabeth Griscom Ross Ashbourn Claypoole (1752–1836)—who worked in her family's flag-making and upholstery business—actually lived here and whether she really made the first Stars and Stripes is debatable. Nonetheless, the house, built about 1760, is a splendid example of a Colonial Philadelphia home and is fun to visit. Owned and maintained by the city, the eight-room house overflows with artifacts such as a family Bible and Betsy Ross's chest of drawers and reading glasses. The small rooms hold period pieces that reflect the life of this hardworking Quaker (who died at the age of 84, outliving three husbands). You may have to wait in line, as this is one of the city's most popular attractions. The house, with its winding narrow stairs, is not accessible to people with disabilities. Alongside the house is a courtyard with a fountain, benches, and the graves of Betsy Ross and her third husband, John Claypoole. ⌂ 239

GREAT EXPERIENCES IN OLD CITY

African American Museum in Philadelphia: One of the nation's first museums created to commemorate Black history, the museum has a special focus on the lives of African-Americans during the nation's first century.

Betsy Ross House: Whether or not you really believe the story of Betsy Ross sewing the first Stars and Stripes flag, her house is worth a visit as an example of a typical Colonial home.

Christ Church: Attend a service at this stately Georgian-style church, whose congregation included 15 signers of the Declaration of Independence.

Christ Church Burial Ground: See the final resting place of Benjamin Franklin and other founder fathers.

Elfreth's Alley: Stroll through this charming, cobblestone lane—the oldest continuously occupied street in the country—and imagine yourself living in Colonial times.

Arch St., Old City ☎ *215/686–4026* ⊕ *www.betsyrosshouse.org* ✉ *$3; $2 charge for audio tour* ⊙ *Jan.–Mar., Wed.–Sun. 10–5; Apr.–Sept., daily 10–5; Oct.–Dec., Tues.–Sun. 10–5.*

㉑ ★ Elfreth's Alley. The alley, the oldest continuously occupied residential street in America, dates to 1702. Much of Colonial Philadelphia resembled this area, with its cobblestone streets and narrow two- or three-story brick houses. These were modest row homes, most built for rent, and lived in by craftsmen, such as cabinetmakers, silversmiths, and pewterers, and their families. They also housed captains and others who made their living in the city's busy shipping industry. The earliest houses (two stories) have pent eaves; taller houses, built after the Revolution, show the influence of the Federal style. The Elfreth's Alley Museum includes two homes that have been restored by the Elfreth's Alley Association: No. 124, home of a Windsor chair maker, and No. 126, a Colonial dressmaker's home, with authentic furnishings and a Colonial kitchen. In early June residents celebrate Fete Day, when some of the 30 homes are open to the public for tours hosted by guides in Colonial garb. On the second Friday evening in December, residents again welcome visitors for a candlelight holiday tour. Both of these special events require advance tickets. ✉ *Front and 2nd Sts. between Arch and Race Sts., Old City* ☎ *215/574–0560* ⊕ *www.elfrethsalley.org* ✉ *Alley free; museum $5* ⊙ *Mar.–Oct., Mon.–Sat. 10–5, Sun. noon–5; Nov.–Feb., Thurs.–Sat. 10–5, Sun. noon–5.*

㉕ United States Mint. The first U.S. mint was built in Philadelphia at 16th and Spring Garden streets in 1792, when the Bank of North America adopted dollars and cents instead of shillings and pence as standard currency; the current mint was built in 1971. During a self-guided tour you can see blank disks being melted, cast, and pressed into coins, which are then inspected, counted, and bagged. The visitors' gallery has an exhibition of medals from the nation's wars, including the Medal of Honor, the Purple Heart, and the Bronze Star. Seven Tiffany glass tile mosaics depict coin making in ancient Rome. A shop in the lobby sells special coins and medals—in mint condition. ⊠ *5th and Arch Sts., Old City* ☎ *215/408–0114* ⊕ *www.usmint.gov* 🎫 *Free* ☾ *Weekdays 9–3.*

WORTH NOTING

㉘ **African American Museum in Philadelphia.** The centerpiece of this museum
★ is "Audacious Freedom: African Americans in Philadelphia 1776–1876," a permanent exhibit that uses video and touch-screen monitors to tell the stories of such pioneers as Frances Ellens Watkins Harper, a conductor on the Underground Railroad and suffragist, Thomas Morris Chester, a journalist and lawyer who was the first black to argue a case before the U.S. Supreme Court, and Elizabeth Taylor Greenfield, a renowned singer who performed for Queen Victoria. The museum's gift shop stocks one of the area's widest selection of books on black culture, history, fiction, poetry, and drama, along with African textiles and sculpture and African-American jewelry, prints, and tiles. Opened in the Bicentennial year of 1976, this is the first museum of its kind funded and built by a city. ⊠ *701 Arch St., Old City* ☎ *215/574–0380* ⊕ *www.aampmuseum.org* 🎫 *$10* ☾ *Tues.–Sat. 10–5, Sun. noon–5.*

㉔ **Arch Street Meeting House.** Constructed in 1804 for the Philadelphia Yearly Meeting of the Society of Friends, this building of simple lines is still used for that purpose, as well as for biweekly services. Among the most influential members in the 19th century was Lucretia Mott (1793–1880), a leader in the women's suffrage, antiwar, and antislavery movements. A small museum in the building presents a series of dioramas and a 14-minute slide show depicting the life and accomplishments of William Penn (1644–1718), who gave the land on which the meeting house sits to the Society of Friends. Quaker guides give tours year-round. ⊠ *320 Arch St., at 4th St., Old City* ☎ *215/627–2667* ⊕ *www.archstreetfriends.org* 🎫 *$2 suggested donation* ☾ *Mon.–Sat. 10–4; worship Wed. at 7 PM and Sun. at 10:30 AM.*

OFF THE BEATEN PATH

Benjamin Franklin Bridge. When the bridge opened in 1926, its 1,750-foot main span made it the longest suspension bridge in the world. Paul Cret, architect of the Rodin Museum, was the designer. The bridge has been having some rust problems of late, but a massive, multiyear project has restored its glorious blue paint job. The bridge is most impressive when it's lighted at night. Start the 1¾-mi walk (one-way) from either the Philadelphia side, two blocks north of the U.S. Mint, or the Camden, New Jersey, side. ⊠ *5th and Vine Sts., Old City* ☎ *215/218–3750* ⊕ *www.drpa.org.*

⑳ **Christ Church.** The Anglicans of the Church of England built a wooden church on this site in 1697. When they outgrew it, they erected a new church, the most sumptuous in the colonies, designed by Dr. John Kearsley and modeled on the work of famed English architect Sir Christopher Wren. The symmetrical, classical facade with arched windows, completed in 1754, is a fine example of Georgian architecture; the church is one of the city's treasures. The congregation included 15 signers of the Declaration of Independence. The bells and the soaring 196-foot steeple, the tallest in the colonies, were financed by lotteries run by Benjamin Franklin. Brass plaques mark the pews of George and Martha Washington, John and Abigail Adams, Betsy Ross, and others. Two blocks west of the church is Christ Church Burial Ground. ⊠ *20 N. American St., 2nd St. north of Market St., Old City* ☎ *215/922–1695* ⊕ *www.oldchristchurch.org* ⊠ *$3 suggested donation* ☉ *Jan. and Feb., Wed.–Sat. 9–5, Sun. 1–5; Mar.–Dec., Mon.–Sat. 9–5, Sun. 1–5; services Sun. 9 and 11, Wed. at noon.*

NEED A BREAK?

Old City Metro Cafe in Farmicia (⊠ *15 S. 3rd St., Old City* ☎ *215/627–6274* ⊕ *www.farmiciarestaurant.com*) serves a wide range of breakfast and lunch dishes, as well as a tantalizing array of brownies and cookies, along with coffee and other beverages.

Christ Church Burial Ground. Weathered gravestones fill the resting place of five signers of the Declaration of Independence and other Colonial patriots. The best-known is Benjamin Franklin; he lies alongside his wife, Deborah, and their son, Francis, who died at age four. According to local legend, throwing a penny onto Franklin's grave will bring you good luck. The burial ground is open to the public—except in January and February—for regular visits for the first time in 150 years. ⊠ *5th and Arch Sts., Old City* ☎ *215/922–1695* ⊕ *www.oldchristchurch.org* ⊠ *$2* ☉ *Mar.–Nov., Mon.–Sat. 10–4, Sun. noon–4; Dec., weekdays noon–4, Sat. 10–4, Sun. noon–4.*

OFF THE BEATEN PATH

Edgar Allan Poe National Historic Site. One of America's most original writers, Edgar Allan Poe (1809–49), lived here from 1843 to 1844; it's the only one of his Philadelphia residences still standing. During that time some of his best-known short stories were published: "The Telltale Heart," "The Black Cat," and "The Gold Bug." You can tour the three-story brick house; to evoke the spirit of Poe, the National Park Service is displaying first-edition manuscripts and has set up painted backdrops in some rooms to provide a sense of how it may have looked in Poe's time. An adjoining house has exhibits on Poe and his family, his work habits, and his literary contemporaries; there's also an eight-minute film and a small Poe library and reading room. A statue of a raven helps set the mood. Special programs include Poetry Month tours (usually March or April) and popular "ghostly" tours in October (reservations required). The site, easily reached from the African American Museum, is five blocks north of Market Street. SEPTA Bus 47 travels on 7th Street to Spring Garden Street, where you should disembark. ⊠ *532 N. 7th St., Northern Liberties* ☎ *215/597–8780* ⊕ *www.nps.gov/edal* ⊠ *Free* ☉ *Wed.–Sun. 9–5.*

㉒ ☾ **Fireman's Hall Museum.** Housed in an authentic 1876 firehouse, this museum traces the history of fire fighting, from the volunteer company founded in Philadelphia by Benjamin Franklin in 1736 to the professional departments of the 20th century. The collection includes early hand- and horse-drawn fire engines, such as an 1815 hand pumper and a 1907 three-horse Metropolitan steamer; fire marks (18th-century building signs marking them as insured for fire); uniforms; and other memorabilia. ⊠ *147 N. 2nd St., Old City* ☎ *215/923–1438* ⊕ *www. firemanshallstore.com* ⊠ *Free* ☉ *Tues.–Sat. 10–4:30 and 1st Fri. of each month 10–9.*

William Penn and His Legacy

William Penn was a rebel with a cause. Born in London in 1644 into a nobleman's family, he attended Oxford University, studied law, and tried a military career (in emulation of his father, an admiral in the British Navy). It was at Oxford that Penn first heard Quaker preachers professing that each life is part of the Divine spirit, and that all people should be treated equally. At age 23, Penn joined the Religious Society of Friends (Quakers), who at the time were considered religious zealots.

Penn was imprisoned in the Tower of London for his heretical pamphlets, but he was spared worse persecution because of his father's support of King Charles II. He petitioned the king to grant him land in the New World for a Quaker colony; he was given a 45,000-square-mi tract along the Delaware River in payment of a debt Charles owed to his late father. Indeed, the king named the land Pennsylvania in honor of the admiral.

On Penn's first visit to his colony, from 1662 to 1664, he began his "Holy Experiment," establishing his haven for Quakers. His laws guaranteed religious freedom and an elected government. He bought land from the Native Americans and established a peace treaty that lasted for 70 years.

Penn was called back to England in 1684 and remained there until 1699, caring for his ill wife, Gulielma Maria Springett, who would die without seeing his beloved Pennsylvania. Penn was suspected of plotting with the former Catholic king, James II, to overthrow the Protestant monarchy of William and Mary, who revoked his charter in 1692 for 18 months.

Penn made his second trip to America with his second wife, Hannah Callowhill Penn, in 1699. The couple moved into Pennsbury Manor along the upper Delaware River, where, while preaching about a life of simplicity, he lived in luxury. Penn issued a new frame of government, the Charter of Privileges, which became a model for the U.S. Constitution. He had to return to England yet again in 1701; there he was consumed by the political and legal problems of his colony, a term in prison for debt, and then illness. Penn died before he could return to Pennsylvania. After his death, his wife honored him by assuming the governorship for nine years.

Although Penn spent only four of his 74 years in Pennsylvania, his legacy is profound. As a city planner, he mapped out a "greene countrie towne" with broad, straight streets. He positioned each house in the middle of its plot, so that every child would have play space; he named its streets—Walnut, Spruce, Chestnut—for trees, not for men. His original city plan has survived. As a reformer, Penn replaced dungeons with workhouses, established the right of a jury to decide a verdict without harassment by a judge; provided schools where boys—and girls—could get a practical education; and limited the death penalty to two offenses—murder and treason—rather than the 200 mandated by English criminal law.

Welcome Park (✉ *2nd St. just north of Walnut, Old City*) has a time line of Penn's life and a map of Penn's Philadelphia carved in the pavement.

Free Quaker Meeting House. This was the house of worship for the Free "Fighting" Quakers, a group that broke away from the Society of Friends to take up arms against the British during the Revolutionary War. The building was designed in 1783 by Samuel Wetherill, one of the original leaders of the group, after they were disowned by their pacifist brothers. Among the 100 members were Betsy Ross (then Elizabeth Griscom) and Thomas Mifflin, a signer of the Constitution. After the Free Quaker group dissolved (many left to become Episcopalian), the building was used as a school, library, and warehouse. The meeting house, built in the Quaker plain style with a brick front and gable roof, has been carefully restored. ⊠ *500 Arch St., at 5th St., Old City* ☎ *215/965–2305* ⊕ *www.nps.gov/inde/free-quaker.htm* ⊠ *Free* ☉ *Wed.–Sun. 10–4.*

Loxley Court. One of the restored 18th-century houses in this lovely court was once home to Benjamin Loxley, a carpenter who worked on Independence Hall. The court's claim to fame, according to its residents, is as the spot where Benjamin Franklin flew his kite in his experiment with lightning; the key tied to it was the key to Loxley's front door. ⊠ *321–323 Arch St., Old City* ☉ *Closed to public.*

㉗ Mikveh Israel. Nathan Levy, a Colonial merchant whose ship, the *Myrtilla,* brought the Liberty Bell to America, helped found this Jewish congregation in 1740, making it the oldest in Philadelphia and the second oldest in the United States. The original synagogue was at 3rd and Cherry streets; the congregation's current space (1976) is in the Sephardic style (following Spanish and Portuguese Jewish ritual). The synagogue's Spruce Street Cemetery (about eight blocks away, beyond Old City) dates from 1740 and is the oldest surviving Jewish site in Philadelphia. It was the burial ground for the Spanish-Portuguese Jewish community. Guided tours, arranged through the synagogue, are given mid-June through mid-August, Tuesday to Friday and Sunday 10 to 3, and by appointment the rest of the year. ⊠ *Synagogue: 44 N. 4th St., Old City* ☎ *215/922–5446* ⊕ *www.mikvehisrael.org* ☉ *Mon.–Thurs. 10–5, Fri. 10–3, Sun. noon–5* ⊠ *Cemetery: Spruce St. between 8th and 9th Sts., Old City .*

NEED A BREAK? Located next door to its popular namesake restaurant, Fork: etc. (⊠ *308 Market St., Old City* ☎ *215/625–9425* ⊕ *www.forkrestaurant.com/forketc.htm*) offers an ever-changing array of gourmet salads, soups, sandwiches, and pastries. You can dine in or take food out for a picnic in nearby Independence National Historical Park.

㉖ National Museum of American Jewish History. Established in 1976, this museum is scheduled to move to a new 100,000-square-foot building on a high-profile corner near Independence Hall in the fall of 2010. The core exhibits will tap the museum's collection of 20,000 objects to trace the history of American Jews from 1654 to the present. A ground floor gallery, "*Only in America,*" will be a multimedia showcase of the accomplishments of Jewish Americans. Until the fall 2010 move, the museum shares a building with **Mikveh Israel.** ⊠ *55 N. 5th St.,*

Old City ☎ *215/923–3811* ⊕ *www.nmajh.org* ✉ *Free* ☉ *Mon.–Thurs. 10–5, Fri. 10–3, Sun. noon–5.*

**OFF THE
BEATEN
PATH**

☾ **Insectarium.** In Northeastern Philly, a neighborhood not known for its tourist attractions, is this bug lover's heaven. Revel in this ugly, yet beautiful collection of thousands of creepy crawlers—tarantulas, giant centipedes, assassin bugs, and metallic beetles that look like pieces of gold jewelry. Started by an exterminator, the mustum is home to more than 50 live species and mounted insects from around the world. The 5,000-square-foot space has one of the largest butterfly and moth collections in North America, a working beehive, a tank filled with glow-in-the-dark scorpions, and a kitchen teeming with live cockroaches. It's definitely a place for screaming kids, but it's hard not to enjoy at any age. It's easier to drive here than to take public transportation. By public transit: take the Market-Frankford subway to the end (Bridge Street); transfer to SEPTA Bus 66 to Welsh Road. ⊠ *8046 Frankford Ave., Northeast Philadelphia* ☎ *215/335–9500* ⊕ *www.myinsectarium. com* ✉ *$6* ☉ *Mon.–Sat. 10–4.*

SOCIETY HILL

During the 18th century Society Hill was Philadelphia's showplace. A carefully preserved district, it remains the city's most photogenic neighborhood, filled with hidden courtyards, delightful decorative touches such as chimney pots and brass door knockers, wrought-iron foot scrapers, and other remnants from the days of horse-drawn carriages and muddy, unpaved streets. Here time has not quite stopped but meanders down the cobblestone streets, whiling away the hours.

A trove of Colonial- and Federal-style brick row houses, churches, and narrow streets, Society Hill stretches from the Delaware River to 8th Street, south of Independence National Historical Park. Those homes built before 1750 in the Colonial style generally have 2½ stories and a dormer window jutting out of a steep roof. The less heavy, more graceful houses built after the Revolution were often in the Federal style, popularized in England during the 1790s.

Here lived the "World's People," wealthier Anglicans who arrived after William Penn and loved music and dancing—pursuits the Quakers shunned when they set up their enclave in Old City, north of Market Street, in a less desirable commercial area. The "Society" in the neighborhood's moniker refers, however, to the Free Society of Traders, a group of business investors who settled here on William Penn's advice.

Today many Colonial homes in this area have been lovingly restored by modern pioneers who moved into the area nearly 50 years ago and rescued Society Hill from becoming a slum. Inspired urban renewal efforts have transformed vast empty factory spaces into airy lofts; new town houses were carefully designed to blend in with the old. As a result, Society Hill is not just a showcase for historic churches and mansions but a living, breathing neighborhood.

GREAT EXPERIENCES IN SOCIETY HILL

Head House Square: On weekends from May through December, peruse the wares from local farmers and artisans at this historic marketplace.

House museums: See how well the Colonial era's movers and shakers lived by touring two of the city's most gracious residences, the Physick and Powel houses.

Mother Bethel African Methodist Episcopal Church: This house of worship also served as a stop on the Underground Railroad.

South Street: Stroll the city's funkiest shopping district.

Washington Square: Have a picnic or kick back on a bench at this lush park, one of the city's original squares and also the graveyard for 2,600 British and American soldiers who died in the Revolutionary War.

PLANNING YOUR TIME

You'll need about one hour to walk through Society Hill, more if you tour the Powel and Physick houses. If walking is your main interest, save this excursion for a warm day, because it can be quite windy along the waterfront. On summer weekends Penn's Landing bustles with festivals and Head House Square turns into a farmers' market with locally grown products and baked goods and a marketplace for fine arts and crafts.

TOP ATTRACTIONS

❺ Head House Square. This open-air Colonial marketplace, extending from Pine Street to Lombard Street, is a reminder of the days when people went to central outdoor markets to buy food directly from farmers. It was first established as New Market in 1745. George Washington was among those who came here to buy butter, eggs, meat, fish, herbs, and vegetables. The Head House, a boxy building with a cupola and weather vane, was built in 1803 as the office and home of the market master, who tested the quality of the goods. Today, every weekend from May through December, it is the site of a farmer's market, featuring about a dozen vendors on Saturdays and 30 on Sunday. On some summer weekends the square also is home to a crafts and fine arts fair featuring the work of more than 30 Delaware Valley artists. ⊠ *2nd and Pine Sts., Society Hill* ☎ *215/790–0782* ⊗ *May–Dec., Sat–Sun. 10–2.*

❶ Physick House. Built in 1786, this is one of two remaining freestand-
★ ing houses from this era in Society Hill (you will see plenty of the famous Philadelphia row houses here). It's also one of the most beautiful homes in America, with elegantly restored interiors and some of the finest Federal and Empire furniture in Philadelphia. Touches of Napoléon's France are everywhere: the golden bee motif woven into upholstery; the magenta-hue Aubusson rug (the emperor's favorite color); and stools in the style of Pompeii, the Roman city rediscovered at the time of the house's construction. Upstairs in the parlor, note the inkstand that still retains Benjamin Franklin's fingerprints. The house's most famous owner was Philip Syng Physick, the "Father of American

Surgery" and a leading physician in the days before anesthesia. His most celebrated patient was Chief Justice John Marshall. The garden planted on three sides of the house is filled with plants common during the 19th century: complete with an Etruscan sarcophagus, a natural grotto, and antique cannon, it is considered by some to be the city's loveliest. ⊠ *321 S. 4th St., Society Hill* ☎ *215/925–7866* ⊕ *www.philalandmarks.org* ⊠ *$5* ◷ *Thurs.–Sat., noon–5, Sun. 1–5; guided tours on hr, last tour at 4.*

> ### WORD OF MOUTH
>
> "I hope your visit includes a Sunday, as Head House Market, one of the best outdoor farmer's markets in the city, re-opens in May and is open on Sundays from 10–2. I love this place—brimming with fresh fruits, veggies, cheeses, baked goods, and flowers, not to mention people running into friends with some shrieks and hugs...a great place to people watch and take in the local scene."　　　　—go_laura

❾ ★ Powel House. The 1765 brick Georgian house purchased by Samuel Powel in 1769 remains one of the most elegant homes in Philadelphia. Powel—the "Patriot Mayor"—was the last mayor of Philadelphia under the Crown and the first in the new republic. The lavish home, a former wreck saved from demolition in 1930, is furnished with important pieces of 18th-century Philadelphia furniture. A mahogany staircase from Santo Domingo embellishes the front hall, and there is a signed Gilbert Stuart portrait in the parlor. In the second-floor ballroom Mrs. Powel—the city's hostess-with-the-mostest—served floating islands and whipped syllabubs to distinguished guests (including Adams, Franklin, and Lafayette) on Nanking china that was a gift from George and Martha Washington. Today the ballroom can be rented for parties and special events. ⊠ *244 S. 3rd St., Society Hill* ☎ *215/627–0364* ⊕ *www. philalandmarks.org* ⊠ *$5* ◷ *Thurs.–Sat. noon–5, Sun. 1–5; guided tours on hr, last tour at 4.*

WORTH NOTING

⑫ Athenaeum. Housed in a national landmark Italianate brownstone dating from the mid-1800s and designed by John Notman, the Athenaeum is a research library specializing in architectural history and design. Its American Architecture Collection has close to a million items. The library, founded in 1814, contains significant materials on the French in America and on early American travel, exploration, and transportation. Besides books, the Athenaeum has notable paintings and period furniture; changing exhibits are presented in the gallery. ⊠ *219 S. 6th St., Society Hill* ☎ *215/925–2688* ⊕ *www.philaathenaeum.org* ⊠ *Free* ◷ *Gallery, weekdays 9–5, first Sat. of each month 10–2; tours by appointment.*

❷ Mother Bethel African Methodist Episcopal Church. Society Hill holds a notable landmark in the history of African-Americans in the city. In 1787 Richard Allen led fellow blacks who left St. George's Methodist Church as a protest against the segregated worship. Allen, a lay minister and former slave who had bought his freedom from the Chew family of Germantown, purchased this site in 1791. It's believed to be the country's oldest parcel of land continuously owned by African-Americans.

When the African Methodist Episcopal Church was formed in 1816, Allen was its first bishop. The current church, the fourth on the site, is an example of the 19th-century Romanesque Revival style, with broad arches and a square corner tower, opalescent stained-glass windows, and stunning woodwork. The earlier church buildings were the site of a school where Allen taught slaves to read and also a stop on the Underground Railroad. Allen's tomb and a small museum are on the lower level. ⊠ *419 Richard Allen Ave., S. 6th St. between Pine and Lombard Sts., Society Hill* ☎ *215/925–0616* ⊕ *www.motherbethel.org* ✉ *Donation requested* ⊙ *Museum Tues.–Sat. 10–3.*

❸ **Old Pine Street Presbyterian Church.** Designed by Robert Smith in 1768 as a simple brick Georgian-style building, Old Pine is the only remaining Colonial Presbyterian church and churchyard in Philadelphia. Badly damaged by British troops during the Revolution, it served as a hospital and then a stable. In the mid-19th century its exterior had a Greek Revival face-lift that included Corinthian columns. In the 1980s the interior walls and ceiling were stenciled with thistle and wave motifs, a reminder of Old Pine's true name—Third, Scots, and Mariners Presbyterian Church, which documented the congregation's mergers. The beautifully restored church is painted in soft shades of periwinkle and yellow. In the churchyard are the graves of 100 Hessian soldiers from the Revolution—and of Eugene Ormandy, former conductor of the Philadelphia Orchestra. ⊠ *412 Pine St., Society Hill* ☎ *215/925–8051* ⊕ *www.oldpine.org* ✉ *Free* ⊙ *Weekdays 10–noon and 2–3; Sun. worship late Sept.–late June 10:30, late June–mid-Sept. 9:30.*

❿ **Old St. Joseph's Church.** In 1733 a tiny chapel was established by Jesuits for Philadelphia's 11 Catholic families. It was one of the first places in the English-speaking colonies where Catholic mass could be legally celebrated, a right granted under William Penn's 1701 Charter of Privileges, which guaranteed religious freedom. But freedom didn't come easy; on one occasion Quakers had to patrol St. Joseph's to prevent a Protestant mob from disrupting the service. The present church, built in 1839, is the third on this site. The late-19th-century stained-glass windows are notable. ⊠ *321 Willings Alley, Society Hill* ☎ *215/923–1733* ⊕ *www. oldstjoseph.org* ✉ *Free* ⊙ *Daily 9:30–4:30; mass Mon.–Sat. 12:05, Sat. 5:30, Sun. 7:30, 9:30, 11:30, 6:30.*

❽ **Old St. Mary's Church.** The city's second-oldest Catholic church, circa 1763, became its first cathedral when the archdiocese was formed in 1808. A Gothic-style facade was added in 1880; the interior was redone in 1979. The stained-glass windows, a ceiling mural of St. Mary, and brass chandeliers that hung in the Founders Room of Independence Hall until 1967 are highlights. Commodore John Barry, a Revolutionary War naval hero, and other famous Philadelphians are buried in the small churchyard. ⊠ *252 S. 4th St., Society Hill* ☎ *215/923–7930* ⊕ *www.ushistory.org/tour/tour_stmary.htm* ✉ *Free* ⊙ *Daily 9–4; mass Sat. 4:30, Sun. 10.*

⓫ **Philadelphia Contributionship for the Insurance of Houses from Loss by Fire.** The Contributionship, the nation's oldest fire insurance company, was founded by Benjamin Franklin in 1752; the present Greek Revival

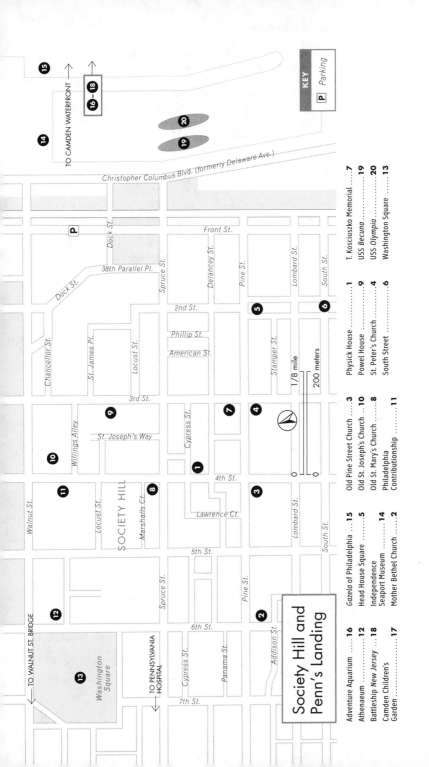

Society Hill and Penn's Landing

Adventure Aquarium **16**
Athenaeum **12**
Battleship *New Jersey* ... **18**
Camden Children's
Garden **17**

Gazela of Philadelphia ... **15**
Head House Square **5**
Independence
Seaport Museum **14**
Mother Bethel Church **2**

Old Pine Street Church **3**
Old St. Joseph's Church .. **10**
Old St. Mary's Church **8**
Philadelphia
Contributionship **11**

Physick House **1**
Powel House **9**
St. Peter's Church **4**
South Street **6**

T. Kosciuszko Memorial **7**
USS *Becuna* **19**
USS *Olympia* **20**
Washington Square **13**

KEY

P Parking

building with fluted marble Corinthian columns dates from 1836 and has some magnificently elegant salons (particularly the boardroom, where a seating plan on the wall lists Benjamin Franklin as the first incumbent of seat Number One). The architect, Thomas U. Walter, was also responsible for the dome and House and Senate wings of the U.S. Capitol in Washington, D.C. This is still an active business, but a small museum is open to the public. ⊠ *212 S. 4th St., Society Hill* ☏ *215/627–1752* ⊕ *www.contributionship.com* ⊡ *Free* ☉ *Weekdays 9–4.*

❹ **St. Peter's Episcopal Church.** Founded by members of Christ Church in ★ Old City who were living in newly settled Society Hill, St. Peter's has been in continuous use since its first service on September 4, 1761. William White, rector of Christ Church, also served in that role at St. Peter's until his death in 1836. The brick Palladian-style building was designed by Scottish architect Robert Smith, who was responsible for Carpenters' Hall and the steeple on Christ Church. William Strickland's simple steeple, a Philadelphia landmark, was added in 1842. Notable features include the grand Palladian window on the chancel wall, high-back box pews that were raised off the floor to eliminate drafts, and the unusual arrangement of altar and pulpit at either end of the main aisle. The design has been called "restrained," but what is palpable on a visit is the silence and grace of the stark white interior. In the churchyard lie Commodore John Hazelwood, a Revolutionary War hero, painter Charles Willson Peale, and seven Native American chiefs who died of smallpox on a visit to Philadelphia in 1793. A guide is on hand Saturday from 11 to 5 and on Sunday to answer questions. Call ahead for tours. ⊠ *313 Pine St., Society Hill* ☏ *215/925–5968* ⊕ *www.stpetersphila.org* ☉ *Weekdays 8:30–4, Sat. 8:30–5, Sun. 1–3; services Sun. 9 and 11.*

❻ **South Street.** Philadelphia's most bohemian neighborhood is crammed with craft shops and condom stores, coffee bars and tattoo parlors, ethnic restaurants, and New Age bookshops. At night it's crammed with people—those who hang out, and those who come to watch them, giving South Street the offbeat feel of Greenwich Village mixed with Bourbon Street. To some, it's still "the hippest street in town," as the Orlons called it in their 1963 song, although flower children have been replaced by teens with pierced eyebrows, and the crowds can get rowdy, especially late on weekend nights. ⊠ *South St. from Front St. to about 10th St., Lombard St. to Bainbridge St., Society Hill / Queen Village* ⊕ *www.southstreet.com.*

❼ **Thaddeus Kosciuszko National Memorial.** A Polish general who later became a national hero in his homeland, Kosciuszko came to the United States in 1776 to help fight in the Revolution; he distinguished himself as one of the first foreign volunteers in the war. The plain three-story brick house, built around 1776, in 2009 launched a series of new exhibits that feature a rotating collection of artifacts from six museums in Poland to help depict Kosciuszko's life in his homeland. An eight-minute film (in English and Polish) portrays the general's activities during the Revolution. ⊠ *301 Pine St., Society Hill* ☏ *215/597–9618* ⊕ *www.nps.gov/ thko* ⊡ *Free* ☉ *Wed.–Sun. noon–4.*

⑬ Washington Square. This leafy area resembling a London park has been through numerous incarnations since it was set aside by William Penn. From 1705 until after the Revolution, the square was lined on three sides by houses and on the fourth by the Walnut Street Prison. The latter was home to Robert Morris, who went to debtors' prison after he helped finance the Revolution. The square served as a burial ground for victims of the 1793 yellow fever epidemic and for 2,600 British and American soldiers who perished during the Revolution. The square holds a Tomb of the Unknown Soldier, erected to the memory of unknown Revolutionary War soldiers. By the 1840s the square had gained prestige as the center of the city's most fashionable neighborhood. It later became the city's publishing center. ⊠ *Bounded by 6th and 7th Sts. and Walnut and Locust Sts., Society Hill.*

NEED A BREAK?

Philadelphia Java Co. (⊠ *518 S. 4th St., Society Hill* ☎ *215/928–1811*) offers respite from the bustle of nearby South Street. Inside is a cozy space with exposed brick walls and magazines and newspapers to peruse while you sip a favorite caffeinated beverage with a bagel or scone. Or you can dine alfresco on the cafe's signature *labneh,* an open-face sandwich with creamy Lebanese yogurt topped with green olives and olive oil.

PENN'S LANDING AND CAMDEN WATERFRONT

The spot where William Penn stepped ashore in 1682 is the hub of a 37-acre riverfront park that stretches from Market Street south to Lombard Street. Walk along the waterfront and you can see scores of pleasure boats moored at the marina and cargo ships chugging up and down the Delaware River. Philadelphia's harbor, which includes docking facilities in New Jersey and Delaware, is one of the world's largest freshwater ports. Attractions at Penn's Landing include historic vessels like the world's largest four-masted tall ship, the *Moshulu,* which doubles as a restaurant. The waterfront is also the scene of the annual Memorial Day Jam on the River and July 4 fireworks, as well as jazz and big band concerts, ethnic festivals, and children's events. Camden, New Jersey, has also been sprucing up its waterfront and building attractions to lure visitors across the Delaware River. The lineup at Camden Waterfront includes the Adventure Aquarium, the Camden Children's Garden, the Battleship *New Jersey,* and Campbell's Field, a minor-league park where the Camden Riversharks play.

GETTING HERE AND AROUND

Penn's Landing is within easy walking distance of the Historic Area, Old City, and Society Hill, or can be accessed by SEPTA. To reach Penn's Landing, cross the Walnut Street Bridge at Front Street, which deposits you at the Independence Seaport Museum. The RiverLink Ferry connects Penn's Landing to Camden, New Jersey.

ESSENTIALS

RiverLink Ferry. This passenger ferry makes a 12-minute trip across the Delaware River; it travels back and forth between the Independence Seaport Museum at Penn's Landing and Camden's waterfront attractions, including the New Jersey State Aquarium, the Camden Children's Museum, and the Battleship *New Jersey*. You can get a picturesque view of Philadelphia's skyline and the Ben Franklin Bridge. Besides its daytime schedule, the ferry runs express service before and after Tweeter Center concerts and Camden Riversharks baseball games. ⊠ *Penn's Landing near Walnut St., Penn's Landing* ☎ *215/925–5465* ⊕ *www.riverlink-ferry.org* 🖭 *$6 round-trip* ☉ *May and Sept., weekends only; June–Aug., daily; departs from Camden on half hr 9:30–5:30; last ferry at 6:30 on Fri., Sat., and Sun.; from Philadelphia on hr 10–6, last ferry at 7 on Fri., Sat., and Sun.*

> **GREAT EXPERIENCES ON THE DELAWARE**
>
> **Adventure Aquarium:** Swim with the sharks—if you dare—at this comprehensive, hands-on science center.
>
> **Battleship** *New Jersey:* Walk the decks of this World War II–era ship, one of the U.S. Navy's most decorated military vessels.
>
> **Camden Children's Garden:** Go green in this interactive urban oasis.
>
> **Independence Seaport Museum:** Philadelphia's rich maritime heritage is celebrated at this museum.

PLANNING YOUR TIME

You could easily spend a whole day here. If your kids are in tow, allow an hour and a half for the Independence Seaport Museum and its historic boats and another two or three hours for the ferry ride and visit to the aquarium, followed by a tour of the Battleship *New Jersey*.

TOP ATTRACTIONS

⓰ Adventure Aquarium. This high-tech, hands-on science education center
Ⓒ is the home of "Shark Realm," a 550,000-gallon tank stretching two
★ stories high and thick with sharks, stingrays, and sawfish. The daring can "swim with the sharks" by snorkeling along the tank's perimeter under the careful supervision of aquarium staff. In the "West African River Experience" hippopotamuses cohabit with birds, crocodiles, and porcupines. There are also daily seal shows, penguin feedings, live animal talks, and "4-D" theater presentations, in which the 3-D on-screen action is choreographed to motion in the theater's seats. To get here, drive or take the ferry from Penn's Landing. ⊠ *1 Riverside Dr., Camden Waterfront, Camden, NJ* ☎ *856/365–3300* ⊕ *www.adventureaquarium. com* 🖭 *$19.95; $31.50 for combination ticket with Battleship New Jersey* ☉ *Daily 9:30–5.*

⓮ Independence Seaport Museum. Philadelphia's maritime museum houses
Ⓒ many nautical artifacts, figureheads, and ship models, as well as interac-
★ tive exhibits that convey just what the Delaware and Schuylkill rivers have meant to the city's fortunes over the years. You can climb in the gray, cold wooden bunks used in steerage, unload cargo from giant container ships with a miniature crane, weld and rivet a ship's hull, or even

hop in a scull and row along the Schuylkill. Enter the museum by passing under the three-story replica of the Benjamin Franklin Bridge. ⊠ *211 S. Columbus Blvd., at Walnut St., Penn's Landing* ☎ *215/925–5439* ⊕ *www.phillyseaport.org* ✉ *$12, includes admission to USS Becuna and USS Olympia; free Sun. 10–noon* ⊙ *Daily 10–5.*

WORTH NOTING

⑱ **Battleship *New Jersey*.** The World War II–era USS *New Jersey*, one of ☺ the most decorated battleships in the history of the U.S. Navy, is now a floating museum. It's docked in Camden, New Jersey, south of the Tweeter Center. A 2½-hour guided tour takes you around the upper and lower decks of the ship, or you can explore on your own. Families with at least one child between 7 and 17 can arrange for a sleepover on the ship. ⊠ *Beckett St., Camden Waterfront, Camden, NJ* ☎ *856/966–1652* ⊕ *www.battleshipnewjersey.org* ✉ *$18.50–$19.95 for guided tour; $35.50 for combination ticket with Adventure Aquarium* ⊙ *Feb.–mid-Mar., Fri.–Mon. 10–3; mid-Mar.–Apr., daily 9:30–3; May–Aug., daily 9:30–5, and Sept.–Dec., daily 9:30–3.*

⑰ **Camden Children's Garden.** Located adjacent to the Adventure Aquarium ☺ on the Camden waterfront, this delightful 4-acre garden is an interactive horticultural playground with theme exhibits. You can smell, hear, touch, and even taste some of the elements in the Dinosaur, Butterfly, Picnic, Tropical, and World's Kitchen gardens. The Storybook Gardens have a maze, carousel, and tree house. To get here, drive or take the ferry from Penn's Landing. ⊠ *3 Riverside Dr., Camden Waterfront, Camden, NJ* ☎ *856/365–8733* ⊕ *www.camdenchildrensgarden. org* ✉ *$6; $3.50 if you enter via the gate inside Adventure Aquarium* ⊙ *Daily 10–5.*

⑮ ***Gazela* of Philadelphia.** Built in 1883 and formerly named *Gazela Primeiro*, this 177-foot square-rigger is the last of a Portuguese fleet of cod-fishing ships. Still in use as late as 1969, it's the oldest and largest wooden square-rigger still sailing. As the Port of Philadelphia's ambassador of goodwill, the *Gazela* sails up and down the Atlantic coast from May to October to participate in harbor festivals and celebrations. It's also a ship school and a museum. An all-volunteer crew of 35 works on ship maintenance from November to April, while it's in port. ⊠ *Penn's Landing at Market St., Penn's Landing* ☎ *215/238–0280* ⊕ *www.gazela.org* ⊙ *Call ahead for tours.*

⑲ **USS *Becuna*.** You can tour this 318-foot-long "guppy class" submarine, ☺ which was commissioned in 1944 and conducted search-and-destroy missions in the South Pacific. The guides—all World War II vets—tell amazing stories of what life was like for a crew of 88 men, at sea for months at a time, in these claustrophobic quarters. Then you can step through the narrow walkways, climb the ladders, and glimpse the torpedoes in their firing chambers. Children love it, and it's fascinating for adults, too. The ticket booth by the boats is closed in winter; tickets must be purchased at the Independence Seaport Museum mid-November–mid-April. ⊠ *Spruce St., Penn's Landing* ☎ *215/922–1898* ⊕ *www.phillyseaport.org/Becuna.html* ✉ *$12, includes admission to USS Olympia and the Independence Seaport Museum* ⊙ *Daily 10–5.*

②⓪ **USS** *Olympia.* Commodore George Dewey's flagship at the Battle of Manila in the Spanish-American War is the only remaining ship from that war. Dewey entered Manila Harbor after midnight on May 1, 1898. At 5:40 AM he told his captain, "You may fire when ready, Gridley," and the battle began. By 12:30 the Americans had destroyed the entire Spanish fleet. The *Olympia* was the last ship of the "New Navy" of the 1880s and 1890s, the beginning of the era of steel ships. You can tour the entire restored ship, including the officers' staterooms, engine room, galley, gun batteries, pilothouse, and conning tower. The ticket booth by the boats is closed in winter; tickets must be purchased at the Independence Seaport Museum mid-November–mid-April. ⊠ *Spruce St., Penn's Landing* ☎ *215/922–1898* ⊕ *www.phillyseaport.org/Olympia.html* ☎ *$12, includes admission to USS Becuna and Independence Seaport Museum* ⊙ *Daily 10–5.*

QUEEN VILLAGE AND SOUTH PHILADELPHIA

Two of the city's most interesting neighborhoods lie south of South Street—Queen Village (also known as Southwark) and South Philadelphia. Queen Village, stretching from Front to 6th Street and from South Street to Washington Avenue, was the center of the commercial and ship-building activity that made Philadelphia the biggest port in the colonies and in the young United States. One of the oldest sections of the city, Queen Village was already settled by the Swedes when the English arrived; the Swedish influence shows in street names such as Swanson, Christian, and Queen.

Directly south of Society Hill, Queen Village is neither as glamorous nor as historically renowned as its neighbor. Chiseled in stone on one facade are these words: ON THIS SITE IN 1879, NOTHING HAPPENED! But like Society Hill, Southwark's Queen Village and South Philadelphia's Bella Vista neighborhoods have been gentrified by young professionals; the restoration attracted chic, hip bars, restaurants, and interesting shops.

Through the years South Philadelphia has absorbed boatloads of immigrants—European Jews, Italians, and most recently, Asians and Mexicans. The city's Little Italy is a huge area of identical row houses, many with gleaming white-marble steps, stretching south and west of Queen Village. At the heart of the neighborhood's Bella Vista section, along 9th Street, is the outdoor Italian Market, packed with vendors hawking crabs and octopus, eggplants, and tomatoes. From butcher-shop windows hang skinned animals; cheese shops are crammed with barrels of olives. Sylvester Stallone walked along 9th Street in *Rocky* and *Rocky II,* and almost every campaigning president has visited the market on his swing through Philadelphia. It's a great photo op for them—and for you.

Although there are chic eateries in South Philadelphia, the majority of the neighborhood's Italian restaurants are not fancy (red-check vinyl tablecloths and plastic grapes hanging from plastic vines are common sights), but the food can be terrific and—more important—authentic. You'll wonder if Mama is in the kitchen preparing a southern

Italian specialty just for you. This is the neighborhood that gave the world Mario Lanza, Bobby Rydell, Frankie Avalon, and Fabian, and some area restaurants proudly display gold records earned by these neighborhood celebrities. Plenty of locals and visitors alike head for South Philly's competing culinary shrines, Pat's King of Steaks and Geno's, both at the corner of 9th Street and Passyunk Avenue. One of their cheesesteaks makes a perfect prelude to an evening at the city's sports complexes, at the southern end of South Philadelphia.

GETTING HERE AND AROUND

You can reach the Italian Market on foot from Center City, or you may take SEPTA bus route 47, which runs south on 8th Street and makes a return loop north on 7th Street. Free parking is available in municipal lots located on the 800 block of Christian Street and the 1000 block of S. 8th Street, just north of Washington Avenue.

> ### GREAT EXPERIENCES IN SOUTH PHILLY
>
> **Italian Market:** Rocky ran through it, but you should plan on a more leisurely exploration of the outdoor stalls and shops.
>
> **Samuel S. Fleisher Art Memorial:** Take a detour from the Italian Market to view the latest exhibit at the gallery of this community-based art school.
>
> **Mummers Museum:** See the highlights from this uniquely Philly New Year's Day parade.
>
> **Pat's and Geno's:** Grab a cheesesteak at both famed purveyors to weigh in on which cheesesteak reigns supreme.

PLANNING YOUR TIME

It's best to visit this neighborhood Tuesday through Saturday, because the Italian Market is closed Sunday afternoon and Monday, and the Mummers Museum is closed Sunday in July and August and every Monday. Start early—the Italian Market winds down by late afternoon—and allow three to four hours.

TOP ATTRACTIONS

3 Italian Market. It's more Naples than Philadelphia: vendors crowd the sidewalks and spill out onto the streets; live crabs and caged chickens wait for the kill; picture-perfect produce is piled high. The market dates to the turn of the last century, when it was founded by Italian immigrants. You'll find fresh pastas, cheeses, spices, meats, fruits and vegetables, and dry goods and kitchen equipment, as well as junky dollar-stores and funky boutiques. These days the market has become more diversified, with the addition of several Mexican grocers, a natural foods grocer, taquerias, and a wine and cheese bar. ⊠ *9th St. between Washington Ave. and Christian St., Bella Vista/S. Philadelphia* ⊕ *www. phillyitalianmarket.com* ☉ *Tues.–Sat. 9–late afternoon, Sun. 9–12:30.*

2 Mummers Museum. Even if you aren't in Philadelphia on New Year's Day, you can still experience this unique local institution. Famous for extravagant sequin-and-feather costumes and string bands, the Mummers spend the year preparing for the all-day parade up Market Street. A 45-inch screen shows filmed highlights of past parades.

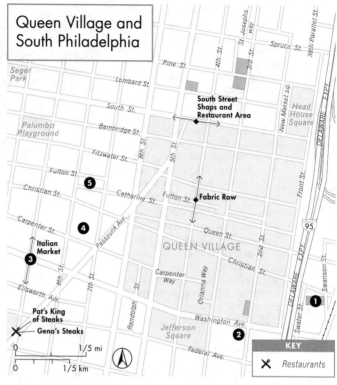

Early English settlers brought to the colonies their Christmastime custom of dressing in costume and performing pantomimes—the name Mummers derives from the German *Mumme*, meaning "mask or disguise." In Philadelphia, families would host costume parties on New Year's Day; on January 1, 1876, the first individual groups paraded informally through the city. The parade caught on, and by 1901 the city officially sanctioned the parade and 42 Mummers' clubs strutted for cash prizes.

These days the Mummers also stage a summer Mummers Parade around July 4 (during the city's Welcome America! celebration); in late February they present the "Show of Shows" at the Spectrum. The latter is a chance to hear the original 16 string bands perform indoors. The museum presents free outdoor concerts (weather permitting) on most Thursday evenings 8–10 from May to September. ✉ *1100 S. 2nd St., at Washington Ave., South Philadelphia* ☎ *215/336–3050* ⊕ *www.mummersmuseum.com* 🗺 *$3.50* ⊙ *Oct.–Apr., Wed.–Sat. 9:30–4:30; May–Sept., Wed., Fri.–Sat. 9:30–4:30; Thurs. 9:30–9:30.*

WORTH NOTING

⑤ Samuel S. Fleisher Art Memorial. The result of founder Samuel S. Fleisher's invitation to the world "to come and learn art," this school and gallery has offered tuition-free classes since 1898. Now administered by the

Philadelphia Museum of Art, the Fleisher offers regular exhibits of contemporary art, which are selected through its competitive "Challenge" series, as well as works by faculty and students. The Memorial consists of four connected buildings on Catharine Street—including the Sanctuary, a Romanesque Revival Episcopal church designed by the architectural firm of Frank Furness and featuring European art from the 13th to the 15th centuries—as well as a satellite building at 705 Christian Street dedicated to works on paper. ⊠ *709–721 Catharine St., Southwark* ☎ *215/922-3456* ⊕ *www.fleisher.org* ⊡ *Free* ⊙ *Weekdays 10–5; additional hrs when school is in session, Mon.–Thurs. 6:30–9:30 PM.*

❶ Gloria Dei. One of the few relics of the Swedes who settled Pennsylvania before William Penn, Gloria Dei, also known as Old Swedes' Church, was organized in 1642. Built in 1698, the church has numerous intriguing religious artifacts, such as a 1608 Bible once owned by Sweden's Queen Christina. The carvings on the lectern and balcony were salvaged from the congregation's first church, which was destroyed by fire. Models of two of the ships that transported the first Swedish settlers hang from the ceiling—right in the center of the church. Grouped around the church are the parish hall, the caretaker's house, the rectory, and the guild house. The church sits in the center of its graveyard; it forms a picture that is pleasing in its simplicity and tranquillity. ⊠ *916 Swanson St., near Christian St. and Columbus Blvd., Queen Village* ☎ *215/389-1513* ⊕ *www.nps.gov/glde* ⊡ *Free* ⊙ *Daily 9–5, but call first.*

NEED A BREAK?
When you're ready for an atmospheric break, stop by **Anthony's Italian Coffee House** (⊠ *903 S. 9th St., Bella Vista/S. Philadelphia* ☎ *215/627-2586*) in the heart of the Italian Market. Here, to the strains of Frank Sinatra, you can sample a fresh panino with prosciutto and mozzarella or indulge in homemade cannoli or gelati imported from Italy.

❹ Mario Lanza Museum. In this museum you'll find memorabilia devoted to the famous tenor and Hollywood star (1921–59). Lanza was supposedly moving a piano into the Academy of Music when he seized the opportunity to sing from its stage—and was discovered. Arturo Toscanini said that Lanza had perhaps the greatest natural voice of the century. Lanza's birthplace, at 634 Christian Street, is about a block away. ⊠ *712 Montrose St., Bella Vista/S. Philadelphia* ☎ *215/238-9691* ⊕ *www.mario-lanza-institute.org* ⊡ *Free* ⊙ *Mon.–Sat. 11–3.*

OFF THE BEATEN PATH
Bartram's Garden. Begun in 1728 by the pioneering botanist John Bartram (1699–1777), this is America's oldest surviving botanical garden. Bartram, with his son William, introduced into cultivation more than 200 native plants from species up and down the east coast. John became the royal botanist for King George III, and made a fortune selling plants to England. Today the 10-acre historical site along the river has lots of flowering shrubs and trees, including various azaleas, rhododendrons, and magnolias, and the Franklinia, a tree from South Georgia that became extinct in its native habitat and survived only because Bartram gathered it. Although there is almost always something flowering, the best time to come is in May and June, when the gardens are fragrant and filled with the lively chatter of birds. The original 1728 farmhouse still

stands, and you can take a tour through its rooms, which have various exhibits, including Native American artifacts from the property dating back 3,000 years. Prince Charles's former gardener David Howard has taken on Bartram's garden as a pet project of sorts. ■TIP➡ It's tucked **down a driveway in an impoverished neighborhood of Southwest Philadelphia; drive or take a cab.** ✉ *54th St. and Lindbergh Blvd., Southwest Philadelphia* ☎ *215/729–5281* ⊕ *www.bartramsgarden.org* ⌨ *Garden, free; house tour, $5* ⊘ *Garden: daily 10–5. House: Mar.–mid-Dec., Tues.–Sun. noon–4; tours at 12:10, 1:10, 2:10, and 3:10.*

Fort Mifflin. There are number of strange, forgotten sights in Philadelphia that in any other city would be *a* major, if not the major tourist attraction. Fort Mifflin may be the best of these sights in Southwest Philadelphia. The fort is enormous and nearly always empty. Within its walls, spread out on a huge lawn, are cannons and carriages, officers' quarters, soldiers' barracks, an artillery shed, a blacksmith shop, a bomb shelter, and a museum. The exhibits are dated, but the stories are fascinating, from the 40-day battle in 1777 to hold off British ships coming up the Delaware to the use of the site as a prison during the Civil War. The fort was almost totally destroyed during the Revolution, but was rebuilt in 1798 from plans by French architect Pierre L'Enfant, who also designed Washington, D.C. If you wander off beyond the fort and into the other parts of the 49-acre national historic landmark, you will find a long embankment of overgrown and unexcavated battlements from the 1800s. From Penn's Landing it's an easy jaunt on I–95. ✉ *Island and Hog Island Rds., on Delaware River near Philadelphia Int'l Airport, Southwest Philadelphia* ☎ *215/685–4167* ⊕ *www.fortmifflin. us* ⌨ *$6* ⊘ *Mar.–Nov., Wed.–Sun. 10–4.*

CENTER CITY

For a grand introduction to the heart of the downtown area, climb the few steps to the plaza in front of the Municipal Services Building at 15th Street and John F. Kennedy Boulevard. You'll be standing alongside a 10-foot-tall bronze statue of the late Frank L. Rizzo waving to the people. Rizzo, nicknamed the "Big Bambino," was the city's police commissioner, two-term mayor (in the 1970s), and a five-time mayoral candidate. He shaped the political scene just as the structures that surround you—City Hall, the Philadelphia Saving Fund Society Building, the Art Museum, the skyscrapers at Liberty Place, Oldenburg's *Clothespin,* and more—shape its architectural landscape.

The story behind this skyline begins with Philadelphia's historic City Hall, which reaches to 40 stories and was the tallest structure in the metropolis until 1987. No law prohibited taller buildings, but the tradition sprang from a gentleman's agreement not to build higher. In May 1984, when a developer proposed building two office towers that would break the 491-foot barrier, it became evident how entrenched this tradition was: the proposal provoked a public outcry. The traditionalists contended that the height limitation had made Philadelphia a city of human scale, given character to its streets and public places, and showed respect for tradition. The opposing camp thought that a dramatic new skyline would shatter the city's conservative image and encourage economic growth. After painstaking debate the go-ahead was granted. In short order the midtown area became the hub of the city's commercial center, Market Street west of City Hall became a district of high-rise office buildings, and the area became a symbol of the city's ongoing transformation from a dying industrial town to a center for service industries. Here, too, are a number of museums, the excellent Reading Terminal Market and the convention center, and Chinatown.

GETTING HERE AND AROUND

The heart of Center City is an easy 10- to 15-minute stroll from the Historic Area, or about a 20- to 25-minute walk from Penn's Landing. To orient yourself, Broad Street (the name for what would be 14th Street) serves as a delineation for Center City East and Center City West, while City Hall, located at Broad and Market streets, is the diving line for north-south addresses on the numbered streets. You also can use SEPTA bus lines on Market or Walnut streets, or the underground Blue line on Market Street, to reach points west of the Historic Area or take the PHLASH, which runs seasonally. The City Hall SEPTA station is a major hub that includes connections for the north-south Orange Line, as well as the east-west Blue and Green lines.

PLANNING YOUR TIME

To get a feel for the city at work, save this neighborhood for a weekday, when the streets are bustling (on weekends, especially Sunday, the area is quiet). Besides, the City Hall Observation Tower is open weekdays only, and the Masonic Temple is closed on Sunday. You could walk through the neighborhood in 45 minutes, but reserve about half a day, with an hour each at the Masonic Temple, City Hall Tower, and the Pennsylvania Academy of the Fine Arts. If you get an early start, you can finish with lunch at the Reading Terminal Market.

TOP ATTRACTIONS

❶ **City Hall.** Topped by a 37-foot bronze statue of William Penn, City
★ Hall was Philadelphia's tallest building until 1987; you can study the trappings of government and also get a panoramic view of the city here. With 642 rooms, it's the largest city hall in the country and the tallest masonry-bearing building in the world: no steel structure supports it. Designed by architect John McArthur Jr., the building took 30 years to build (1871–1900) and cost taxpayers more than $23 million. The result has been called a "Victorian wedding cake of Renaissance styles." Placed about the facade are hundreds of statues by Alexander Milne Calder, who also designed the statue of William Penn at the top. Calder's 27-ton cast-iron statue of Penn is the largest single piece of sculpture on any building in the world.

Not only the geographic center of Penn's original city plan, City Hall is also the center of municipal and state government. Many of the magnificent interiors—splendidly decorated with mahogany paneling, gold-leaf ceilings, and marble pillars—are patterned after the Second Empire salons of part of the Louvre in Paris. On a tour each weekday at 12:30 you can see the Conversation Hall, the Supreme Court of Pennsylvania, the City Council chambers, and the mayor's reception room.

GREAT EXPERIENCES IN CENTER CITY

Reading Terminal Market: Sample a wide range of ethnic foods at dozens of stalls at this bustling market.

City Hall: Take the elevator to the observation deck for commanding views of the city.

The Comcast Center: The city's tallest building—and most green-friendly office tower—offers a seasonal sidewalk café and an entertaining video installation in its lobby.

Macy's: The former John Wanamaker flagship store is a city landmark and home to the world's largest pipe organ.

Pennsylvania Academy of the Fine Arts: The High Victorian building housing this collection of American art is worth a visit in itself.

Chinatown: Stop by this colorful district to sample authentic Asian cuisine or shop for ingredients to make your own meal at home.

You can attend the frequently heated City Council meetings, held each Thursday morning at 10.

To top off your visit, take the elevator from the seventh floor up the tower to the observation deck at the foot of William Penn's statue for a 30-mi view of the city and surroundings. The elevator holds only six people per trip and runs every 15 minutes; the least-crowded time is early morning. The 90-minute building tour, including a trip up the tower, steps off weekdays at 12:30. The tour office is in Room 121. ✉ *Broad and Market Sts., Center City* ☎ *215/686–1776, 215/686–2840 tour information* ⊕ *www.philadelphiacityhall.org* ☜ *$10 for tour and tower visit; $5 for tower only* ☉ *Tower: weekdays 9:30–4:15; 2–3* PM *reserved for tour participants.*

❸ **Pennsylvania Academy of the Fine Arts.** This High Victorian Gothic struc★ ture is a work of art in itself. Designed in 1876 by the noted, and sometimes eccentric, Philadelphia architects Frank Furness and George Hewitt, the multicolor stone-and-brick exterior is an extravagant blend of columns, friezes, and Richardsonian Romanesque and Moorish flourishes. The interior is just as lush, with rich hues of red, yellow, and blue and an impressive staircase. The nation's first art school and museum (founded in 1805) displays a fine collection that ranges from the Peale family, Gilbert Stuart, Benjamin West, and Winslow Homer to Andrew Wyeth and Red Grooms. *Fox Hunt* by Winslow Homer, *The Artist in His Museum* by Charles Willson Peale, and *Interior with Doorway* by Richard Diebenkorn are just a few notable works. The academy faculty has included Thomas Sully, Charles Willson Peale, and Thomas Eakins. The latter painted what is now the museum's most prized work, *The Gross Clinic,* a dramatic depiction of Samuel D. Gross, a celebrated 19th-century surgeon, presiding over an operation under a skylighted roof; the masterwork is co-owned with the Philadelphia Museum of Art, and is displayed for six months at a time at each institution.

Supplementing the permanent collection are constantly changing exhibitions of sculptures, paintings, and mixed-media artwork in the adjacent

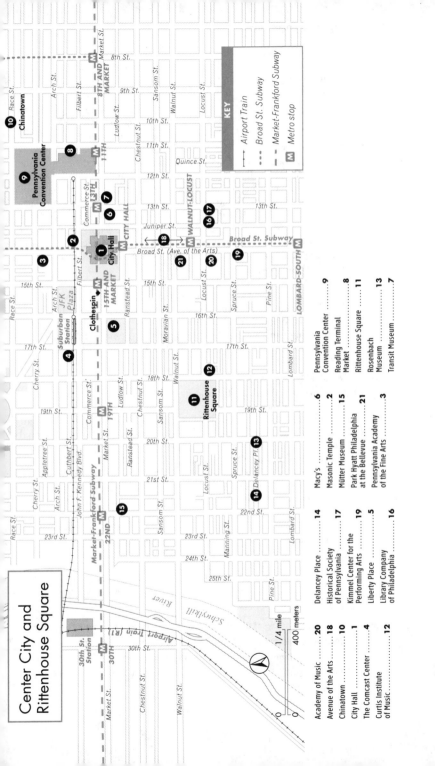

Center City and Rittenhouse Square

KEY

- ┼┼┼ Airport Train
- ‑‑‑ Broad St. Subway
- ‑ ‑ ‑ Market-Frankford Subway
- Ⓜ Metro stop

Samuel M. V. Hamilton Building; the 11-story facility, which opened for the academy's 200th anniversary, is also the home to the Sculpture Study Center, which offers changing displays from the permanent collection, classrooms, group and private studios for more than 300 students, and Portfolio, the museum's gift shop. ⊠ *118–128 N. Broad St., at Cherry St., Center City West/Avenue of the Arts* ☎ *215/972–7600* ⊕ *www.pafa. org* 🖾 *$10* ☉ *Tues.–Sat. 10–5, Sun. 11–5.*

❽ **Reading Terminal Market.** The market is nothing short of a historic trea-
Fodor's Choice — sure, and a food heaven to Philadelphians and visitors alike. One floor
★ beneath the former Reading Railroad's 1891 train shed, the sprawling market has more than 75 food stalls and other shops, selling items from hooked rugs and handmade jewelry to South American and African crafts. Here, amid the local color, you can sample Bassett's ice cream, Philadelphia's best; down a cheesesteak, a hoagie, a bowl of snapper soup, or a soft pretzel; or nibble Greek, Mexican, Thai, and Indian specialties. From Wednesday through Saturday the Amish from Lancaster County cart in their goodies, including Lebanon bologna, shoofly pie, and scrapple. Many stalls have their own counters with seating; there's also a central eating area. An open kitchen offers regular demonstrations by some of the region's top chefs. The entire building is a National Historic Landmark, and the train shed is a National Engineering Landmark. ⊠ *12th and Arch Sts., Center City East/Market East* ☎ *215/922–2317* ⊕ *www.readingterminalmarket.org* ☉ *Mon.–Sat. 8–6, Sun. 9–5.*

WORTH NOTING

❿ **Chinatown.** Centered on 10th and Race streets two blocks north of Market Street, Chinatown serves as the residential and commercial hub of the city's Chinese community. Chinatown has grocery stores, souvenir and gift shops, martial arts studios, a fortune cookie store, bilingual street signs, red-and-green pagoda-style telephone booths, and more than 50 restaurants. Over the past 20 years Chinatown's population has become more diverse, reflecting the increase in immigration from other parts of Southeast Asia. As a result, the dining options are more varied; there now are restaurants serving authentic Vietnamese, Thai, Cambodian, and Burmese cuisine. One striking Chinatown site is the **Chinese Friendship Gate,** straddling 10th Street at Arch Street. This intricate and colorful 40-foot-tall arch—the largest authentic Chinese gate outside China—was created by Chinese artisans, who brought their own tools and construction materials. The citizens of Tianjin, Philadelphia's sister city in China, donated the building materials, including the ornamental tile. ⊠ *9th to 11th Sts., Arch to Vine Sts., Chinatown* ⊕ *www.phillychinatown.com.*

NEED A BREAK?
For a savory or sweet Chinese snack, stop at the **Hong Kong Bakery** (⊠ *917 Race St., Chinatown* ☎ *215/925–1288*). Sample the "Hong Kong Hotdog," a smallish wiener encased in puff pastry, or a sweet egg custard tart. Most items are cheap (usually under $1), and you might just find a new favorite snack.

❹ The Comcast Center. Now Philadelphia's tallest building, the 975-foot Comcast Center is also one of its most eco-friendly: The 58-story design by Robert A.M. Stern Architects uses 40 percent less water than a traditional office building and also deploys its glass-curtain wall facade to reduce energy costs significantly. Not to be missed is *The Comcast Experience*, a 2000-square-foot high-definition video "wall" in the building's "winter garden" lobby, which also features "Humanity in Motion," an installation of 12 life-sized figures by Jonathan Borofsky that appear to be striding along girders 110 feet above. The building is also the site of an upscale food court, a high-end Italian restaurant and steak house, and a seasonal, outdoor café. ☒ *1701 John F. Kennedy Blvd., Center City West/Market West.*

Clothespin. Claes Oldenburg's 45-foot-high, 10-ton steel sculpture stands in front of the Center Square Building. Lauded by some and scorned by others, this pop art piece contrasts with the traditional statuary so common in Philadelphia. ☒ *15th and Market Sts., Center City West.*

❺ Liberty Place One and Two. One Liberty Place is the 945-foot office building designed by Helmut Jahn that propelled Philadelphia into the "ultrahigh" skyscraper era. Built in 1987, it became the city's tallest structure; however, that distinction now belongs to the 975-foot Comcast Center. Vaguely reminiscent of a modern version of New York's Chrysler Building, One Liberty Place is visible from almost everywhere in the city. In 1990 the adjacent tower, **Two Liberty Place,** opened. Zeidler Roberts designed this second building, which now holds the Westin Philadelphia, luxury condominiums, and a restaurant on the 37th floor. ☒ *One Liberty Pl., 1650 Market St., Center City West/Market West* ☒ *Two Liberty Pl., 1601 Chestnut St., Center City West/Market West .*

NEED A BREAK? **The Shops at Liberty Place** (☒ *1625 Chestnut St., between Liberty One and Liberty Two, Market West* ☎ *215/851–9055* ⊕ *www.shopsatliberty. com*) houses a large international food court on the second level, above the upscale stores. You can find anything from salad to sushi to those familiar Philly cheesesteaks.

❻ Macy's. The former John Wanamaker department store, this building is almost as prominent a Philadelphia landmark as the Liberty Bell. Wanamaker began with a clothing store in 1861, and became one of America's most innovative and prominent retailers. The massive building, which occupies a city block with grace, was designed by the noted Chicago firm of D.H. Burnham and Company. Its focal point is a 2,500-pound statue of an eagle, a remnant of the 1904 Louisiana Purchase Exposition in St. Louis. "Meet me at the Eagle" remains a popular way for Philadelphians to arrange a rendezvous. The store's 30,000-pipe organ—the largest ever built—is used for free concerts Monday, Tuesday, Thursday, and Saturday at noon and 5:30 and Wednesday and Friday at noon and 7. ☒ *13th and Market Sts., Center City East* ☎ *215/241–9000* ⊕ *www.macys.com* ☼ *Mon.–Sat. 10–8, Sun. 11–7.*

❷ Masonic Temple. The temple is one of the city's architectural jewels, but ★ it remains a hidden treasure even to many Philadelphians. Historically, Freemasons were skilled stoneworkers of the Middle Ages who relied

Philadelphia Flower Show

It takes one week; 7,000 Belgian blocks; 3,500 volunteers; thousands of plumbers, carpenters, and electricians; more than a million plants; and 50 tractor-trailer loads of mulch to transform the Pennsylvania Convention Center into the annual **Philadelphia Flower Show** (☎ 215/988–8899 ⊕ www.theflowershow.com), the world's largest indoor horticultural event. But the exhibitors—nursery owners, landscapers, and florists from the region and from Africa, Japan, and Europe—spend the better part of a year planning their displays. The astonishing, fragrant results of their efforts arrive in the city as a touch of spring in early March.

It's a fitting tribute to William Penn that Philadelphia hosts this extravaganza, for this was Penn's "greene countrie town," which he laid out on a grid punctuated with tree-lined streets, pocket parks, small squares, and large public parks. It's also appropriate that this city gave root to the Pennsylvania Horticultural Society, the nation's first such organization. In 1829, two years after its founding, the society hosted its first show at the Masonic Hall in an 82- by 69-foot exhibition space; 25 society members showed off their green thumbs.

Today the show fills 10 acres of exhibition space at the convention center and spills throughout the area as local restaurants, hotels, and attractions offer special deals. (The show's Web site may have discounts and coupons.) Along with the more than 50 major exhibits, amateur gardeners contribute more than 2,000 entries in 330 competitive categories—from pressed plants and miniature settings to spectacular jewelry designs that use flowers. There are free cooking and gardening demonstrations, lectures, and an area where you can try out the latest gardening gadgets. Hundreds of vendors sell plants, birdhouses, topiaries, watering systems, botanical prints, and more.

Each year the show has a theme, and the show's designers think big—very big. Visitors to the 2009 show, called "Bella Italia," got a virtual tour of the country, with stops including the storied canals of Venice, the formal gardens of ancient Rome, the flower fields of San Remo, and the bucolic Tuscan countryside.

If you've made reservations, you can rest your weary feet during **Garden Tea at the Flower Show** (☎ 215/988–8879), a proper English tea served at 12:30 and 3:45. For a more substantial lunch break, you can head across the street to the **Reading Terminal Market** (✉ 12th and Arch Sts., Center City East/Market East), which has more than 80 stalls, shops, and lunch counters. Or walk two blocks east to the many restaurants of **Chinatown.**

Many people plan trips to Philadelphia during the run of the flower show, so be sure to make reservations early. Wear good walking shoes, check your coat, and bring spending money for the many horticultural temptations. To avoid crowds, which can be daunting, arrive after 4 on weekdays and stay until the 9:30 closing, or show up when the doors open on weekend mornings at 8.

on secret signs and passwords. Their worldwide fraternal order—the Free and Accepted Masons—included men in the building trades, plus many honorary members; the secret society prospered in Philadelphia during Colonial times. Brother James Windrim designed this elaborate temple as a home for the Grand Lodge of Free and Accepted Masons of Pennsylvania. The trowel used here at the laying of the cornerstone in 1868, while 10,000 brothers looked on, was the same one that Brother George Washington used to set the cornerstone of the U.S. Capitol. The temple's ornate interior consists of seven lavishly decorated lodge halls built to exemplify specific styles of architecture: Corinthian, Ionic, Italian Renaissance, Norman, Gothic, Oriental, and Egyptian. The Egyptian room, with its accurate hieroglyphics, is the most famous. The temple also houses an interesting museum of Masonic items, including Benjamin Franklin's printing of the first book on Freemasonry published in America and George Washington's Masonic Apron, which was embroidered by Madame Lafayette, wife of the famous marquis. ✉ *1 N. Broad St., Center City East/Avenue of the Arts* ☏ *215/988–1917* ⊕ *www.pagrandlodge.org/tour/onsite.html* 🎟 *$3 for library and museum only, $8 for tour* ⊙ *45-min tours Sept.–June, Tues.–Fri. 10, 11, 2, 3, and 4, Sat. 10, 11, and 12.*

❾ **Pennsylvania Convention Center.** It's big: the area of the main exhibition hall equals seven football fields. And it's beautiful: the 1.9 million square feet of space are punctuated by the largest permanent collection of contemporary art in a building of its kind. Many city and state artists are represented in the niches, nooks, and galleries built to house their multimedia works. To see the architectural highlight of the building—the Reading Terminal's magnificently restored four-story-high Victorian train shed, which has been transformed into the Convention Center's Grand Hall—enter the building through the century-old Italian Renaissance Headhouse structure on Market Street between 11th and 12th streets and ride up the escalator. The facility is undergoing a major expansion that will boost exhibit space by 60 percent when completed in 2011. ✉ *1101 Arch St., Center City East/Market East* ☏ *215/418–4700* ⊕ *www.paconvention.com* 🎟 *Free* ⊙ *45-min tours by appointment only.*

❼ **Transit Museum.** Located, appropriately enough, in the headquarters of the Southeastern Pennsylvania Transportation Authority, this small museum showcases the history and development of public transportation in the region and its impact on social, political, and economic life. ✉ *Concourse level, 1234 Market St., Market East* ☏ *215/580–7168* ⊕ *www.septa.org/store* 🎟 *Free* ⊙ *Weekdays 10–5, Sat. 10–3.*

RITTENHOUSE SQUARE AND AVENUE OF THE ARTS SOUTH

Rittenhouse Square, at 18th and Walnut streets, has long been one of the city's swankiest addresses. The square's entrances, plaza, pool, and fountains were designed in 1913 by Paul Cret, one of the people responsible for the Benjamin Franklin Parkway. The square was named in honor of one of the city's 18th-century stars: David Rittenhouse, president of the American Philosophical Society and a professor of astronomy at the University of Pennsylvania. The first house facing the square was erected in 1840, soon to be followed by other grand mansions. Almost all the private homes are now gone, replaced by hotels, apartments, and cultural

WORD OF MOUTH

"Another great area is Rittenhouse Square—plenty of great restaurants and side streets—and pulling up a bench or lazing in the grass in the middle of the square is a favorite activity, watching the world go by."   —teaberry

institutions, and elegant restaurants and stylish cafés dot the neighborhood. The former home of banker George Childs Drexel was transformed into the Curtis Institute, alma mater of Leonard Bernstein and Gian Carlo Menotti. The former Samuel Price Wetherill mansion is now the Philadelphia Art Alliance, sponsor of exhibitions, drama, dance, and literary events.

The area south and west of the square is still largely residential and lovely, with cupolas and balconies, hitching posts and stained-glass windows. You can also find some small shops and the Rosenbach Museum and Library. In the heart of the city there are green places, too. Peek in the streets behind these homes or through their wrought-iron gates, and you can see well-tended gardens. On Delancey Place, blocks alternate narrow and wide. The wide blocks had the homes of the wealthy, and the smaller ones held dwellings for servants or horses (today these carriage houses are prized real estate). When he saw 18th Street and Delancey Place, R. F. Delderfield, author of *God Is an Englishman,* said, "I never thought I'd see anything like this in America. It is like Dickensian London." Today the good life continues in Rittenhouse Square. Annual events include the Rittenhouse Square Flower Show and the Fine Arts Annual, an outdoor juried art show.

Four blocks east of the square is the Avenue of the Arts, also known as Broad Street. "Let us entertain you" could be the theme of the ambitious cultural development project that has transformed North and South Broad Street from a commercial thoroughfare to a performing arts district. Dramatic performance spaces have been built, old landmarks have been refurbished, and South Broad Street has been spruced up with landscaping, cast-iron lighting fixtures, special architectural lighting of key buildings, and decorative sidewalk paving.

PLANNING YOUR TIME

This is one of the city's loveliest neighborhoods for strolling. Two hours would allow you enough time to wander through the Rittenhouse Square area and visit the Rosenbach Museum and Library (get there before 2:45). Add at least another hour for a stroll along South Broad Street, including a cool drink or snack at the Ritz-Carlton's tony 10 Arts lounge.

GREAT EXPERIENCES IN RITTENHOUSE SQ.

Academy of Music: Take in an opera, ballet, or theatrical performance at this magnificent concert hall, whose interior is modeled on Milan's La Scala.

Delancey Place: Stroll the 2000 block to check out some of the city's most elegant town houses.

Kimmel Center for the Performing Arts: Pop into this contemporary arts facility, which holds free public performances in its glass-enclosed plaza.

Park Hyatt Philadelphia at the Bellevue: Built in the early 20th century, this grande-dame hotel still evokes the opulence of a bygone era.

Rittenhouse Square: This lush park offers a lovely retreat in the heart of the city.

TOP ATTRACTIONS

❶ Rittenhouse Square. Once grazing ground for cows and sheep, Philadelphia's most elegant square is reminiscent of a Parisian park. One of William Penn's original five city squares, the park was named in 1825 to honor David Rittenhouse, 18th-century astronomer, clock maker, and the first director of the United States Mint. Many of Philadelphia's celebrities have lived here. Extra paths were made for Dr. William White, a leader in beautifying the square, so he could walk directly from his home to the exclusive Rittenhouse Club across the square and lunch with author Henry James. Until 1950 town houses bordered the square, but they have now been replaced on three sides by swank apartment buildings and hotels. Some great houses remain, including the former residence of Henry P. McIlhenny on the southwest corner. If you want to join the office workers who have lunch-hour picnics in the park, you can find many eateries along Walnut, Sansom, and Chestnut streets east of the square. Or you can dine alfresco at one of several upscale open-air cafés across from the square on 18th Street between Locust and Walnut. The term "Rittenhouse Row" describes the greater Rittenhouse Square area, bordered by Pine, Market, 21st, and Broad streets. ⊠ *Walnut St. between 18th and 19th Sts., Rittenhouse Square.*

Fodor'sChoice
★

NEED A BREAK?

Di Bruno Bros. (⊠ *1730 Chestnut St., Rittenhouse Square* ☎ *215/665–9220* ⊕ *www.dibruno.com*) **is a two-level gourmet shop with a dazzling array of prepared foods, mouth-watering pastries, and creamy gelato. Sampling the wares can make for a good snack, but if you require something more substantial, head to the dining room upstairs.**

❸ Rosenbach Museum and Library. This 1863 three-floor town house and an adjoining building are filled with Persian rugs and 18th-century British, French, and American antiques (plus an entire living room that once belonged to poet Marianne Moore), but the real treasures are the artworks, books, and manuscripts here. Amassed by Philadelphia collectors Philip H. and A. S. W. Rosenbach, the collection includes paintings

★

by Canaletto, Sully, and Lawrence; drawings by Daumier, Fragonard, and Blake; book illustrations ranging from medieval illuminations to the works of Maurice Sendak, author of *Where the Wild Things Are*; the only known copy of the first issue of Benjamin Franklin's *Poor Richard's Almanack*; and the library's most famous treasure, the original manuscript of James Joyce's *Ulysses*. The Rosenbach celebrates "Bloomsday" on June 16 with readings from *Ulysses* by notable Philadelphians. The library has more than 130,000 manuscripts and 30,000 rare books. ⊠ *2010 Delancey Pl., Rittenhouse Square* ☎ *215/732–1600* ⊕ *www.rosenbach.org* ⊠ *$10* ☉ *Tues., Thurs., and Fri. 10–5, Wed. 10–8, weekends 10–5; guided tours on the hr 10–4; additional tours Wed. at 5 and 6.*

WORTH NOTING

⑳ Academy of Music. The only surviving European-style opera house in America is the current home of the Opera Company of Philadelphia and the Pennsylvania Ballet; for the past century, it was home to the Philadelphia Orchestra. Designed by Napoleon Le Brun and Gustav Runge, the 1857 building has a modest exterior; the builders ran out of money and couldn't put marble facing on the brick, as they had intended. The lavish interior, modeled after Milan's La Scala, has elaborate carvings, murals on the ceiling, and a huge Victorian crystal chandelier. ⊠ *Broad and Locust Sts., Avenue of the Arts* ☎ *215/893–1999 box office* ⊕ *www. academyofmusic.org.*

⑱ Avenue of the Arts. Broad Street, the city's main north–south thoroughfare, has been reinvented as a performing arts district. Although most of the cultural institutions are situated along South Broad Street from City Hall to Spruce Street, the avenue's cultural, education, and arts organizations reach as far south as Washington Avenue in South Philadelphia and as far north as Dauphin Street in North Philadelphia. The main venue is the Kimmel Center for the Performing Arts, at Broad and Spruce streets, which includes a 2,500-seat concert hall designed for the Philadelphia Orchestra. The newest addition is the Suzanne Roberts Theatre, a 365-seat facility that is home to the Philadelphia Theatre Company. ⊠ *Broad St., Avenue of the Arts* ☎ *215/731–9668* ⊕ *www. avenueofthearts.org.*

⑫ Curtis Institute of Music. Graduates of this tuition-free school for outstanding students include Leonard Bernstein, Samuel Barber, Ned Rorem, and Anna Moffo. The school occupies four former private homes; the main building is in the mansion that belonged to banker George W. Childs Drexel. Built in 1893 by the distinguished Boston firm of Peabody and Stearns, it's notable for Romanesque and Renaissance architectural details. Free student and faculty concerts are given from October through May, usually at 8 PM on Monday, Wednesday, and Friday. ⊠ *1726 Locust St., Rittenhouse Square* ☎ *215/893–5261 recital hot line, 215/893–7902 ticket office* ⊕ *www.curtis.edu.*

⑭ Delancey Place. This fine residential area southwest of Rittenhouse Square was once the **address of Pearl S. Buck** (⊠ *2019 Delancey Pl., Rittenhouse Square*) and Rudolf Serkin. At one corner there's an interesting **sea captain's house** (⊠ *320 S. 18th St., Rittenhouse Square*). At

No. 2010 is the **Rosenbach Museum and Library.** Cypress Street, north of Delancey Place, and Panama Street (especially the 1900 block, one block south of Delancey) are two of the many intimate streets lined with trees and town houses characteristic of the area.

⑰ Historical Society of Pennsylvania. Following a merger with the Balch Institute for Ethnic Studies, this superlative special-collections library now contains more than 500,000 books, 300,000 graphic works, and 19 million manuscript items; the emphasis is on Colonial, early national, and Pennsylvania history, as well as immigration history and ethnicity. Founded in 1824, the society also owns one of the largest family history libraries in the nation. This is the place to go to trace your family roots. Notable items from the collection include the Penn family archives, President James Buchanan's papers, a printer's proof of the Declaration of Independence, and the first draft of the Constitution. The library is open to anyone over 13 years old. ✉ *1300 Locust St., Washington Square West* ☎ *215/732–6200* ⊕ *www.hsp.org* ✍ *$6* ⊙ *Tues. and Thurs. 12:30–5:30, Wed. 12:30–8:30, Fri. 10–5:30.*

NEED A BREAK?

Capogiro (✉ *119 S. 13th St.19107* ☎ *215/351-0900* ⊕ *www.capogiro.com*) is Italian for "swooning," so be sure to grab a chair before tasting the gelato at this popular spot. The daily list of flavors ranges from the trendy (rosemary honey goat's milk, Thai iced tea) to the classic (pistachio, chocolate).

⑲ Kimmel Center for the Performing Arts. Intended to make a contemporary design statement, the Kimmel Center for the Performing Arts has some architectural oomph with its dramatic vaulted glass roof. The 450,000-square-foot facility by architect Rafael Viñoly includes the 2,500-seat Verizon Hall, the more intimate 650-seat Perelman Theater, a restaurant, a café, a gift shop, and a rooftop terrace. Making their home at the Kimmel are the Philadelphia Orchestra, Philadanco, Philadelphia Chamber Music Society, Concerto Soloists Chamber Orchestra, and American Theater Arts for Youth. Free performances are given before some performances and on many weekends in the center's Commonwealth Plaza. ✉ *Broad and Spruce Sts., Avenue of the Arts* ☎ *215/790–5800 or 215/893–1999* ⊕ *www.kimmelcenter.org* ✍ *Free* ⊙ *Daily 10–6, general tour Tues.–Sun. at 1, art and architecture tour Sat. at 10:30.*

⑯ Library Company of Philadelphia. Founded in 1731, this is one of the oldest cultural institutions in the United States and the only major Colonial American library that has survived virtually intact, despite having moved from building to building. From 1774 to 1800 it functioned as the de facto Library of Congress, and until the late 19th century it was the city library. Ten signers of the Declaration of Independence were members, among them Benjamin Franklin, Robert Morris, Benjamin Rush, and Thomas McKean. The 500,000-volume collection includes 200,000 rare books. Among the first editions—many acquired when they were first published—are Herman Melville's *Moby-Dick* and Walt Whitman's *Leaves of Grass*. The library is particularly rich in Americana up to 1880, black history to 1915, the history of science, and women's history. Changing exhibits showcase the library's holdings.

✉ *1314 Locust St., Washington Square W* ☎ *215/546–3181* ⊕ *www.librarycompany.org* ✉ *Free* ☉ *Weekdays 9–4:45.*

⑮ Mütter Museum. Skulls, antique microscopes, and a cancerous tumor removed from President Grover Cleveland's mouth in 1893 form just part of the unusual medical collection in the Mütter Museum, in the College of Physicians of Philadelphia. The museum has hundreds of anatomical and pathological specimens, medical instruments, and organs removed from patients, including a piece of John Wilkes Booth's neck tissue. The collection contains 139 skulls; items that belonged to Marie Curie, Louis Pasteur, and Joseph Lister; and a 7-foot, 6-inch skeleton, the tallest on public exhibition in the United States. ✉ *19 S. 22nd St., Rittenhouse Square* ☎ *215/563–3737* ⊕ *www.collphyphil.org* ✉ *$14* ☉ *Mon.–Thurs. and weekends 10–5, Fri. 10–9.*

㉑ Park Hyatt Philadelphia at the Bellevue. Though its name has been changed many times, this building will always be "the Bellevue" to Philadelphians. The hotel has had an important role in city life, much like the heroine of a long-running soap opera. The epitome of the opulent hotels characteristic of the early 1900s, the Bellevue Stratford was the city's leading hotel for decades. It closed in 1976 after the first outbreak of Legionnaires' disease, which spread through the building's air-conditioning system during an American Legion convention. The hotel has reopened several times since then, and now includes upscale shops and restaurants and a food court in its basement, but its character seems to have remained the same. ✉ *200 S. Broad St., at Walnut St., Avenue of the Arts* ☎ *215/893–1776* ⊕ *www.hyatt.com.*

NEED A BREAK?

For a most civilized break from touring, enter the luxurious world of the Ritz-Carlton's soaring rotunda, now the site of famed chef Eric Ripert's **10 Arts** restaurant-lounge (✉ *10 S. Broad St., Avenue of the Arts* ☎ *215/735–7700* ⊕ *www.10arts.com*). Here the stately marble columns and classical architecture nicely contrast with modern, upholstered furniture and other contemporary design touches. You can take it all in with a cool drink or cocktail and a gourmet Philly-style snack, like housemade soft pretzel bites with cheddar sauce, Dijon mustard, and jalapeño jam.

THE BENJAMIN FRANKLIN PARKWAY

Alive with colorful flowers, flags, and fountains, the Benjamin Franklin Parkway stretches northwest from John F. Kennedy Plaza to the Kelly (East) and West River drives. This 250-foot-wide boulevard is crowned by the Philadelphia Museum of Art. French architects Jacques Greber and Paul Cret designed the parkway in the 1920s. Today a distinguished assemblage of museums, institutions, hotels, and apartment buildings line the street, competing with each other in grandeur.

Here you can find the Free Library of Philadelphia and the Family Court, housed in buildings whose designs are copied from the palaces on Paris's Place de la Concorde. A newer addition is the Four Seasons Hotel, though its dignified design has made it look like a local

GREAT EXPERIENCES NEAR THE PARKWAY

Eastern State Penitentiary: Gangster Al Capone lived in this model prison, which in the 19th century influenced the designs of penitentiaries around the world.

The Franklin Institute: Walk through a giant artificial heart, gaze at the stars in the planetarium, and learn all about science and technology at this interactive museum honoring founding father, inventor, and scientist Benjamin Franklin.

Logan Circle: One of William Penn's original four squares is now a circle with the graceful Swann Fountain, representing the Delaware and Schuylkill rivers and Wissahickon Creek, as its centerpiece.

Philadelphia Museum of Art: Modeled after a Greek temple, the building itself is a work of art, but you'll want to head inside to see one of the nation's greatest art collections.

Rodin Museum: This jewel box of a museum houses the largest collection of Rodin sculptures outside of his native France.

institution since the day it opened. A grand processional path, the parkway occasionally lets down its hair as the route for city parades and the site of many festivals and events, including the Thanksgiving and Columbus Day parades and the TD Bank Philadelphia International Cycling championship.

GETTING HERE AND AROUND

The parkway is easily reached on foot from Rittenhouse Square, but is 30-minute walk from the far eastern sections of the Historic Area. SEPTA or the PHLASH also are good options to reach this neighborhood, particularly if you're planning on visiting the Philadelphia Museum of Art. If you have a car, it's also fairly easy to find parking on metered spaces along the parkway or north of the museum on Pennsylvania Avenue. The museum also has a parking structure with hundreds of spaces.

PLANNING YOUR TIME

The parkway is at its most colorful in spring, when the trees and flowers are in bloom. Start early in the morning and plan to spend an entire day—and possibly the evening—in this area. On Friday you can cap off your day of culture with dinner and entertainment at the Philadelphia Museum of Art. If it's a Friday or Saturday, save the Franklin Institute for midafternoon, head out to dinner in the neighborhood, and return for a film on the giant screen of the Omniverse Theater, which usually has a final show at midnight. How much time you spend at each museum depends on your interests; be aware that the Philadelphia Museum of Art and the Rodin Museum are closed on Monday.

TOP ATTRACTIONS

8 **Eastern State Penitentiary Historic Site.** Designed by John Haviland and built in 1829, Eastern State was at the time the most expensive building in America; it influenced penal design around the world and was the model for some 300 prisons from China to South America. Before it closed in 1971, the prison was home to Al Capone, Willie Sutton, and Pep the Dog, who killed the cat that belonged to a governor's wife. The audio tour of this ruin features narration by former guards and inmates—punctuated by cell doors slamming and other sounds of prison life. The penitentiary, just a half mile north of the Rodin Museum, hosts changing art exhibitions, haunted house tours around Halloween, and a Bastille Day celebration the Sunday before July 14, with a reenactment of the storming of the Bastille. ⊠ *22nd St. and Fairmount Ave., Fairmount* ☎ *215/236–3300* ⊕ *www.easterstate.org* ✉ *$12* ◷ *Daily 10–5; last entry at 4.*

NEED A BREAK?

Across the street from the brooding Eastern State Penitentiary is a more welcoming spot—**Mugshots Coffeehouse and Cafe** (⊠ *2100 Fairmount Ave., Fairmount* ☎ *267/514–7145*), a neighborhood hangout offering organic fair-trade coffee, fresh juices, and smoothies, as well as an all-day chalkboard menu of bagel-and-egg sandwiches, soups, mini-frittatas, veggie wraps, and even good-old-reliable peanut butter and jelly.

❹ ☾ ★ **The Franklin Institute.** Founded more than 175 years ago to honor Benjamin Franklin, this science museum is as clever as its namesake, thanks to an abundance of dazzling hands-on exhibits. To make the best use of your time, study the floor plan before exploring. You can sit in the cockpit of a T-33 jet trainer, trace the route of a corpuscle through the world's largest artificial heart (15,000 times life size), and ride to nowhere on a 350-ton Baldwin steam locomotive. You'll also be able to explore **Sir Isaac's Loft,** which combines lessons in art and science, delve into the mechanics of more than two-dozen mechanical devices in **Amazing Machine,** and see Franklin's famous lightning rod. One don't-miss: the 30-foot-tall statue of Franklin.

The **Franklin Air Show** celebrates powered flight with the Wright Model B Flyer. **The Sports Challenge** conveys the physics, physiology, and material science behind your favorite sport by simulating surfing, climbing a rock wall, and comparing your sneakers to Shaquille O'Neal's size 22s. The **Fels Planetarium**—which has a state-of-the-art aluminum dome, lighting and sound systems, and a related astronomy exhibit, "Space Command"—has shows about the stars, space exploration, comets, and other phenomena. **Franklin Theater** is a venue for 3-D films. The **Mandell Center** includes the Tuttleman IMAX Theater, with a 79-foot domed screen and a 56-speaker sound system; recent movies include *Star Trek, Van Gogh: Brush with Genius,* and *Pulse: A Stomp Odyssey.*

Run by the Franklin Institute, the **Kids Science Park** (⊠ *21st St. between Winter and Race Sts., Logan Circle* ✉ *Free with admission to Franklin Institute or Please Touch Museum* ◷ *May–Sept., daily 10–3*) presents interactive displays in an outdoor setting—which means children get a chance to run around and play while they learn. Swings demonstrate the laws of gravity and energy, and golf illustrates physics in motion. ⊠ *20th St. and Benjamin Franklin Pkwy., Logan Circle* ☎ *215/448–1200* ⊕ *www.fi.edu* ✉ *$14.75–$22.25* ◷ *Daily 9:30–5.*

❼ **Philadelphia Museum of Art.** The city's premier cultural attraction is one

Fodor's Choice ★

of the country's leading museums. One of the greatest treasures of the

Benjamin Franklin's Spark

Unlike the bronze statue of William Penn perched atop City Hall, a marble likeness of Benjamin Franklin is within **The Franklin Institute.** Perhaps that's as it should be: noble-born Penn above the people and common-born Franklin sitting more democratically among them.

Franklin (1706–90) was anything but a common man. In fact biographer Walter Isaacson called him "the most accomplished American of his age." Franklin's insatiable curiosity, combined with his ability to solve problems in his own life, inspired his invention of bifocals, an odometer to measure postal routes, a "long arm" to reach books high on his shelves, and a flexible urinary catheter for his brother who was suffering with kidney stones. His great intellect inspired his launching of the American Philosophical Society, the oldest learned society in America. He was the only Founding Father who shaped and signed all of the nation's founding documents, including the Declaration of Independence, the Constitution, and treaties with France and England. He was a citizen of the world—a representative in the Pennsylvania General Assembly, a minister to France.

It's fortunate for Philadelphians that Franklin spent so many of his 84 years here. That might have been an act of fate or early recognition that "time is money," as he wrote in *Advice to a Young Tradesman* in 1748. Born in Boston in 1706, Franklin ran away from home and the oppression of his job as a printer's apprentice at his brother's shop. When he couldn't find work in New York, he didn't waste time; he moved on to Philadelphia. Within 10 years Franklin had opened his own printing office. His *Pennsylvania Gazette* was the most successful newspaper in the colonies; his humor propelled his *Poor Richard: An Almanack* to best-seller status in the colonies. In Franklin's Print Shop in the **Franklin Court** complex, site of Ben's first permanent home in Philadelphia, you can get a letter hand-stamped with a "B. Free Franklin" cancellation.

Franklin had time and passion for civic duties. As postmaster, he set up the city's postal system. He founded the city's first volunteer fire company and the **Library Company of Philadelphia,** its first subscription library. After his famous kite experiment, he opened the first fire-insurance company, the **Philadelphia Contributionship for the Insurance of Houses from Loss by Fire.** He proposed the idea for the **University of Pennsylvania** and personally raised money to finance **Pennsylvania Hospital,** the nation's first.

Franklin was laid to rest alongside his wife, Deborah, and one of his sons, Francis, in the **Christ Church Burial Ground.**

museum is the building itself. Constructed in 1928 of Minnesota dolomite, it's modeled after ancient Greek temples but on a grander scale. The museum was designed by Julian Francis Abele, the first African-American to graduate from the University of Pennsylvania School of Architecture. You can enter the museum from the front or the rear; choose the front and you can run up the 99 steps made famous in the movie *Rocky.*

Once inside, you'll see the grand staircase and Saint-Gaudens's statue *Diana;* she formerly graced New York's old Madison Square Garden. The museum has several outstanding permanent collections: the John G. Johnson Collection covers Western art from the Renaissance to the 19th century; the Arensberg and A. E. Gallatin collections contain modern and contemporary works by artists such as Brancusi, Braque, Matisse, and Picasso. Famous paintings in these collections include Van Eyck's *St. Francis Receiving the Stigmata,* Rubens's *Prometheus Bound,* Benjamin West's *Benjamin Franklin Drawing Electricity from the Sky,* Van Gogh's *Sunflowers,* Cézanne's *The Large Bathers,* and Picasso's *Three Musicians.* The museum has the world's most extensive collection of works by Marcel Duchamp, including the world-famous *Nude Descending a Staircase* and *The Bride Stripped Bare by Her Bachelors, Even.* Among the American art worth seeking out is a fine selection of works by 19th-century Philadelphia artist Thomas Eakins, including *The Gross Clinic,* which the museum co-owns with the Pennsylvania Academy of the Fine Arts.

Perhaps the most spectacular objects in the museum are entire structures and great rooms moved lock, stock, and barrel from around the world: a 12th-century French cloister, a 16th-century Indian temple hall, a 16th-century Japanese Buddhist temple, a 17th-century Chinese palace hall, and a Japanese ceremonial teahouse. Among the other collections are costumes, Early American furniture, and Amish and Shaker crafts. An unusual touch—and one that children especially like—is the Kienbusch Collection of Arms and Armor.

The Ruth and Raymond G. Perelman Building, across the street in the former Reliance Standard Life Insurance Building, is home to the museum's permanent collection of photography, costume, and contemporary design.

Friday evenings feature live jazz and world music performances in the Great Hall. The museum has a fine restaurant and a surprisingly good cafeteria. A short stroll away is the Fairmount Waterworks and Boathouse Row, as well as a path well-used by bikers and joggers that connects the museum to Center City's Fitler Square neighborhood. ⊠ *26th St. and Benjamin Franklin Pkwy., Fairmount* ☎ *215/763–8100* ⊕ *www. philamuseum.org* ✉ *$16, Sun. pay what you wish* ☉ *Tues., Thurs., and weekends 10–5; Wed. and Fri. 10–8:45.*

❻ **Rodin Museum.** This jewel of a museum holds the biggest collection out-
★ side France of the work of sculptor Auguste Rodin (1840–1917). You'll pass through a newly re-landscaped courtyard to reach Rodin's *Gates of Hell*—a 21-foot-high sculpture with more than 100 human and animal

2

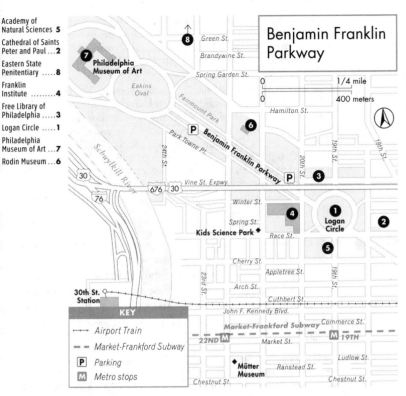

figures. In the exhibition hall, the sculptor's masterworks are made even more striking by the use of light and shadow. Here are *The Kiss, The Burghers of Calais,* and *Eternal Springtime.* A small room is devoted to one of Rodin's most famous sitters, the French novelist Balzac. Photographs by Edward Steichen showing Rodin at work round out the collection. The museum occupies a 20th-century building designed by French architects Jacques Greber and Paul Cret. ⌷ *22nd St. and Benjamin Franklin Pkwy., Fairmount* ☏ *215/763–8100* ⊕ *www.rodinmuseum.org* ⌷ *$5 donation suggested* ☉ *Tues.–Sun. 10–5.*

WORTH NOTING

⑤ Academy of Natural Sciences. The dioramas of animals from around the world displayed in their natural habitats give this natural history museum an old-fashioned charm. The most popular attraction is Dinosaur Hall, with reconstructed skeletons of a Tyrannosaurus rex and some 30 others of its ilk. Other draws are "Butterflies!," where colorful, winged creatures take flight in a tropical rain-forest setting; the "Big Dig, where you can hunt for real fossils; and "Outside-In, an interactive area where kids can crawl through a log, investigate a real beehive, and touch a legless lizard. If you're keeping track of Philadelphia firsts, note that the academy, the oldest science-research institution in the western hemisphere and a world leader in the fields of natural-science research, education, and exhibition, was founded in 1812; the present building dates from 1868. That history is celebrated in the Ewell Sale Stewart Library, a trove of natural-history books and artworks. ⊠ *19th St. and Benjamin Franklin Pkwy., Logan Circle* ☎ *215/299–1000* ⊕ *www.ansp. org* ☜ *$12* ☉ *Weekdays 10–4:30, weekends 10–5.*

❷ **Cathedral of Saints Peter and Paul.** The basilica of the archdiocese of Philadelphia is the spiritual center for the Philadelphia area's 1.4 million Roman Catholics. Topped by a huge copper dome, it was built between 1846 and 1864 in the Italian Renaissance style. Many of the interior decorations are by Constantino Brumidi, who painted the dome of the U.S. Capitol. Six Philadelphia bishops and archbishops are buried beneath the altar. ⊠ *18th and Race Sts., Logan Circle* ☎ *215/561– 1313* ⊕ *www.sspeterpaulcathedral.catholicweb.com* ☜ *Free* ☉ *Daily 7–5. Sept.–May, mass weekdays 7:15, 8, 12:05, and 12:35; June–Aug. 7:30, 12:05, and 12:35; Sat. 12:30 and 5:15; Sun. 8, 9:30, 11, 12:30, and 5.*

NEED A BREAK? At the eastern end of the parkway sits the **Capriccio Café and Espresso Bar at Café Cret** (⊠ *16th St. and the Benjamin Franklin Pkwy., Center City* ☎ *215/735–9797* ⊕ *www.capricciocafe.com*), which, from its glass-enclosed indoor pavilion or alfresco seating, offers commanding views of the famed LOVE statue and City Hall. On the menu are a range of hot and cold coffee-based drinks, along with breakfast items, pastries, sandwiches, and salads.

❸ **Free Library of Philadelphia.** Philadelphia calls its vast public-library system the Fabulous Freebie. Founded in 1891, the central library has more than 1 million volumes. With its grand entrance hall, sweeping marble staircase, and enormous reading rooms, this Greek Revival building looks the way libraries should. It's also the site of regular author readings and other book-related fairs and events. With more than 12,000 musical scores, the Edwin S. Fleisher collection is the largest of its kind in the world. Tormented by a tune whose name you can't recall? Hum it to one of the music room's librarians, and he or she will track it down. The department of social science and history has nearly 100,000 charts, maps, and guidebooks. The rare-book room is a beautiful suite housing first editions of Dickens, ancient Sumerian clay tablets, illuminated medieval manuscripts, and more modern manuscripts, including Poe's "The Raven." The children's department houses the city's largest collection of children's books in a made-for-kids setting. In the works for a tentative 2012 opening is a 130,000-square-foot addition designed by acclaimed architect Moshe Safdie that will house a new children's department, an area for teens, a self-publishing center, exhibition galleries, and a 550-seat auditorium. ⊠ *19th St. and Benjamin Franklin Pkwy., Logan Circle* ☎ *215/686–5322* ⊕ *www.library.phila.gov* ☜ *Free* ☉ *Mon.–Wed. 9–9, Thurs.–Fri. 9–6, Sat. 9–5, Sun. 1–5; closed Sun. late May–Sept.; tours of rare book room weekdays at 11.*

❶ **Logan Circle.** One of William Penn's five squares, Logan Circle was originally a burying ground and the site of a public execution by hanging in 1823. It found a fate better than death, though. In 1825 the square was named for James Logan, Penn's secretary; it later became a circle and is now one of the city's gems. The focal point of Logan Circle is the **Swann Fountain** of 1920, designed by Alexander Stirling Calder, son of Alexander Milne Calder, who created the William Penn statue atop City Hall. You can find many works by a third generation of the family, noted modern sculptor Alexander Calder, the mobile- and stabile-maker, in the nearby **Philadelphia Museum of Art.** The main figures in the fountain symbolize Philadelphia's three leading waterways: the Delaware and Schuylkill rivers and Wissahickon Creek. Around Logan Circle are some examples of Philadelphia's magnificent collection of outdoor art, including *General Galusha Pennypacker,* the Shakespeare Memorial (*Hamlet and the Fool,* by Alexander Stirling Calder), and *Jesus Breaking Bread.*

FAIRMOUNT PARK

Stretching from the edge of downtown to the city's northwest corner, Fairmount Park is the largest landscaped city park in the world. With more than 8,500 acres and 2 million trees (someone claims to have counted), the park winds along the banks of the Schuylkill River—which divides it into west and east sections—and through parts of the city. Quite a few city dwellers consider the park their backyard. On weekends the 4-mi stretch along Kelly Drive is crowded with joggers, bicycling moms and dads with children strapped into kiddie seats atop the back wheel, hand-holding senior citizens out for some fresh air, collegiate crew teams sculling on the river, and budding artists trying to capture the sylvan magic just as Thomas Eakins once did.

Fairmount Park encompasses natural areas—woodlands, meadows, rolling hills, two scenic waterways, and a forested 5½-mi gorge. It also contains tennis courts, ball fields, playgrounds, trails, exercise courses, several celebrated cultural institutions, and some historic Early American country houses that are operated by the Philadelphia Museum of Art and open to visitors. Philadelphia has more works of outdoor art than any other city in North America, and more than 200 of these works—including statues by Frederic Remington, Jacques Lipchitz, and Auguste Rodin—are scattered throughout Fairmount Park. Some sections of the park that border depressed urban neighborhoods are neglected; it's better maintained along the Schuylkill.

GETTING HERE AND AROUND

Boathouse Row on Kelly Drive and portions of West River are easily reached on foot from the Philadelphia Museum of Art. To reach the Zoo or the Please Touch Museum, you will need to use a car or take SEPTA or the PHLASH. Both the zoo and Please Touch are less than 15-minutes' drive from Center City West.

PLANNING YOUR TIME

You can tour by car (get a good city map), starting near the Philadelphia Museum of Art. Signs point the way, and the historic houses have free parking. Before you set out, call **Park House Information** (☎ 215/683–0200 or 215/988–9334 ⊕ *www.fairmountpark.org*) to find out which

GREAT EXPERIENCES IN FAIRMOUNT PARK

Boathouse Row: Join the masses strolling, jogging, biking, or roller-blading near this collection of rowing clubs along Kelly Drive.

Fairmount Park Houses: Experience early American country life by visiting one or several of these period homes scattered around the park.

Philadelphia Zoo: Lions and tigers and bears—oh, my—as well as giraffes, birds, and all kinds of wildlife prowl around the nation's oldest zoo.

Please Touch Museum: Ride the carousel and schedule a play date at this fun, interactive facility located in one of the last remaining buildings from the 1876 Centennial Exhibition.

Japanese House: Get your serenity now at this 16th-century samurai's home and its exquisite garden, complete with pond, waterfall, and Japanese plantings.

historic houses are open that day. Another option is to take the narrated tour given by Philadelphia Trolley Works (board it at the Philadelphia Museum of Art or at John F. Kennedy Plaza, at 16th Street and John F. Kennedy Boulevard). The trolley bus visits many of the sites, and you can get on and off all day for $27. If you leave the driving to the Philadelphia Trolley Works, your narrated tour will take 40 minutes. If you drive yourself, you'll need about two hours. Add another 20–30 minutes for each historic house you tour. Animal lovers can spend half a day at the Philadelphia Zoo, while parents of children 9 and under will want to spend a full morning or afternoon at the Please Touch Museum at Memorial Hall, the hub of a new district celebrating sites that were part of the 1876 Centennial Exhibition.

TOP ATTRACTIONS

❸ **Boathouse Row.** These architecturally varied 19th-century buildings—in

Fodor's Choice Victorian Gothic, Gothic Revival, and Italianate styles—are home to
★ the rowing clubs that make up the Schuylkill Navy, an association of boating clubs organized in 1858. The view of the boathouses from the west side of the river is splendid—especially at night, when they're outlined with hundreds of small lights. The row's newest addition, Lloyd Hall, has a gymnasium, bicycle and skate rentals in season, and a two-story café. ⊠ *Kelly Dr., E. Fairmount Park, Fairmount Park* ⊕ *www. boathouserow.org.*

⓱ **Philadelphia Zoo.** Opened in 1874, America's first zoo is home to more
☾ than 2,000 animals representing six continents. It's small and well landscaped enough to feel pleasantly intimate, and the naturalistic habitats allow you to get close enough to hear the animals breathe. At each exhibit an old-fashioned Talking Storybook provides narration when activated by an elephant-shaped key. The Amphibian and Reptile House houses 87 species, from 15-foot-long snakes to frogs the size of a dime. The 2½-acre Primate Reserve is home to 11 species from around the world. Notable attractions include Big Cat Falls, where you'll find leopards, jaguars, mountain lions, tigers, and more than a dozen rare

white lions; the McNeil Avian Center, the state-of-the-art nest for some 100 birds; and African Plains, stomping ground of giraffes and zebras. The Tastykake Children's Zoo has a bunny village; two exercise yards with macaws, porcupines, hedgehogs, and owls; and a barnyard-animal petting-and-feeding area. You can get a bird's-eye view of the zoo and Fairmount Park on the Channel 6 Zooballoon, a 30-passenger helium balloon anchored by a high tensile-steel cable. ⊠ *34th St. and Girard Ave., W. Fairmount Park, Fairmount Park* ☎ *215/243–1100* ⊕ *www. phillyzoo.org* ✉ *$12.95–$18* ⊙ *Mar.–Oct., daily 9:30–5; Nov.–Feb., daily 9:30–4.*

⓭ **Please Touch Museum.** Philadelphia's children's museum occupies one of the city's most stately buildings, a gorgeous example of Beaux Arts–style architecture constructed for the 1876 Centennial Exhibition and one of just two public buildings still standing from the event. The facility, which is aimed at children 9 and younger, instills a sense of wonder from the get-go, with its marble-floored Great Hall, which has an 80-foot-high ceiling and a 40-foot-tall sculpture of the torch of the Statue of Liberty at its centerpiece. (The real statue's torch was displayed here for the nation's 100th birthday celebration.) The 38,000-square-foot facility is set up as six discovery zones, where kids can learn through hands-on play at exhibits including a mock supermarket, a child-sized television studio, a hospital area, Alice's Adventures in Wonderland, and a theater with interactive performances. Another highlight is a circa-1908 Dentzel Carousel ride with 52 gleaming and colorful horses, pigs, cats, and rabbits that's housed in an adjacent, enclosed glass pavilion; separate tickets can be purchased for carousel rides. There also is a café serving lunch items and snacks. ⊠ *4231 Ave. of the Republic, W. Fairmount Park, Fairmount Park* ☎ *215/581–3181* ⊕ *www.pleasetouchmuseum. org* ✉ *$15* ⊙ *Mon.–Sat. 9–5, Sun. 11–5.*

NEED A BREAK?

Situated in one of two remaining public structures built for the 1876 Centennial Exhibition, the **Centennial Café-The Ohio House** (⊠ *4700 States Dr., W. Fairmount Park, Fairmount Park* ☎ *215/877–3055* ⊕ *www. thecentennialcafe.com*) features a menu of breakfast and lunch dishes such as omelets, salads, and sandwiches—notably its house-smoked brisket—as well as homemade cookies and cakes and other snacks. The high-ceilinged, sunny space also offers the very modern amenity of free Wi-Fi access.

WORTH NOTING

⓾ **Belmont Plateau.** Literally the high point of your park tour, Belmont Plateau has a view from 243 feet above river level. In front of you is the park, the Schuylkill River winding down to the Philadelphia Museum of Art, and, 4 mi away, the Philadelphia skyline. ⊠ *2000 Belmont Mansion Dr., W. Fairmount Park, Fairmount Park.*

⓯ **Cedar Grove.** Five styles of furniture—Jacobean, William and Mary, Queen Anne, Chippendale, and Federal—reflect the accumulations of five generations of the Paschall-Morris family. The house stood in Frankford, in northeastern Philadelphia, for 180 years before being moved to this location in 1927. ⊠ *Lansdowne Dr. off N. Concourse*

Dr., W. Fairmount Park, Fairmount Park ☎ *215/235–7469* ⊕ *www.fairmountparkhouses.org* ✉ *$5* ☉ *Tues.–Sun. 10–5.*

❹ Ellen Phillips Samuel Memorial Sculpture Garden. Bronze and granite sculptures by 16 artists stand in a series of tableaux and groupings on riverside terraces. Portraying American themes and traits, they include *The Quaker,* by Harry Rosen; *Birth of a Nation,* by Henry Kreis; and *Spirit of Enterprise,* by Jacques Lipchitz. ⊠ *Kelly Dr., E. Fairmount Park, Fairmount Park.*

❶ Faire Mount. This is now the site of the Philadelphia Museum of Art. In 1812 a reservoir was built here to distribute water throughout the city.

❷ Fairmount Waterworks. Designed by Frederick Graff, this National His-
★ toric Engineering Landmark built in 1815 was the first steam-pumping station of its kind in the country. The notable assemblage of Greek Revival buildings—one of the city's most beautiful sights—sits just behind the Philadelphia Museum of Art; it includes an interpretive center with original machinery on display, an art gallery, an upscale restaurant, and an information center. ⊠ *Waterworks Dr., off Kelly Dr., Fairmount Park* ☎ *215/685–0719* ⊕ *www.fairmountwaterworks.org* ✉ *Free* ☉ *Interpretive center Tues.–Sat. 10–5, Sun. 1–5.*

⑪ Horticulture Center. On the Horticulture Center's 27 wooded acres are a butterfly garden, a greenhouse where plants and flowers used on city property are grown, and a pavilion in the trees for bird-watching from the woodland canopy. Don't miss the whimsical *Seaweed Girl* fountain in the display house. The center stands on the site of the 1876 Centennial Exposition's Horticultural Hall. ⊠ *N. Horticultural Dr., W. Fairmount Park, Fairmount Park* ☎ *215/685–0096* ⊕ *www.fairmountpark.org/HortCenter.asp* ✉ *Free* ☉ *Visitor center and greenhouses daily 9–3. Grounds July–Sept., daily 8–6; Oct.–June, daily 8–5.*

⑫ Japanese House. This reconstructed 16th-century samurai's dwelling was reassembled here in 1958. The architectural setting and the waterfall, gardens, Japanese trees, and pond are a serene contrast with the busy city. The house is called Shofu-So, which means "pine breeze villa," and has a roof made of the bark of the hinoki, a cypress that grows only in the mountains of Japan. The facility also features 20 murals by acclaimed Japanese contemporary artist Hiroshi Senju, and is the site of monthly tea ceremonies, for which reservations are required. ⊠ *Lansdowne Dr. east of Belmont Ave., W. Fairmount Park, Fairmount Park* ☎ *215/878–5097* ⊕ *www.shofuso.com* ✉ *$6* ☉ *May–Oct., Tues.–Fri. 10–4, weekends 11–5.*

❼ Laurel Hill. Built around 1767, this Georgian house on a laurel-covered hill overlooking the Schuylkill River once belonged to Dr. Philip Syng Physick (also owner of Society Hill's Physick House). On some Sunday evenings in summer, Women for Greater Philadelphia sponsors candlelight chamber music concerts here. ⊠ *E. Edgely Dr., E. Fairmount Park, Fairmount Park* ☎ *215/235–1776* ⊕ *www.fairmountparkhouses.org* ✉ *$5* ☉ *Apr.–June, weekends 10–4; July–mid-Dec., Wed.–Sun. 10–4.*

**OFF THE
BEATEN
PATH**
Laurel Hill Cemetery. John Notman, architect of the Athenaeum and many other noted local buildings, designed Laurel Hill in 1836. The cemetery is an important example of an early rural burial ground and the first

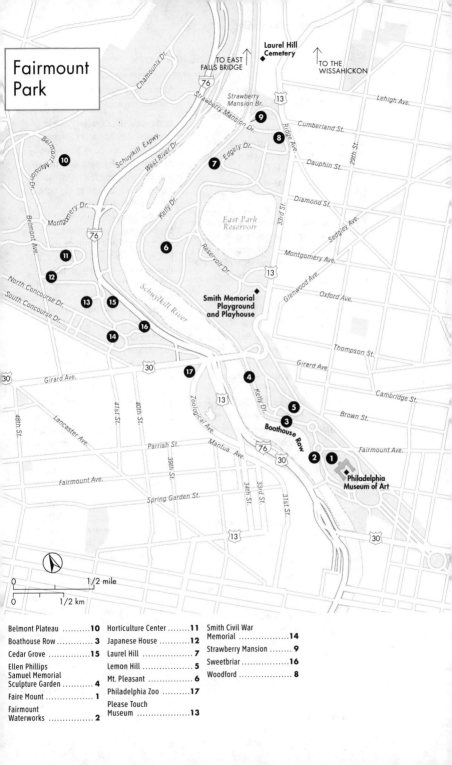

Fairmount Park

Laurel Hill Cemetery

TO EAST
FALLS BRIDGE

TO THE
WISSAHICKON

Strawberry
Mansion Br.

Chamounix Dr.

Schuylkill Expwy.

West River Dr.

Belmont Mansion Dr.

Montgomery Dr.

Kelly Dr.

Edgley Dr.

Strawberry Mansion Dr.

Ridge Ave.

Cumberland St.

Lehigh Ave.

Dauphin St.

Diamond St.

Sedgley Ave.

29th St.

33rd St.

East Park
Reservoir

Reservoir Dr.

Montgomery Ave.

Glenwood Ave.

Oxford Ave.

Belmont Ave.

North Concourse Dr.

South Concourse Dr.

Schuylkill River

Smith Memorial
Playground
and Playhouse

Thompson St.

Girard Ave.

Girard Ave.

Zoological Ave.

Mantua Ave.

Lancaster Ave.

48th St.

41st St.

40th St.

39th St.

34th St.

33rd St.

31st St.

Parrish St.

Fairmount Ave.

Spring Garden St.

Boathouse Row

Cambridge St.

Brown St.

Fairmount Ave.

Philadelphia
Museum of Art

0   1/2 mile
0   1/2 km

Driving Around Fairmount Park

Your visit can start where the park began, at **Faire Mount.** Begin this outing with a walk before you set off by car. Park behind the art museum and walk down the stairs. To your right is the Azalea Garden. Straight ahead, overlooking the Schuylkill, is the **Fairmount Waterworks,** an elegant group of Greek Revival buildings. North of the Waterworks you can see the Victorian structures of **Boathouse Row**; watch for rowers on the river here, too. Walking north along Kelly Drive, you soon reach the **Ellen Phillips Samuel Memorial Sculpture Garden.**

Now's the time to walk back to your car for a driving tour of East Fairmount Park. Follow Kelly Drive to the end of Boathouse Row; turn right up the hill to a Federal-style country house, **Lemon Hill.** Head back to Kelly Drive, turn right, pass through the rock archway, and turn right again at the equestrian statue of Ulysses S. Grant. The first left takes you to **Mt. Pleasant,** a Georgian mansion. Continue along the road that runs to the right of the house (as you face it) past Rockland, a handsome Federal house that's currently closed. At the dead end turn left onto Reservoir Drive. You'll pass the redbrick Georgian-style Ormiston, also closed. Take the next left, Randolph Drive, to another Georgian house, **Laurel Hill,** on Edgely Drive, which becomes Dauphin Street. Just about 10 feet before reaching 33rd Street, turn left on Strawberry Mansion Drive, and you're at **Woodford,** which has an interesting collection of household goods. A quarter-mile northwest of Woodford stands the house that gave its name to the nearby section of Philadelphia,

Strawberry Mansion. It has furniture from three periods of its history.

Visit Laurel Hill Cemetery before you cross the river to West Fairmount Park. Drive back down the driveway of Strawberry Mansion, turn left at the stop sign, and follow the narrow road as it winds right to the light. Turn left onto Ridge Avenue and follow it to the entrance gate, which sits between eight Greek columns. To skip the cemetery and continue your tour, proceed down the Strawberry Mansion driveway to the stop sign, turn left, and follow the road as it loops down and around to the Strawberry Mansion Bridge. Cross the river and follow the road; when it splits, stay left. You'll come to Chamounix Drive, a long straightaway. Turn left and then left again on Belmont Mansion Drive for a fine view from **Belmont Plateau.** Follow Belmont Mansion Drive down the hill. Where it forks, stay to the left, cross Montgomery Drive, and bear left to reach the **Horticulture Center** with its greenhouse and garden. Loop all the way around the Horticulture Center to visit the serene **Japanese House** and its waterfall and gardens.

Drive back around the Horticulture Center and continue through the gates to Montgomery Drive. Turn left and then left again at the first light (Belmont Avenue). Turn left again on North Concourse Drive. On your left is **Memorial Hall,** which now houses the **Please Touch Museum.** The two towers ahead are part of the **Smith Civil War Memorial.** Turn left just past them to see **Cedar Grove.** Just south of Cedar Grove is a Federal mansion, **Sweetbriar.** Continue past the house, make the first left, and turn left again at the stop sign onto Lansdowne Drive. Follow signs to the **zoo.**

2

cemetery in America designed by an architect. Its rolling hills overlooking the Schuylkill River, its rare trees, and its monuments and mausoleums sculpted by Alexander Milne Calder, Alexander Stirling Calder, William Strickland, and Thomas U. Walter made it a popular picnic spot in the 19th century; today it's a great place for a stroll. Among the notables buried in this 99-acre necropolis are prominent Philadelphians and Declaration of Independence signers. Burials still take place here. ⊠ *3822 Ridge Ave., Fairmount Park* ☎ *215/228–8200* ⊕ *www. laurelhillcemetery.com* ▣ *Free* ⊙ *Weekdays 8–4:30, Sat. 9:30–5.*

❺ **Lemon Hill.** An impressive example of a Federal-style country house, Lemon Hill was built in 1800 on a 350-acre farm. Its most distinctive features are oval parlors with concave doors and the entrance hall's checkerboard floor of Valley Forge marble. ⊠ *Poplar Dr., E. Fairmount Park, Fairmount Park* ☎ *215/232–4337* ⊕ *www.fairmountparkhouses. org* ▣ *$5* ⊙ *Apr.–mid-Dec., Wed.–Sun. 10–4.*

❻ **Mt. Pleasant.** Built in 1761 by John Macpherson, a Scottish sea captain, Mt. Pleasant is one of the finest examples of Georgian architecture in the country. The historically accurate furnishings are culled from the Philadelphia Museum of Art's collection of Philadelphia Chippendale furniture. According to legend, Revolutionary War traitor Benedict Arnold purchased this house as an engagement gift for Peggy Shippen, but he was banished before the deal was signed. ⊠ *3800 Mt. Pleasant Dr., E. Fairmount Park, Fairmount Park* ☎ *215/235–7469* ⊕ *www. fairmountparkhouses.org* ▣ *$5* ⊙ *Tues.–Sun. 10–5.*

⑭ **Smith Civil War Memorial.** Built between 1897 and 1912 with funds donated by wealthy foundry owner Richard Smith, the memorial honors Pennsylvania heroes of the Civil War. Among those immortalized in bronze are generals Meade and Hancock—and Smith himself. At the base of each tower is a curved wall with a bench. If you sit at one end and listen to a person whispering at the other end, you can understand why they're called the Whispering Benches. Unfortunately, litter is a constant problem here. ⊠ *N. Concourse Dr., W. Fairmount Park, Fairmount Park.*

Smith Memorial Playground and Playhouse. Founded in 1899, this beloved facility has been completely refurbished in recent years with state-of-the-art, age-specific equipment; the centerpiece of the 6½-acre site is the aptly named Giant Slide, which measures 40 feet long, 12 feet wide, and 10 feet tall, and can accommodate up to 12 children at a time. ⊠ *33rd and Oxford Sts., E. Fairmount Park, Fairmount Park* ☎ *215/765–4325* ⊕ *www.smithplayhouse.org* ▣ *Free* ⊙ *Giant slide Apr.–Oct., Tues.–Sun. 10–4; playhouse Tues.–Sun. 10–4.*

❾ **Strawberry Mansion.** The largest mansion in Fairmount Park, which is scheduled to reopen in the summer of 2010 after undergoing major structural repairs including new windows and wiring, has furniture from the three main phases of its history: Federal, Regency, and Empire. In the parlor is a collection of rare Tucker porcelain; the attic holds fine antique dolls. ⊠ *Near 33rd and Dauphin Sts., E. Fairmount Park, Fairmount Park* ☎ *215/228–8364* ⊕ *www.historicstrawberrymansion. org* ▣ *$5* ⊙ *Tues.–Sun. 10–4.*

⑯ Sweetbriar. This three-story Federal mansion dating from 1797 was the first year-round residence in what is now Fairmount Park. It was built by Samuel and Jean Breck to escape the yellow fever epidemic that ravaged the city. ⊠ *Lansdowne Dr. off N. Concourse Dr., W. Fairmount Park, Fairmount Park* ☎ *215/222–1333* ⊕ *www.fairmountparkhouses. org* 🔄 *$5* ⊙ *July–mid-Dec., Wed.–Sun. 10–4.*

❽ Woodford. The Naomi Wood collection of antique household goods, including Colonial furniture, unusual clocks, and English delftware, can be seen in this fine Georgian mansion built about 1756. ⊠ *Near 33rd and Dauphin Sts., E. Fairmount Park, Fairmount Park* ☎ *215/229– 6115* ⊕ *www.fairmountparkhouses.org* 🔄 *$5* ⊙ *Tues.–Sun. 10–4.*

UNIVERSITY CITY

University City is the portion of West Philadelphia that includes the campuses of the University of Pennsylvania, Drexel University, and the Philadelphia College of Pharmacy and Science. It also has the University City Science Center (a leading think tank), the Annenberg Center performing arts complex (part of the University of Pennsylvania), an impressive collection of Victorian houses, and a variety of moderately priced restaurants, movie theaters, stores, and lively bars catering to more than 32,000 students and other residents. The neighborhood stretches from the Schuylkill River west to 44th Street and from the river north to Powelton Avenue.

This area was once the city's flourishing western suburbs, where wealthy Philadelphians built grand estates and established summer villages. It officially became part of the city in 1854. Twenty years later the University of Pennsylvania moved its campus here from the center of the city. The university moved into many of the historic homes, and others were adopted by fraternities. **Penn's Information Center** (☎ *215/898–4636*) is at 34th and Walnut streets.

GETTING HERE AND AROUND
Unless you're a big walker or have access to a bike, you'll want to take either a SEPTA bus or underground Blue or Green line to University City. If you're driving, street parking can be easier to find here than in Center City, although it can be tight near the Penn campus when school is in session.

PLANNING YOUR TIME
University City is at its best when college is in session; the students rushing to classes give this area its flavor. Allow half an hour each in the Arthur Ross Gallery and the Institute of Contemporary Art, two hours in the University Museum, and an hour exploring the campus. If your time is limited, skip all but the University Museum, a don't-miss for the archaeologically inclined.

TOP ATTRACTIONS
❹ University Museum of Archaeology and Anthropology. Rare treasures from
Ⓒ the deepest jungles and ancient tombs make this one of the finest
★ archaeological and anthropological museums in the world. The collection of more than 1 million objects includes the world's third-largest

sphinx from Egypt, a crystal ball once owned by China's Dowager Empress, the world's oldest writing—Sumerian cuneiform clay tablets—and the 4,500-year-old golden jewels from the royal tombs of the kingdom of Ur. The museum's Worlds Intertwined galleries showcase its Greek, Roman, and Etruscan collections; the latter is the only comprehensive exhibit of its kind in the United States. Children run to "The Egyptian Mummy: Secrets and Science" and to "Living in Balance: The Universe of the Hopi, Zuni, Navajo, and Apache." ⊠ *33rd and Spruce Sts., University City* ☎ *215/898–4001* ⊕ *www.upenn.edu/museum* ⊠ *$10, free Sun.* ☉ *Labor Day–Memorial Day, Tues.–Sat. 10–4:30, Sun. 1–5, except the Sunday before Memorial Day and Labor Day.*

> **GREAT EXPERIENCES IN UNIVERSITY CITY**
>
> **Institute of Contemporary Art:** Andy Warhol, Robert Mapplethorpe, and Laurie Anderson are among the cutting-edge artists to show their work at this exhibition space.
>
> **University Museum of Archaeology and Anthropology:** Check out the world's third-largest sphinx and other treasures from the ancient world.
>
> **University of Pennsylvania:** This Ivy League school's leafy campus offers a nice contrast to its urban surroundings.

WORTH NOTING

❷ Arthur Ross Gallery. Penn's official art gallery showcases treasures from the university's collections and traveling exhibitions. The gallery shares its historic-landmark building, designed by Frank Furness, with the **Fisher Fine Arts Library.** ⊠ *220 S. 34th St., University City* ☎ *215/898–2083* ⊕ *www.upenn.edu/ARG* ⊠ *Free* ☉ *Tues.–Fri. 10–5, weekends noon–5.*

❸ Fisher Fine Arts Library. One of the finest examples remaining of the work of Philadelphia architect Frank Furness, this was the most innovative library building in the country when it was completed in 1890. It was the first library to separate the reading room and the stacks. Peek into the catalog room, dominated by a huge fireplace, and the reading room, with study alcoves lit from the leaded-glass windows above. The unusual exterior stirred controversy when it was built: note the terracotta panels, short heavy columns, and gargoyles on the north end. ⊠ *220 S. 34th St., University City* ☎ *215/898–8325* ⊕ *www.library.upenn.edu/finearts* ⊠ *Free* ☉ *Sept.–mid-May, Mon.–Thurs. 8:30 AM–midnight, Fri. 8:30–8, Sat. 10–8, Sun. noon–midnight; mid-May–Aug., Mon.–Thurs. 9–7, Fri. 9–5.*

NEED A BREAK?

A popular hangout for the Penn crowd, the sleek **Marbar** (⊠ *40th and Walnut sts., University City* ☎ *215/222-0100* ⊕ *www.marathongrill.com*), serves from early morning through late night, with breakfast items offered all day, along with burgers, sandwiches, salads, and more substantive main dishes such as a turkey dinner with all the trimmings and grilled salmon. For a pan-Asian fix, grab a stool at the sushi bar at the futuristic **Pod** (⊠ *3636 Sansom St., University City* ☎ *215/387-1803*

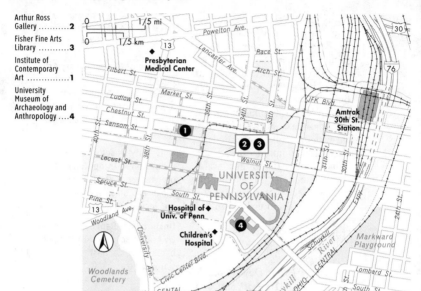

University
City

⊕ *www.podrestaurant.com*), where you can select your favorite raw fish
from a conveyor belt.

❶ **Institute of Contemporary Art.** This museum, part of the University of
Pennsylvania, has established a reputation for identifying promising
artists and exhibiting them at a critical point in their careers. Among the
artists who have had shows at ICA and later gone on to international
prominence are Andy Warhol, Robert Mapplethorpe, and Laurie Ander-
son. ✉ *118 S. 36th St., at Sansom St., University City* ☎ *215/898–7108*
⊕ *www.icaphila.org* 🎫 *Free* ⊙ *Wed.–Fri. noon–8, weekends 11–5.*

Manayunk, Germantown, and Chestnut Hill

Updated by
Josh McIlvain

In 1683, at the founding of Germantown by German settlers, the county encompassed present day Germantown, Mount Airy, and Chestnut Hill. It played an important role in the nation's founding: during the American Revolution, it was the sight of the Battle of Germantown, which marked the first attack by American armed forces on the British. Originally intended as a farming community, the land turned out to be too rocky for anything but subsistence farming. Instead the Germans turned to making textiles, milling, and printing.

Germantown became fashionable for wealthy Philadelphians wanting to escape the city's heat in the mid-1700s. There are more than 70 homes dating from the 1700s here, as well as some of the oldest mills in the country. Germantown was also the seat of government for two summers during Washington's presidency, when yellow fever epidemics raged in the city.

Mount Airy and Chestnut Hill were not developed until the 19th century, when they became desirable as the location for summer homes for Philadelphia business owners drawn to Germantown's booming textile industry. Indeed, Philadelphia University had been the Philadelphia College of Textiles from the late 1800s to 1999. Germantown township was incorporated into Philadelphia in 1854, by which point local trains were already servicing the area, making travel to the city convenient.

Today Chestnut Hill and Mount Airy are very pleasant, predominantly residential neighborhoods. Travel to downtown Philadelphia is easy by car or train. Restaurants and shops run all along Germantown Avenue in Chestnut Hill. Mount Airy is a little more sprawling, but there are a number of good restaurants and bars there as well.

Manayunk has little of its history on display, unless you follow the tow path up the Schuykill to see the last remnants of decaying mills. This predominantly Polish and Irish neighborhood renovated its Main Street in the 1980s into a quaint avenue with restaurants, funky shops, and a few good bars, perfect for a pleasant afternoon. It's also the sight of a well-known professional bike race that includes a brutal ascent up a road called "The Wall." During the race, bikers must climb "The Wall" *10 times*.

TOP REASONS TO GO

American History: More than 70 buildings dating to the 1700s still stand in Germantown, including the Germantown White House, which for two summers was the seat of government. The history of the neighborhood and the nation are told within these structures.

The Schmitter: Head to McNallly's Tavern at the top of Chestnut Hill for one of the great bar sandwiches of all time, the Schmitter. It's a cheesesteak on a Kaiser roll with the added goodness of fried salami, fried onions, and a special sauce.

Mountain biking: Believe it or not, there are some serious mountain bike trails along the steep wooded hillsides near Valley Green, one of the best areas in the city's massive Fairmount Park system.

Main Street Manayunk: Spend a pleasant afternoon in Manayunk, ambling along the tow path, window shopping, and refueling in bars along the way.

Walking Chestnut Hill: If you like strolling around neighborhoods, looking at people's homes, and deciding which ones you'd like to live in, the residential streets of Chestnut Hill are right up your alley. They house everything from the gracious homes of the turn of the 19th century to 1960s funky glass boxes.

ORIENTATION AND PLANNING

GETTING ORIENTED

Northwest Philadelphia includes Germantown, Mount Airy, and Chestnut Hill, all of which run along Germantown Avenue, the East–West divider. The easiest way to get to this area from downtown is to take Kelly Drive, Martin Luther King Boulevard (formerly West River Driver), or the Schuylkill Expressway and either take Lincoln Drive or head east through East Falls on Midvale Avenue or Schoolhouse Lane to the Germantown area. Be warned that these roads are windy, and locals sometimes treat them as speedways. Manayunk is just down the river from East Falls, about a 10-minute drive from the Philadelphia Museum of Art. Going north along Germantown Avenue, Germantown becomes Mount Airy (somewhat fuzzy dividing line) and then becomes Chestnut Hill at Cresheim Valley Drive. Valley Green, an extension of Fairmount Park and Wissahicken Par, divides Mount Airy and Chestnut Hill from the Roxborough, Andorra, and Manayunk sections of the city.

Manayunk. Main Street is like a vacation village, with boutiques, sports bars, and restaurants. Sitting along the Schuylkill River, the rest of the neighborhood rises steeply up the hill, with houses crammed together up twisting streets.

Germantown. Nearly all of the area's 18th-century homes are here, most of which are along Germantown Avenue, which is alternately historic and ramshackle. There are a lot of beautiful residential houses in the area, but it's not a suitable place to wander alone at night.

Chestnut Hill and Mount Airy. Chestnut Hill is Philadelphia's most relaxed neighborhood as well as one of its greenest . People gather here to eat and wander about the precious shops on Germantown Avenue. It's a great neighborhood for peering into people's homes as well. In recent years Mount Airy has seen an increase in dining, drinking, and shopping establishments. Although its businesses are less concentrated than in Chestnut Hill, there are a number of hidden corners with charming cafés, and some great beer at Earth Bread and Brewery

PLANNING

WHEN TO GO

It's no secret that, like the rest of Philadelphia, spring and fall are the best times to visit. However, Chestnut Hill and Mount Airy, the leafiest sections of the city, are also noticeably cooler during the summer. During the winter, most of the historical sites in Germantown are closed (due to a lack of heaters). On weekends, Germantown Avenue in Chestnut Hill and Manayunk can be congested with traffic. If you've never driven on cobblestones before, now's your chance—Germantown Avenue is still full of them.

GETTING HERE AND AROUND

BIKE TRAVEL

You can bike from the Philadelphia Museum of Art all the way to Chestnut Hill, about 12 mi, only having to cross one road, thanks to the bike paths along both sides of the Schuylkill and the paths and trails that lead into the park where East Falls and Manayunk collide (at Ridge Avenue and Main Street).

BUS TRAVEL

Although the 23 Bus travels from the top of Chestnut Hill all the way to the stadiums in deep South Philly, getting to the Germantown–Chestnut Hill area by bus from Center City is a long, winding route that is not recommended. Traveling between Chestnut Hill, Mount Airy, and Germantown, however, is convenient. The fare is $2. There is no convenient bus to Manayunk.

CAR TRAVEL

A car is helpful to really take advantage of the area. Manayunk, however, can be nightmare for parking, especially as the backstreets can be somewhat intimidating with random one ways and steep two-lane roads that only have space for one car at a time. Chestnut Hill, Mount Airy, and Germantown have abundant streetside parking.

TAXI TRAVEL

A cab from downtown to Chestnut Hill is about $30, Mount Airy $25, Germantown $20–$25, and Manayunk $15.

TRAIN TRAVEL

SEPTA's Regional Rail connects Center City Philadelphia to the various outlying neighborhoods. The R7 Chestnut Hill East and the R8 Chestnut Hill West both service Germantown through to Chestnut Hill (20–30 minutes, depending on your stop), each following it's respective side of Germantown Avenue. The trains run about every hour, more

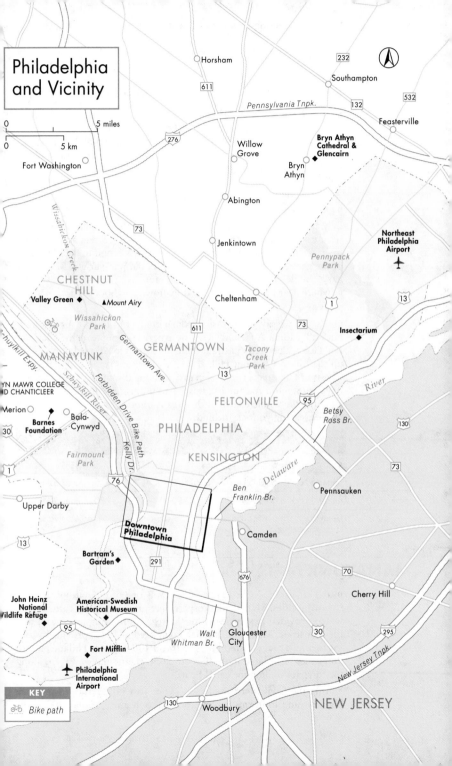

during rush hour. The R7 runs the latest train into and out of the city. The R5 Norristown services Manayunk, and the train station is very convenient to the action.

Train Contacts **SEPTA** (☎ 215/580–7800 ⊕ www.septa.com).

PLANNING YOUR TIME

Manayunk and the Germantown/Chestnut Hill areas are two separate trips that will occupy the better part of a day. Manayunk has more of a nightlife scene, including a couple of bars with decks over the river, so you'll find yourself delayed there longer. Stationing yourself in Chestnut Hill for a weekend and using that as your base for the area and the city is another option.

RESTAURANTS

In Manayunk and Chestnut Hill, friendly neighborhood taverns, ethnic restaurants, and tiny storefront startups line Main Street and German-town Avenue. Some of the best food is actually found in bars, whether of the gastro-pub variety or just the plain old pub variety. Manayunk has a couple of good fine-dining restaurants, but the restaurant scene is nowhere near as good as that of downtown neighborhoods.

HOTELS

Or should we say, hotel? Aside from a number of tiny B&Bs in Chestnut Hill, Mount Airy, and Germantown, the only hotel is the Chestnut Hill Hotel, a perfectly pleasant option in a great location about halfway up the hill in Chestnut Hill. If you are keen on staying at a B&B in Chestnut Hill, make sure it is in easy walking distance of Germantown Avenue (Stenton Avenue is a busy road that is far enough away to be a pain)—the whole charm of the area is to be able to walk out on the avenue leaving your car behind.

WHAT IT COSTS					
	¢	$	$$	$$$	$$$$
Restaurant	under $10	$10–$14	$15–$19	$20–$24	over $24
Hotel	under $100	$100–$150	$151–$200	$201–$250	over $250

Restaurant prices are for one main course at dinner. Hotel prices are for two people in a standard double room.

MANAYUNK

In the mid-1800s, when Philadelphia was one of the nation's leading industrial cities, Manayunk prospered because of its many cotton mills, which provided raw material for the region's thriving paper and textile industries. Manayunk's canal, completed in 1819, provided water for the mills and allowed boats to travel 108 mi from Philadelphia to Pottsville. Mills lined both sides of the canal, and mules walked along the towpath pulling the canal boats.

During the Civil War the mills switched to wool textiles to produce blankets and uniforms for the troops. Soon after, Manayunk's mills closed because of competition from cheaper labor in the South. It took about 100 years for its luck to change. In the mid-1980s the neighborhood was designated a historic district. This new status provided a golden opportunity for business owners, who transformed the old mills into apartments and stores.

About 5 mi down the Schuylkill from the Phialdelphia Museum of Art, Manayunk's Main Street is like an oasis with alfresco dining, dozens of one-of-a-kind stores, including art galleries, antiques shops, and clothing boutiques, and plenty of bars. This urban neighborhood, with its distinctive architecture, brick row houses, and narrow streets, is a good destination for a leisurely stroll with dinner and shopping; many stores stay open late.

Up from Main Street is a decidedly different vibe. The hill rises steeply and houses are jammed together along twisted streets that are narrow and often end up nowhere near where you thought you were headed. Though it is less pronounced now than in the past, the blue-collar veneer of the rest of Manayunk is still a striking contrast to Main Street, but there is also something of a European hill town to the community.

The Manayunk Tow Path—part dirt and part wooden boardwalk— follows the canal, which runs between Main Street and the Schuylkill River. Old rail lines, textile mills, canal locks, and the ruins of the locktender's house are still visible. Bicycling is very popular in Manayunk. You can ride to Center City or the opposite way, all the way to Valley Forge National Park. You are also near the bike path that leads through Wissahickon Park to Chestnut Hill. You can rent bikes at Human Zoom Bikes & Boards in Manayunk or at Bike Line downtown.

GETTING HERE AND AROUND
If you're driving from Center City, follow I–76 west (the Schuylkill Expressway) to the Belmont Avenue exit. Turn right across the bridge and right again onto Main Street and park. On weekends you can be strolling with hundreds of visitors—and fighting with them for parking spaces. The town has been working to remedy that; there are parking lots off Main Street toward the river. Participating stores offer validation stickers for reduced rates. From 6 PM on, valet parking is available for diners and shoppers for $10. You can also take the SEPTA R6 (Norristown) train from Market East, Suburban Station, or 30th Street Station to the Manayunk Station (on Cresson Street) and walk downhill to Main Street.

ESSENTIALS
Bike Rentals **Bike Line** (*1028 Arch St.* ☎ *215/923–1310* ⊕ *bikeline.com*). **Human Zoom Bikes & Boards** (*4159 Main St.* ☎ *215/487–7433* ⊕ *www.human-zoom.com*).

Visitor Information **Manayunk Development Corporation** (☎ *215/482–9565* ⊕ *www.manayunk.com*).

WHERE TO EAT

$$ ✕**Chabaa.** This Thai bistro is a nice, calming escape from the noisy
THAI restaurant scene of Main Street. Enjoy authentic Thai flavors in your
lime-infused Thai sausage, Po Tek (a spicy seafood hotpot with basil
and lemongrass), or the various face-flushing curries. They have quite
good Pad Thai, including one with crispy duck. It's BYOB, but there is
a small corkage fee ($3 for one bottle, $5 for two 'til infinity). ⊠ *4371
Main St.* ☎ *215/483–1979* ⊕ *www.chabaathai.com* ⊟ *AE, D, DC, MC,
V* ⌷ *BYOB* ☉ *No lunch Mon. or Fri.*

$–$$ ✕**Le Bus.** It's loud, it's crowded, but something about Le Bus has always
AMERICAN kept it upbeat. The longtime Philly bakery and restaurant got its start
★ many years ago selling out of a van at the University of Pennsylvania,
and the quality has always remained high. It's mostly comfort food,
but with a variety of influences, such as the asparagus and wild mushroom risotto or the cilantro roasted chicken American. Le Bus is a good
choice for a Manayunk lunch, as the menu is reasonably priced, and
their Cuban and turkey Reuben sandwiches go well with midafternoon
beers. ⊠ *4266 Main St.* ☎ *215/487–2663* ⊕ *www.lebusmanayunk.com*
⊟ *AE, D, DC, MC, V.*

$$$–$$$$ ✕**Jake's.** The restaurant that started Main Street's transformation into
AMERICAN a place to go follows a pretty simple approach of making good food
★ that won't leave you hungry. From the cheesy potato puree that com-
pliments the braised short ribs to the apple-cider barbecued chicken,
chef Bruce Cooper (his wife is Jake) does not shy away from bold, rich
flavors. The crab cakes are outstanding, and the signature cookie taco
makes a great ending. The dining room is a little noisy, but it's done up
nicely. Next door they've opened the lower-priced, open-to-the-street
Cooper's Brick Oven Wine Bar, serving brick oven pizza (try the ham
and egg or the pear with Roquefort) in a more casual atmosphere, as
well as some tasty small plates like the andouille-stuffed sea scallops;
you can also order from Jake's menu and vice versa. ⊠ *4365 Main St.*
☎ *215/483–0444* ⊟ *AE, DC, MC, V.*

NIGHTLIFE

Manayunk Brewery & Restaurant. It's a large establishment with plenty of
TVs, but the home-brew beers are good, the food decent, and there's an
outdoor patio that's along the canal. ⊠ *4120 Main St.* ☎ *215/482–8220*
⊕ *www.manayunkbrewery.com.*

Thomas' Restaurant & Bar. This may be the only real neighborhood bar
on Main Street. There's a friendly, easygoing vibe here that's lacking
in some of the other drinking establishments nearby. ⊠ *4201 Main St.*
☎ *215/483–9075.*

SHOPPING

Manayunk's Main Street is a mix of national chains (Nicole Miller, Pot-
tery Barn, Restoration Hardware), clothing boutiques, gift shops, and
furniture stores. Many stores stay open until 9 on Friday and Saturday

nights. On the last weekend in June the Manayunk Arts Festival lines Main Street with the region's largest outdoor arts and crafts show.

Antiques Provençcal. The beautiful French countryside furniture from the 18th–19th centuries found here is worth looking at even if you can't afford the price tag. ⊠ *4303 Main St.* ☎ *215/483–1269* ⊕ *www. antiquesprovencal.com* ⊗ *Closed Sun.–Mon.*

Dwelling. Modern, exciting furniture that will make you want to redecorate your pad into the coolest, most comfortable apartment in town. A must, even if you're not planning to buy. *4050 Main St.* ☎ *215/487-7400* ⊕ *www.dwellinghome.com.*

Goldmine Unlimited. A retro hipster den with all sorts of fun, mainly '60s and '70s items that have become artful junk. Occasionally, it's also a tea lounge. ⊠ *4223 Main St., Manayunk* ☎ *917/945–9466* ⊕ *www. goldmine-unlimited.com.*

Octavio Miles. A Bichon Frise stands guard at this purveyor of colorful ladies handbags, hats, and accessories. There are a few men's items for sale as well, like novelty cufflinks. ⊠ *4251 Main St., Manayunk* ☎ *215/482–0678* ⊕ *www.octaviomiles.com* ⊗ *Closed Mon.*

Propper Brothers. A half-block away from Main Street, this store has two floors filled with chairs, sofas, and tables, and everything in between. The style is classic, and the pieces are all chosen with great taste. ⊠ *115 Levering St.* ☎ *215/483-0544* ⊕ *www.propperbrothers.com.*

Shades of Africa. Part gallery, part fabric store, part safari travel agency, this store sells some great African sculptures, fabrics, and jewelry, including large wooden hippos. ⊠ *4345 Main St., Manayunk* ☎ *215/487–0675.*

Showing with Style. Formerly "From Belly to Baby" this is a maternity store for mothers-to-be who don't want to lose their style. ⊠ *4321 Main St., Manayunk* ☎ *267/297–7035* ⊕ *www.maternityonmain.com.*

GERMANTOWN

In its transformation from Indian trail to toll road to main street, Germantown Avenue has woven a path through history. Germantown, about 6 mi northwest of Center City, has been an integrated, progressive community since 13 German Quaker and Mennonite families moved here in 1683. They soon welcomed English, French, and other European settlers seeking religious freedom. The area has a tradition of free thinking—the first written protest against slavery in America came from its residents. Today it houses a wealth of exceptionally well-preserved architectural masterpieces.

The Germantown area is rich in history. It was the site of Philadelphia's first gristmill (1683) and America's first paper mill (1690). The American colonies' first English-language Bible was printed here (1743). In 1777 Colonial troops under George Washington attacked British forces here and fought the Battle of Germantown, the first time Washington led the rebel troops in an attack. After the Revolutionary War, Germantown became a rural retreat for wealthy city residents who could afford a "vacation home." For information on Germantown's historic attractions, visit ⊕ *www.freedomsbackyard.com.*

GETTING HERE AND AROUND

The best way to tour the area is by car. From Center City follow Kelly Drive to Midvale Avenue and turn right. Follow Midvale up the hill and all the way to Germantown Avenue. To get to Mount Airy and Chestnut Hill from Germantown, follow Germantown Avenue north. SEPTA's Regional Rail trains R8 Chestnut Hill West and R7 Chestnut Hill East are easy options to get to Germantown. The 23 Bus runs along Germantown Avenue—use this bus only between Germantown and Chestnut Hill; it is a very long ride if you pick it up downtown.

EXPLORING GERMANTOWN'S HISTORIC HOMES

Nearly every historic house has its own administration, so there has traditionally been little coordination between them. This is starting to improve, particularly with the "Passport," which allows year-long access to 14 historical sites. The Passport is $15 for individuals and $25 for families. You can purchase the Passport at The Germantown Historical Society, any of the historic homes, and at Independence Visitor Center (downtown at 6th and Market streets). It's best to do two houses in one day; three is probably the maximum. Cliveden is close to Wyck and the Johnson House, the Germantown White House (formerly the Deshler-Morris house) is across the street from the Germantown Historical Society, and a block away is Grumblethrope.

Visiting these homes is nearly always about the stories you are told, and the sense that you're standing upon history more than any wow-factor of the artifacts or houses themselves (though Cliveden is an impressive estate). The gardens of many of these houses are also impressive, especially as they are often completely hidden from the street. This is not an accident: the homes were originally taxed for their frontage, and so would be as narrow as possible up front, and then expand at an angle in the back. In winter, all of Germantown's historic houses, except the Johnson House, are closed. Always call ahead to ensure a tour—even if you're just around the corner.

If you are visiting the Germantown homes, you will likely want to visit Chestnut Hill to unwind. The business section of Germantown is still struggling to get its legs, and some areas are not safe at night.

Germantown Historical Society. The headquarters of the society has a historical and genealogical library and a museum showcasing noteworthy furniture, textile, and costume collections, from Colonial highboys and Peale paintings to Quaker samplers and mourning clothes. It's also an orientation point for anyone visiting the Germantown houses. The society doesn't function as well as it should as a gateway to the various sights, but you can collect most of the information that you'll need here. ⊠ *5501 Germantown Ave.* ☎ *215/844–1683* ⊕ *www.freedomsbackyard.com* ▧ *Museum $5, museum and library $7.50* ☉ *Tues. 9–1, Thurs. 1–5, Sun. 1–5; closed 2nd Sun. of each month.*

TOP ATTRACTIONS

Cliveden. The grounds take up an entire block, and its unique history, impressive architecture, and the guides who spin a good yarn combine to make Cliveden perhaps the best of the historic Germantown homes. The elaborate country house was built in 1763 by Benjamin Chew (1722–1810), a Quaker and Chief Justice of the Colonies, and something of a fence-straddler during the Revolution. Cliveden was at the center of the Battle of Germantown, occupied by British troops, and the walls still bear the marks of American cannon fire. Except for a brief period of time in the late 1700s when it was owned by a privateer (legalized pirating), the house remained in the Chew family until 1972, when it was donated to the National Trust for Historic Preservation. The original house has been completely opened to the public. A shining example of Georgian style, it has Palladian windows and an elegant entrance hall. The family-owned furniture includes a mahogany sofa by Thomas Affleck and looking glasses by James Reynolds. Special events, such as a beer festival, jazz festival, and an elaborate reenactment of the Battle of Germantown (in October) are held here. The house, on 6 acres, can be seen on a 45-minute guided tour. ⊠ *6401 Germantown Ave.* ☎ *215/848–1777* ⊕ *www.cliveden.org* ⊠ *$8* ☉ *Apr.–Dec., Thurs.– Sun. noon–4.*

Germantown White House. Formerly called the Deshler-Morris House, the Germantown home was where President Washington lived and held Cabinet meetings during the yellow fever epidemic of 1793–94, making it the seat of government of the new republic for a short time, and also the oldest "official" residence of an American president. A major renovation completed in 2009 has put new life into the house. Interpretive exhibits are displayed in the house next door, and the house itself has been restored to the time Washington was there. The emphasis has also shifted to telling the stories of the entire household, from the slaves who worked there to the President and his wife. In October 1777, during the Battle of Germantown, the house was the headquarters for British general Sir William Howe. As one of the many Germantown houses built flush with the road, it has enchanting side and back gardens. The house, which has moved beyond its "Washington slept here" renown into something much more interesting, is part of the Independence National Historical Park. ⊠ *5442 Germantown Ave.* ☎ *215/596–1748* ⊕ *www.nps.gov/demo/index.htm* ⊠ *Free* ☉ *Apr.–mid-Dec., Wed.–Sun. 1–4; other times by appointment.*

Grumblethorpe. The blood of General James Agnew, who died after being struck by musket balls during the Battle of Germantown, stains the floor in the parlor of this Georgian house. Built by Philadelphia merchant and wine importer John Wister in 1744, Grumblethorpe is one of Germantown's leading examples of early-18th-century Pennsylvania-German architecture. The Wister family lived here for 160 years, and during the Revolution a teenage Sally Wister kept a diary that has become an important historical source for what that time was like. On display are period furnishings and family mementos, but probably the best part of the house is the large garden. Wisteria, the flowering vine, is named after Charles Wister (John's grandson), who was an avid botanist and amateur scientist, and there is plenty of it in the garden. There are also an enormous hundred-year-old rose bush, a peony alley, a two-story arbor with climbing clematis and a grape vine working its way across its base, and a number of tulips. ✉ *5267 Germantown Ave.* ☎ *215/843–4820* ⊕ *www.philalandmarks.org* ✑ *$5, $12 per family* ☉ *Apr.–Dec., call ahead for appointment.*

WORTH NOTING

Ebenezer Maxwell Mansion. Philadelphia's only mid-19th-century house-museum is a Victorian Gothic extravaganza of elongated windows and arches. This gorgeous 1859 suburban villa is used to illustrate the way Victorian social mores were reflected through its decoration. The downstairs highlights the Rococo Revival (circa 1860), the upstairs is fashioned after the Renaissance Revival (1880s), and the difference is striking, especially the Art Deco–like wall details you may not associate with the time. Also striking is the chamber pot in the dining room that the men used after the ladies retired to the parlor. What makes this house particularly interesting is that it was home to middle-upper class residents, and so much of the decoration represents the norm of what. people in that class strove to be. Tours on how the Industrial Revolution affected the household and on Victorian women's lives are in development. Numerous Victorian-themed events, such as picnics and faux furnishing workshops, are held here. The house is two blocks from the Tulpehocken stop on the R8 Chestnut Hill West. ✉ *200 W. Tulpehocken St.* ☎ *215/438–1861* ⊕ *www.ebenezermaxwellmansion.org* ✑ *$10* ☉ *Apr.–Dec., Thurs.–Sat. noon–4.*

Johnson House. After bringing visitors through the hidden back entrance of this 1768 home, guides retrace the experience of slaves who found a haven here when the Johnson House was a key station on the Underground Railroad. They weave the story of the Johnson family, Quakers who worked to abolish slavery, with that of Harriet Tubman, who was sheltered here with runaway slaves and later guided them to freedom. Visitors see hiding places, including the third-floor attic hatch that runaways would use to hide on the roof when the sheriff came by, learn Underground Railroad code words, and view slavery artifacts, such as ankle shackles and collars. The home has contained the gamut of American history; in 1777 the house was in the line of fire during the Battle of Germantown; the shutters still show the impact of the musket rounds. In the early 1900s it was saved from demolition when it became a women's club. The house itself does not amaze, but hearing the stories of the home when you are standing within it is interesting. It's best to call ahead for tours. ✉ *6306 Germantown Ave.* ☎ *215/438–1768* ⊕ *www.johnsonhouse.org* ✑ *$8* ☉ *Thurs. and Fri. 10–4, Sat. 1–4.*

Stenton. James Logan may not be a household name, but he was a seminal figure in pre-Revolutionary America. He was secretary to William Penn and managed the daily affairs of the colony. Logan, who went on to hold almost every important public office in the colonies, designed the 1730 Georgian manor himself and named it for his father's birthplace in Scotland. He used it to entertain local luminaries and Native American tribal delegates. It was also where he kept one of the area's first libraries, at a time when books were looked upon with suspicion.

George Washington was a guest of James's grandson on his way to the Battle of Brandywine, and British General Howe claimed it for his headquarters during the Battle of Germantown. The Stenton mansion is filled with family and period pieces; the site also includes a kitchen wing, barn, and Colonial-style garden. The guided 45-minute tour interprets the life of three generations of the Logan family and the life of the region from the 1720s through the American Revolution. This house has one of the best interiors of any of the Germantown homes. It's best to call ahead for a tour. ✉ *4601 18th St.* ☎ *215/329–7312* ⊕ *www.stenton.org* ✉ *$5* ⏲ *Apr.–Dec., Tues.–Sat. 1–4.*

3

Wyck. Between the 1690s and 1973, Wyck sheltered nine generations of the Wistar-Haines family. Their accumulated furnishings are on display, along with ceramics, children's needlework, dolls, and artifacts generally contemporary with the mid-1800s. On one side is a garden of old roses, dating to the 1820s, which bloom in late May, as well as a magnolia tree from that time. Out back are a large lawn, where you can picnic, and a vegetable garden—the land has been continuously farmed since 1690. Known as the oldest house in Germantown, Wyck was used as a British field hospital after the Battle of Germantown. The home's current form dates to 1824, when William Strickland made alterations. The grounds are open for wandering, but it's best to call ahead for a house tour. ✉ *6026 Germantown Ave.* ☎ *215/848–1690* ⊕ *www.wyck. org* ✉ *$5* ⏲ *Apr.–mid-Dec., Tues. and Thurs.–Sat. 1–4.*

CHESTNUT HILL AND MOUNT AIRY

Northwest of Germantown are Mount Airy and then Chestnut Hill. Although it's part of the city, Chestnut Hill is a leafy neighborhood that seems much like its own village. Beyond cobblestoned Germantown Avenue, lined with restaurants, galleries, and boutiques, you can find lovely examples of Colonial Revival and Queen Anne houses. Wissahickon Park runs adjacent to Chestnut Hill and Mount Airy.

GETTING HERE AND AROUND

To get to Mount Airy or Chestnut Hill by car, follow Kelly Drive to Lincoln Drive and take that road to its end, making a right on Allen's Lane and then a left on Germantown Avenue. SEPTA's Regional Rail trains R8 Chestnut Hill West and R7 Chestnut Hill East are good options as well.

ESSENTIALS

Visitor Information Chestnut Hill Business Association (✉ *8426 Germantown Ave., Chestnut Hill* ☎ *215/247–6696* ⊕ *www.chestnuthillpa.com* ⏲ *Weekdays 8:30–5, Sat. 10–4, Sun. noon–4*).

EXPLORING

★ **Morris Arboretum.** This is one of the best arboretums in the country, and ⏲ makes for a great stroll. Begun in 1887 and bequeathed to the University of Pennsylvania in 1932, this 166-acre arboretum was based on Victorian-era garden and landscape design, with its romantic winding paths, hidden grotto, a fernery, a koi pond, and natural woodland. The highlights are the spectacular rose garden and the swans. Large modern sculptures, some of which are spectacular, are sprinkled throughout the property. The arboretum has 3,500 trees and shrubs from around the world, including one of the finest collections of Asian plants outside Asia. An elaborate model

WORD OF MOUTH

"Chestnut Hill/Wissahickon has some great hiking/picnic areas if they want a nature day, and there's also the Schuylkill Center and the Tinicum Wildlife Center for more involved eco-days."

—Amy

railroad with dozens of miniature buildings attracts many children. You may want to drive, as it's a good hike from the top of Chestnut Hill and a very hilly, but short bike ride. ⊠ *100 E. Northwestern Ave., Chestnut Hill* ☏ *215/247-5777* ⊕ *www.upenn.edu/arboretum* ☑ *$14, $7 for bicyclists* ☉ *Apr.–Oct., weekdays 10–4, weekends 10–5, open until 8 on Thurs. in summer; Nov.–Mar., daily 10–4; guided tours weekends at 2.*

Fodor'sChoice **Valley Green (Wissahickon Park).** There are many great sections of Fair-
★ mount Park, but the 1,800 acres around Valley Green known as Wisssahickon Park may be the most stunning. Miles and miles of trails running along and above the river lead to covered bridges, a statue of an Indian chief, 17th century caves of a free-love cult, large boulders that drip water, and ducks. Forbidden Drive, on which cars are forbidden, runs from Northwestern Avenue (the westernmost part of Chestnut Hill) all the way to Lincoln Drive, where it connects to a bike and walking path. This leads eventually to Manayunk and Kelly Drive, where there are additional bike paths that can take you to the city or out along the Schuylkill. At the very end of Forbidden Drive, if you make a left, you will find **Historic Rittenhouse Town** (⊠ *206 Lincoln Dr., Philadelphia* ☏ *215/438–5711* ⊕ *www.rittenhousetown.org* ☑ *$5* ☉ *Tours: June–Sept., weekends noon–4, last tour at 3; Oct.–May, by appointment only)* , which is where the first printing press in colonial North America was built in 1690. Only six buildings remain of the original 40. A couple of stables adjoin the park at different entrances: in Mount Airy are **Montesary Stables** (☏ *215/848–4088* ⊕ *www.monasterystables.org*), off Kitchen's Lane (turn downhill from Wissahickon Drive), and **Northwestern Stables** (☏ *215/685–9286* ⊕ *www.northwesternstables.com*) at Northwestern and Germantown avenues. There are also many miles of surprisingly difficult mountain-bike trails. The Valley Green Inn is a decent restaurant located on Forbidden Drive and Valley Green Road, and there is a refreshment stand there as well. ⊠ *Valley Green Rd., Chestnut Hill* ⊕ ☑ *Free* ☉ *Daily dawn–dusk.*

NEED A BREAK?   **Cake** (⊠ *8501 Germantown Ave., entrance on Evergreen Ave., Chestnut Hill* ☏ *215/247–6887*) is a café specializing in made-from-scratch baked goods. Since it's moved into Robertson's Flowers old greenhouse, they've become more of a restaurant, but you can still enjoy your coffee and scones while reading the paper.

Woodmere Art Museum. This modest-sized museum has trouble draw-ing a crowd due to its location halfway down the other side of the hill from Chestnut Hill's shops and restaurants. You can spend a pleasant half-hour here, however, taking in the varied modern, 20th-century, and 19th-century art from artists mostly based in the region. Perhaps the best collection is of mid-1900s woodcut and other prints, and the museum has been doing a good job of rotating exhibits and bringing in special exhibitions. There are also some interesting 19th-century Pennsylvania landscapes, and the rooms dedicated to the founder of the museum have spectacularly gaudy vases and furniture from 19th-century Europe. The grounds have varied modern outdoor sculpture. After nearly 10 years of neighborhood battles, Woodmere looks like it will finally be able to break ground on an expansion that will double its size, which it plans to open in 2012. ⊠ *9201 Germantown Ave., Chestnut Hill* ☎ *215/247–0476* ⊕ *www.woodmereartmuseum.org* ✉ *Free* ⊙ *Tues.–Sat. 10–5, Sun. 1–5.*

WHERE TO EAT

Chestnut Hill has the largest selection of restaurants, with Mount Airy not far behind, though Mount Airy is more spread out. You may have to wait at times, but rarely do you need reservations.

$$
AMERICAN
✕ **Caffette.** Inside this funky little bungalow are an open kitchen, tables crammed together, and old Parisian posters lining the walls. Outside, the garden and outdoor seating area provide an extremely pleasant spot in good weather. Try the Philadelphia style crabcake, which mixes in cream cheese and a soft-pretzel crusting, or the roasted chicken with apple-cider gravy. For an imaginative vegetarian choice, try the spicy battered tofu over a roasted portabella mushroom and greens. Lunch consists of salad and sandwiches geared toward working folks, with a few interesting exceptions like the egg-salad sandwich with thick bacon and curried chickpea cakes. They also have a good brunch. ⊠ *8134 Ardleigh, Chestnut Hill* ☎ *215/242–4220* ⊕ *www.cafette.com* ▭ *No credit card* ⊙ *Closed Mon.*

$–$$
AMERICAN
✕ **Campbell's Place.** A longtime cozy local tavern, Campbell's now has a legitimate gastro-pub kitchen to go with the downstairs bar's charm. The difference is in the details—from the purple potatoes next to the rosemary pork chop to the Hoegaarten broth for the mussels. There is hefty fare like the large Black Angus burger and meatloaf, but it's nice to dine tapas style on appetiziers like the excellent Asian wings, beet and goat cheese salad, and calamari. The specials tend to be more adventurous and quite good. Upstairs is almost shockingly character-less, with beige wall-to-wall carpeting. They also have a Sunday brunch. ⊠ *8337 Germantown Ave., Chestnut Hill* ☎ *215/242–1818* ▭ *AE, D, MC, V.*

$–$$
AMERICAN
★
✕ **Earth Bread & Brewery.** Although primarily a restaurant—families are welcome and ever-present—not a bar, this is a beer geek destination. Run by the former owners of Heavyweight Brewery, it always has four specialty brews made on the premise available. The rest of the taps are almost entirely local craft beers (Victory, Stoudts, Sly Fox, etc.). Once a month they dedicate all their taps to one local brewery and pour all

their specialty brews. If you want grub to go with your suds, the flat-bread pizzas are light and crispy with all natural ingredients (there is an earth-friendly emphasis) and topped with unique flavors like pumpkin seeds, black beans, and banana-pepper pesto. Meat lovers need not fear—there's also sausage. The salads are excellent, as are snack plates of olives and cheeses. There's also a good and unusual wine list. ⊠ *7136 Germantown Ave., Mount Airy* ☎ *215/242–6666* ⊕ *www.earthbread-brewery.com* ⊟ *AE, D, MC, V* ⊘ *No lunch except Sat. Closed Mon.*

$$$

JAPANESE

✕ **Hokka Hokka.** This sushi joint has very friendly service and particularly good rolls, including some fun ones like the "Hollywood"—a massive creation with tempura shrimp, avocado, salmon, and eel sauce. Near the bottom of the hill, Hokka Hokka is a nice alternative to the mostly pub-inspired comfort food around this area. ⊠ *7830 Germantown Ave., Chestnut Hill* ☎ *215/242–4489* ⊕ *www.restauranthokka.com* ⊟ *AE, D, MC, V.*

$

AMERICAN

★

✕ **McNally's.** Welcome to the home of the Schmitter. People come to McNally's more for the food than the beer (families are welcome), and generally order one of the six featured sandwiches. The Schmitter, a cheesesteak on a Kaiser roll with fried salami, fried onions, and a special sauce, is insanely delicious. Rivaling the Schmitter is the vegetarian sandwich option, the G.B.S. (George Bernard Shaw), which has mushrooms, peppers, tomato, and lettuce draped in cheese and special sauce. ■TIP→ **For an even more heavenly taste, ask for fried veggies on the G.B.S.** At a close third is the Dickens—hot turkey, stuffing, and cranberry sauce on a Kaiser roll. Soups and turkey chili are also worth trying. Citizens Bank ballpark has a Schmitter booth, but they are a poor substitute for the real thing. ⊠ *8634 Germantown Ave., Chestnut Hill* ☎ *215/247–9736* ⊕ *mcnallystavern.com* ⊟ *AE, D, MC, V* ⊘ *Closes at 8 PM Sunday.*

WHERE TO STAY

$

▥ **Chestnut Hill Hotel.** This is the place to rest if you are looking for a mellow Philadelphia stay, or looking to stay in Northwest Philadelphia. The rooms are quiet, and resemble comfortable guest rooms in your friend's nicely furnished home. There's nothing fancy about the adequately sized rooms, but there's nothing missing either. ■TIP→ **Make sure to call for room rates, as they are often lower than the advertised price.** Chestnut Grille, a decent restaurant with an outdoor seating area, is attached to the hotel, but is not owned by it. **Pros:** low-key; on the avenue with all the shops, bars, and restaurants. **Cons:** not for those who like all-encompassing hotels. ⊠ *8229 Germantown Ave., Chestnut Hill* ☎ *215/242–5905* ⊕ *www.chestnuthillhotel.com* ⇆ *32 rooms, 4 suites* ♤ *In-room: Wi-Fi. In-hotel: laundry service, Wi-Fi, parking (free)* ⊟ *AE, D, DC, MC, V* ❶❂ *CP.*

NIGHTLIFE

Tavern on the Hill. This popular hangout has an excellent kitchen and friendly vibe. ⊠ *8636 Germantown Ave., Chestnut Hill* ☎ *215/247–9948.*

McMenamins. This Mount Airy favorite has a fantastic choice of craft beer on tap, plus good burgers and fish-and-chips. ⊠ *7170 Germantown Ave., Mount Airy* ☎ *215/247–9920.*

Mermaid Inn. Head to the Mermaid, as the locals do, to hear excellent live music (folk, blues, rock, and jazz) and drink from an interesting selection of bottled beers. ⊠ *7673 Germantown Ave., Chestnut Hill* ☎ *215/247–9797* ⊕ *www.themermaidinn.net/home.html* ⊠ *Free–$10.*

WORD OF MOUTH

"Chestnut Hill is just gorgeous. The main drag is cobblestone lined with 200+-year-old buildings that house quaint little shops."
—GoTravel

3

SHOPPING

Bredenbreck's Ice Cream Parlor. The bakery half of the store is nothing to write home about, but on the ice-cream side they scoop Bassetts ice cream. If you've tried Bassetts—there's also a counter in Reading Terminal Market—you'll know why this is important information. ⊠ *8126 Germantown Avenue, Chestnut Hill* ☎ *215/247–7374* ⊕ *www.bredenbecks.com* ☉ *Mon.–Sun. noon–10.*

Caleb Meyer's. You'll find elegant and distinctive jewelry in gold and platinum. They also have a curated collection of crafts in wood, glass, pottery, and silver. ⊠ *8250 Germantown Ave., Chestnut Hill* ☎ *215/248–9250* ⊕ *www.calebmeyer.com* ☉ *Tues.–Fri. 10–5:30, Sat. 10–5.*

Chestnut Hill Farmer's Market. Even if you can't take advantage of the local butchers, you can still grab fresh take-out from the good Mexican, hoagie (from Ranck's Meats), Indian, and Caribbean stalls. ⊠ *8229 Germantown Ave., Chestnut Hill* ☎ *215/242–5905* ☉ *Thurs.–Fri. 9–6, Sat. 8–5.*

Eye Candy. Kids candy for grown-ups—there are jellies, gummies, and hard candy as well as nostalgic goodies like Necco candy dots. ⊠ *8127 Germantown Ave., Chestnut Hill* ☎ *215/247–8787* ☉ *Closed Sun.–Mon.*

Metropolitan Bakery. Stop by for a bit of goodness, from the fresh breads and breakfast sweets to the great cheeses. ⊠ *8607 Germantown Ave., Chestnut Hill* ☎ *215/753–9001* ⊕ *www.metropolitanbakery.com* ☉ *Mon.–Fri. 7:30–7, Sat. 8–6, Sun. 8–5.*

Side Trip Along the Main Line

In March 1823 the Pennsylvania legislature passed a charter for the construction of the Pennsylvania Railroad, the state's first railroad, linking Philadelphia to Columbia via Lancaster. After the Civil War, genteel suburbs sprang up around the stations. The gracious estates with endless lawns, debutante balls, and cricket clubs, were the province of wealthy families.

The 1939 film *Philadelphia Story*, a depiction of Main Line society life, starred Katharine Hepburn, a graduate of **Bryn Mawr College** (✉ *101 N. Merion Ave., Bryn Mawr* ☎ *610/526–5000* ⊕ *www.brynmawr.edu*), the first college for women that offered B.A. degrees. Founded in 1885 and modeled after Cambridge and Oxford colleges, Bryn Mawr introduced the "collegiate Gothic" style of architecture to the United States.

However, the main attraction of the Main Line is the Barnes Foundation.

 Barnes Foundation. The Barnes will soon be moving to its new home near the Philadelphia Museum of Art, but it will still be in Merion at least through 2010. Do not miss this museum while it still exists, but plan ahead, because tickets are limited. Although they promise to expand their hours in 2010, every lover of impressionism will want to visit before this unique experience disappears. Renoirs (181), Cézannes (69, including his *Card Players*), Matisses (59), and masterpieces by Van Gogh, Degas, Seurat, Picasso, Gauguin, Tintoretto, Modiglianni, Soutine, and others are wallpapered floor-to-ceiling alongside household tools, Amish chests, and New Mexican folk icons. That was the way Albert C. Barnes wanted it: all the

artwork is set up to be viewed in relation to each other. The son of a Philadelphia butcher made millions by inventing Argyrol (a completely ineffective but popular medicine used to treat eye inflammations) and selling his pharmaceutical company right before the stock market crash of 1929, leaving him with a lot of cash with which to buy art on the cheap during the Great Depression. His tastes, particularly for impressionists, were frowned upon by the establishment at the Philadelphia Museum of Art at the time, but of course now it is the envy of the art world. Reservations are required, and should be made at least two months in advance. If you don't arrive in time to join the limited first-come, first-served docent tours, at 10, 1, and 2, opt for the $7 audio tour. Aside from driving (parking at the Barnes is expensive—up to $15), you can take SEPTA's R5 Paoli train from 30th Street Station to the Merion Station stop, turn right on Merion Road and left on Latch's Lane, and walk ½ mi to the museum. ✉ *300 Latches La., Merion* ☎ *610/667–0290 (for reservations press 5)* ⊕ *www. barnesfoundation.org* 🎟 *$15* ☉ *Sept.–June, Fri.–Sun. 9:30–5; July and Aug., Wed.–Fri. 9:30–5.*

Chanticleer. At this 35-acre pleasure garden circling a country estate even the old tennis court has been transformed into a garden. If you enjoy flowers and paths, this is a great stop. It's lavish, but its over-the-top opulence is part of what makes it so enjoyable. ✉ *786 Church Rd., Wayne* ☎ *610/687–4163* ⊕ *www.chanticleer-garden.org* 🎟 *$5* ☉ *Apr.–Oct., Wed.–Sun. 10–5; May–Aug., Wed.–Thurs. and weekends 10–5, Fri. 10–8.*

Where to Eat

By Caroline
Tiger

We could begin by talking about how Philadelphia was once a gourmet backwater, about how, culinarily speaking, visitors to this city were once limited to cheesesteaks, scrapple, and pepper pot. But by now that's such old news that it doesn't even seem worth mentioning. Over the last decade or so, Philadelphia has evolved into a bona fide dining destination, one that boasts every type of culinary experience, from authentic ethnic cuisine to chef-owned storefront bistros to high-profile four-star dining rooms. And there's no indication the surge is slowing.

You can trace the current explosion back to the 1970s and '80s, when the openings of Le Bec-Fin, Friday Saturday Sunday, and the White Dog Café snuffed out the dark ages and heralded the beginning of a protracted dining renaissance. Soon, neighborhood by neighborhood, lights turned on and kitchens fired up. The march of the restaurants followed the march of development.

Exhibit A is mega-restaurateur Stephen Starr, who has opened more than a dozen of Philadelphia's most buzzed-about restaurants. He triggered the boom in Old City when he opened the Continental Martini Bar and Lounge in 1995. Since that year, more than 100 restaurants have opened in a five-block radius. Hipster neighborhood Northern Liberties began to hum with *restaubars* once artists started moving there from Old City. South Philadelphia continues to be a haven for downhome Italian cooking and recently for more complex Italian flavors even as clusters of ethnicities who are newer to the city—Vietnamese, Mexican, Ethiopian—form new dining pockets there.

In fact, the formation of dining pockets is the newest chapter in the Philadelphia dining story. Some of the culinary landmarks on Walnut Street's Restaurant Row—Susanno Foo, Striped Bass, Brasserie Perrier—have closed, but tens of restaurants opened during the same period. Some, such as Eric Ripert's 10 Arts and Stephen Starr's Barclay Prime, fill the fine-dining void left by the departing marquee restaurants, but most are more casual, ambitious spots grouped in less centrally located neighborhoods. East Passyunk Avenue in South Philadelphia is one example—what was formerly the place to go to find spaghetti with gravy is now home to Paradiso, a sleek sophisticated place where chef and owner Lynne Marie Rinaldi cooks rabbit cacciatore and offers a wine list to rival any in the city. In Northern Liberties, Peter McAndrews' Modo Mio has become a destination unto itself. Thirteenth Street bustles with energetic, eclectic eateries like El Vez and Lolita; and the 700 block of Chestnut has a new restaurant row since Chifa and Union Trust joined stalwart Morimoto.

Philadelphia has also emerged as a national leader in restaurant design. At Chifa, Distrito, and Amada, New York designer Jun Aizaki has created wholly distinct environments based on the research trips he's taken to Spain, Mexico, and Peru with restaurateur Jose Garces during each project's conception phase. The New Yorker also manages to match the tone of each joint to its distinct neighborhood—Amada in Old City exudes a grown-up kind of cool while Distrito is trendy, playful, and over-the-top like its young clientele in University City. At XIX (Nineteen) at the top of the Park Hyatt at the Bellevue, local design doyenne Meg Rodgers updated the former Founders Room to create something iconic and modern. And it's not surprising to discover that the owner of Bar Ferdinand, Owen Kamihira, has a splashy design pedigree—he put the Buddha in Buddakan and the pop-art olives in the Continental.

Two free weekly local papers, the *City Paper* and *Philadelphia Weekly,* have restaurant reviews and numerous listings. These "freebies" are available in metal sidewalk dispensers on nearly every Center City street corner. There are also plenty of local foodie blogs, the best and most informative of which are *Foobooz* (⊕ *www.foobooz.com*) and Messy and Picky (⊕ *www.messyandpicky.com*). And the most feared food critic (by restaurants) in town is the *Philadelphia Inquirer's* Craig LaBan, whose reviews appear in that paper every Friday.

MEALTIMES

Unless otherwise noted, the restaurants listed in this guide are open daily for lunch and dinner. Philadelphia's starting to keep later hours: restaurants used to close by 10 PM on weekdays and stay open an hour or two later on weekends; you can find a few late-night eats as well. As in many other cities, brunch is a weekend ritual and is generally served from 11:30 to 2:30, with Sunday being the big day.

RESERVATIONS AND DRESS

Reservations are noted when they're essential or not accepted. (Le Bec-Fin and Buddakan are generally booked a month ahead for Saturday night. Vetri is almost always booked two months ahead.)

Most of Philadelphia's restaurants can be classified as business casual, with the exception of inexpensive spots or the University City area where jeans and sneakers are de rigueur. Dress is mentioned in reviews only when men are required to wear a jacket or a jacket and tie.

USING THE MAP

Throughout the chapter, you'll see mapping symbols and coordinates (✛ *B4*) at the end of each review. The property's coordinate will point you to where the property is located on the map grid.

WINE, BEER, AND SPIRITS

The most popular local brew is, of course, Yuengling, one of the oldest breweries in the country. Other area breweries include Victory, Flying Fish, and Yard's.

One happy development to come from Pennsylvania's somewhat arcane alcohol laws is the proliferation of BYOB restaurants—where you can bring your own bottle(s) of wine, beer, or liquor and enjoy them with your meal free of corkage fees. Many different cuisines are available, including Italian, Mexican, Thai, French, and Mediterranean. They are found throughout the city but are perhaps most highly concentrated in the Bella Vista and Queen Village neighborhoods in South Philly. Look out for the 🍷 *BYOB* symbol at the end of our restaurant reviews so you know when to bring a bottle along.

State-run liquor stores, called state stores, sell wine and other spirits. Beer is sold on a take-out basis by some bars and restaurants, but is otherwise available only by the case from certain distribution centers.

PRICES

		WHAT IT COSTS			
	¢	$	$$	$$$	$$$$
Restaurant	under $10	$10–$14	$15–$19	$20–$24	over $24

Price per person for a median main course or equivalent combination of smaller dishes.

RESTAURANT REVIEWS

Listed alphabetically within neighborhoods. Use the coordinate ⊕ G4 at the end of each listing to locate a site on the corresponding map.

HISTORIC AREA AND OLD CITY

The Historic Area around Independence National Historical Park and Old City have a concentration of restaurants, especially around Market and Chestnut streets and along 2nd Street.

$$$
SPANISH
Fodor's Choice
★

✕ **Amada.** Since his debut with Amada in 2005, chef-restaurateur Jose Garces has opened three more restaurants in the city, all of them instant and enduring hits. The young Ecuadorian-American chef has taken Philadelphia by storm, and it was at Amada where he set the stage for his modus operandi of elevating authentic regional cuisine with choice ingredients and a modern touch. On offer are more than 60 tapas, each one worth trying, especially the white-bean stew with escarole and chorizo, and the flatbread topped with fig jam, Spanish blue cheese, and shredded duck. Ingredients—including glorious cheeses—are sourced from northern Spain. The large, festive front room can skew loud; for a quieter meal, ask for a table in the second dining room, beyond the open kitchen. ✉ *217–19 Chestnut St., Old City* ☎ *215/625–2450* ⊕ *www.amadarestaurant.com* ⌖ *Reservations essential* ▭ *AE, D, MC, V* ⊗ *No lunch weekends* ⊕ *G4.*

$$$
ASIAN

✕ **Buddakan.** This post office turned stylish restaurant is presided over by a 10-foot-tall gilded Buddha who seems to approve of the sake cocktails and the fusion food that pairs Asian ingredients with various cooking styles. The edamame

WORD OF MOUTH

"The 'angry lobster' entree at Buddakan is one of the best dishes I've had anywhere, anytime. I'm not sure if it's a special or always on the menu—but if you see it and like lobster, order it." —Gekko

BEST BETS FOR PHILADELPHIA DINING

With hundreds of restaurants to choose from, how will you decide where to eat? Fodor's writers and editors have selected their favorite restaurants by price, cuisine, and experience in the Best Bets lists below. In the first column, Fodor's Choice properties represent the "best of the best" in every price category. You can also search by neighborhood for excellent eats—just peruse our reviews on the following pages.

Fodor'sChoice ★

Amada, p. 110
Ansill, p. 117
Fountain, p. 136
James, p. 121
Le Bec-Fin, p. 129
Marigold Kitchen, p. 135
Morimoto, p. 113
PARC, p. 132
Vetri, p. 124
Zahav, p. 116

By Price

¢

Jim's Steaks, p. 118
La Lupe, p. 121
Reading Terminal Market, p. 124

$

Jamaican Jerk Hut, p. 128
Lee How Fook, p. 125
Sabrina's Café, p. 122

$$

Chifa, p. 112
Continental Restaurant and Martini Bar, p. 112
Dmitri's, p. 119
Monk's, p. 129

$$$

Horizons, p. 118
Osteria, p. 130
Snackbar, p. 133
Tria, p. 133

$$$$

Tangerine, p. 116
Union Trust, p. 116

By Cuisine

AMERICAN

XIX (Nineteen), p. 127
Fork, p. 113

CHINESE

Lee How Fook, p. 125
Sang Kee Peking Duck House, p. 125

FRENCH

Bistrot La Minette, p. 117
PARC, p. 132

ITALIAN

Modo Mio, p. 138
Paradiso, p. 121
Ristorante Panorama, p. 116

MEXICAN

Lolita, p. 123
Xochitl, p. 119

VEGETARIAN

Beau Monde, p. 117
Horizons, p. 118

By Experience

BEST BYOBS

Matyson, p. 129
Mercato, p. 123
Pumpkin, p. 131

BEST CHEESESTEAKS

Geno's Steaks, p. 120
Jim's Steaks, p. 118
Pat's King of Steaks, p. 121
Tony Luke's, p. 122

GOOD FOR GROUPS

Oceanaire, p. 123
Osteria, p. 130
Zahav, p. 116

NEIGHBORHOOD JOINT

London Grill, p. 136
Monk's, p. 129
Pub & Kitchen, p. 130
Standard Tap, p. 138

GREAT VIEW

XIX (Nineteen), p. 127
Water Works, p. 136

MOST ROMANTIC

Lacroix, p. 132
Le Bar Lyonnais (part of Le Bec-Fin), p. 129
Water Works, p. 136

BEST FOR LOCAVORES

Marigold Kitchen, p. 135
Pumpkin, p. 131
White Dog Café, p. 135

PRE-THEATER

Bliss, p. 127
Ernesto's 1521 Café, p. 128

4

ravioli appetizer and chocolate bento-box dessert are tasty, but most of the appeal is in the theatrical decor and people-watching also in evidence at Buddakan's outposts in New York City and Atlantic City. A long "community table" provides an opportunity to dine with anyone else fortunate enough to snag this center-stage space. Be prepared for a loud and lively atmosphere as the evening wears on. ⊠ *325 Chestnut St., Old City* ☎ *215/574-9440* ⊕ *www.buddakan.com* ⚖ *Reservations essential* ☲ *AE, DC, MC, V* ☺ *No lunch weekends* ⊹ *G4.*

$$
PERUVIAN
★

✕ **Chifa.** The newest in wunderkind Jose Garces's stable of small-plate restaurants serves Peruvian-Asian fusion—hard to say out loud but very easy on the eyes, the palate, and the wallet. Since it opened in early 2009, diners have been raving about Chifa's ceviche—the Hiramasa is slices of hamachi accented with ginger and charred pineapple. Most dishes have a spicy zing and embody the surprising synthesis of Peruvian and Asian flavors—the Red Curry del General is a one-bowl meal of jasmine rice with crab, clams, coconut, and red curry, and the Chaufa Rice mixes chorizo with edamame and mango with five-spice. If you prefer an earthy atmosphere, sup in the front dining room's soaring, serene space. To spice up an already spicy experience, choose the second room with its vibrant red and golds. ⊠ *707 Chestnut St., Historic Area* ☎ *215/925-5555* ⊕ *www.chifarestaurant.com* ☲ *AE, MC, V* ☺ *No lunch weekends* ⊹ *G4.*

$$$$
AMERICAN

✕ **City Tavern.** You can time-travel to the 18th century at this authentic re-creation of historic City Tavern, where the atmosphere suggests that Founding Fathers such as John Adams, George Washington, Thomas Jefferson, and the rest of the gang *might* have dined here (they didn't; the restaurant was built under the supervision of the National Park Service in 1994, to the specifications of the original 1773 tavern). The food is heavy and rich—West Indies pepper-pot soup, Martha Washington's turkey potpie, and braised rabbit are prepared from enhanced period recipes and served on handsome Colonial-patterned china or pewter. Happily all is not authentic—the restaurant makes good use of refrigeration and electricity. Reservations are recommended. ⊠ *138 S. 2nd St., Old City* ☎ *215/413-1443* ⊕ *www.citytavern.com* ☲ *AE, D, DC, MC, V* ⊹ *H4.*

$$
ECLECTIC

✕ **Continental Restaurant & Martini Bar.** Light fixtures fashioned like olives pierced with toothpicks are a tip-off to the theme at this cool watering hole. It's installed in a classic diner shell in the center of Old City's action. This is the first of Stephen Starr's trendy restaurants, where he serves lively (but not outré) food in generous portions to people who know how to enjoy it. Don't miss the addictive Szechuan french-fried potatoes with hot-mustard sauce and the crispy calamari salad. ⊠ *138 Market St., Old City* ☎ *215/923-6069* ⊕ *www.continentalmartinibar. com* ☲ *AE, DC, MC, V* ⊹ *H3.*

$$$$
LATIN AMERICAN

✕ **Cuba Libre.** People who have been in Havana swear this place is a dead ringer. In any event, it's lovely, with balconies and fancy streetlights, and even a leaded-glass window—on the interior. An entire menu is devoted to rum from everywhere in the Caribbean and Central and South America, including Cuba Libre's own brand. The appetizers, like lobster empanadas and crab cakes, taste fairly authentic; rice and black beans are served with just about everything, of course, and the mojitos are renowned. It's lively and everyone seems to be having a good time, especially during the salsa-dance shows on Friday and Saturday nights. Reservations are recommended. ✉ *10 S. 2nd St., Old City* ☎ *215/627–0666* ⊕ *www.cubalibrerestaurant.com* ▭ *AE, D, DC, MC, V* ✛ *H3.*

$$$ ✕ **Fork.** Happy sounds have always emanated from diners in this com-
AMERICAN fortable, elegant eatery, but the menu of bistro-style fare went from tasty to transcendental when Terence Feury took over the kitchen in early 2009. The chef is known for his masterfully light touch with seafood—in evidence here with succulent North Carolina bay scallops poached in tarragon butter and flavorful pan-roasted New England cod—but the lamb-belly confit is the menu item not to miss. Sit as far back in the restaurant as possible to watch Feury and his colleagues at work in the open kitchen. Next door, Fork:etc is a great place to grab a quick breakfast or lunch. Reservations are recommended. ✉ *306 Market St., Old City* ☎ *215/625–9425* ⊕ *www.forkrestaurant.com* ▭ *AE, D, DC, MC, V* ⊙ *No lunch Sat.* ✛ *G3.*

$–$$ ✕ **Karma Restaurant and Bar.** Lots of Old City restaurants are all bark
INDIAN and no bite, but Karma's the opposite. The interior is nothing more than a good effort, but the food will stick in your memory long after it's unstuck from your chops. Fresh naan, flavorful tikka masala—the menu is full of Indian standards that are done well. ✉ *114 Chestnut St., Old City* ☎ *215/925–1444* ▭ *AE, DC, MC, V* ✛ *H4.*

$$ ✕ **La Locanda del Ghiottone.** Literally "the place of the gluttons," the
ITALIAN small L-shaped dining room gets loud and crowded as patrons arrive and waiters shout orders from tableside into the open kitchen. It's all part of the charm. The server will forbid you from putting cheese on fish (a house rule), then he'll ask sweetly after your mother. This is homey food, comfort food—tender gnocchi, platters of pasta brimming with fresh seafood, and osso buco, to name a few of the amply proportioned dishes. ✉ *130 N. 3rd St., Old City* ☎ *215/829–1465* ⌂ *Reservations essential* ▭ *No credit cards* ⌦ *BYOB* ⊙ *Closed Mon. No lunch* ✛ *G3.*

$$$$ ✕ **Morimoto.** Stunningly expensive dishes created by celebrity chef Masa-
JAPANESE haru Morimoto (of the Food Network's *Iron Chef*) are served in an
Fodor's Choice elegant, slightly futuristic setting. White plastic tables and benches
★ glow beneath multi-colored lights; the ceiling is undulating bamboo. *Omakase* (tasting menus), $40–$80 at lunch and $80–$120 at dinner, are well worth the expense, as is the sushi, sliced with special knives Morimoto has handcrafted in Japan. Authentic and creative à la carte dishes include *toro* (tuna) with caviar and wasabi and tempura with Gorgonzola sauce. Reservations are recommended. ✉ *723 Chestnut St., Historic Area* ☎ *215/413–9070* ⊕ *www.morimotorestaurant.com* ▭ *AE, D, DC, MC, V* ⊙ *No lunch weekends* ✛ *F4.*

$$ ✕ **Plough and the Stars.** The cheery first floor of a renovated bank feels
IRISH like a genuine Irish pub. A long bar with a dozen spigots is invariably spouting several imported and a few local brews. This is the place to get a Guinness poured the correct way. In winter, patrons crowd around a blazing fireplace on stools set around small tables. It's possible to munch on good Irish smoked salmon on grainy bread while imbibing; you can also head to the upstairs dining room for some respite from the crush

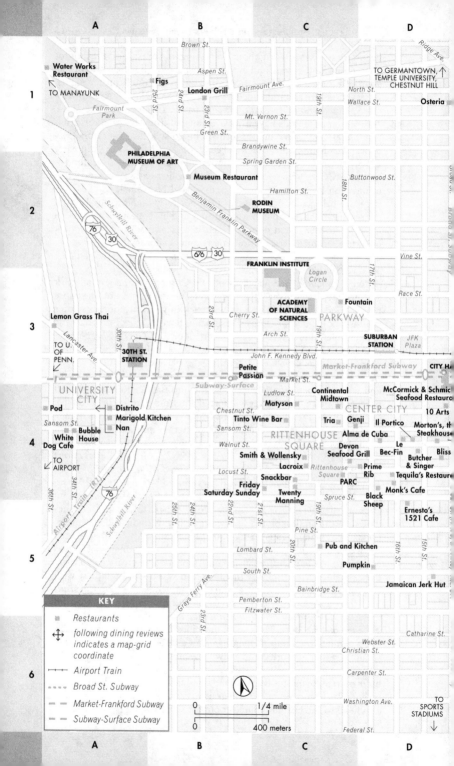

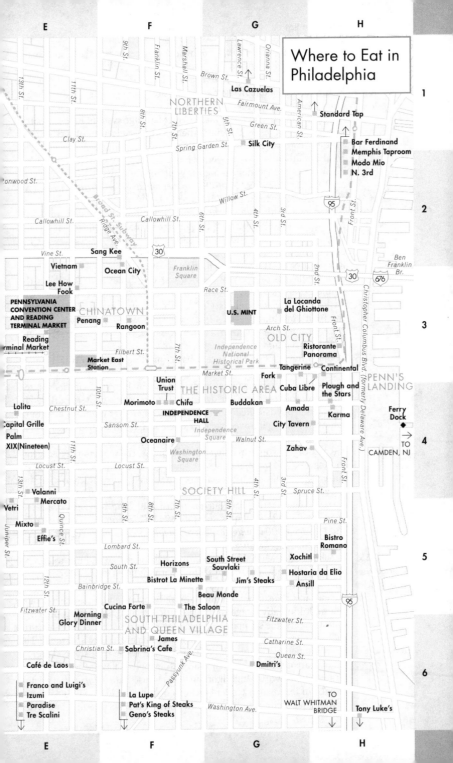

and choose from a panoply of worldly appetizers, salads, and main courses. ⊠ *123 Chestnut St., enter on 2nd St., Old City* ☎ *215/733–0300* ⊕ *www.ploughstars.com* ▭ *AE, DC, MC, V* ✛ *H4.*

$$$$
ITALIAN

✕ **Ristorante Panorama.** The name refers to a lovely mural rather than a window view from this lively spot inside the Penn's View Hotel. The restaurant has the largest wine cruvinet (storage system) in the country. Besides 150 wines by the glass, there's a huge selection of well-chosen bottles. You can sip them in Il Bar or in the main dining room. The food is authentic Italian—simple and hearty. The ambience is either noisy or animated, depending on your tolerance level. ⊠ *14 N. Front St., Old City* ☎ *215/922–7800* ⊕ *www.pennsviewhotel.com* ⌲ *Reservations essential* ▭ *AE, DC, MC, V* ✛ *H3.*

$$$$
MOROCCAN

✕ **Tangerine.** Although neither the interior nor the food is authentic Moroccan, there's enough of the genuine to make people feel as though they're in that beautiful, exotic country. Take the wall of twinkling candle-filled niches and the backlit velvet curtains. Take the *tagines* (cone-topped clay pots) that hold some of the oven-cooked dishes, and take the flavors of many of the richly spiced dishes and, somehow, the whole experience adds up to a trip to North Africa—in spirit, at least. Dishes are served family style. An abbreviated menu is available in the twinkling lounge. ⊠ *232 Market St., Old City* ☎ *215/627–5116* ⊕ *www.tangerinerestaurant.com* ⌲ *Reservations essential* ▭ *AE, DC, MC, V* ⊗ *No lunch* ✛ *G3.*

$$$$
STEAK
★

✕ **Union Trust.** What was once a bank building has been transformed, $12 million later, into a super-swanky steak house. You'll need a minute to take it all in when you enter the soaring main room with its vaulted blue-and-gold ceilings. The details are impressive—waiters outfitted in suits from Boyds (Philadelphia's elite clothier that employs a team of Italian tailors); engraved steak knives; salted caramel truffles served with the check—and so is the service. The upbeat vibe is established by the mix of hip youngsters in expensive jeans, the women they're trying to pick up, and groups in power suits. Prices are high, in the $60-an-entrée range, but the food delivers. The steak, from Chicago's sterling Allen Brothers, is the star, and steak lovers' mouths will water over the vertical steak-tasting for four people of four long bone rib-eyes, dry-aged for 35, 42, 49, and 56 days. ⊠ *717 Chestnut St., Historic Area* ☎ *215/925–6000* ⊕ *www.uniontruststeakhouse.com* ▭ *AE, D, MC, V* ⊗ *No lunch weekends* ✛ *F4.*

$$$
MEDITERRANEAN
Fodor's Choice
★

✕ **Zahav.** Chef Michael Solomonov has brought great buzz to several restaurant locations in Philadelphia. With his latest entry, steeped in the milk and honey and hummus and lamb of his native Israel—as well as the cultures that have left a mark on that Promised Land—he's done it again. Taking advantage of its dramatic perch above one of the city's oldest streets, the stripped-down Zahav relies on architectural features such as picture windows and soaring ceilings to create spectacle. The open kitchen, on view behind leaded glass, is the true stage. There, a small staff mixes and matches a melting pot of flavors for a modern Israeli menu whose highlights include house-baked *laffa* (flatbread), kebabs of impossibly tender chicken cooked over hot coals and served with sumac onions and Israeli couscous, and addictive florets of fried

Best Brunch

Just as Philadelphians are famous for their disputes over who makes the best cheesesteak, the best hoagie roll, the best water ice, and the best cannoli, each neighborhood has its own ongoing debate for "best brunch." Here are some of the contenders:

- Beau Monde, South Street

- LaCroix at the Rittenhouse, Rittenhouse Square

- Mixto, Center City East

- Morning Glory, Center City West

- PARC, Rittenhouse Square

- Sabrina's Café, Center City West

- Valanni, Center City East

4

cauliflower served with a lemon- and dill-spiked *lebneh* (yogurt cheese). Cap off your meal with truly innovative cocktails and desserts like pistachio baklava. ⊠ *237 St. James Place, Old City* ☎ *215/625–8800* ⊕ *www.zahavrestaurant.com* ▤ *AE, D, MC, V* ✛ *H4.*

SOCIETY HILL AND SOUTH STREET

Small clusters of restaurants appear in Society Hill and along South Street.

$$$
ECLECTIC
Fodor's Choice
★
✕ **Ansill.** Foodies clamor for David Ansill's inventive, sophisticated small plates and his much lauded use of such adventurous items as bone marrow, lamb's tongue, and duck eggs. But all of the hullabaloo over scary ingredients subsides once you sample the exquisite bites that arrive one after another from the kitchen—feathery, perfectly shirred eggs; sumptuous pork belly pieces on a bed of spaetzle twists; tender grilled octopus with a tang of sherry vinaigrette. Ansill's wife, Catherine, makes the desserts. Nothing beats her dark-chocolate panino on a buttery brioche served with a mound of mascarpone. ■TIP→ **Bring your own bottle along Tuesday to Friday (no BYOB at the bar).** ⊠ *627 S. 3rd St., South Street* ☎ *215/627–2485* ⊕ *www.ansillfoodandwine.com* ▤ *AE, MC, V* ☖ *BYOB optional* ☾ *No lunch. Closed Mon.* ✛ *G5.*

$$
FRENCH
✕ **Beau Monde.** Imported cast-iron griddles are the secret to this crêperie's paper-thin wrappers. In this city, at least, this is the closest you'll find to the crepes of Brittany, where the owners of this casual bistro traveled to study. The menu is split into savory crepes (made with buckwheat flour) and sweet crepes (made with wheat flour). Some tried-and-true combos are ratatouille, goat cheese, and andouille sausage; and ham and gruyère. The cheese plate is a great value, and there's plenty on the menu for vegetarians. When the weather behaves, alfresco dining is an option. ⊠ *624 S. 6th St., South Street* ☎ *215/592–0656* ⊕ *www.creperie-beaumonde.com* ▤ *AE, D, MC, V* ☾ *Closed Mon.* ✛ *F4.*

$$$
FRENCH
✕ **Bistrot La Minette.** The cheery atmosphere inside the long, narrow bistro and in the outside courtyard illuminated by candles and twinkling

strings of lights exudes warmth and attention to detail, from the flea-market knickknacks picked out by Chef Peter Woolsey and his French wife in Burgundy to the ceramic pitchers of house wine delivered to your table. Woolsey studied at the Cordon Bleu, fell in love with French food, culture, and his wife, a Frenchwoman, and came back to his native Philadelphia to share the bistro experience with his countrymen. The place has quickly become a neighborhood favorite, with regulars swearing by some standouts including the Alsatian-style Flammenkuchen appetizer of caramelized onions, bacon lardoons, and crème fraiche on flatbread; the perfectly simple lemon sole in white-wine butter sauce; and the light and airy beignets that speak to Woolsey's extensive training as a pastry chef. ⊠ *623 S. 6th St., South Street* ☎ *215/925–8000* ⊕ *www.bistrolaminette.com* ⊟ *AE, D, MC, V* ⊘ *Closed Sun. No lunch Mon.* ⊹ *G5.*

$$–$$$ ✕ **Bistro Romano.** Copious portions of regional Italian cuisine are served
ITALIAN   in the brick-walled dining room of this early-18th-century granary. Don't miss the acclaimed Caesar salad prepared tableside by the genial owner, who thoroughly enjoys animated conversations with his guests. Tuesday-night lobster specials make the trip to the Society Hill area more than worthwhile. ⊠ *120 Lombard St., South Street* ☎ *215/925–8880* ⊕ *www.bistroromano.com* ⊟ *AE, D, DC, MC, V* ⊘ *No lunch* ⊹ *H5.*

$$$ ✕ **Horizons.** Vegan food is hardly ever associated with fine dining, but
VEGETARIAN   chef-owner Rich Landau effortlessly pulls off that mix in this bright,
★   airy dining room off bustling South Street. This is vegetarian food that's not afraid to be vegetarian—there's no faux "meat" on the menu. Instead, the chef relies on seasonal ingredients and inventive techniques that infuse tofu and tempeh with complex flavors. Choices change with the seasons, but the artfully plated edamame hummus and spicy gochujang-glazed tofu are available more often than not. The knowledgeable servers will steer even the biggest cheesesteak lovers toward something they'll devour. The wine and beer are vegan, too, as are the desserts, which are surprisingly delectable. ⊠ *611 S. 7th St., South Street* ☎ *215/923–6117* ⊕ *www.horizonsphiladelphia.com* ⋒ *Reservations essential* ⊟ *AE, DC, MC, V* ⊘ *Closed Sun. and Mon. Lunch on Sat. only* ⊹ *F5.*

$$ ✕ **Hostaria da Elio.** The simple surroundings belie the sophistication of
ITALIAN   the chef, who prepares light-as-a-feather pastas with complex sauces. Spinach gnocchi with homemade tomato sauce and gnocchi with Gorgonzola-cheese sauce are both excellent. Go early to avoid the crowds. ⊠ *615 S. 3rd St., South Street* ☎ *215/925–0930* ⊟ *AE, D, DC, MC, V* ⌯ *BYOB* ⊘ *Closed Mon.* ⊹ *G5.*

¢ ✕ **Jim's Steaks.** You'll know you're nearing Jim's when the scent of fry-
AMERICAN   ing onions overwhelms your senses—or when you see people lined up around the corner. Big, juicy, drippy sandwiches of Philly steaks—shaved beef piled high on long crusty rolls—come off the grill with amazing speed when the counter workers hit their stride; but be aware that no matter how hard you beg, they will not toast the rolls. Yell "wit' wiz" (meaning: "with Cheese Whiz, please") for major *cred* and extra authenticity. Jim's is mostly takeout, but there are some tables and

chairs upstairs. ✉ *400 South St., South Street* ☎ *215/928–1911* ⊕ *www. jimssteaks.com* ▭ *No credit cards* ✛ *G5.*

$ ✕ **South Street Souvlaki.** The first thing you'll see is the large rotisserie,
GREEK trumpeting the ubiquitous gyro—tasty slices of meat are stuffed inside a large fresh pita, with tangy yogurt and some exemplary fresh veggies. Other Greek specialties, such as stuffed grape leaves, moussaka, and, of course, souvlaki, round out the menu. No pomp and circumstance here—just casual taverna fare and service that's often indifferent. But they must be doing something right—Souvlaki has been going strong since 1977, definitely a record on this mercurial street. ✉ *509 South St., South Street* ☎ *215/925–3026* ▭ *MC, V* ☉ *Closed Mon.* ✛ *G5.*

$$–$$$ ✕ **Xochitl.** Don't be fooled by the guacamole made tableside—this is
MEXICAN no Tex-Mex joint. Newcomer Dionicio Jimenez is so passionate about
★ his ambitious Neuvo Mexican cooking that he often brings the dishes out from the kitchen himself. There's plenty of glory for his basking. A scallop-watermelon ceviche is refreshing perfection, and the slow-cooked lamb leg marinated in avocado leaves and agave nectar slides off the bone. From happy hour on, the tiny dining room can get a bit noisy, as revelers in the adjacent bar sip Sr. Barrigas (Mexican mojitos) and sample flights of top-shelf tequila served in carved-out cucumber cups. The best advice is to join in on the fun. Reservations are recommended. ✉ *408 S. 2nd St., South Street* ☎ *215/938–7280* ⊕ *www.xochitlphilly. com* ▭ *AE, D, MC, V* ☉ *Closed Mon. No lunch* ✛ *H5.*

SOUTH PHILADELPHIA

In addition to the fabulous Italian Market, South Philadelphia is a great place for cheap, hearty eats.

$ ✕ **Café de Laos.** Wonderfully rendered *kalagas* (beaded and sequined
THAI wall hangings) set the tone at this elegant eatery. The staffers are often bedecked in elegant silk fabrics embroidered with gold thread. When you walk in the door you might think you've arrived in Southeast Asia, a feeling reinforced by tasty, authentic Thai and Laotian food such as fiery green curry and fragrant noodle-based entrées. ✉ *1117 S. 11th St., South Philadelphia* ☎ *215/467–1546* ▭ *MC, V* ⏁ *BYOB* ☉ *Closed Mon.* ✛ *E6.*

$$$ ✕ **Cucina Forte.** Chef Maria Forte turns out plenty of Italian classics,
ITALIAN including heavenly homemade gnocchi plus fanciful dishes such as Maria's Dream Soup (a mix of pork, chicken, and seafood with pasta), a true delight. A cream cake makes a delectable finish. Cucina Forte serves lunch by appointment only. ✉ *768 S. 8th St., South Philadel-phia* ☎ *215/238–0778* ▭ *AE, D, DC, MC, V* ⏁ *BYOB* ☉ *Closed Mon.* ✛ *F5.*

$$ ✕ **Dmitri's.** This no-frills eatery has developed a loyal following thanks
SEAFOOD to its light Mediterranean touch with the freshest of seafood. Locals
★ happily withstand long waits and sitting elbow-to-elbow with their neighbors in order to dip pita wedges into airily whipped hummus and to fork tender chunks of grilled octopus brushed with olive oil and lemon juice. ✉ *795 S. 3rd St., Queen Village* ☎ *215/625–0556* ▭ *No credit cards* ⏁ *BYOB* ✛ *G6.*

CLOSE UP

Philly Cheesesteaks

Philly's best-known culinary creation is simple in theory but complex in the details of its execution. Begin with the basic hoagie roll, which should be slightly crusty with a good amount of chew—Amoroso's is a popular choice. Add to that extremely thin-sliced strips of top round, grilled over a bed of onions until well browned. Then, if you want the full effect, order your sandwich "Whiz wit," meaning with a ladle of Cheez Whiz and friend onions. Other cheeses may also be used, including American and provolone, depending on the cultural etiquette of the particular establishment. As befitting a cultural touchstone, there are many other homages on Philly menus, including chicken cheesesteaks, cheesesteak egg rolls, even vegetarian cheesesteaks. In fact, Philadelphians are so enamored of their signature sandwich that even high-end restaurants pay their respects—including a famous $100 version at Stephen Starr's steak house, Barclay Prime.

$$
ITALIAN
✕ **Franco and Luigi's High Note Cafe.** Arias from classic operas, sung mostly by fresh-faced young singers who are in training or have done professional stints around Philadelphia and other cities, accompany somewhat unusual, but unquestionably Italian, dishes such as veal, shrimp, and scallops sautéed in scampi sauce over a bed of shredded radicchio. Reserve well in advance to ensure seating on weekends. ⊠ *1547 S. 13th St., South Philadelphia* ☎ *215/755–8903* ⊕ *www.francoandluigis. com* ⊟ *AE, DC, MC, V* ⌂ *BYOB* ⊘ *Closed Mon and Tues. No lunch* ✛ *E6.*

¢
AMERICAN
✕ **Geno's Steaks.** Geno's is a regular upstart compared to rival Pat's. The latter's been serving sandwiches since 1930; Geno's opened in 1966. That divide manifests itself visually in the contrast between Pat's understated aesthetic and Geno's over-the-top use of neon. The place is lit up so brightly that astronauts can probably see it from space. The other big difference is that Geno's meat is sliced (not chopped). Some aficionados claim that the two serve wildly dissimilar products; others just don't get it, but it's always fun to taste-test, as the buses full of tourists who frequently make their way down Passyunk to Pat's and Geno's can attest. ⊠ *1219 S. 9th St., South Philadelphia* ☎ *215/389–0659* ⊕ *www. genosteaks.com* ⊟ *No credit cards* ✛ *F6.*

$$$
JAPANESE
✕ **Izumi.** It's a bit surprising to find a sophisticated sushi spot in this part of town that has never seen a shortage of cheesesteaks, water ice, spaghetti, or red gravy, but not when you tie it to the recent hipster and yuppie influx to South Philly. The tiny restaurant wraps around a busy corner of East Passyunk's burgeoning restaurant row, a few blocks south of Pat's and Geno's, and is always packed with South Phillyites toting everything from Pabst to Santa Margherita to drink with Izumi's maki. The rolls range from simple to ambitious—from the solid spicy tuna to the Passyunk Avenue roll, with a spicy layer of crab salad atop shrimp tempura. ⊠ *1601 E. Passyunk Ave., South Philadelphia* ☎ *215/271–1222* ⊕ *www.izumiphilly.com* ⊟ *AE, MC, V* ⊘ *Closed Mon* ✛ *E6.*

$$$$ ✕ **James.** Chef Jim Burke repeatedly wins "best chef" accolades from
ITALIAN   local and national magazines for his contemporary takes on Northern
Fodor's Choice   Italian fare—favorites are the hand-cut tagliatelle with a duck ragu
★   seasoned with shavings of Valhrona chocolate and orange peel; and a
slow-roasted Four Story Hill Farm poularde that's the perfect antidote
to a chilly evening. He cooks, and his wife Kristina does everything else
in the sleek and chic little restaurant, including setting an effusive tone
that comes out in the servers' enthusiastic descriptions of the kitch-
en's offerings. ✉ *824 S. 8th St., Bella Vista* ☎ *215/629–4980* ⊕ *www.
jameson8th.com* ▭ *AE, D, MC, V* ☾ *Closed Sun.* ✢ *F6.*

¢–$ ✕ **La Lupe.** This little place is only a few blocks from the Italian Market
MEXICAN   and is adjacent to the famous Pat's and Geno's cheesesteakeries, but
it couldn't be more authentic in its Mexican flavors. The proof of its
authenticity: local Mexican-American families dine here on weekends.
Hand-pressed tortillas cradle ingredients that are surprising for street
food—*huitlacoche (Mexican corn truffle),* pickled pumpkin blossoms,
salty queso fresco, and roasted slow-cooked goat. Try the enchiladas
suizas, which drip with genuine Mexican cheese. ✉ *1201 S. 9th St., Italian Market* ☎ *215/551–9920* ▭ *AE, D, MC, V* ⛛ *BYOB* ✢ *F6.*

¢–$ ✕ **Morning Glory Diner.** The Morning Glory bills itself as a "finer diner,"
AMERICAN   and offers traditional touches such as big mugs of steaming coffee
(although the mugs are pewter). But the "finer" comes in the updated,
wholesome versions of diner fare such as homemade catsup on every
table; grilled ahi tuna with wasabi mayo on a brioche bun; thick pecan
waffles with whipped peach butter; and enormous, flaky biscuits that
accompany breakfast. Unless you're an early weekend riser, weekdays
are a better bet. The wait for weekend brunch can be epic. ✉ *735 S. 10th
St., South Philadelphia* ☎ *215/413-3999* ⊕ *www.themorninggorydiner.
com* ▭ *No credit cards* ☾ *No dinner* ✢ *F5.*

$$$ ✕ **Paradiso.** When chef Lynne Marie Rinaldi opened Paradiso in 2005
ITALIAN   two blocks from where she grew up, she sparked a restaurant renais-
sance in a section of South Philadelphia formerly known as a source for
spaghetti with gravy. By proving that an upscale, sleek eatery can flour-
ish in what was once Rocky country, Rinaldi has developed a reputation
as a pioneer and a devoted following. Favorites are the remarkably light
potato gnocchi with tomato and basil; rabbit cacciatore with mascar-
pone polenta; and any of the pastas, made fresh—of course—nearby at
the Italian Market. The extensive wine list includes some varieties even
oenophiles may never have heard of. ✉ *1627 E. Passyunk Ave., South
Philadelphia* ☎ *215/271-2066* ⊕ *www.paradisophilly.com* ▭ *AE, D,
MC, V* ☾ *Closed Mon. No lunch Sat. or Sun.* ✢ *E6.*

¢ ✕ **Pat's King of Steaks.** New cheesesteak restaurants come and go all the
AMERICAN   time, but two of the oldest—Pat's and Geno's, at the corner of 9th and
Passyunk—have a longstanding feud worth weighing in on. It comes
down to a matter of taste. Both serve equally generous portions of rib-
eye steak, grilled onions, and melted Provolone, American, or Cheese
Whiz on freshly baked Italian rolls. The main differences as far as we
can tell: Pat's claims to have invented the cheesesteak; Pat's meat is
chopped; and Pat's exterior is more, ahem, understated than Geno's
neon extravaganza. ✉ *1237 E. Passyunk Ave., South Philadelphia*
☎ *215/468-1546* ⊕ *patskingofsteaks.com* ▭ *No credit cards* ✢ *F6.*

4

$–$$ ✕ **Sabrina's Cafe.** If there's one thing
AMERICAN   you can count on, it's a two-hour
wait for Sunday brunch at this
cozy former bakery around the
corner from the Italian Market.
■ **TIP→** Locals know to phone in their
names and wait it out with coffee and
the paper at home, and you can, too.
Here's what everyone is waiting

for: apple and sharp cheddar omelets, stuffed and caramelized challah
French toast with vanilla-bean maple syrup, and the barking Chihuahua
breakfast (a burrito filled with scrambled eggs, black beans, red peppers,
and pepper-jack cheese). Brunch overshadows lunch and dinner, but
it shouldn't—those are delicious and hearty, too. ⊠ *910 Christian St.,
South Philadelphia* ☎ *215/574–1599* ⊕ *www.sabrinascafe.com* ⊟ *AE,
MC, V* ⊗ *No dinner Sun. and Mon.* ✛ *F6.*

$$$$ ✕ **The Saloon.** For many years this classic wood-panel restaurant has
STEAK   been a favorite among Philadelphia's most discerning diners, who
enjoyed steaks and chops in more-than-generous portions and the
always-true-to-their-roots Italian specialties. The superior quality of
ingredients still shines, but with the help of an inspired chef, Gene Betz,
a few more innovative twists sneak into the outstanding preparations,
although not so many that they intrude on the sensibilities of the regulars. Reservations are recommended. ⊠ *750 S. 7th St., South Philadelphia* ☎ *215/627–1811* ⊕ *www.saloonrestaurant.net* ⊟ *AE* ⊗ *Closed
Sun. No lunch Sat. and Mon.* ✛ *F5.*

¢   ✕ **Tony Luke's.** The original location—nearly under I–95—earned such a
AMERICAN   reputation from truckers who stopped for huge beef or pork sandwiches
with Italian greens and cheese that locals finally caught on and adopted
the dinerlike establishment for their own. The lines are long, though
they move quickly, and seating (outside only, under cover) is relatively
scarce; still, people flock here from early morning to closing time for
generous breakfasts and tasty sandwiches. For large orders, it's possible
to call ahead for takeout. ⊠ *39 E. Oregon Ave., South Philadelphia*
☎ *215/551–5725* ⊕ *www.tonylukes.com* ⊟ *No credit cards* ⊗ *Closed
Sun.* ✛ *H6.*

$$ ✕ **Tre Scalini.** When this restaurant in South Philadelphia, a locus of
ITALIAN   down-home Italian, moved from a cozy town house to a generic store-
front around the corner, patrons worried that the food would suffer.
Happily the old favorites, which are more homey than trendy, are
intact. Signature dishes like the grilled polenta with broccoli rabe and
bruschetta calamari with cannellini beans are carefully prepared and
amply plated. Pasta dishes—such as lobster- and cheese-filled ravioli and
black pasta with prawns and crabmeat—are best. ⊠ *1915 E. Passyunk
Ave., South Philadelphia* ☎ *215/551–3870* ⊟ *MC, V* ⍟ *BYOB* ⊗ *Closed
Mon. No lunch* ✛ *E6.*

CENTER CITY EAST

In Center City East (meaning the blocks east of Broad Street), most restaurants are near Washington Square and a few blocks west, along the bustling 13th Street corridor.

$$
GREEK

✕ **Effie's.** This restaurant doesn't get the attention it deserves, probably because it's been here so long. The Greek taverna in a 19th-century brownstone in the middle of Pine Street's Antique Row serves casual country Greek basics that are consistently satisfying. There's always a selection of fresh fish that can be simply grilled and seasoned with olive oil and lemon. Ask for a seat in the courtyard if the weather's nice. ✉ *1127 Pine St., Center City East* ☎ *215/592–8333* ⊕ *www.effies-restaurant.com* ▭ *MC, V* 🍴 *BYOB* ☽ *No lunch* ✛ *E4.*

$$$
MEXICAN

✕ **Lolita.** In a town where liquor licenses are few and far between, lots of restaurants are BYOB (bring your own bottle). Lolita's twist is BYOT, or bring your own tequila. They'll use it to blend a pitcher of some exotic-sounding margarita—try fresh strawberry puree and purple basil. The food—nouveau Mexican prepared with locally sourced ingredients—is pretty good, too. Lolita, one of the first in Philly's recent wave of ambitious Mexi-fusion restaurants, has a loyal following. ✉ *106 S. 13th St., Center City East* ☎ *215/546–7100* ⊕ *www.lolitabyob.com* ▭ *No credit cards* 🍴 *BYOB* ☽ *No lunch* ✛ *E4.*

$$$
ITALIAN

✕ **Mercato.** This BYOB in a former corner food market is noisy, cramped, and cash-only. Because of its no-reservation policy, people waiting for a table stand pressed up against the door. Still, they keep packing them in. Why? It's the Italian/New American bistro's attention to detail, visible in the exquisite artisanal cheese plate, the perfectly seared scallops, the separate olive-oil menu, and the homemade triangle-shaped pasta. ✉ *1216 Spruce St., Center City East* ☎ *215/985–2962* ⊕ *www.mercato-byob.com* ▭ *No credit cards* 🍴 *BYOB* ☽ *No lunch* ✛ *E4.*

$$
LATIN-AMERICAN

✕ **Mixto.** Latin American and Caribbean cuisine mix in an airy, two-story space on historic Antique Row, a few blocks below Broad Street. The place feels like a well-loved neighborhood joint, with its friendly vibe, heaping portions of slightly greasy food, and Latin music that sets the mood for some of the city's best mojitos. Occasionally the food reaches new heights, as with their paella Valenciana and some solid brunch offerings, including a delicious smoked salmon frittata. ✉ *1141-43 Pine St., Center City East* ☎ *215/592–0363* ⊕ *www.tierra-mixtophilly.com* ▭ *AE, D, MC, V* ✛ *E5.*

$$$$
SEAFOOD

✕ **Oceanaire Seafood Room.** Everything about this place is enormous, from the vast dining room to the Baked Alaska the size of your head. The '40s supper club atmosphere is festive, and the seafood-heavy menu would be impressive even if this weren't a chain. David Wiederholt is the fourth chef since the place opened in 2006, but the revolving door doesn't seem to affect the solid preparation of hard-to-find fish like Dover sole, Copper River salmon, and barramundi. The extensive raw bar, flashy decor, and snappy service all recommend the place for special occasions. Reservations are recommended. ✉ *700 Walnut St., Center City East* ☎ *215/652–8862* ⊕ *www.theoceanaire.com* ▭ *AE, MC, V* ☽ *No lunch* ✛ *F4.*

4

¢ ✕ **Reading Terminal Market.** When the
ECLECTIC Reading Company opened its train
★ shed in 1892, it was the only one in
the country with a market tucked
away in its cellar. The trains are
long gone, but the food remains.
And while disagreeing over the best
cheesesteak is a popular pastime in
Philly, pretty much everyone can

agree on pancakes at the Dutch Eating Place, the roast pork sandwich
at Dinic's, cupcakes at the Flying Monkey, and double chocolate-chip
cookies at Famous 4th Street. Get here early to beat the lunch rush.
Hours are 8–6 Monday–Saturday, and 9–4 Sunday. Seventy-five-minute
tours every Wednesday and Saturday highlight the market's history and
offerings (call ☎ 215/545–8007 to make a reservation). ■TIP→ **The
Amish shops, which sell pastries, fresh cheeses, honey and jams, and more,
are only open Wednesday through Saturday.** ✉ *12th and Arch Sts., Center
City East* ☎*215/922–2317* ⊕ *www.readingterminalmarket.org* ⊹ *F3.*

$$$ ✕ **Valanni.** One of the few eateries in Center City to offer food service
MEDITERRANEAN until 1 AM, Valanni can accommodate double the number of revelers
since expanding into the neighboring town house in 2008. This hip
lounge-restaurant has a chic, casual interior of exposed brick, polished
black surfaces, purple velvet banquettes, and funky, undulating white
walls. The decor, lively outdoor-seating scene, and long cocktail list
sometimes obscure the excellent food, which include tasty tapas and
ambitious cheese plates for those who can't commit to an entrée. Much
of the late-night crew returns late morning for Sunday brunch and some
of the chef's new twists on old favorites, like lemon ricotta pancakes
with fresh berries and cheddar and pear omelets. ✉ *1229 Spruce St.,
Center City East* ☎*215/790–9494* ⊕ *www.valanni.com* ⊟ *AE, D, MC,
V* ⊹ *E4.*

$$$$ ✕**Vetri.** Chef Mark Vetri blew into town from New York, where his
ITALIAN cooking had garnered all sorts of kudos. This tiny space was formerly
Fodor's Choice home to such stellar restaurants as Le Bec-Fin. The magic of the loca-
★ tion seems to be working again as Vetri's deft hands turn out such spe-
cialties as spinach gnocchi, wild boar ragu on chestnut fettucine, and
a strange-sounding but exquisite dessert known as chocolate polenta
soufflé. Friday and Saturday dinners are limited to a $135 *degustazione*
(tasting menu), where you receive a hand-painted menu and a series of
small courses of Vetri's design. Some complain that the portions are too
small, and all complain that reservations are too hard to come by—the
average backlog is two months. ✉ *1312 Spruce St., Center City East*
☎*215/732–3478* ⊕ *www.vetriristorante.com* ⚲ *Reservations essential*
⊟ *AE, DC, MC, V* ☉ *Closed Sun. No lunch. Closed 2 weeks in Aug.,
1 week in Jan.* ⊹ *E4.*

CHINATOWN

The restaurants of Chinatown are located north of Market Street, near Reading Terminal Market.

$ ✕ **Lee How Fook.** Literally translated as "good food for the mouth,"

CHINESE this unprepossessing spot is now being run by a second generation of restaurateurs. They do an excellent job with the most straightforward fare, like General Tso's chicken, hot-and-sour soup, and steamed dumplings filled with pulled pork, but they are best known for their salt-baked seafood and their hot pots. ✉ *219 N. 11th St., Chinatown* ☎ *215/925–7266* ⊕ *www.leehowfook.com* ▭ *AE, MC, V* 🈺 *BYOB* ☾ *Closed Mon.* ✛ *E3.*

¢–$ ✕ **Ocean City.** It's mostly all locals eating at this smallish banquet space

CHINESE almost on the edge of Chinatown. Things can get a bit hectic with big-screen TVs hanging from every corner, spangly chandeliers overhead, and dim sum carts racing through the aisles. Snag a seat next to the kitchen to flag down the carts as they emerge. You won't often know what's inside until you take a bite, but the dim sum is excellent and definitely a bargain. ✉ *234 N. 9th St., Chinatown* ☎ *215/829–0688* ⊕ *www.oceancityrestaurant.com* ▭ *AE, MC, V* ✛ *F2.*

$$$ ✕ **Penang.** The juxtaposition of bamboo and exposed pipes is indicative

MALAYSIAN of the surprising mix of flavors in this perennially busy restaurant. A taste of India creeps into a scintillating appetizer of handkerchief-thin crepes served with a small dipping dish of spicy chicken curry. Other preparations are redolent of flavors from several other Asian countries. Soups with various types of noodles are unusual, tasty, and filling. ✉ *117 N. 10th St., Chinatown* ☎ *215/413–2531* ⊕ *www.penangusa. com* ▭ *No credit cards* ✛ *F3.*

$–$$ ✕ **Rangoon.** Burmese food is somewhat Chinese and somewhat Indian,

ASIAN with a touch of other tastes that make the mixture intriguing. The spring ginger salad and thousand-layer bread served with a potato-curry dipping sauce are both excellent. Portions are somewhat small, but because of the fullness of the flavors, diners usually leave satisfied. ✉ *112 N. 9th St., Chinatown* ☎ *215/829–8939* ▭ *MC, V* ☾ *Closed Mon.* ✛ *F3.*

$ ✕ **Sang Kee Peking Duck House.** Although the decor is getting a bit tired,

CHINESE this Chinatown stalwart continues to dish up delicious noodle soups. Egg or rice noodles come in different widths and are simmered with duck, pork, or beef brisket. If you wish, you can have your soup with both noodles *and* overstuffed, tender wontons. Other traditional foods, besides the house specialty, duck, are carried from the kitchen with more speed than style. Beer is available. ✉ *238 N. 9th St., Chinatown* ☎ *215/925–7532* ▭ *No credit cards* ✛ *F2.*

¢–$ ✕ **Vietnam.** Owner Benny Lai took what started as a noodle shop

VIETNAMESE founded by his immigrant parents, bought up the building and the surrounding property, and turned it into a chic restaurant with an upstairs lounge serving small plates and wacky cocktails like the Flaming Volcano (two straws included). In the dining room the best bets are the crispy spring rolls, salted squid, barbecue platter, and soups with rice noodles. ✉ *221 N. 11th St., Chinatown* ☎ *215/592–1163* ⊕ *www.eatat-vietnam.com* ▭ *No credit cards* ✛ *E2.*

4

Where to Refuel Around Town

For those times when all you want is a quick bite—and you just can't face another cheesesteak or slice of pizza—consider these alternatives.

DiBruno Bros.: This uptown outpost of the original Italian Market location is a one-stop gourmet shop where office workers, students, and ladies who lunch rub elbows midday to choose from the eat-in or take-out options. It's well-placed for a picnic, with Rittenhouse Square just a few blocks away.

Downstairs at the Bellevue: This centrally located, upscale food court beneath the Park Hyatt at the Bellevue at Broad and Walnut streets features some local vendors, such as 12th Street Cantina and Rocco's Italian Hoagies.

Italian Market: At 9th and Christian are a few lunch spots featuring hot pork and tripe sandwiches in addition to many varieties of hoagies. If you prefer fish, Anastasio's Fish Market at 9th and Washington also serves lunch and dinner.

Marathon Grill: In eight (and counting) locations around the city, this local chain serves an enormous selection of comfort foods, much of which is customizable (wraps, sandwiches, salads). It's a great place to stop in for a quick, cheap lunch—or a smoothie to go.

Market at Comcast Center: The newest, tallest skyscaper in Philadelphia hides its sweet spot underground at the Market at Comcast Center, the best grab-a-bite scenario this side of Reading Terminal Market. Choose from sandwiches and salads from DiBruno Bros., dumplings by Susanno Foo, and sushi by Tokyo Express.

Street Vendors: A number of lunch carts in Center City offer ethnic food, including Chinese, Japanese, Middle Eastern, and Italian, as well as the more standard hot dogs, hamburgers, and fresh fruit. In University City the block between 37th and 38th on Sansom Street has various ethnic vendors catering to Penn students.

CENTER CITY WEST

Many of the places in Center City West are high-price dazzlers like Le Bec-Fin, though the variety here is notable—dining can be a multicourse extravaganza or as simple as grabbing a falafel.

$$$$

FRENCH

✕ **10 Arts by Eric Ripert.** Even in a town filled with nationally acclaimed chefs, the arrival of a new Ripert outpost in Philadelphia hasn't gone unnoticed. The Frenchman and his chef-de-cuisine Jennifer Carroll have met the high expectations of his eagerly waiting fans with an expertly crafted menu that includes the expected staples—roast chicken, bouillabaisse, and butter-smothered trout—then exceeded them with inspired local touches such as a lip-smacking soft pretzel appetizer and malted "TastyKake" ice cream. Perhaps more noteworthy, however, is the jazzy makeover given to the Jeffersonian rotunda of the Ritz-Carlton Hotel, which hosts the restaurant's varied nooks. Gone are the lounge's overstuffed jacquard sofas, and in is a streamlined deco look, accented with striking, albeit rather jarring, towers lit in jewel tones. In a separate dining room all is sedate, sophisticated, and tryst-ready. ⊠ *10 Avenue of the Arts, Center City West* ☎ *215/523–8273* ⊕ *www.10arts.com* ⊟ *AE, MC, V* ✛ *D4.*

$$$
AMERICAN
✕ **XIX (Nineteen).** The highest restaurant in Philadelphia—with panoramic views through floor-to-ceiling windows to prove it—recently underwent a major renovation. Seeing the before and after was like watching a stuffy society lady loosen up and trade in her Chanel suits for Armani couture. The menu also underwent an overhaul, emerging with a focus on seafood, with preparation that blends in Thai and Indian influences. The raw bar is the centerpiece of both the menu and the main dining room, where dinner and Sunday brunch are served. All-day dining is available in the chic, comfortable café, which is more casual but benefits from those same bird's-eye views. ⊠ *200 S. Broad St., Center City West* ☎ *215/893–1234* ⊕ *www.hyatt.com* ⚑ *Reservations essential* ⊟ *AE, DC, MC, V* ✛ *E4.*

$$$
LATIN-AMERICAN
✕ **Alma de Cuba.** A bit of scrolled ironwork greets diners, followed by a swank bar pulsating with Cuban music that lets everyone know this is a happening place. Find a seat here because you may wait a while, even with a reservation. The service is a bit chaotic, but the mojitos are refreshing and you won't be easily bored. The decor is evocative of pre-Castro Havana, with dim lighting, mod seating, and larger-than-life images of tobacco fields projected onto the walls. The menu contains a few genuine dishes, such as *lechon asado* (crispy roasted pork) and a wide selection of ceviche, all prepared by star chef Douglas Rodriguez. Although oysters are not generally considered Cuban, they're a knockout here, served fried over *fufu* (mashed sweet plantains studded with bacon). ⊠ *1623 Walnut St., Center City West* ☎ *215/988–1799* ⊕ *www.almadecubarestaurant.com* ⚑ *Reservations essential* ⊟ *AE, DC, MC, V* ☽ *No lunch* ✛ *D4.*

$$–$$$
IRISH
✕ **Black Sheep.** Converted from a private club with blacked-out windows, this Dublin-style pub has been packing them in for rivers of Irish draft and kitchen specialties. Guinness-battered fish-and-chips could have been produced on the "auld sod," and the malt vinegar to sprinkle over it all does little to dampen the crisp crust. The first-floor bar is noisy and spirited—show up before happy hour to snag a seat—but the mood gets a bit quieter as you climb the steps to the dining room. ⊠ *247 S. 17th St., Center City West* ☎ *215/545–9473* ⊕ *www.theblacksheeppub.com* ⊟ *AE, D, DC, MC, V* ✛ *D4.*

$$$
AMERICAN
✕ **Bliss.** Multatented chef Francesco Martorella exercises his imagination in this somewhat stark space—think of it as a blank canvas that allows him to create wonderful dishes ranging from grilled garlic-rubbed skirt steak with pomme frites to crispy ginger chicken breast with wasabi jasmine rice. The patrons, many of them music stars from the nearby Academy of Music, are drawn to this place where the chef is clearly in command and enjoys his position. An early crowd gives way to a more sophisticated group as the evening wears on and more and more bottles from the excellent wine list are poured. ⊠ *220–24 S. Broad St., Center City West* ☎ *215/731–1100* ⊕ *www.bliss-restaurant.com* ⚑ *Reservations essential* ⊟ *AE, D, DC, MC, V* ☽ *Closed Sun. No lunch weekends* ✛ *D4.*

$$$$ ✗**Butcher & Singer.** Restaurateur Stephen Starr's latest venture, Butcher
STEAK   & Singer, is housed in an old wood-paneled and marbled brokerage
(from which it borrows its name). Here the dishes are traditional rather
than fancy (surf-and-turf rather than Kobe beef), portions are hefty
(even the chocolate fudge cake is huge), and the sides classic (stuffed
hash browns, and gravy mushrooms and onions). A pair of showstopper chandeliers, a *New Yorker*–style mural depicting tony pooches clad
in pencil skirts and smoking robes, and leather banquettes skew closely
to the restaurant's avowed 1940s supper club aesthetic. ⊠ *1500 Walnut
Street, Center City West* ☎ *215/732–4444* ⊕ *www.butcherandsinger.
com* ▤ *AE, MC, V* ⊗ *No lunch Sat. and Sun.* ✢ *D4.*

$$$$ ✗**Capital Grille.** It's only fair to question whether this is a restaurant or
STEAK   an art gallery. When you first enter the stunning dining room, you'll find
walls covered with exquisitely framed paintings and pedestals bearing
bronze statues. Steaks and chops come in two sizes: large and larger. A
baby lobster (about a pound) makes an excellent appetizer along with
the requisite green salad and shrimp cocktail. The wine cellar is ample
and fairly priced for a selection of excellent bottles. ⊠ *1338 Chestnut
St., at Broad St., Center City West* ☎ *215/545–9588* ⊕ *www.thecapital-
grille.com* ▤ *AE, D, DC, MC, V* ⊗ *No lunch weekends* ✢ *D4.*

$-$$ ✗**Continental Mid-town.** You're not sure what decade you're in once
ECLECTIC   you enter the vast, retro playground that shares a name with the Old
City martini lounge, also from blockbuster restaurateur Stephen Starr.
Line up for a spot on the popular rooftop lounge or sit inside, in a
swinging wicker basket chair, a sunken banquette, or a baby-blue vinyl
booth. The global tapas menu includes shoestring fries drizzled with
Chinese mustard, a gargantuan crispy calamari salad, and a cheesesteak
egg roll. Of the retro cocktails, the most popular is the Tang-rimmed
Buzz Aldrin. ⊠ *1801 Chestnut St., Center City West* ☎ *215/567–1800*
⊕ *www.continentalmidtown.com* ▤ *AE, MC, V* ✢ *C4.*

$$$ ✗**Ernesto's 1521 Cafe.** A devoted clientele has helped transform this
ITALIAN   simple café into a sophisticated bistro. The location across from the
Kimmel Center hasn't hurt, either. The food is creative, with hints of
French and other cuisines mingling with the standard Italian flavors.
The fried calamari, for example, is served with mango chutney. The
vegetable Napoleon satisfies vegetarians; carnivores might prefer the
chicken osso buco served with polenta or the seafood cioppino. Desserts
made by the owner's mother, Livia, are outstanding. ⊠ *1521 Spruce St.,
Center City West* ☎ *215/546–1521* ⊕ *www.ernestos1521.com* ▤ *MC,
V* ⊗ *Closed Mon. No dinner Sun.* ✢ *D4.*

$$$ ✗**Il Portico.** This elegant restaurant is next door to flashy Le Bec-Fin,
ITALIAN   so it doesn't get the attention it deserves. Service is excellent, as is the
food: beef carpaccio, black *tagliolini* (long, flat pasta) with salmon in
a brandy sauce, chicken breast stuffed with fontina cheese and Parma
ham, and a simple pasta sautéed with broccoli and sausage. Some dishes
are a bit pricey. ⊠ *1519 Walnut St., Center City West* ☎ *215/587–7000*
⊕ *www.il-portico.com* ⌂ *Reservations essential* ▤ *AE, MC, V* ⊗ *No
lunch weekends* ✢ *D4.*

$ ✗ **Jamaican Jerk Hut.** The liquid of choice at this BYOB is rum, to mix
CARRIBBEAN   with the Hut's selection of tropical juices. Chef Nicola Shirley lovingly

tends to jerk pork and chicken over an authentic pit; the culinary school grad also serves exemplary versions of her homeland's curries and *roti* (pancakes with fillings such as curried chickpeas or chicken). When weather permits, eat in a charming back garden; the tiny storefront is primarily takeout. ✉ *1436 South St., Center City West* ☎ *215/545–8644* ⊕ *www.jamaicanjerkhutinc.com* 🖃 *No credit cards* 🍴*BYOB* ✚ *D5.*

$$$$ ✕**Le Bec-Fin.** A few years ago Georges Perrier took the Versailles-style
FRENCH decor down to a 19th-century Parisian salon motif and the servers' uni-
Fodor's Choice forms down from tuxedoes to blazers. In 2008 the front of the house
★ loosened up even more with an à la carte menu replacing set seating times and a prix-fixe degustation menu and—mais, oui!—a dress code that allows jeans. The prix-fixe options—$35 for three courses or $150 for the traditional seven courses plus all-you-can-eat dessert cart—are still available as are signature Le Bec dishes like the popular *galette de crab* (a sublime crab cake) and the magnificent dessert cart. You can order the dessert cart à la carte for $15. This outpost of Lyonnais cuisine continues to set a stratospherically high standard for Philadelphia, and there's still sufficient acclaim to require an advance reservation of a month or more to garner a table on Saturday night. If dinner is out of your price range, Le Bar Lyonnais—down a flight of stairs from the main dining room—is a cozy, charming space that features the chef's specialty dishes for entrées that range $15–$40. ✉ *1523 Walnut St., Center City West* ☎ *215/567–1000* ⊕ *www.lebecfin.com* 🍴 *Reservations essential* 🖃 *AE, D, DC, MC, V* ☾ *Closed Sun.* ✚ *D4.*

$$$ ✕ **Matyson.** At one of many BYOBs in the city where the partners in
AMERICAN the kitchen are also partners in life, Matt and Sonjia Spector (they joined the first syllables of their names) turn out a menu of eclectic, fused American cuisine. Steak frites and herb-roasted chicken are favorites, as are any of Sonjia's desserts. ✉ *37 S. 19th St., Center City West* ☎ *215/564–2925* ⊕ *www.matyson.com* 🍴 *Reservations essential* 🖃 *MC, V* 🍴*BYOB* ☾ *Closed Sun.* ✚ *C4.*

$$ ✕**McCormick & Schmick's Seafood Restaurant.** "Big, bold, and beautiful"
SEAFOOD might be the best way to describe this fish house, especially when you're talking about the ceiling with its remarkable Art Deco chandeliers. There are more than 40 daily specials brought in from many ports, such as Maine (lobsters) and Washington (red king salmon). Of course, there are oysters galore. The food is prepared by a knowledgeable kitchen crew and served by a well-trained staff, and the crowd is predictable—businesspeople entertaining clients and families from out of town. ✉ *1 S. Broad St., Center City West* ☎ *215/568–6888* ⊕ *www.mccormickandschmicks.com* 🖃 *AE, D, DC, MC, V* ✚ *D4.*

$$ ✕**Monk's Cafe.** Mussels are practically the national dish of Belgium.
BELGIAN Whether steamed in classic style with wine and shallots or with cream, they're a high point at this casual, lively bar and restaurant. The fries that accompany them draw raves from the regulars who crowd the place. Burgers, too, are favorites. Add to these an outstanding assortment of Belgian specialty dishes and beers and you get the picture. ✉ *264 S. 16th St., Center City West* ☎ *215/545–7005* ⊕ *www.monkscafe.com* 🖃 *MC, V* ✚ *D4.*

4

$$$$ ✕ **Morton's, the Steakhouse.** This classic steak house attracts many visitors
STEAK familiar with its outposts in other cities, as well as a devoted coterie
of local business executives. Etched glass and wood paneling provide a
semblance of privacy in the large dining room, and there's an intimate
stand-up bar and cigar lounge for postprandial puffing. The house specialty, a 24-ounce porterhouse, puts the most determined carnivore to
the test. Pristine whole fish and lobsters are priced by the pound. Sides
are steak house–style huge. Reservations are recommended. ✉ *1411
Walnut St., Center City West* ☎ *215/557–0724* ⊕ *www.mortons.com*
⚑ *Reservations essential. Jacket required* ▭ *AE, DC, MC, V* ⊘ *No
lunch* ✛ *D4.*

$$$ ✕ **Osteria.** Osteria is more than a consolation prize for the many who
ITALIAN are thwarted by the two-month back-up in reservations at Marc Vetri's
★ eponymous fine-dining restaurant. His long-awaited second restaurant
is a little more affordable and decidedly more casual and versatile with
its wide-ranging menu of Italian comfort food. The menu has everything
from amazing brick-oven pizzas (try the Lombarda, with cotechino
sausage and a soft-cooked egg) to a charred rib-eye for two served
over white beans. The lively North Broad Street setting with red con-
crete floors, rustic wooden tables, and soaring ceilings blends loft and
country, industry and art. ✉ *640 N. Broad St., Center City West/North
Philadelphia* ☎ *215/763–0920* ⊕ *www.osteriaphilly.com* ⚑ *Reserva-
tions essential* ▭ *AE, D, MC, V* ⊘ *No lunch Sat. to Wed.* ✛ *D1.*

$$$$ ✕ **Palm.** Local movers and shakers broker deals here in the beige space
STEAK off the lobby of the Park Hyatt at the Bellevue and beneath their own
caricatures hanging on the wall. The steak-house ambience comes
complete with bare floors, harried waiters, and huge steaks, chops,
and salads whizzing by. The flavorful New York strip steak is fine at
dinner, and the stupendous steak sandwich (*no* relation to a chees-
esteak) is a lunchtime value. ✉ *200 S. Broad St., Center City West*
☎ *215/546–7256* ⊕ *www.thepalm.com* ▭ *AE, D, DC, MC, V* ⊘ *No
lunch weekends* ✛ *E4.*

$$$ ✕ **Petite Passion.** You can eat like a king at paupers' prices at this inti-
ECLECTIC mate 50-seat restaurant inside the Art Institute of Philadelphia. On
Wednesday and Thursday the four-course lunch is $15; the six-course
dinner, $30. The menu changes weekly, depending on what's fresh in
the market and what inspires the culinary arts students and instructors.
Through a large picture window you can see and hear them at work.
✉ *2300 Market St., Center City West* ☎ *215/405–6766* ⚑ *Reservations
essential* ▭ *No credit cards* ⛬ *BYOB* ⊘ *Closed Fri.–Tues. Closed when
the Art Institute isn't in session* ✛ *B3.*

$$ ✕ **Pub and Kitchen.** Local food groupies are all a-chatter about Chef
BRITISH Johnny Mac's sophisticated UK-inspired fare—the "white fish roll
mops" on the bar snacks menu are pickled bits of pollack tossed with
dilled sour cream and diced apples atop little toasts. The flaky fish in his
"fish and chips" is coated with beer batter and served with crispy fries
on a generous mound of vivid green, buttered mushy peas. But people
flock to the energetic (and noisy) *restaubar* to unwind with friends
after a long day as much as they do for the food. In what used to be a
dive bar, Pub is an unpretentious, attractive hangout with hardwood

Bring Your Own, Buddy

The scarcity and high cost of liquor licenses available to Pennsylvania restaurateurs combined with the absence of a law prohibiting patrons from bringing liquor into a restaurant has resulted in an active bring-your-own-bottle (BYOB) scene in Philadelphia. Natives know that BYOBs have the most flavorful food and atmosphere, not to mention a bill that is easier to digest. Bringing your own is penalty-free—there's no extra charge for corkage. Here are some of our favorite BYOBs:

■ Dmitri's, Queen Village

■ Effie's, Center City East

■ Marigold Kitchen, West Philadelphia

■ Matyson, Rittenhouse Square

■ Modo Mio, Fishtown

■ Pumpkin, Center City West

4

---

floors, exposed brick walls, tables fashioned from reclaimed floor joists, and familiar rock music playing from the speakers. ⊠ *1946 Lombard St., Center City West* ☎ *215/545–0350* ⊕ *www.thepubandkitchen.com* ⌀ *No reservations* ▭ *AE, D, MC, V* ☉ *No lunch weekdays* ✛ *C5.*

$$$
AMERICAN
✕ **Pumpkin.** This funky foodie favorite has spawned a casual café and a small market selling locally produced products one block away from the original BYOB. Dinner at Pumpkin's produce-driven menu changes daily depending on what has inspired self-taught chef Ian Moroney on that particular day. A $35 five-course tasting menu on Sundays highlights such fresh, eclectic fare as crispy sweetbreads with ramps vinaigrette, grilled quail with citrus and fig balsamic, and salmon with chimichurri sauce, pineapple, and Serrano salsa. Calling ahead is essential to snagging a spot in the 28-seat, elbow-to-elbow dining room. ⊠ *1713 South St., Center City West* ☎ *215/545–4448* ⊕ *www.pumpkinphilly.com* ▭ *No credit cards* ⌀ *BYOB* ☉ *Closed Mon.* ✛ *D5.*

$$$
MEXICAN
✕ **Tequila's Restaurant.** Chef Carlos Molina's menu includes authentic Mexican dishes such as *chiles rellenos* (moderately spicy poblano peppers stuffed with cheese or ground meat) and chicken *mole poblano* (a sauce with many ingredients, including dried chili peppers, cloves, and bitter chocolate). The entryway is brightly painted with Day of the Dead figures and the dining rooms feature a long hardwood bar, Mexican glassware, and colorful ceramics. You can choose from tangy margaritas—if you order enough, they bring you your own personal tankard—plus a dozen different Mexican beers and 52 types of tequila. Reservations are recommended. ⊠ *1602 Locust St., Center City West* ☎ *215/546–0181* ⊕ *www.tequilasphilly.com* ▭ *AE, DC, MC, V* ☉ *Closed Sun. No lunch Sat.* ✛ *D4.*

RITTENHOUSE SQUARE

Rittenhouse Square, naturally, has its share of flash, with few budget options.

$$$$
SEAFOOD

✕ **Devon Seafood Grill.** Once you get past the crowded bar and into the vast dining room (the bar is so popular with young business types that it's nearly impossible to get in the door on Friday), you enter a quintessential fish house with all the classic dishes and then some. Lobster in several sizes is always on the menu and generally available in all of them, beautifully cooked to order. Hot biscuits delivered to the table are runaway favorites. Reservations are recommended. ⊠ *225 S. 18th St., Center City* ☎ *215/546–5940* ⊕ *www.devonseafood.com* ▭ *AE, DC, MC, V* ⊹ *C4.*

$$$
AMERICAN

✕ **Friday Saturday Sunday.** This neighborhood favorite was a player in Philadelphia's 1970s restaurant renaissance, and though the menu (like the decor) is somewhat dated, the finished product is generally pleasing. Entrées are simple compared with today's inventive fusion cuisines—grilled tuna steak, chicken Dijon, filet mignon—but will nonetheless leave you feeling satisfied. The restaurant is known (and loved) for charging just $10 above cost for wine, and for having excellent banquettes for serious canoodling. Reservations are recommended. ⊠ *261 S. 21st St., Rittenhouse Square* ☎ *215/546–4232* ⊕ *www.frisatsun.com* ▭ *AE, DC, MC, V* ⊗ *No lunch* ⊹ *C4.*

$$$
JAPANESE

✕ **Genji.** For more than 20 years, Genji has earned a loyal following for the consistently high quality of its fish, its classic sushi preparation, and its relatively down-to-earth prices. The place is cozy and casual, with exposed-brick walls and a low-ceiling room upstairs. Eel lovers get their fix here with the Double Eel (an inside out eel roll topped with eel and avocado). ⊠ *1720 Sansom St., Rittenhouse Square* ☎ *215/564–1720* ▭ *AE, D, DC, MC, V* ⊗ *No lunch weekends* ⊹ *C4.*

$$$$
ECLECTIC

✕ **Lacroix.** Eyebrows were raised in early 2009 when Jason Cichonski took over from gastronomically adventurous Matthew Levin, who in turn raised eyebrows when *he* took over from legendary Jean-Marie Lacroix. But Cichonski has proven himself to be a worthy successor and one who's true to Levin's mix of cutting-edge techniques with quality ingredients for inventive, sometimes playful, dishes like tomato-cheddar soup garnished with a wistful drizzle of charcoal oil and diver scallops accented with carrot jam. Combined with a 500-plus-label cellar of high-end bottles and a gorgeous dining room overlooking Rittenhouse Square, a meal here is guaranteed to be one of your most memorable. There's also the $52 blowout Sunday brunch—a tremendous value. ⊠ *210 W. Rittenhouse Sq., Rittenhouse Square* ☎ *215/790–2533* ⊕ *www.lacroixrestaurant.com* ⌲ *Reservations essential. Jacket required* ▭ *AE, D, DC, MC, V* ⊹ *C4.*

$$$
FRENCH
Fodor's Choice
★

✕ **PARC.** Restaurateur Stephen Starr's fondness for themes (a giant golden Buddha in his pan-Asian restaurant, Buddakan, and a mid-country, mid-century feel at the comfort food eatery Jones) has reached perfection in this vast but meticulous stage set placed on Philadelphia's most desirable corner. Brass rails, silvered mirrors, claret-hued banquettes, and oak wainscoting reclaimed from now-shuttered Parisian restaurants, imbue patina—while small touches like newspapers on wooden poles, create extra realism. Similarly, standard menu items (roasted chicken, trout amandine) hold their own, but the little things—desserts and salads, fresh-baked goods (including housemade macaroons), and excellent onion soup—stand out. Ask for an indoor-outdoor table overlooking the park: you'll get generous views and the pleasant din of the 150 diners behind you without the deafening buzz that is the restaurant's one true downside. ⊠ *227 S. 18th St., Rittenhouse Square* ☎ *215/545–2262* ⊕ *www.parc-restaurant.com* ⊟ *AE, MC, V* ⊹ *C4.*

$$$$
STEAK
★
✕ **Prime Rib.** The glamorous 1940s atmosphere sets this steak house apart from the rest—sleek leopard-print carpeting, nightly jazz piano and bass, and black-lacquer walls trimmed with gold all add up to a convivial atmosphere. Habitués (of whom there are many) admire the gigantic slabs of dry-aged prime beef, glistening fresh seafood (also served in more than generous portions), addictive baked potato skins, and other sit-up-and-take-notice dishes that keep this handsome restaurant hopping. ⊠ *Warwick Hotel, 1701 Locust St., Center City West* ☎ *215/772–1701* ⊕ *www.theprimerib.com* ⊟ *AE, D, DC, MC, V* ⊗ *No lunch* ⊹ *D4.*

$$$$
STEAK
✕ **Smith & Wollensky.** Adjacent to the Rittenhouse Hotel, this lively outpost of a New York classic steak house is on two levels—a café-type bar on the first floor and a traditional dining room upstairs. The restaurant serves a typical steak-house menu with some unique variants: all the steaks are dry-aged on the premises, a roasted pork shank is a permanent menu special, and a 28-ounce Cajun rib eye is the runaway favorite of locals. A baby lobster is a delightful appetizer. ⊠ *210 Rittenhouse Sq., Rittenhouse Square* ☎ *215/545–1700* ⊕ *www.smithandwollensky. com* ⊟ *AE, D, DC, MC, V* ⊹ *C4.*

$$$
AMERICAN
✕ **Snackbar.** With a vivid red palette, a flickering fireplace suspended midway up one wall, and a sparkling clientele, this tiny restau-lounge is both an avant-garde eatery and a theatrical backdrop for the goings-on of a certain slice of the city's movers and shakers. Go early to grab a sidewalk table without having to wait. ⊠ *253 S. 20th St., Rittenhouse Square* ☎ *215/545–5655* ⊕ *www.snackbarltd.com* ⊠ *Reservations not accepted* ⊟ *AE, D, MC, V* ⊹ *C4.*

$$
SPANISH
★
✕ **Tinto Wine Bar.** Chef Jose Garces went to Spain to research food and wine for Amada, his Old City tapas restaurant, and while he was there he fell in love with Basque Country. Tinto is his ode to the bars in San Sebastian that serve up *pinxtos* (small plates), *bocadillos* (sandwiches), charcuterie, and cheeses. Always inventive and never showy, Garces's take on the regional cuisine is defined by surprising combinations—chorizo chips with lobster cream; lamb loin skewered and served in shot-glasses of onion cream and sherry jus; a morsel of duck confit topped with a black cherry and served on blue cheese–smeared toasted bread. The Basque wine list pairs perfectly. ⊠ *114 S. 20th St., Rittenhouse Square* ☎ *215/665–9150* ⊕ *www.tintorestaurant.com* ⊠ *Reservations essential* ⊟ *AE, MC, V* ⊹ *C4.*

$$
AMERICAN
★
✕ **Tria.** Tria's brown interior and minimalist signage give off a wallflower vibe, but the tables packed with chic urbanites grazing lightly belie its inner beauty. The knowledgeable staff is serious about the restaurant's focus—the "fermentation trio" of wine, cheese, and beer—but not in a

snobby way. They'll casually toss off suggestions for a cheese plate that's a phenomenal medley of textures and flavors. Then they'll recommend a zippy white wine that sets it off perfectly. ⊠ *123 S. 18th St., Rittenhouse Square* ☎ *215/972–8742* ⊕ *www.triacafe.com* ⊟ *AE, MC, V* ⊹ *C4.*

$$$
AMERICAN

╳ **Twenty Manning.** The second venture from local girl made good Audrey Claire Taichman was a hit from the moment it opened in 2000. Large French windows open up onto the sidewalk where tables are always packed in the warmer months with chic young couples and klatches sipping pomegranate martinis and supping on Pan-Asian small plates like black tea house-smoked tuna and grilled prawns with roasted yams. Inside, the space is half-bar/lounge, half-restaurant, and all glass, leather, and luxe minimalism. Reservations are recommended. ⊠ *261 S. 20th St., Rittenhouse Square* ☎ *215/731–0900* ⊕ *www.twentymanning. com* ⊟ *AE, MC, V* ⊗ *No lunch* ⊹ *C4.*

UNIVERSITY CITY

In University City you can enjoy the many affordable, funky eateries geared toward Penn students.

$–$$
ASIAN

╳ **Bubble House.** This bright, casual university hangout across from the U. of Penn law school is spread out in two adjoining town houses with lots of tables and booths in adjoining rooms. Named for "bubble tea," a Taiwanese drink made with tapioca pearls and served with a straw wide enough to accommodate those pearls, this place is about much more than tea. Its extensive menu of pan-Asian fare is consistently tasty and provides lots of options for vegetarians. ⊠ *3404 Sansom St., University City* ☎ *215/243–0804* ⊕ *www.thebubblehouse.com* ⊟ *AE, D, MC, V* ⊹ *A4.*

$$$
MODERN
MEXICAN

╳ **Distrito.** Star chef Jose Garces's latest joint is colorful, energetic, and enormous—just like Mexico City, the place that inspired it. Distrito's "modern Mexican" menu, made up entirely of small plates, includes cuisine from all over Mexico as well as the capital city's hierarchy of street food to fine food—but always with a Garces twist. The Los Hongos huarache is topped with earthy mushrooms spiked with black truffle and tempered by corn shoots. Slices of buttery yellowtail in hamachi ceviche are plated with a dollop of sangrita sorbet and a dash of mint. Urban (and, on the weekend, suburban) fans of Garces's downtown restaurants, Amada and Tinto, rub elbows with packs of Penn and Drexel students who flock here for the delicious food as well as the karaoke room, 60 tequilas, nightly DJ, and a movie screen flashing scenes from the hit film *Nacho Libre.* Ask for one of the huge rattan booths on the second floor for a truly moving experience—the spinning structures are jury-rigged with wheels. ⊠ *3945 Chestnut St., University City* ☎ *215/222–1657* ⊕ *grg-mgmt.com/distritorestaurant.com* ⊗ *No lunch* ⊟ *AE, D, DC, MC, V* ⊹ *A4.*

$$
THAI

╳ **Lemon Grass Thai.** With occasional deviations (mostly the lunchtime specials), the Thai food here is about as authentic as you can get in town. It's conscientious in its presentation, but down-to-earth enough to be a favorite among Penn students. Pad thai with baby shrimp is among the most popular choices. ⊠ *3626 Lancaster Ave., West Philadelphia*

☎ *215/222–8042* ▭ *AE, D, DC, MC, V* ☻ *Closed Sun. No lunch weekends* ✛ *A3.*

$$$ ✕ **Marigold Kitchen.** This former boardinghouse more than a few blocks
SOUTHERN west of Penn's campus is a surprising foodie haven buried among, and
Fodor's Choice nearly indiscernible from, a sea of Victorian town houses. The homey
★ goldenrod interior is a simple backdrop for the chef's New Southern fare,
artfully plated on spare, white dinnerware. Regulars show up clutching
their best bottles of wine to complement such inspired comfort food
as the signature appetizer of creamy, stone-ground grits topped with a
few plump mussels. The menu is seasonal in ingredients and in tone—in
spring the food actually tastes springy. Case in point: a large morsel of
vivid orange salmon, seared to perfection and served on a tangle of soft,
buttery, fresh-picked leeks. The cheeses and desserts don't disappoint
either; in fact those with the time and appetite should spring for the $60
six-course tasting menu. Reservations recommended. ⊠ *501 S. 45th St.,
West Philadelphia* ☎ *215/222–3699* ⊕ *www.marigoldkitchenbyob.com*
▭ *AE, DC, MC, V* ⛾ *BYOB* ☻ *Closed Mon.* ✛ *A4.*

$$$ ✕ **Nan.** Long before "fusion" was an official foodie term, the inspired
THAI chef here took a wholly different approach to his native Thai cuisine,
pairing it with French ingredients and techniques. As a result, you're
just as likely to find escargots on the menu as chicken *saté.* Others
have followed suit, but Nan is still bewitching diners with an intoxicating mix of flavors: salmon with lemongrass, pork cooked with thyme
and dried fruits, and pheasant with tamarind, to name just a few.
The simple three-course lunch is a bargain; the fruit tart is ethereal.
The service, however, can be spotty. ⊠ *4000 Chestnut St., University
City* ☎ *215/382–0818* ⊕ *www.nanrestaurant.com* ▭ *MC, V* ⛾ *BYOB*
☻ *Closed Sun. No lunch weekends* ✛ *A4.*

$$$ ✕ **Pod.** The futuristic atmosphere of this restaurant (all-white tables and
JAPANESE chairs and partially enclosed booths—or pods—whose lighting changes
color with the touch of a button) is a fitting setting for food with strong
Asian overtones that ultimately defies precise description. The sushi
conveyor is an entertaining touch. Dim sum, stir fry, and crab pad thai
share the menu with entrées such as crispy scallion chicken, wasabi-
crusted filet mignon, and the amusingly named "Lobzilla," a 3-pound
lobster served with risotto and soba noodle salad. There's an extensive
sake bar—you can get it warm or cold. Reservations are essential on
the weekend. ⊠ *3636 Sansom St., University City* ☎ *215/387–1803*
⊕ *www.podrestaurant.com* ▭ *AE, DC, MC, V* ☻ *No lunch weekends*
✛ *A4.*

$$$$ ✕ **White Dog Cafe.** A favorite among University of Pennsylvania students
AMERICAN and professors, this stalwart specializes in locally sourced, sustainable
★ foods including free-range chicken with sage-roasted cheese pump-
kin *panzanella* and pasture-raised pork chops stuffed with apples and
pears. At first reading, seasonings and sides can seem comically com-
plicated, but the combos do work. The small, lively bar has a number
of American beers on tap and in bottles; the wine list, too, is all-Amer-
ican. Vegetarians will find plenty to please them here. Reservations are
recommended. ⊠ *3420 Sansom St., University City* ☎ *215/386–9224*
⊕ *www.whitedog.com* ▭ *AE, D, DC, MC, V* ✛ *A4.*

BEN FRANKLIN PARKWAY AND FAIRMOUNT PARK

$$$ ✕**Figs.** A large fig tree sets the tone for this simple restaurant. Some
MEDITERRANEAN Moroccan specialties are woven through the menu. Otherwise, the
flavors of the Mediterranean permeate. The baked Brie in clay pot
appetizer with honey, lavender, and almonds is a standout; usually
there's a good *tagine* (stew of meat or poultry simmered with veg-
etables, olives, garlic, and spices) on the menu. ✉ *2501 Meredith St.,
Fairmount* ☎ *215/978–8440* ⊕ *www.figsrestaurant.com* ▭ *No credit
cards* ⌗♟ *BYOB* ⊘ *No lunch. Closed Mon.* ✛ *B1.*

$$$$ ✕**Fountain.** Dining here is a cosmopolitan experience, blending unpar-
AMERICAN   alleled service with gorgeous surroundings—gold-rimmed Bernaudad
Fodor's Choice china, sumptuous linens, elegant flower arrangements, handsome wood-
★   paneled walls, and a view of Logan Circle's graceful fountain. The peak
of the experience, however, is unquestionably the food. Miami-bred
Rafael Gonzalez said he'd bring the wow factor when he took over the
kitchen in early 2009, and he does. French techniques and high-quality
ingredients combine to create modern, light masterpieces like an amuse
bouche of hamachi ceviche on a light cracker and an entrée of perfectly
prepared Atlantic wild king salmon perched in a pool of vibrant spinach
nage. Of course, it all pales in comparison to the magnificently deca-
dent chocolate soufflé. The restaurant is off the lavish but understated
lobby of the Four Seasons—a culinary oasis for travelers and a favorite
dining location for well-heeled locals. Especially popular is the Sunday
brunch, a knockout in bounty, elegance—and, at $68 per person, price.
✉ *1 Logan Sq., Benjamin Franklin Parkway* ☎ *215/963–1500* ⊕ *www.
fourseasons.com* ⌕ *Reservations essential. Jacket required* ▭ *AE, D,
MC, V* ✛ *C3.*

$$ ✕**London Grill.** Serving modern takes on old favorites, such as sea scal-
AMERICAN   lops poached in lobster oil with potato blinis, this longtime favorite
keeps locals interested with its seasonally changing menus, which are
imaginative and consistently good. It returns the favor with its commit-
ment to buying local. The bar menu— mussels, wings, and quesadillas—
is popular, especially the burger, which is more often than not in the
running for the city's best. Because it's so close to the Art Museum,
the restaurant often offers special menus to coincide with blockbuster
exhibits. ✉ *2301 Fairmount Ave., Fairmount* ☎ *215/978–4545* ⊕ *www.
londongrill.com* ▭ *AE, D, DC, MC, V* ⊘ *No lunch Sat.* ✛ *B1.*

$$$ ✕**Museum Restaurant.** The venerable Philadelphia Museum of Art gives
AMERICAN   visitors an opportunity to feed their bodies while nourishing their souls
at lunch as well as at Friday dinner and Sunday brunch. The restaurant
is bright, white, and hung with a rotating display of paintings. Dining
options include a prix-fixe menu inspired by a current exhibition and
the Artist's Table, a buffet with unlimited returns, artfully arranges
foodstuffs such as a daily rotisserie, roasted salmon, grilled vegetables,
and a fine cheese board. ✉ *26th St. and Benjamin Franklin Pkwy., Ben-
jamin Franklin Parkway* ☎ *215/684–7990* ⊕ *www.philamuseum.org/
dining* ▭ *AE, DC, MC, V* ⊘ *Closed Mon.* ✛ *B2.*

$$$$ ✕**The Water Works Restaurant.** In the late 1800s these neoclassical struc-
AMERICAN   tures on the river were a trendy hangout for Victorians passing through.
★   After lying fallow for many years, the place was recently reopened as

a restaurant and bar that makes full use of the magnificent view from the grand columned terrace. The food impresses, too. Highlights from the menu, American with touches of the Mediterranean and Greece (the owners are Greek), are the grilled haloumi cheese appetizer, pan-seared bass in saffron-infused tomato broth, and vanilla-butter poached lobster with truffled mashed potato. This place calls for dressing up—no jeans or sneakers. ⊠ *640 Water Works Dr., Benjamin Franklin Parkway* ☎ *215/236–9000* ⊕ *www.thewaterworksrestaurant.com* 🕸 *Reservations essential* ▤ *AE, DC, MC, V* ⊗ *Closed Mon. Brunch on weekends* ✚ *A1.*

NORTHERN LIBERTIES

4

Northern Liberties is a taxi ride from Old City, and therefore not convenient for a lunch stop, but the neighborhood has a burgeoning nightlife scene—and funky restaurants to boot.

⇨ *For restaurants in Manayunk and Germantown, see Chapter 3: Manyunk, Germantown, and Chestnut Hill.*

$$ ✕ **Bar Ferdinand.** Owner Owen Kamihira came to this venture with an
SPANISH impressive design pedigree—he put the Buddha in Buddakan. So it's not
★ surprising that Bar Ferdinand has spectacular decor. What is surprising is that a first-time restaurateur got the food so right—the hot and cold tapas, *bocadillos* (sandwiches), and *pinchos* (skewers) are almost good enough to distract you from the dramatic cut-glass mosaic of Ferdinand the Bull. ⊠ *1030 N. 2nd St., Northern Liberties* ☎ *215/923–1313* ⊕ *www.barferdinand.com* ▤ *MC, V* ⊗ *No lunch* ✚ *H1.*

$–$$ ✕ **Las Cazuelas.** This authentically Mexican family-run place is an anom-
MEXICAN aly in a rather industrial neighborhood. The colors, both inside and out, are warm and bright. The food is simple and rather gently spiced, apropos the family's roots in the town of Puebla. Reservations are essential for groups larger than four. ⊠ *426–28 W. Girard Ave., Northern Liberties* ☎ *215/351–9144* ⊕ *lascazuelas.net* ▤ *MC, V* ✚ *G1.*

$$ ✕ **N. 3rd.** Is it a bar or a restaurant? It seems most like a bar until the
AMERICAN food comes and you taste chef Peter Dunmire's food, which is quite a few steps above pub fare, with steamed mussels in white wine and crispy Atlantic salmon in Thai coconut curry sauce. Weekend brunch here—challah French toast, arugula and beet salad, smoked salmon club sandwich—is one of the best in the neighborhood. ⊠ *801 N. 3rd St., Northern Liberties* ☎ *215/413–3666* ⊕ *www.norththird.com* ▤ *AE, D, MC, V* ⊗ *No lunch weekdays* ✚ *H1.*

$$ ✕ **Silk City Diner Bar & Lounge.** Mark Bee, the local restaurateur behind
AMERICAN favorite gastropub N. 3rd, bought the Silk City Diner in 2006, polished off its grease-coated, 1950s-era pink Formica counter, and started serving updated comfort food including a fierce plate of buttermilk fried chicken, cilantro-spiked calamari, the city's best bowl of mac-and-cheese (baked with a garlic bread crust), and some lighter fare (a honey-roasted beet salad) should you want to go next door to the bar and lounge and dance 'til dawn beneath the disco ball. ⊠ *435 Spring Garden St., Northern Liberties* ☎ *215/592–8838* ⊕ *www.silkcityphilly. com* ▤ *AE, D, MC, V* ✚ *G1.*

$ ✕ **Standard Tap.** This neighborhood gastropub is a Northern Liberties
AMERICAN   fixture, popular with the hipsters who populate this particular neighborhood and for good reason. The menu, presented unpretentiously
on a chalkboard, is much more ambitious—and much tastier—than
you'd expect from average bar food, and since you're in a bar, you can
wash down the grilled octopus, duck confit salad, and roasted beets
with one of the local microbrews on tap. Sunday brunch (think Bloody
Mary's and fried oysters) is always busy. ✉ *901 N. 2nd St., Northern
Liberties* ☎ *215/238–0630* ⊕ *www.standardtap.com* ▭ *AE, DC, MC,
V* ⊙ *No lunch* ✛ *H1.*

BEYOND NORTHERN LIBERTIES

$ ✕ **Memphis Taproom.** Beer aficionado Brendan Hartranft is the master-
AMERICAN   mind behind Philadelphia's newest gastropub. Beef and onion pasties,
short ribs, and sweet-onion-filled fried pastry dough are addictively
good options for soaking up the many tasty brews available. Vegans
swear by the ALT, a version of the BLT with smoked avocado that tastes
better than bacon. Desserts come from neighborhood micro-bakery
BAKED. Expect a rotating list of 30-plus American craft beers in addition to Belgian, German, and English selections by the bottle. Although
the space evokes the air of classic Parisian bistros and Belgian beer cafés,
its decor is a nod to the traditional Philadelphia working-class neighborhood corner taprooms (once called "Tappys"). Artwork is modern, and
much of the building has been restored to its original splendor. Cask ale
lovers come out Saturday mornings, when a different firkin of beer (or
11 gallons) is tapped and gravity poured at room temperature. ✉ *2331
E. Cumberland St., Port Fishington* ☎ *212/425–4460* ⊕ *www.memphi-
staproom.com* ⊳ *Reservations not accepted* ▭ *AE, MC, V* ✛ *H1.*

$$ ✕ **Modo Mio.** Chef/owner Peter McAndrews's narrow, bustling BYOB
ITALIAN   on the Northern Liberties/Fishtown divide lures even Main Line cou-
★   ples into formerly uncharted territory (the restaurant is way north of
Center City). The meal is worth the trek, however, beginning with the
homemade bread—a 15-pound Umbrian loaf sliced thick and served
with olive oil and ricotta cheese. The small plates menu is a menag-
erie of rustic Italian flavors with modern twists, like grilled frogs' legs
accented with green apple and herbed mayonnaise and thin-sliced duck
breast in a cherry-spiked wine sauce. ✉ *161 W. Girard Ave., Fishtown*
☎ *215/203–8707* ⊕ *www.modomiorestaurant.com* ▭ *No credit cards*
⊙ *Closed Sun. and Mon.* ✛ *H1.*

Where to Stay

By Bernard
Vaughan

From historic digs with four-poster beds to grand hotels serving room-service foie gras, Philadelphia has lodgings for every style of travel. Thanks to the Pennsylvania Convention Center and a hotel-building boom in the late 1990s, some mid-price chains have moved into town or have spruced up their accommodations. If you have greater expectations, you need look no further than the city's handful of swank hotels, each with its own gracious character.

Budget, moderate, and luxury properties are spread throughout the downtown area. The Historic Area, on the east side of downtown, centers on Independence Hall and extends to the Delaware River, and is a good base for sightseeing. Old City and Society Hill lodgings are also convenient for serious sightseeing; Society Hill is the quietest of the three areas. For business-oriented trips, Center City encompasses the heart of the downtown business district, centered around Broad and Market streets, and Rittenhouse Square hotels are also nearby.

If you prefer to keep your distance from the tourist throngs, check out the Benjamin Franklin Parkway–Museum Area along the parkway from 16th Street to the Philadelphia Museum of Art. There are also a couple of hotels in University City—just across the Schuylkill River in West Philadelphia and close to the University of Pennsylvania and Drexel University—a 5- to 10-minute drive or taxi ride from Center City.

FACILITIES

Assume that all rooms have private baths unless otherwise noted. Assume that hotels operate on the **European Plan** (EP, with no meals) unless we specify that they use the **Continental Plan** (CP, with a continental breakfast), **Breakfast Plan** (BP, with a full breakfast), **Modified American Plan** (MAP, with breakfast and dinner), or the **Full American Plan** (FAP, with all meals).

RESERVATIONS

Even with the large number of hotel rooms, sometimes it's difficult to find a place to stay, so advance reservations are advised. Philadelphia has no real off-season, but many hotels offer discount packages for weekends, when the demand from business travelers and groups subsides. Besides substantially reduced rates, these packages often include an assortment of freebies, such as breakfast, parking, cocktails, and the use of exercise facilities. Tickets to popular museum shows have become part of many packages, too.

PARKING

Most downtown hotels charge an average of $25 a day for parking, but some include it in the rate. You can find street parking if you're willing to put in the effort, but it is extremely difficult—even for natives. The best time to try is in the early evening, before the nightlife starts

BEST BETS FOR PHILADELPHIA LODGING

Fodor's offers a selective listing of quality lodging experiences in every price range, from the city's best budget beds to its most sophisticated luxury hotels. Here we've compiled our top recommendations by price and experience. The very best properties—in other words, those that provide a particularly remarkable experience in their price range—are designated in the listings with the Fodor's Choice logo.

Fodor's Choice ★

Four Seasons, p. 156
Penn's View Inn, p. 143
Rittenhouse 1715, p. 155
Ritz-Carlton Philadelphia, p. 152
Westin Philadelphia, p. 153

Best by Price

¢

Apple Hostels, p. 142
Chamounix Mansion, p. 158

$

Alexander Inn, p. 147
Best Western Center City, p. 156
Penn's View Inn, p. 143
Thomas Bond House, p. 146

$$

Hampton Inn Philadelphia Center City-Convention Center, p. 149
Hilton Garden Inn Philadelphia Center City, p. 149
Latham, p. 152

$$$

Four Points by Sheraton Philadelphia City Center, p. 148
Lippincott House, p. 154
Loews Philadelphia Hotel, p. 150

$$$$

Four Seasons, p. 156
Park Hyatt Philadelphia at the Bellevue, p. 152
Hotel Sofitel Philadelphia, p. 154
Radisson Plaza Warwick Hotel, p. 154
Ritz-Carlton Philadelphia, p. 152
The Rittenhouse, p. 155
Westin Philadelphia, p. 153

By Experience

BEST LOCATION

Ritz-Carlton Philadelphia, p. 152
The Rittenhouse, p. 155

BEST KEPT SECRET

Four Points by Sheraton Philadelphia City Center, p. 148
The Gables, p. 157
Lippincott House, p. 154

HIPSTER HOTELS

Hotel Sofitel Philadelphia, p. 154
Westin Philadelphia, p. 153

BEST SPA

Four Seasons, p. 156
The Rittenhouse, p. 155

BEST FOR ROMANCE

Four Seasons, p. 156
Loews Philadelphia Hotel, p. 150
Penn's View Inn, p. 143
Rittenhouse 1715, p. 155
The Rittenhouse, p. 155
Ritz-Carlton Philadelphia, p. 152

BEST FOR KIDS

Four Seasons, p. 156
Loews Philadelphia Hotel, p. 150
The Rittenhouse, p. 155
Ritz-Carlton Philadelphia, p. 152
Westin Philadelphia, p. 153

BEST GYM

Loews Philadelphia Hotel, p. 150
Park Hyatt Philadelphia at the Bellevue, p. 152
Sheraton University City, p. 158

BUSINESS TRAVEL

Sheraton University City, p. 158
Four Points by Sheraton Philadelphia City Center, p. 148
The Rittenhouse, p. 155

BEST HOTEL BARS

Loews Philadelphia Hotel, p. 150
Radisson Plaza Warwick Hotel, p. 154
Ritz-Carlton Philadelphia, p. 152

5

up. However, many streets have two-hour time limits until 8 PM—and even midnight in some cases—and the two-hour rule goes into effect at 8 AM, even on Sundays in many places. ■TIP→ **The Best Western Center City near the Philadelphia Museum of Art has free parking.**

USING THE MAP

Throughout the chapter, you'll see mapping symbols and coordinates (✛ E4) at the end of each review. The property's coordinate will point you to where the property is located on the map grid.

PRICES

We always list the facilities that are available, but we don't specify whether they cost extra. When pricing accommodations, always ask what's included and what costs extra.

WHAT IT COSTS					
	¢	$	$$	$$$	$$$$
Hotel	under $100	$100–$150	$151–$200	$201–$250	over $250

Prices are for a standard double room in high season.

HOTEL REVIEWS

Listed alphabetically within neighborhoods. Use the coordinate ✛ G4 at the end of each listing to locate a site on the corresponding map

OLD CITY

¢ 🏨 **Apple Hostels.** This independently owned hostel is downtown's best bargain. It's on the edge of the historic district in a 140-year-old factory and in the center of the most bustling part of Old City. Clean and brightly painted dormitory-style rooms, segregated by gender, have enough bunk beds to accommodate 70 people. Rooms for couples are also available. Guests often gather around the pool table and watch nightly videos in the common area. The facility is a member of Hostelling International. **Pros:** great for the young traveler looking to meet new people; great location for nightlife. **Cons:** dormitory style rooms; can be noisy at night; fee for Wi-Fi. ⊠ *32 S. Bank St., Old City* 🕾 *215/922–0222 or 877/275–1971* ⊕ *www.applehostels.com* 🛏 *70 beds* ⌂ *In-hotel: laundry facilities, Wi-Fi* ▤ *MC, V* ✛ *G4.*

$$$ 🏨 **Best Western Independence Park Hotel.** Surrounded by key historic sites ☾ as well as many nightlife options, this five-story hotel is within walking distance of just about everything you need. Built in 1856, it has been run as a hotel since 1988. The high-ceiling guest rooms have a few period touches; some also have modern conveniences like CD players and docks for your MP3 player. Deluxe rooms have parlors and king-size beds. Complimentary continental breakfast is served in a glass atrium, and afternoon tea and freshly baked cookies are available in the lobby. A complimentary wine and cheese reception is held every Wednesday at 5:30. **Pros:** free snacks and wine; intimate boutique hotel near restaurants, nightlife, and tourist attractions. **Cons:** can be noisy at night;

some rooms have views of brick walls. ✉ *235 Chestnut St., Old City* ☎ *215/922–4443 or 800/624–2988* ⊕ *www.independenceparkinn.com* ⮩ *36 rooms* ♿ *In-room: refrigerator (some), DVD (some), Internet, Wi-Fi. In-hotel: room service, laundry service, Wi-Fi, parking (paid), some pets allowed, no-smoking rooms* ▭ *AE, D, DC, MC, V* ⦙⦿⦙ *CP* ⊹ *G4.*

$$ ⊞ **Holiday Inn Historic District.** This eight-story hotel sits within what is billed as the country's "most historic square mile," within a block and a half of the Liberty Bell and Independence Hall. The rooms are pleasant, and a bargain for this part of the city. **Pros:** relative bargain located close to major tourist attractions. **Cons:** lots of tourists and large groups. ✉ *400 Arch St., Old City* ☎ *215/923–8660 or 800/843–2355* ⊕ *www. holiday-inn.com/phlhistoric* ⮩ *364 rooms, 7 suites* ♿ *In-room: refrigerator (some), Internet, Wi-Fi. In-hotel: 2 restaurants, room service, bar, pool, gym, laundry facilities, laundry service, Internet terminal, Wi-Fi, parking (paid), no-smoking rooms* ▭ *AE, D, DC, MC, V* ⊹ *G4.*

$$$$ ⊞ **Omni Hotel at Independence Park.**
☾ An ornate fireplace dominates the breathtaking marble lobby of this towering hotel in the historic district. Enjoy cocktails in the adjoining lounge, which occasionally features live music. The spacious rooms, many of which overlook bustling Old City, have basic traditional furniture, flat-screen televisions, and sofas. All are decorated in clean whites, deep blues, and cream colors. Bathrooms have large marble baths and lighted makeup mirrors. Children are treated to complimentary cookies and milk.

This is a pleasant base for visiting the nearby art galleries and cafés, as well as the Liberty Bell, Independence Hall, and other sights. **Pros:** excellent location for historic touring and Old City revelry; boutique feel; good service; nice views; known to offer good sale rates. **Cons:** some rooms can get noisy at night from proximity to nightlife. ✉ *401 Chestnut St., Old City* ☎ *215/925–0000 or 800/843–6664* ⊕ *www. omnihotels.com* ⮩ *150 rooms, 2 suites* ♿ *In-room: safe, refrigerator, Internet, Wi-Fi. In-hotel: restaurant, room service, bar, pool, gym, spa, laundry service, parking (paid), Wi-Fi, no-smoking rooms* ▭ *AE, D, DC, MC, V* ⊹ *G4.*

$$ ⊞ **Penn's View Inn.** This cosmopolitan little hotel in a refurbished 19th-century commercial building on the fringe of Old City has its own brand of urban charm. The owner is a well-regarded Italian-born restaurateur who also runs Ristorante Panorama, the downstairs eatery, and Il Bar, with perhaps the best wine cellar in the city. Accommodations are comfortable and rather European looking, with Chippendale-style furniture, floral wallpaper, and queen beds; 20 rooms have fireplaces, and 12 of

Fodor's Choice
★

5

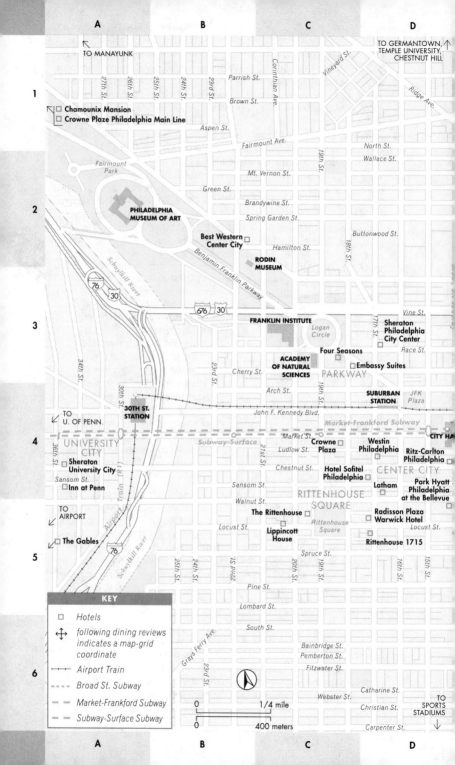

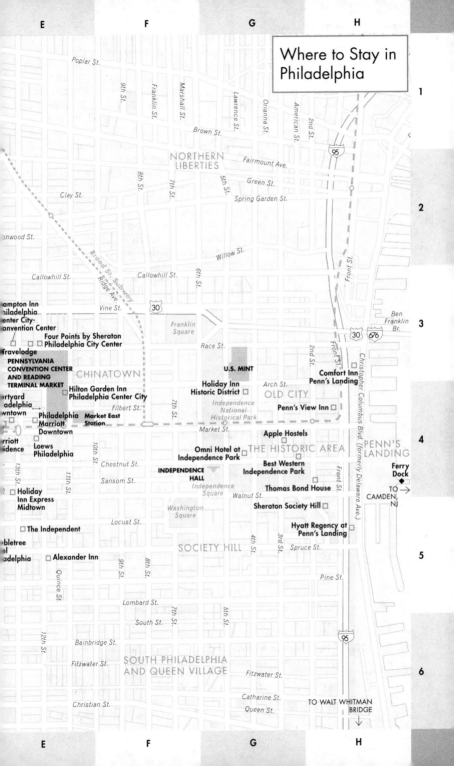

Where to Stay in Philadelphia

E   **F**   **G**   **H**

1

Poplar St.

9th St.

Franklin St.

Marshall St.

Lawrence St.

Orianna St.

American St.

2nd St.

Brown St.

95

NORTHERN
LIBERTIES

Fairmount Ave.

Clay St.

8th St.

7th St.

5th St.

Green St.

Spring Garden St.

2

onwood St.

Broad St. Subway

Ridge Ave.

Willow St.

Front St.

Callowhill St.

Callowhill St.

6th St.

Ben
Franklin
Br.

ampton Inn
hiladelphia
enter City-
onvention Center

Vine St.

30

Four Points by Sheraton
Philadelphia City Center

Franklin
Square

Race St.

30 676

Front St.

3

Travelodge

PENNSYLVANIA
CONVENTION CENTER
AND READING
TERMINAL MARKET

CHINATOWN

Hilton Garden Inn
Philadelphia Center City

Filbert St.

7th St.

U.S. MINT

Holiday Inn
Historic District

Arch St.

Independence
National
Historical Park

2nd St.

Front St.

Comfort Inn
Penn's Landing

OLD CITY

Penn's View Inn

Christopher Columbus Blvd. (formerly Delaware Ave.)

rtyard
adelphia
wntown

Philadelphia
Marriott
Downtown

Market East
Station

Market St.

Apple Hostels

THE HISTORIC AREA

PENN'S
LANDING

4

rriott
idence

Loews
Philadelphia

10th St.

11th St.

Chestnut St.

Sansom St.

Omni Hotel at
Independence Park

INDEPENDENCE
HALL

Independence
Square

Best Western
Independence Park

Thomas Bond House

Front St.

Ferry
Dock

TO →
CAMDEN,
NJ

13th St.

Holiday
Inn Express
Midtown

Locust St.

Washington
Square

Walnut St.

Sheraton Society Hill

Hyatt Regency at
Penn's Landing

4th St.

3rd St.

Spruce St.

5

bletree
el
adelphia

The Independent

Alexander Inn

9th St.

8th St.

Quince St.

SOCIETY HILL

Pine St.

12th St.

Lombard St.

South St.

7th St.

5th St.

Bainbridge St.

Fitzwater St.

SOUTH PHILADELPHIA
AND QUEEN VILLAGE

Fitzwater St.

95

6

Christian St.

Catharine St.

Queen St.

TO WALT WHITMAN
BRIDGE

↓

E   **F**   **G**   **H**

them also have whirlpool baths. Some have views of the Delaware River. **Pros:** good service, generous continental breakfast including waffles, romantic atmosphere. **Cons:** gym is tiny; rooms facing I–95 can be noisy. ⊠ *14 N. Front St., Old City* ☎ *215/922–7600 or 800/331–7634* ⊕ *www.pennsviewhotel.com* ➥ *51 rooms, 2 suites* ⚭ *In-room: Internet, Wi-Fi. In-hotel: restaurant, room service, bar, gym, Wi-Fi, parking (paid), no-smoking rooms* ═ *AE, D, DC, MC, V* ⧉⊙⧉ *CP* ✛ *H4.*

$–$$ ⬚ **Thomas Bond House.** This bed-and-breakfast in the heart of Old City is great for travelers who want an authentic taste of historic Philadelphia. Built in 1769 by a prominent local physician (an enormous family tree detailing his descendents hangs from a wall in a common living room), the four-story Georgian house has undergone a faithful, meticulous restoration. Everything from the home's molding and wall sconces to the woodwork and flooring has been restored. Rooms have reproduction period furnishings (there are also a few antiques), including four-poster beds, and two have marble fireplaces. In keeping with the Colonial theme, some rooms are a tad cold in winter. Continental breakfast is served weekdays; a full breakfast is served on weekends. Complimentary coffee, tea, and ice water are always on hand, and wine and cheese is served nightly. **Pros:** historic home; good service. **Cons:** some guests complain of noise when nearby bars let out at 2 AM, there are also some complaints about closet space and hot water; no elevator. ⊠ *129 S. 2nd St., Old City* ☎ *215/923–8523 or 800/845–2663* ⊕ *www. thomasbondhousebandb.com* ➥ *10 rooms, 2 suites* ⚭ *In-room: Internet, Wi-Fi. In-hotel: laundry service, Wi-Fi, parking (paid), no-smoking rooms* ═ *AE, D, MC, V* ⧉⊙⧉ *CP* ✛ *H4.*

SOCIETY HILL AND PENN'S LANDING

$–$$ ⬚ **Comfort Inn at Penn's Landing.** The reasonable price is the main attraction at this 10-story hotel. Near several busy streets, the location has more noise than charm—but if you have a room on an upper floor facing the river you can enjoy a good view of the Benjamin Franklin Bridge lighted up at night. A bar helps enliven the small, nondescript lobby. Old City is a long walk (there is a pedestrian bridge on Market Street) or a short cab ride across busy I–95, but the courtesy van service to Center City is a nice plus. The hotel is a good location and value if you're visiting for a concert at the Susquehanna Bank Center across the Delaware River in Camden. **Pros:** cheaper downtown alternative; nice views of the river and Benjamin Franklin Bridge; free shuttle to Center City. **Cons:** a bit isolated from Center City. ⊠ *100 N. Columbus Blvd., Penn's Landing* ☎ *215/627–7900 or 800/228–5150* ⊕ *www.comfortinn.com* ➥ *185 rooms, 2 suites* ⚭ *In-room: safe, Internet, Wi-Fi. In-hotel: bar, pool, gym, laundry service, Wi-Fi, parking (paid), no-smoking rooms* ═ *AE, D, DC, MC, V* ⧉⊙⧉ *CP* ✛ *H3.*

$$$$ ⬚ **Hyatt Regency at Penn's Landing.** The theme here is "room with a view." ⟳ The first hotel to open on the banks of the Delaware River offers dramatic river views from both back and front rooms of the 22-story tower. The fourth-floor fitness center overlooks the city and the waterfront; after you swim in the indoor pool, you can lounge on the outdoor terrace. Likewise, Keating's River Grill has both indoor seating and

alfresco dining on a deck above the river. The guest rooms are contemporary and well sized. **Pros:** nice indoor pool with option to sit outside; great views. **Cons:** separated from Old City by I–95; it can feel a tad isolated. ✉ *201 S. Columbus Blvd., Penn's Landing* ☎ *215/928–1234 or 800/233–1234* ⊕ *www.pennslanding.hyatt.com* ⟲ *350 rooms, 10 suites* ♿ *In-room: safe, kitchen (some), refrigerator (some), Internet, Wi-Fi. In-hotel: restaurant, room service, bar, pool, gym, laundry service, parking (paid)* ▤ *AE, D, DC, MC, V* ✛ *H5.*

> **WORD OF MOUTH**
>
> "We stay at the Alexander Inn every time we visit Philly, which is a couple times a year. The location is great and within walking distance to everything you would want to do in Center City. The staff is friendly, and the continental breakfast setup is one of the best I've seen in a long while."
>
> —bryanc75

$$$–$$$$ ⊞ **Sheraton Society Hill.** Convenient to downtown sights, this Colonial-style building is two blocks from Penn's Landing, three blocks from Head House Square, and four blocks from Independence Hall. Framed by archways, the pleasant atrium lobby is flooded with natural light during the day and lighted by wrought-iron lanterns at night. Guest rooms, completely renovated in 2007, are done in restful shades of beige, brown, and maroon. The fourth-floor rooms facing east toward the Delaware River have the best views. The glass ceiling over the indoor pool provides an outdoor feel year-round. A Starbucks is in the lobby, and in-room coffeemakers feature the popular brand. **Pros:** natural light and abundant plant life make for a pleasant, outdoorsy lobby; choice of two restaurants and a bar on premises; within walking distance of Old City nightlife, but not bothered by its noise at night; $10 shuttle available to airport. **Cons:** can be a bit of a walk to Old City attractions; fee for Wi-Fi. ✉ *1 Dock St., Society Hill* ☎ *215/238–6000 or 800/325–3535* ⊕ *www.sheraton.com* ⟲ *365 rooms, 13 suites* ♿ *In-room: Internet, Wi-Fi. In-hotel: 2 restaurants, room service, bar, pool, gym, laundry service, Internet, Wi-Fi, parking (paid), some pets allowed, no-smoking rooms* ▤ *AE, D, DC, MC, V* ✛ *H5.*

CENTER CITY EAST

$–$$ ⊞ **Alexander Inn.** The nicely refurbished rooms at this small hotel have an Art Deco feel. The property is close to the Pennsylvania Convention Center, the Avenue of the Arts, and most downtown attractions. Though straight-friendly, it has a largely gay clientele, and is near some of the city's gay bars. ▮TIP→ **For the lone budget traveler, the Alexander offers rooms with twin beds for $119 a night.** **Pros:** great location between Rittenhouse Square and historic district; quiet yet near lively nightlife; away from touristy spots; great service; Web specials on room rate. **Cons:** older building; no laundry facilities or services; bar downstairs can get noisy; tiny gym. ✉ *12th and Spruce Sts., Center City East* ☎ *215/923–3535 or 877/253–9466* ⊕ *www.alexanderinn.com* ⟲ *48 rooms* ♿ *In-room: safe, Wi-Fi. In-hotel: gym, Internet terminal, Wi-Fi, parking (paid), no-smoking rooms* ▤ *AE, D, DC, MC, V* ⓘ◎ *CP* ✛ *E5.*

$$$ 🍴 **Courtyard Philadelphia Downtown.** This hotel is in the historic City Hall Annex, and the original brass, copper, and bronze details on the elevators and staircases have been lovingly refinished. It's across the street from its sister property, the Philadelphia Marriott; both provide easy access to the Pennsylvania Convention Center. The hotels share some facilities—meeting rooms, for example. The comfortable guest rooms—renovated in 2007—have business-friendly amenities like full-size desks. Some rooms have excellent views of City Hall's elaborate

Victorian architecture. The new fitness center gets plenty of natural light and features machines equipped with flat-screen televisions. **Pros:** centrally located; architecturally beautiful; good service. **Cons:** central location can make for difficulty in picking up and dropping off car. ⊠ *21 N. Juniper St., Center City East* ☎ *215/496–3200 or 800/321–2211* ⊕ *www.marriott.com* ⇆ *427 rooms, 61 suites* ⚐ *In-room: refrigerator (some), DVD (some), Internet, Wi-Fi. In-hotel: restaurant, room service, bar, pool, gym, laundry facilities, laundry service, Internet terminal , Wi-Fi, parking (paid), no-smoking rooms* ▭ *AE, D, DC, MC, V* ✛ *E4.*

$$$ 🍴 **Doubletree Hotel Philadelphia.** The hotel's sawtooth design ensures that each room has a peaked bay window with an eye-popping 180-degree view. Rooms on the east side look out toward the Delaware River, while west-side rooms overlook Broad Street. The four-story atrium lobby lounge observes one of the busiest corners of Philly's theater district, directly across the street from the handsome Academy of Music and a short walk from the Kimmel Center. Refurbished contemporary guest rooms are decorated in white and blond tones, with separate vanities. Academy Café has good contemporary food and pleasant service. The Standing O Bar/Bistro serves burgers, sandwiches, and lighter fare. **Pros:** great location for the theatergoer; good views; sunny and unique lobby. **Cons:** lots of groups can make for a hectic lobby. ⊠ *237 S. Broad St., Center City East* ☎ *215/893–1600 or 800/222–8733* ⊕ *www.doubletree.com* ⇆ *432 rooms, 5 suites* ⚐ *In-room: Internet. In-hotel: 2 restaurants, room service, bar, pool, gym, laundry service, Internet terminal, Wi-Fi, parking (paid), no-smoking* ▭ *AE, D, DC, MC, V* ✛ *E5.*

$$$ 🍴 **Four Points by Sheraton Philadelphia City Center.** With its understated boutique-like charms, this Four Points, opened in December 2008, offers a practical yet homey alternative to some of its larger neighbors in the convention center area. A hardwood-floor foyer with wall coat hangers sets the tone, and an enormous work area featuring slide-out desks and flat-screen televisions is conducive to work and rest. Bathrooms with glass-enclosed showers—but no tubs—have a sharp modern feel, and there is ample closet space. A gym with brand new exercise machines is open 24 hours. Chase Lounge and Restaurant is a popular spot for local professionals as well as hotel guests. **Pros:** affordable; new; modern yet intimate. **Cons:** no tub for those who like baths; low-key signage has caused some confusion. ⊠ *1201 Race St., Center City East* ☎ *215/496-2700* ⊕ *www.starwoodhotels.com* ⟿ *92 rooms* ⌂ *In-room: refrigerator (some), Internet, Wi-Fi. In-hotel: restaurant, room service, bar, gym, laundry service, Internet terminal, Wi-Fi, parking (paid), no-smoking rooms* ▭ *AE, D, DC, MC, V* ⊕ *E3.*

$$ ⊡ **Hampton Inn Philadelphia Center City-Convention Center.** This hotel bills itself as the "best value hotel in Center City" and backs it up with a gym, business center, and, weather permitting, complimentary break-fast on a patio facing 13th Street. Rooms have full-length mirrors and spacious bathrooms with long marble countertops. The hotel is a short walk away from the Convention Center, Reading Terminal Market, and Chinatown. **Pros:** excellent value for convention center events; friendly service. **Cons:** not much nightlife within walking distance. ⊠ *1301 Race St., Center City East* ☎ *215/665–9100 or 800/426–7866* ⊕ *www.hamptoninn.com* ⟿ *250 rooms, 20 suites* ⌂ *In-room: Internet, Wi-Fi, In-hotel: pool, gym, laundry facilities, laundry service, Internet terminal, Wi-Fi, parking (paid), no-smoking rooms* ▭ *AE, D, DC, MC, V* ⦿❘ *BP* ⊕ *E3.*

$$ ⊡ **Hilton Garden Inn Philadelphia Center City.** This hotel is an affordable alternative to other hotels near the Pennsylvania Convention Center. It's within walking distance of the Reading Terminal Market, the Gal-lery Mall, Chinatown, and many historic sites. Rooms are spacious and simply designed, with comfortable beds that allow you to adjust firmness, spacious desks, and flat-screen televisions. The "Stay Fit Kit" provides an in-room Pilates band, yoga mat, abs ball, resistance rope, and light weights. Like its neighbors near the convention center, it sits in an area that can be desolate after dark. **Pros:** nice rooms; good value; a central location. **Cons:** convention center neighborhood can be quiet and dark at night. ⊠ *1100 Arch St., Center City East* ☎ *215/923–0100 or 800/774–1500* ⊕ *www.hiltongardenphilly.com* ⟿ *159 rooms, 120 suites* ⌂ *In-room: refrigerator, Internet, Wi-Fi. In-hotel: restaurant, room service, bar, pool, gym, laundry facilities, laundry service, Inter-net terminal, Wi-Fi, parking (paid), no-smoking rooms* ▭ *AE, D, DC, MC, V* ⊕ *E4.*

$$$ ⊡ **Holiday Inn Express Midtown.** What this hotel lacks in frills it more than makes up for with its central location, free access to a nearby health club, and complimentary breakfast bar. Rooms are surprisingly spacious, with contemporary furnishings, large work desks, and sepa-rate vanity areas. A pungent odor of carpet deodorizer in the hall-ways thankfully does not seem to seep into the rooms. The location is excellent: one block from the Broad Street subway, near the theater and shopping district, and three blocks from the Pennsylvania Con-vention Center. During busy hours, be prepared to wait in line in a small lobby with lots of kids and groups. **Pros:** location; big rooms; free continental breakfast. **Cons:** small lobby can get cramped with groups; funky smells in common areas; lots of congested traffic during daylight hours. ⊠ *1305 Walnut St., Center City East* ☎ *215/735–9300*

5

or 800/564–3869 ⊕ *www.himidtown.com* 🛏 *168 rooms* ⚄ *In-room: Wi-Fi. In-hotel: pool, laundry service, Wi-Fi, parking (paid), no-smoking rooms* ⊟ *AE, D, DC, MC, V* ⦿*CP* ⊕ *E4.*

$ ⚄**The Independent.** The Independent meets Philadelphia's desperate need for alternatives to big convention hotels. This boutique property features 24 well-appointed, hip, high-tech rooms that are all uniquely furnished, but share a warm butterscotch and ochre palette with funky accents, such as leopard-print rugs, exposed brick walls, and copper-tiled ceilings. Touchpad screens on the in-room telephones allow guests to control temperature and lights from their bedside, and are pre-set for dialing hand-picked local restaurants. The hotel's corridors ring a skylighted four-story atrium adorned with a well-known local muralist's work. Complimentary wine and cheese is served every evening in the cozy lobby, and a continental breakfast is served there each morning. **Pros:** even on a busy street, there is not a smidgen of street noise. **Cons:** the brand-new hotel still has some kinks to work out, such as lights that flicker on and off without warning, but the staff is highly attentive to fixing these snafus. ⊠ *1234 Locust St., Center City East* ☎ *215/772–1440* ⊕ *www.theindependenthotel.com* 🛏 *24 rooms* ⚄ *In-room: safe, kitchen (some), refrigerator, Internet, Wi-Fi. In-hotel: room service, Wi-Fi, no-smoking rooms* ⊟ *AE, D, DC, MC, V* ⊕ *E5.*

$$$ ⚄ **Loews Philadelphia Hotel.** Topped by the red neon letters PSFS (for the
↻ former tenant, Pennsylvania Savings Fund Society), this 1930s building was the country's first skyscraper in the ultramodern international style. With an attitude that is decidedly contemporary, the hotel has guest rooms equipped with comfortable chaise lounges and flat-screen televisions. ■TIP→ **Complimentary toys and games are available for children.** There are three levels of concierge rooms with a private library and lounge. The lobby lounge and Sole Food, an eclectic, fusion seafood restaurant, both have Art Deco touches. A 15,000-square-foot state-of-the-art fitness center includes a sauna, steam room, and indoor lap pool. Be sure to check out the 33rd floor for sweeping views of the city and beyond. **Pros:** architectural gem; cool style throughout; amazing views, nice bathrobes and coffeemakers. **Cons:** some guests have complained about the smell of smoke in rooms; you might need a cab to get to nightlife destinations. ⊠ *1200 Market St., Center City East* ☎ *215/627–1200 or 800/235–6397* ⊕ *www.loewshotels.com* 🛏 *568 rooms, 15 suites* ⚄ *In-room: safe, refrigerator, Wi-Fi. In-hotel: restaurant, room service, bar, pool, gym ,spa, laundry service, Wi-Fi, parking (paid), some pets allowed, no-smoking rooms* ⊟ *AE, D, DC, MC, V* ⊕ *E4.*

$$$$ ⚄ **Marriott Residence Inn.** Originally the Market Street National Bank,
↻ this building from the 1920s has a beautifully restored Art Deco facade. (The rooms remain mostly Marriott.) You can choose between studios or one- or two-bedroom suites; all have full kitchens, living rooms, and work areas. Novel amenities include grocery shopping (the staff will pick up items for you) and complimentary dinner Monday to Thursday. The hotel is a big hit with families with small children. Across from City Hall, this hotel is close to all major downtown destinations. **Pros:** centrally located; novel amenities; nice option for families. **Cons:** pricey

parking; central location makes it hard to drop off and pick your car. ⊠ *1 E. Penn Sq., corner of Market and Juniper Sts., Center City East* ☎ *215/557–0005 or 800/331–3131* ⊕ *www.residenceinn.com* ⤴ *269 suites* ♿ *In-room: kitchen, refrigerator, Wi-Fi. In-hotel: bar, gym, laundry facilities, laundry service, Internet terminal, Wi-Fi, parking (paid), pets allowed, no-smoking rooms* ▭ *AE, D, DC, MC, V* ⦙◯⦙ *BP* ✢ *E4.*

$$$-$$$$ ⛆ **Philadelphia Marriott Downtown.** This bustling convention hotel—the biggest in Pennsylvania—fills an entire city block. It has so many corridors that even the staff sometimes gets lost. For an intrinsically impersonal type of place, the Marriott tries hard to meet special needs; it also offers some of the lowest rates in its price category. The five-story lobby atrium has a water sculpture and comfortable seating areas with modern furniture. The more than 1,400 guest rooms are brightly decorated. You can request, at no additional cost, one of the 250 "rooms that work," with adjustable desks and extra lighting and outlets. The hotel has a sushi bar and a Starbucks. The hotel restaurant, 13, serves contemporary American food. ▮TIP➜ **If you're driving, you may want to park in a public parking lot, as the hotel charges upwards of $43 a night.** **Pros:** centrally located; clean rooms; potential for good deals; good for traveling families or businesspeople. **Cons:** crowds, crowds, and more crowds; parking is a whopping $43 a night. ⊠ *1201 Market St., Center City East* ☎ *215/625–2900 or 800/228–9290* ⊕ *www.philadelphiamarriott.com* ⤴ *1,408 rooms, 76 suites* ♿ *In-room: refrigerator (some), Internet. In-hotel: 2 restaurants, room service, bar, pool, gym, spa, laundry facilities, laundry service, Wi-Fi, parking (paid), no-smoking rooms* ▭ *AE, D, DC, MC, V* ✢ *E4.*

$-$$ ⛆ **Travelodge.** On the edge of Chinatown, this small hotel has a location as good as many other downtown hotels but charges much less. There's not much in the way of amenities, but the bare-bones accommodations are fine for a brief stay. Rooms are done in a green-and-beige color scheme and have small bathrooms (a separate sink and mirror are in the bedroom). All rooms have work areas with high-speed Internet access. A skylight from the fourth-story ceiling floods the corridors with natural light. **Pros:** affordable, bare-bones option for Center City. **Cons:** small; bare-bones; dominated by convention-goers. ⊠ *1227–29 Race St., Center City East* ☎ *215/564–2888 or 800/578–7878* ⊕ *www.travelodge. com* ⤴ *50 rooms* ♿ *In-room: safe, Internet, Wi-Fi. In-hotel: Wi-Fi, parking (paid), no-smoking rooms* ▭ *AE, D, MC, V* ⦙◯⦙ *CP* ✢ *E3.*

CENTER CITY WEST

$$$$ ⛆ **Crowne Plaza Philadelphia Downtown.** Located in the heart of the city's financial district, the Crowne Plaza is also a short walk from Rittenhouse Square and the Market Street shopping area, as well as historic City Hall. Guest rooms have a contemporary beige and deep gold color scheme and sinks in some of the rooms are separate from the bathroom. Guests on the Club Level share a private lounge. The Elephant & Castle serves British food and an extensive selection of draft beers. ▮TIP➜ **If you're looking for a serene stay, there's a "quiet floor" that bans children and tour groups and housekeeping dares not enter before 10** AM. Large groups can make checking in and out taxing, but the refurbished lobby

features comfy seating areas with large flat-screen televisions, and a coffee shop and bar are steps away. **Pros:** great central location; can be a bargain compared to other Center City options; $10 shuttle to airport. **Cons:** some guests complain about careless service. ⊠ *1800 Market St., Center City West* ☎ *215/561–7500 or 800/227–6963* ⊕ *www.crowneplaza.com* ➥ *445 rooms, 2 suites* ⟁ *In-room: Internet. In-hotel: restaurant, room service, bar, pool, gym, laundry facilities, laundry service, Internet terminal, Wi-Fi, parking (paid), no-smoking rooms* ⊟ *AE, D, DC, MC, V* ⊹ *C4.*

$$ ⬚ **Latham.** Overlooking the bustling Walnut Street shopping area and a block from Rittenhouse Square, this small, elegant boutique offers a relatively good value for its location. The Victorian-style rooms, which are on the small side, are done up in traditional hunter green or contemporary black and tan and are furnished with marble-top bureaus, Louis XV–style writing desks, and full-wall mirrors; bathrooms have marble showers. **Pros:** great location; decent price. **Cons:** small rooms; some guests find it old and run down. ⊠ *135 S. 17th St., Center City West* ☎ *215/563–7474 or 877/528–4261* ⊕ *www.lathamhotel.com* ➥ *138 rooms, 1 suite* ⟁ *In-room: Internet, Wi-Fi. In-hotel: gym, laundry service, parking (paid), no-smoking rooms, Internet terminal, Wi-Fi* ⊟ *AE, D, DC, MC, V* ⊹ *D4.*

$$$$ ⬚ **Park Hyatt Philadelphia at the Bellevue.** A Philadelphia institution for
★ almost a century, the Bellevue continually offers elegant lodging at the very heart of the city. The spacious rooms, done in bright prints, have large walk-in closets and the high ceilings and moldings typical of older buildings; some mark-ups and peeling suggest the rooms and hallways could use an update. The posh restaurant, XIX (Nineteen), features excellent food and stunning views of the city from its 19th-floor perch. Topped by a 30-foot stained-glass dome, XIX is also great for tea and cocktails. The hotel's lower floors feature a food court, an upscale sports bar, and high-end stores like Tiffany and Ralph Lauren. The 93,000-square-foot gym, featuring a running track, squash courts, racquetball courts, and a basketball court, is the best hotel gym in the city. A few blocks away from City Hall, the Bellevue is within walking distance of most attractions. **Pros:** centrally located; shopping downstairs; old-school elegance; amazing gym. **Cons:** rooms and hallways could use an upgrade; fee for Wi-Fi. ⊠ *200 S. Broad St., Center City West* ☎ *215/893–1234 or 800/233–1234* ⊕ *www.parkhyatt.com* ➥ *172 rooms, 13 suites* ⟁ *In-room: safe, DVD, Internet, Wi-Fi. In-hotel: 4 restaurants, room service, bars, pool, spa, laundry service, Internet terminal, Wi-Fi, parking (paid), some pets allowed, no-smoking rooms* ⊟ *AE, D, DC, MC, V* ⊹ *D5.*

$$$$ ⬚ **Ritz-Carlton Philadelphia.** You'll feel like you're checking into the Pan-
Fodor'sChoice theon when you enter this neoclassical hotel set in a century-old bank
★ building. More than 60,000 square feet of Georgian white marble is
☾ sparsely decorated with palms, classical statues, comfortable contemporary seating arrangements, and well-chosen antiques. Ionic columns ascending the height of nine stories dwarf the lobby lounge, and natural light cascades through the oculus of the 140-foot dome ceiling. A drink in the lobby is a treat, even if you're not staying here. Guest rooms

are surprisingly small and could use some better soundproofing, but have modern touches like flat-screen televisions, glass-enclosed showers, and lighted makeup mirrors. Let them know if it's your birthday or another special occasion, and they should greet you with champagne. The hotel also offers an iPod walking tour. 10 Arts by Eric Ripert, the hotel restaurant, uses organic local ingredients for its take on contemporary American cuisine. The hotel offers toys for children. **Pros:** stunning architecture (the lobby bar is unparalleled); attentive and friendly service; modern in-room amenities. **Cons:** rooms are smaller than some luxury competitors; street noise can be a problem; some room outlets do not work; fee for Wi-Fi ($9.95 per day); elevators can be slow; gym is spare. ⊠ *10 S. Broad St., Center City West* ☎ *215/523–8000 or 800/241–3333* ⊕ *www.ritzcarlton.com* 🛏 *303 rooms, 36 suites* 🛆 *In-room: safe, DVD, Internet, Wi-Fi. In-hotel: restaurant, room service, bar, gym, spa, laundry service, Internet terminal, Wi-Fi, parking (paid), some pets allowed, no-smoking rooms* ▭ *AE, D, DC, MC, V* ✛ *D4.*

> ## THE RITZ-CARLTON BUILDING
>
> Originally home to the Girard Trust Company—named after early-19th-century Philadelphia shipping magnate Stephen Girard—this building was designed and built between 1905 and 1908 by the famed architecture firm McKim, Meade & White, which also designed the Pennsylvania Station in New York, the Algonquin Club in Boston, and the West and East Wings of the White House, among numerous other notable landmarks. The gleaming marble in the elegant lobby supposedly comes from the same Italian quarry mined for Michelangelo's David.

$$$$

Fodor's Choice
★
☺

 📺 **Westin Philadelphia.** If luxurious accommodations and plenty of shopping are your top priorities, you're not going to beat the Westin. The 15-story structure sits between the twin blue towers of Liberty Place and near the Shops at Liberty Place, where you can find more than 70 stores, boutiques, and restaurants. The hotel underwent substantial renovations in 2007, adding contemporary touches like sleeker furniture and plasma televisions. The top-notch fitness center features video monitors on each treadmill. ■**TIP→ If you prefer privacy while you work out, ask for a room with its own fitness equipment.** The hotel restaurant serves American fare with locally grown organic products. Kids 12 and under get a Westin Kids Club amenity package upon check-in. **Pros:** close to best shopping areas; excellent beds; comfortable furniture; quiet. **Cons:** pricey parking; fee for Internet. ⊠ *99 S. 17th St., at Liberty Pl., Center City West* ☎ *215/563–1600 or 800/937–8461* ⊕ *www.westin.com/philadelphia* 🛏 *275 rooms, 19 suites* 🛆 *In-room: safe, refrigerator (some), Internet, Wi-Fi. In-hotel: restaurant, room service, bar, gym, laundry service, Internet terminal, Wi-Fi, parking (paid), some pets allowed, no-smoking rooms* ▭ *AE, D, DC, MC, V* ✛ *D4.*

RITTENHOUSE SQUARE

$$$$ **Hotel Sofitel Philadelphia.** In the middle of the city's French Quarter,
★ this luxury hotel has more of a hip feeling than some of its stuffier Federal-style neighbors. The simplicity of Shaker quilts inspired the lobby
floor, done in seven types of granite and marble. Shades of brown, gold,
green, and blue hues give the rooms a warm, tranquil feel. Rooms have
large desks, flat-screen televisions, and spacious bathrooms with glass-
enclosed showers and oversize tubs. The hotel's gym is open 24 hours.
Chez Colette, the trademark brasserie, pays homage to the famous
writer; vintage French advertisements decorate the walls. **Pros:** luxury
with a hipper feel; excellent location; great service. **Cons:** it's central
location can make driving in and out of the hotel a pain. ⊠ *120 S. 17
St., Rittenhouse Square* ☎ *215/569–8300 or 800/763–4835* ⊕ *www.
sofitel.com* ⤳ *306 rooms, 68 suites* ⟨ *In-room: safe, Internet, Wi-Fi.
In-hotel: restaurant, room service, bar, gym, laundry service, Internet
terminal, Wi-Fi, parking (paid), some pets allowed, no-smoking rooms*
⊟ *AE, D, DC, MC, V* ⊕ *D4.*

$$$ **Lippincott House.** Guests at this new B&B get closer to old Ritten-
house Square high society than any of the Lippincott's notable neigh-
borhood rivals. A prominent publisher built this mansion, a block off
Rittenhouse Square, in 1897, and a law firm crowded into its rooms
until proprietor Jack Eldridge bought it in 1997. Before opening as a
B&B in 2008, Eldridge installed an elevator as well as new bathrooms
and a modernized kitchen, from which hot breakfast is served daily.
Eldridge kept intact the building's many charms, including a lounge
graced with stunning rosewood wall paneling, an enormous mahogany
fireplace, and an 1887 grand piano; common areas also include an
antique Brunswick pool table. Original artwork lines the hallways, and
one room features an original wall mural of a village in Tuscany where
the original owner's daughter married. Guests are known to take a good
deal of photos before they leave the building. All rooms have original
fireplaces, though they don't work. **Pros:** historic yet intimate; quiet;
attentive service. **Cons:** it can seem a little dark in some areas. ⊠ *2023–25
Locust St., Rittenhouse Square* ☎ *215/523–9251* ⊕ *www.lippincotthouse.
com* ⤳ *4 rooms* ⟨ *In-room: no phone (some), refrigerator (some), no
TV (some), Wi-Fi (some). In-hotel: Internet terminal, Wi-Fi, some pets
allowed* ⊟ *AE, D, DC, MC, V* ⊌ *BP* ⊕ *C5.*

$$$$ **Radisson Plaza Warwick Hotel.** This classic hotel, first opened in 1926,
has returned to claim its place among the best Philadelphia hotels after
extensive renovations in 2007. The ornate lobby's off-white colors,
sky-motif ceiling, and enormous chandelier lend it an airy vibe; it's a
relaxing spot to read the paper with a coffee before heading out for
the day. The pleasant, bright guest rooms are decorated in soft earth
tones. Though it's a Radisson with more than 300 rooms, it feels like
a boutique thanks to friendly service and rooms with modern touches
like large work desks, flat-screen televisions, and Sleep Number beds.
There's also a new gym and the Plaza Club Level, which pampers you
with complimentary hors d'oeuvres and drinks every evening. The hotel
is around the corner from Rittenhouse Square and Walnut Street. On
weekend nights an adjoining new restaurant, Tavern 17, welcomes you

with live music. **Pros:** historic hotel with modern amenities; great location; great service. **Cons:** smallish bathrooms. ✉ *1701 Locust St., Rittenhouse Square* ☎ *215/735–6000 or 800/333–3333* ⊕ *www.radisson. com/philadelphiapa* ⟳ *301 rooms, 4 suites* ⚬ *In-room: safe (some), Internet, Wi-Fi. In-hotel: 3 restaurants, room service, bar, gym, laundry facilities, laundry service, Wi-Fi, parking (paid), some pets allowed, no-smoking rooms* ⊟ *AE, D, DC, MC, V* ⊕ *D5.*

$$$–$$$$
Fodor's Choice
★

🔅 **Rittenhouse 1715.** On a small street near Rittenhouse Square, this refined, European-style mansion offers the luxury of a large hotel in an intimate space on the fourth floor. Every room has its own understated personality, with Louis XVI–inspired chairs, vintage mirrors, Chippendale-style tables, and neoclassical rugs; some have skylights. Some rooms have larger, glass-enclosed showers. You can also rent the entire mansion for special occasions, as many celebrities have done to protect their privacy. A wine reception is held daily from 5:30 to 6:30 in the lobby, where you can relax on fauteuil-style chairs. It's also ideal for a romantic weekend. **Pros:** quiet option for downtown; romantic. **Cons:** quiet. ✉ *1715 Rittenhouse Square St., Rittenhouse Square* ☎ *215/546–6500 or 877/791–6500* ⊕ *www.rittenhouse1715. com* ⟳ *19 rooms, 4 suites* ⚬ *In-room: safe, Wi-Fi. In-hotel: laundry service, Internet terminal, Wi-Fi, no-smoking rooms* ⊟ *AE, D, DC, MC, V* ⊚ *CP* ⊕ *D5.*

$$$$
☾
★

🔅 **The Rittenhouse.** Service at this small luxury hotel begins about two weeks before your stay with a handy concierge e-mail asking for any special requests: dining reservations, hometown newspaper (they can print 500 different newspapers), flower arrangement for your loved one, you name it. The hotel also caters to new mothers with their "Anything a mother might have left behind" service. The staff, among the nicest in the city, greets you with a glass of champagne and chocolate-covered strawberries, while children can borrow from a "treasure chest" of toys and teens get a complimentary movie and popcorn. The 33-story building's sawtooth design gives the large guest rooms unusual shapes, with nooks and alcoves; many of the rooms overlook the famous square. Each room has a large marble bathroom with a glass-enclosed shower and small flat-screen television on the sink; many also have whirlpool tubs. The management is deeply involved in community affairs, and promotes local artists at the third-floor Satellite Gallery and with the placement of original art throughout the hotel. The restaurant, Lacroix, puts a sumptuous French spin on local ingredients. **Pros:** great service without the stuffiness; among the largest rooms for luxury hotels; quiet. **Cons:** furniture can seem a bit dated; pricey. ✉ *210 W. Rittenhouse Sq., Rittenhouse Square* ☎ *215/546–9000 or 800/635–1042* ⊕ *www.*

> **KID TIP**
>
> Most hotels in Philadelphia allow children under a certain age to stay in their parents' room at no extra charge, but others charge for kids as extra adults; be sure to find out the cutoff age for children's discounts. Babysitting services, children's toys, cookies, and other amenities are offered at several upscale hotels such as Loews, The Rittenhouse, The Four Seasons, and The Westin.

5

rittenhousehotel.com ⇘ *87 rooms, 11 suites* ⚿ *In-room: safes, kitchen (some), refrigerator (some), DVD (some), Internet, Wi-Fi. In-hotel: 3 restaurants, room service, bars, pool, gym, spa, laundry service, Internet terminal, Wi-Fi, parking (paid), some pets allowed, no-smoking rooms* ▭ *AE, D, DC, MC, V* ✛ *C5.*

BENJAMIN FRANKLIN PARKWAY

$ 🖼 **Best Western Center City.** Close to the Philadelphia Museum of Art and the Rodin Museum, this affordable hotel is perfect for art lovers. Rooms come with all the basics, including coffeemakers, ironing boards, and spacious work areas. The best views are from rooms facing south toward the downtown skyline. **Pros:** affordable option near Art Museum area; free parking. **Cons:** long walk to most Center City destinations; not within walking distance of Old City historical attractions; immediate surroundings can be desolate at night; some guests say it's not very clean and needs updating. ⊠ *501 N. 22nd St., Benjamin Franklin Parkway* ☎ *215/568–8300 or 800/528–1234* ⊕ *www. bestwestern.com* ⇘ *183 rooms, 4 suites* ⚿ *In-room: Wi-Fi. In-hotel: 2 restaurants, bar, pool, gym, laundry facilities, laundry service, Internet terminal, Wi-Fi, parking (free), no-smoking rooms, some pets allowed* ▭ *AE, D, DC, MC, V* ✛ *B2.*

$$$$ 🖼 **Embassy Suites.** On Logan Square, this hotel puts you within walk-
☾ ing distance of Boathouse Row. Suites have separate living rooms with sofa beds, dining areas, and private balconies, many with stunning views of nearby Fairmount Park. Business suites have spacious desks with ergonomic chairs. A hot breakfast is served every morning at an adjacent T.G.I. Friday's, but it can be chaotic; there is a more relaxing evening reception—with complimentary beer, wine, and light snacks daily from 5:30 to 7:30. **Pros:** large rooms; great views. **Cons:** can get noisy; often a wait for the elevators. ⊠ *1776 Benjamin Franklin Pkwy., Benjamin Franklin Parkway* ☎ *215/561–1776 or 800/362–2779* ⊕ *www.embassysuites.com* ⇘ *288 suites* ⚿ *In-room: kitchen, refrigerator, Internet, Wi-Fi. In-hotel: restaurant, room service, bar, gym, laundry facilities, laundry service, Internet terminal, Wi-Fi, parking (paid), no-smoking rooms* ▭ *AE, D, DC, MC, V* ⦿ *BP* ✛ *C3.*

$$$$ 🖼 **Four Seasons.** On the outskirts of the finance district, this landmark
Fodor's Choice is within walking distance of the Philadelphia Museum of Art and
★ the department stores along Walnut Street. Furnishings are in a for-
☾ mal traditional style. The staff indulges you (with in-room exercise equipment and hypoallergenic pillows, upon request), your children (with milk and cookies at bedtime), and your pet (with fresh-baked dog biscuits and bottled water served in a silver bowl). Other amenities include complimentary limousine service within Center City. Rooms on the hotel's north side offer the best views of the Greek Revival public library and family court, Logan Circle, and the Cathedral of Saints Peter and Paul. The Fountain Restaurant is one of the best in town, and the Swann Lounge one of the liveliest at cocktail time. **Pros:** excellent service; comfy beds; good pool. **Cons:** be sure to dress up for the on-site restaurant and bar; rooms are smaller than those of some of its luxury competitors. ⊠ *1 Logan Circle, Benjamin Franklin Parkway*

☎ *215/963–1500 or 800/332–3442* ⊕ *www.fourseasons.com/phila-delphia* ⇌ *364 rooms, 102 suites* ⵣ *In-room: safe, refrigerator, DVD, Internet, Wi-Fi. In-hotel: 3 restaurants, room service, bar, pool, gym, spa, laundry service, Internet terminal, Wi-Fi, parking (paid), some pets allowed, no-smoking rooms* ▭ *AE, D, DC, MC, V* ⵕ *C3.*

$$$$ 🏨 **Sheraton Philadelphia City Center.** Although it's a popular convention hotel, this hotel also caters to both business and leisure travelers. The hotel also features a new business center with laptop computers. Rooms, decorated in beige and dark blue, feature oversize desks, nice touches like full-length mirrors, and complimentary bottled water and Starbuck's coffee. The hotel also has a private health club. **Pros:** good location between Art Museum and convention center; clean contemporary rooms. **Cons:** large convention crowds; long waits to check in and out. ⊠ *17th and Race Sts., Benjamin Franklin Parkway Area* ☎ *215/448–2000 or 800/822–4200* ⊕ *www.starwoodhotels.com* ⇌ *744 rooms, 15 suites* ⵣ *In-room: Internet, Wi-Fi. In-hotel: 2 restaurants, room service, bar, pool, gym, laundry service, Internet terminal, Wi-Fi, parking (paid), some pets allowed, no-smoking rooms* ▭ *AE, D, DC, MC, V* ⵕ *D3.*

UNIVERSITY CITY

$ 🏨 **The Gables.** Built in 1889 for a prominent doctor and his family, this ornate mansion is a wonderful place for a B&B. The ground-floor parlor and entryway feature natural cherry and chestnut wood, and the guest rooms have oak floors with elaborate inlays of mahogany, ash, and cherry. In the dining room, guests are served a hot breakfast. An idyllic wraparound porch is perfect for reading a morning paper. One room has a glass-enclosed sitting porch, and two have working electric fireplaces. The owners—who live in the building—are avid collectors of Victoriana, so just about every knickknack or piece of furniture is more than a century old. **Pros:** off the beaten path; lots of antiques and Victoriana; free parking. **Cons:** off the beaten path; the abundance of Victoriana can be a bit much. ⊠ *4520 Chester Ave., University City* ☎ *215/662–1918* ⊕ *www.gablesbb.com* ⇌ *10 rooms, 1 suite* ⵣ *In-room: DVD, Wi-Fi. In-hotel: parking (free), no-smoking rooms, Internet terminal, Wi-Fi* ▭ *AE, D, MC, V* ⵏ⵿ *BP* ⵕ *A5.*

$$$$ 🏨 **Inn at Penn.** Near the University of Pennsylvania, this hotel is a welcome sight for anyone needing to stay in University City. The hotel, with a grand staircase in the lobby and a beautiful wood-paneled library with working fireplace, has a warm, collegiate atmosphere. Up-to-date amenities abound, such as two phone lines, two-tiered work areas, and digital temperature control. Grab a free *Philadelphia Inquirer* at your door after breakfast at the University Club. The Penne Restaurant and Wine Bar features regional Italian cuisine and an extensive wine list. Rates rise at certain times, including graduations. **Pros:** collegiate feel near major campuses. **Cons:** some guests say the service is lacking. ⊠ *3600 Sansom St., University City* ☎ *215/222–0200 or 800/445–8667* ⊕ *www.theinnatpenn.com* ⇌ *238 rooms, 8 suites* ⵣ *In-room: safe, Internet, WiFi . In-hotel: 2 restaurants, room service, bar, gym, laundry service,*

Internet terminal, Wi-Fi, parking (paid), no-smoking rooms ⊟ *AE, D, DC, MC, V* ⊕ *A4.*

$$$ ⛯ **Sheraton University City.** With plush beds and 36-inch flat-screen televisions, spacious work areas, and free in-room desktop computers with free Internet access, this hotel offers a nice balance of luxury and practicality. For a caffeine fix, there are in-room coffeemakers with Starbucks coffee. The new gym, which is open 24 hours, has top-of-the-line treadmills and elliptical machines. The hotel is within walking distance of 30th Street Station, the University of Pennsylvania, Drexel University, and, on a nice day, downtown Philadelphia. **Pros:** free computer with Internet access; 24-hour gym. **Cons:** check-in during big weekends, such as graduation, can be tiresome. ⊠ *3549 Chestnut St., University City* ☎ *215/387–8000 or 877/459–1146* ⊕ *www.sheraton.com/university-city* ⤴ *332 rooms, 25 suites* ⚙ *In-room: Internet, Wi-Fi. In-hotel: restaurant, room service, bar, pool, gym, laundry service, public Internet, parking (paid), some pets allowed* ⊟ *AE, D, DC, MC, V* ⊕ *A4.*

CITY LINE AVENUE

City Avenue is a 10-minute ride on the Schuylkill Expressway to Center City.

¢   ⛯ **Chamounix Mansion.** This is the cheapest place to stay in Philadelphia—$20 a night if you're a Hostelling International member, $23 if you're not. The restored 1802 Federal-style country estate is loaded with character. Flags line the entrance hall; rooms are styled after an 1850 country villa, and walls are decorated with old maps, sketches, and paintings. There's a self-service kitchen and a tennis court a short walk away. Chamounix Mansion is a 15-minute walk from a bus stop, but access to a car might be best; call for directions. **Pros:** off the beaten path; cheap; scenic. **Cons:** off the beaten path. ⊠ *3250 Chamounix Dr., City Line Avenue* ☎ *215/878–3676 or 800/379–0017* ⊕ *www.phila-hostel.org* ⤴ *80 beds, with shared baths* ⚙ *In-room: no phone, no TV. In-hotel: Wi-Fi, bicycles, laundry facilities, Internet, Wi-Fi* ⊟ *MC, V* ⊙ *Closed mid-Dec.–mid-Jan.* ⊕ *A1.*

$$ ⛯ **Crowne Plaza Philadelphia Main Line.** This eight-story hotel is a good value in a choice location—like its neighbors, it's close to downtown as well as trendy Manayunk. Large groups are known to check in—it's a popular venue for weddings and banquets—so let someone else wait in line for you while you sink into one of the lobby's overstuffed easy chairs. Guest rooms are decorated in earth tones with sharp, contemporary furniture and a spacious work desk. Complimentary newspapers are available in the lobby. The glass-enclosed pool, which becomes an outdoor pool in summer, gets plenty of natural light. **Pros:** affordable option on City Avenue; recently renovated. **Cons:** lots of large groups such as weddings and banquets; some complain of poor service. ⊠ *4100 Presidential Blvd., City Line Avenue* ☎ *215/477–0200 or 800/642–8982* ⊕ *www.cpmainline.com* ⤴ *337 rooms, 3 suites* ⚙ *In-room: safe, Internet, Wi-Fi. In-hotel: restaurant, room service, bar, pool, gym, laundry facilities, laundry service, Internet terminal, Wi-Fi, parking (free), no-smoking rooms* ⊟ *AE, D, DC, MC, V* ⊕ *A1.*

Nightlife and the Arts

By Piers
Marchant

Philadelphia has a rhythm of its own. Whether you're listening to the Philadelphia Orchestra while picnicking on the lawn at the Mann Center for the Performing Arts, or having a jazz brunch at one of the countless fab places all over town, you'll soon be caught up in that rhythm.

You can listen to a chanteuse in a chic basement nightclub, dance till 2 AM in a bustling bistro, or sip cocktails in any number of swank lounges. South Street between Front and 9th streets is still hip, with one-of-a-kind shops, bookstores, galleries, restaurants, and bars that attract the young and the restless in droves. Today, however, those in the know head to the trendy bars and clubs of Old City, where the crowd is a bit more chic and upscale, or to the hipster artist enclave of Northern Liberties. Over the past few years Main Street in Manayunk, in the northwest section of the city, has also arrived as a fashionable nightlife destination. More than a dozen clubs line the Delaware River waterfront, most near the Benjamin Franklin Bridge. Besides its club scene, Philadelphia also has larger venues—and draws big names—for rock, pop, and jazz concerts.

There's no shortage of live entertainment, ranging from the Philly Pops to the Philadelphia Folk Festival. There are also summer concerts of popular and classical music at the Penn's Landing amphitheater, right on the shore of the Delaware River, and at Fairmount Park's Mann Center for the Performing Arts. Huge rock groups stop in Philadelphia on their national tours, playing at the Wachovia Center; the Keswick Theatre, in suburban Glenside; or the Susquehanna Bank Center in Camden, New Jersey. Smaller bands hit great venues like the TLA on South Street, the Trocadero in Chinatown, and the World Cafe Live—home of WXPN's famed radio broadcast—in University City.

This is a city of neighborhoods, and you can find entertainment in all of them. From Broadway shows at the Forrest Theater to performance art and poetry readings at the Painted Bride, there's always something new to explore. The city's Avenue of the Arts cultural district on North and South Broad streets is one significant sign of the continued energy in town. Of the arts facilities on the avenue, some are long-standing, such as the stunning Academy of Music and the Merriam Theater; others, including the Wilma Theater and the Prince Music Theater, are more recent additions, along with the Kimmel Center for the Performing Arts, the spectacular home of the Philadelphia Orchestra. Depending on the time of year, you might also be able to take part in citywide arts festivals like the renowned International Film Festival in spring or the cutting-edge Fringe Festival in autumn.

FIVE GREAT NIGHTLIFE EXPERIENCES

Southwark: The vibe of this Queen Village bar/restaurant is like something out of *Casablanca*, with its throwback cocktails and heavy wood bar, the food—call it French countryside—is just as timeless.

Standard Tap: The array of draft beers is but one of the many draws of this two-floor Northern Liberties mainstay.

Fluid: It remains one of Philly's classic DJ venues, everyone from ?uestlove to Jazzy Jeff has spun their magic here.

32°: This luxe lounge in the heart of Old City attracts a largely European crowd; they even accept euros.

Tria: Casual without being sloppy, knowledgeable without being snooty, this wine and cheese bar has two locations and a fermentation school for vino higher learning.

NIGHTLIFE

6

Generally speaking, you can break down Philly's central nightlife hubs into four distinct areas: South Street offers teens and young twenty-somethings block after block of bars, tattoo parlors, and erotica shops; Old City is very popular with out-of-towners and beautiful party people, with higher-end clubs, bars, and restaurants, and, like South Street, is swarmed on weekends; Northern Liberties is a boho oasis, with artists, hipsters, and the edgily affluent mingling in the burgeoning bar scene there; and, finally, Rittenhouse Square offers high-end libations and refreshment for the well-heeled, or for those wanting to pretend for a night. Outside of Center City, University City has all the standard (and not so standard) college-appropriate bars and clubs; East Passyunk is an up-and-coming neighborhood, replete with an assortment of fine restaurants, hipster bars, and old-school South Philly Italian joints; and Manayunk is one of the spots of choice for those recently graduated from college or working their first professional jobs.

For current information, check the entertainment pages of the *Philadelphia Inquirer*, the free alt-weekly *City Paper* or *Philadelphia Weekly*, the *Philadelphia Gay News* (PGN), and *Philadelphia* magazine.

Bars and clubs can change hands or go out of business faster than a soft pretzel goes stale. Many places are open until 2 AM; cover charges vary from free to about $12. Some may not be open every night, so call ahead. A few places do not accept credit cards, so carry some cash. While Philly tends toward the casual in many of its nightlife venues, there are strict dress codes enforced in some of the clubs along the Delaware Avenue strip and elsewhere. Best to check Web sites to make certain if you're venturing into new territory.

BARS AND LOUNGES

OLD CITY

Home to a large proliferation of bars, clubs, and swank restaurants, Old City was long thought of as the place South Street revelers eventually headed after they got through adolescence. It remains a major lynchpin of out-of-towner socializing, but with such high-end joints as Amada, 32°, and Anjou, the area has accomplished its own kind of maturation.

Continental Restaurant & Martini Bar. This retro former diner draws a hip, twentysomething crowd to its swank setting for cocktails and a tapas-style dinner menu. The design, including lots of stainless steel and lighting fixtures resembling olives stabbed with toothpicks, is worth checking out. ✉ *138 Market St., Old City* ☎ *215/923–6069* ⊕ *www.continentalmartinibar.com.*

★ **Il Bar.** The wine bar at Panorama, a northern Italian restaurant in the Penn's View Inn, stands out for its 120-bottle selection, daily tastings, curved bar, and romantic atmosphere. It's open seven nights a week, with a separate entrance from the restaurant. ✉ *14 N. Front St., Old City* ☎ *215/922–7800* ⊕ *www.pennsviewhotel.com.*

CENTER CITY EAST

Including Society Hill and the Washington Square district, Center City east of Broad offers everything from decadent nightspots to exquisite dining.

Fodor's Choice ★ **Apothecary Lounge.** At Apothecary Lounge, the complex, delicious cocktails are not drinks, they're elixirs. You can saunter into this gorgeous, modern spot and order an absinthe, or have them whip up a Booty Collins, a stunning combination of green tea–infused gin, cayenne, valerian root, and brandied cherries. Chemistry has never been so wickedly delicious. ✉ *102 S. 13th St., Center City East* ☎ *215/735–7500* ⊕ *apothecarylounge.com.*

Dirty Frank's. Frank is long gone, but this place is still dirty, cheap, and a Philadelphia classic. An incongruous mixture of students, artists, journalists, and resident characters crowds around the horseshoe-shaped bar and engages in friendly mayhem. ✉ *347 S. 13th St., Center City East* ☎ *215/732–5010.*

Fergie's Pub. This cozy taproom is a comfortable spot for a burger and a brew. Downstairs there's a fun jukebox with samplings from Sinatra to U2; upstairs, on Tuesday and Thursday, there's always an action-packed round of Quizzo, a team trivia game. ✉ *1214 Sansom St., Center City East* ☎ *215/928–8118* ⊕ *www.fergies.com.*

★ **McGillin's Olde Ale House.** For longevity alone, McGillin's can stand proud. Open continuously since 1860, it remains the oldest such watering hole in the country. But don't assume it's all powdered wigs and wooden flasks—in recent years the joint has installed many flat-screen TVs to go with their monster karaoke nights and continuously updating Twitter account. You can try locally brewed beer here; they have everything from Yards to Flying Fish, in addition to a good-sized list of imports. ✉ *1310 Drury St., Center City East* ☎ *215/735–5562* ⊕ *www.mcgillins.com.*

WORD OF MOUTH

"Some time and a spent tab later, we again hit the road down Chestnut Street towards the packed Continental Mid-town, again with no reservations but steered to a most-satisfying 3rd-floor partially-enclosed rooftop bar. The three-story 'global tapas' restaurant/bar has a brow-raising 70s theme with enough modern spin to avoid James-Lileks-style savagery, but on the 3rd floor the all-Lucite bar in the round complete with the semi-shag carpet, fiberglass Eames-wannabe chairs, wicker papasans in the corners, and white-porcelain-glazed metal fireplace in the round give us all pause, then a bit of the giddies. Which turned into stun when we perused the bar menu and noticed that half the cocktails were based on a diabetic dare. One drink contained Kool-aid with a glass rimmed in crushed Smarties; Pam ordered one containing, I kid you not, Tang."

—Ahaugeto

CENTER CITY WEST

A slightly more swank side of town, encompassing both Rittenhouse and Fitler's squares, as well as Walnut Street's famed Restaurant Row, Center City west of Broad Street conjures up Philly's enduring legacy as a major cosmopolitan destination.

XIX (Nineteen). On the 19th floor of the Park Hyatt at the Bellevue, this high-end lounge bestows beautiful vistas of the city, a seafood-centric menu, a roaring fireplace, and leather and mahogany accents. Stodgy? A bit, and certainly pricey, but the views alone more than make up for it. ⊠ *200 S. Broad St., Center City West* ☎ *215/790–1919* ⊕ *www.hyatt. com/gallery/nineteen/xix.html.*

Black Sheep. This handsome pub is just off Rittenhouse Square in a refurbished town house with a Mission-style fireplace on the main floor and a quiet dining room on the upper level. Beer lovers can choose from nearly a dozen local and imported brews on tap, and many more by the bottle. Bring an appetite, too: the impressive kitchen cooks up delicious comfort food like fish-and-chips and shepherd's pie. ⊠ *247 S. 17th St., Center City West* ☎ *215/545–9473* ⊕ *www.theblacksheeppub.com.*

★ **Continental Mid-Town.** A more audacious incarnation of the Old City staple, the Mid-Town offers much the same as the original but does so on two floors of ambient gorgeousness. A full menu and two bars serve the overflowing crowds of trendy folks looking to make a night of it. ⊠ *1801 Chestnut St., Center City West* ☎ *215/567–1800* ⊕ *www. continentalmidtown.com.*

Happy Rooster. The boys once ruled this venerable, upscale roost—house rules prohibited unescorted women from sitting at the bar. Today, under owner Rose Parrotta, anyone is free to relax at the handsome rosewood bar accented by brass lanterns. Those seeking more privacy may wish to enjoy a cocktail at one of the cozy booths. In either case, be sure to sample a well-prepared dish from the ever-changing blackboard menu—choices might include a classic Caesar salad, a deluxe burger with fries, or scrambled eggs and caviar. ⊠ *118 S. 16th St., Center City West* ☎ *215/963–9311.*

Fodor's Choice
★
The Rotunda and the 10 Arts Lounge. Under the soaring, 140-foot-high rotunda of this former bank building, refashioned as the Ritz-Carlton Philadelphia, is an elegant lobby bar with marble floors and over-stuffed couches—a gracious spot to have a before-or after-dinner cocktail or indulge in a decadent dessert. Just off the lobby is the handsome 10 Arts Lounge, a smaller restaurant/bar, opened by celebrity chef Eric Ripert, that specializes in light fare and cocktails. ⊠ *10 S. Broad St., Broad and Chestnut Sts., Center City West* ☎ *215/523–8000* ⊕ *www.10arts.com.*

Fodor's Choice
★
Swann Lounge. Melodious jazz and luscious desserts are served on Friday and Saturday nights in this extremely elegant lounge in the Four Seasons. You can dance to the trio's music in between sampling confections from the Viennese-style dessert buffet. A Sunday brunch with contemporary jazz and big band music is also offered. ⊠ *18th St. and Benjamin Franklin Pkwy., Center City West* ☎ *215/963–1500* ⊕ *www. fourseasons.com/philadelphia/dining/swann_lounge.*

RITTENHOUSE SQUARE

The Bards. A lively and authentic Irish pub, the Bards has an Irish crowd, Irish food, and a host of full-bodied beers. ⊠ *2013 Walnut St., Rittenhouse Square* ☎ *215/569–9585* ⊕ *www.bardsirishbar.com.*

Tank Bar. This bar is on the second floor of Friday, Saturday, Sunday, a longtime Rittenhouse Square neighborhood restaurant. Tiny white lights, strategically placed mirrors, and a tank full of exotic tropical fish add just the right touches of comfort and sophistication. ⊠ *261 S. 21st St., Rittenhouse Square* ☎ *215/546–4232* ⊕ *www.frisatsun.com.*

★ **Tria.** This is a wine bar, to be sure, but one that manages to disavow the typically snooty aspect of the oenophile. As proof, they also happily offer a great selection of beer, and there is also an elegant menu of cheeses and other snacks—don't miss out on the truffled mushroom bruschetta. They have two locations in Center City plus a Fermentation School where you can learn much more about the art and science of wine. ⊠ *123 S. 18th St., Rittenhouse Square* ☎ *215/972–8742* ⊕ *www. triacafe.com* ⊠ *1137 Spruce St., Penn's Landing* ☎ *215/629–9200.*

Twenty Manning. The intimate lounge area and sleek bar at this chic Rittenhouse Square restaurant-bar make for great people-watching. You'll see a mix of downtown professionals, artistic types, and couples on first dates. Wear something black to feel most at home. ⊠ *261 S. 20th St., Rittenhouse Square* ☎ *215/731–0900* ⊕ *www.twentymanning.com.*

★ **The Walnut Room Redux.** An über-cool vibe permeates this upscale Rittenhouse bar, due in no small part to its penchant for surreptitiousness—the unmarked entrance on Walnut Street leads you up two flights of stairs to the well-heeled front room, overlooking the street. Once inside, you can find your way to the back bar, where sultry, dimly-lighted tables and booths await you. There, you can enjoy a rose-petal martini and discreetly check out the other patrons. ⊠ *1709 Walnut St., Rittenhouse Square* ☎ *215/751–0201* ⊕ *www.walnutroomredux.com.*

SOUTH PHILADELPHIA

Once known primarily for the Italian Market and cheesesteak icons Pat's and Geno's, South Philly has rapidly gentrified and has added much welcome diversity. In Bella Vista, where the famed Italian Market resides, a plethora of new French restaurants have joined the existing Old World pasta houses and bars; in Queen Village new hot spots have sprung up amidst the familiar staples and BYOs.

For Pete's Sake. A friendly neighborhood joint, Pete's could easily be mistaken for just another comfy watering hole, but the menu is eclectic and varied, including tuna tacos, baby back ribs, crab mac and cheese, and several varieties of humus. Part sports bar, part gastro pub, Pete's hits the sweet spot. ⊠ *900 S. Front St., Queen Village* ☎ *215/462–2230* ⊕ *www.forpetes-sakepub.com.*

★ **L'etage.** Upstairs from parent restaurant Beau Monde, a fine French crêperie, this unique spot has a vast selection of wines and liquors. They also offer up some unique entertainments in the form of the regular Martha Graham Cracker Cabaret—a kind of snarky satire show— and monthly excursions with the First Person Arts Association's Story Slams, wherein storytellers get to present their finest in front of a large, adoring crowd. ⊠ *624 S. 6th St., Bella Vista* ☎ *215/592–0656* ⊕ *www. creperie-beaumonde.com.*

★ **New Wave Café.** To its devoted Queen Village clientele the New Wave is more than just the place to wait for a table at Dmitri's, the always-crowded seafood restaurant across the street. The regulars come to this long, narrow bar a few blocks off South Street to unwind with a local Yuengling beer (referred to, simply, as "lager"), play a game of darts, and enjoy a surprisingly innovative and oft-changing menu, including flatbread pizzas, grilled tuna, and homemade gnocchi. ⊠ *784 S. 3rd St., Queen Village* ☎ *215/922–8484* ⊕ *newwavecafe.com.*

Royal Tavern. In the wilds of the Bella Vista neighborhood, the Royal serves both nouveau hipsters and entrenched locals with equal aplomb. Beer—both local and imported—is abundant, but so are fine mixed drinks and better-than-average comfort food. To top it off, there's a great jukebox, rocking Iggy Pop, Serge Gainsbourg, and The Kinks. ⊠ *937 E. Passyunk Ave., Bella Vista* ☎ *215/389–6694* ⊕ *www.royal-tavern.com.*

★ **Southwark.** This place is a throwback to the days before martinis had to be chocolate. That isn't to say the excellent bartenders can't fashion you a fancy, newfangled drink (in fact, the key-lime martini is pretty fabulous), just that you won't necessarily need one, sitting up against the simple-yet-elegant bar. The food—consider it "French countryside"—is also excellent. ⊠ *701 S. 4th St., Queen Village* ☎ *215/238–1888.*

WORD OF MOUTH

"I do recommend as perhaps you're wandering from Independence Hall over toward Rittenhouse Square/Italian Market to check out South Street. Youthful, often trendy, sometimes tacky, not to everyone's taste..nevertheless can be fun and worth a look-see at least to see what it's about, and maybe pick up a cheesesteak while you're at it."

—Daniel_Williams

Philly's Music History

Philly holds a special place in pop music history. *American Bandstand*, hosted by Dick Clark, began here as a local dance show. When it went national in 1957, it gave a boost to many hometown boys, including teen heartthrob Fabian, Bobby Rydell, Frankie Avalon, and Chubby Checker, of "Twist" fame. Sun Ra, the legendary jazz pianist, was from Philly, in keeping with the city's rich tradition of jazz luminaries such as saxophonists Grover Washington Jr., Stan Getz, and John Coltrane, drummer Philly Joe Jones, and vocalist Billie Holiday. In the 1970s the Philadelphia Sound—a polished blend of disco, pop, and rhythm and blues—came alive through producers Kenny Gamble and Leon Huff at the famed

Philadelphia International Records studios for artists like The Ojays, Lou Rawls, Teddy Pendergrass, and Three Degrees, whose mega-hit "Love Train" helps to define the '70s era. That lush sound was kept alive by chart toppers such as Hall and Oates, Patti LaBelle, and Boyz II Men, and, within the last decade, rapper/actor Will Smith, as well as former spoken-word artist Jill Scott, hip-hop pioneers the Roots, R&B/neo-soul stylist Musiq Soulchild, hip-hop pinup girl Ethel Cee, the full-bodied South Philly pipes of Pink, and young R&B sensation Jazmine Sullivan. The Philly DJ scene is also potent, including spinners King Britt, RJD2, Rich Medina, Diplo, and ?uestlove, who keep the party pumping at clubs throughout the city.

NORTHERN LIBERTIES AND BEYOND

Gentrification has brought Northern Liberties and the northern nearby neighborhoods of Port Richmond and Fishtown much more than skyrocketing rents—a nightclub and restaurant renaissance is afoot in this area, which spans from Spring Garden Street past Girard Avenue up through Allegheny Avenue, and from Delaware Avenue to 6th Street. The neighborhoods still have an industrial, working-class feel, though much of the area's old industry—including printing, textiles, and metalworking—is long gone.

The **Northern Liberties Neighborhood Association** (☎ 215/627–6562 ⊕ *www.northernliberties.org*) has information on the burgeoning nightlife scene.

The Abbaye. This neighborhood bar serves five kinds of Belgian beer and a largely Belgian menu that includes clams, meatballs, and steak frites. ✉ *3rd St. and Fairmount Ave., Northern Liberties* ☎ *215/627–6711.*

Bar Ferdinand. Continuing in the neighborhood's delightful Latino-influenced trend, Ferdinand's menu consists of a wide variety of Spanish tapas and an impressive wine list. ✉ *1030 N. 2nd St., Northern Liberties* ☎ *215/923–1313* ⊕ *www.barferdinand.com.*

★ **Johnny Brenda's.** A funky, cozy joint and the epitome of the burgeoning Fishtown neighborhood revitalization, JB's is filled to the gills with hipsters, old-timers, and other denizens of North Philly. This gastro pub offers plenty of edgy live music, Mediterranean chow, and local beer taps. ✉ *1201 N. Frankford Ave., Fishtown* ☎ *215/739–9684* ⊕ *www.johnnybrendas.com.*

Memphis Taproom. Another local favorite, the Taproom offers more than 10 beers on-tap from local and international breweries, in addition to its more than 50 available bottles. Their innovative gastro-pub menu offers plenty of veggie, vegan, and gluten-free items. ✉ *2331 E. Cumberland St., Port Richmond* ☎ *215/425-4460* ⊕ *www.memphistaproom.com.*

North Bowl. For an evening of 10 pins, Galaga, booze, and crunchy tater tots, North Bowl is hard to beat. ✉ *909 N. 2nd St., Northern Liberties* ☎ *215/238-2695* ⊕ *www.northbowlphilly.com.*

North Third. A casual bar and lounge with varied entertainment from Thursday through Saturday—usually live music ranging from acoustic rock and blues to jazz and funk, short films, or comedy shows. ✉ *801 N. 3rd St., Northern Liberties* ☎ *215/413-3666* ⊕ *www.norththird.com.*

Fodor's Choice
★ **Standard Tap.** With its dimly lighted interior, cherrywood bar, and jukebox—not to mention up to 13 beers on tap each night—this neighborhood fixture is prime for conversation, people-watching, or simply sipping your brew. It also has surprisingly good food. ✉ *901 N. 2nd St., Northern Liberties* ☎ *215/238-0630* ⊕ *www.standardtap.com.*

GAY AND LESBIAN BARS

The gay scene in Philadelphia revolves around the "Gayborhood" as it is affectionately referred to, an area in Center City East roughly from Chestnut to Pine and 11th to Broad streets. It is rife with gay-friendly bars, clubs, shops, boutiques, and cafés.

For articles and more on the Philly gay scene, including a map of the Gayborhood, check out the *Philadelphia Gay News* (⊕ *www.epgn.com*).

The Bike Stop. A multi-floored space, down a side alley, the Bike Stop caters specifically to those seeking leather-clad adventures. ✉ *206 S. Quince St., Center City East* ☎ *215/627-1662* ⊕ *www.thebikestop.com.*

Bump. With its futuristic Euro vibe, the joint fits in nicely with the neighborhood's gay scene. They have a full menu, many happy-hour specials, and a big selection of specialty cocktails. ✉ *1234 Locust St., Center City East* ☎ *215/732-1800* ⊕ *www.bumplounge.com.*

Sisters Nightclub. The most popular lesbian spot in the Gayborhood and a destination dance club for all others, its 5,000-square-foot dance floor is commonly described as "epic." ✉ *1320 Chancellor St., Center City East* ☎ *215/735-0735* ⊕ *www.sistersnightclub.com.*

Woody's. Philadelphia's most popular gay bar is spread over two levels, offering several bars—with monitors playing music videos and campy moments from TV shows and movies—and a large dance floor upstairs. On Sunday, two-steppers take over the place for country dancing; on other nights the music is a mix of techno and dance tracks. ✉ *202 S. 13th St., Center City East* ☎ *215/545-1893* ⊕ *www.woodysbar.com.*

COMEDY CLUBS

Blessed with a combative but fun-loving temperament, Philadelphians love nothing more than a good laugh—at someone else's expense.

Comedy Sportz. Anything goes during this once-a-week night of improvisational comedy. There are two shows every Saturday at the Playground

at the Adrienne Theater, and the audience is always welcome to participate. ⊠ *2030 Sansom St., Rittenhouse Square* ☎ *877/985–2844* ⊕ *www.
comedysportzphilly.com.*

Laff House. This 250-seat club offers an open-mike night on Wednesday
and showcases local and national acts Thursday through Sunday. ⊠ *221
South St., South Street* ☎ *215/440–4242* ⊕ *www.laffhouse.com.*

DANCE CLUBS

People from outside the city might be surprised to see just how popular
dancing is here. The persuasive DJ culture has permeated throughout
the city, especially in Old City, Northern Liberties, and on South Street.
There are several must-go-to weekly parties, particularly Tastytreats
at Fluid on Saturdays and King Britt's Back2Basics on Monday nights
at Silk City.

OLD CITY AND CENTER CITY

Fodor'sChoice
★ **32°.** A self-described "luxe lounge" in Old City, the place has Euro-pre-
tensions throughout—in fact, it even accepts euros as currency. Sleek,
modern, and—indeed—luxurious, it serves fine booze by the bottle and
rents private lockers where you can store your unfinished spirits. DJs
spin a blend of house, hip-hop, and R&B grooves. ⊠ *16 S. 2nd St., Old
City* ☎ *215/627–3132* ⊕ *www.32lounge.com.*

★ **Fluid.** This small dance club atop the Latest Dish restaurant is nearly
hidden behind an unmarked door on an alley just off 4th Street near
South. Once inside, follow the funky stairwell to the second floor, where
you'll hear a mix of hip-hop, rap, and techno spun by some of the city's
best DJs. ⊠ *613 S. 4th St., South Street* ☎ *215/629–0565* ⊕ *www.flu-
idnightclub.com.*

Pure Nightclub. A former speakeasy, this gay-friendly after-hours joint
still offers some late-night thrills, courtesy of a extremely potent state-
of-the-art light and sound system. Two massive dance floors are filled
with gyrating bodies, and a third-level catwalk enables those wanting
a rest (or further libations) an excellent vantage point from which to
watch the action. ⊠ *1221 St. James St., Center City East* ☎ *215/735–
5772* ⊕ *www.purephilly.com.*

Tritone. For those seeking some offbeat adventure, this joint, in a refurbished area of upper South Street, is a hipster's dream. During any given
week it offers eclectic live music and cutting-edge DJs. ⊠ *1508 South
St., Center City West* ☎ *215/545–0475* ⊕ *www.tritonebar.com.*

NORTHERN LIBERTIES

700 Club. In the heart of the happening Northern Liberties scene,
the 700 Club remains an approachable, no-frills type of joint. The
ground-floor bar gives way upstairs to an even more atmospheric living
room–type lounge where area DJs tear up the dance floor. The crowd
remains young and hip, and the music can range from straight hip-
hop to obscure French techno. ⊠ *700 N. 2nd St., Northern Liberties*
☎ *215/413–3181.*

★ **The Barbary.** Owned by Philly DJ JHN RDN, the place has quickly
become one of the go-to destination spots for live shows and dancing. There are also a host of special nights including '50s surf punk

Late Night Eats

Greasy spoons abound in Philly. Try one of these late-night haunts after a night of carousing.

SOUTH STREET

If you don't mind making your way through the milling crowds up and down the street, head to South Street in Center City East for cheese fries and a chicken cheesesteak at **Ishk-abibble's** (✉ 337 South St., South Street ☎ 215/923–4337), which is open until 2 AM Friday and Saturday.

The primo late-night haunt for the pizza-minded remains **Lorenzo's** (✉ 305 South St., South Street ☎ 215/627–4110), which stays open until 3 AM or later every night but Sunday. Expect long, rowdy lines, and basic slices to go—they don't do toppings. They have a small dining area in the back, but you're much better off enjoying your slice on the street, or going south on 3rd Street and sitting at one of the little benches at Bainbridge Street.

SOUTH PHILADELPHIA

For a regular cheesesteak 24/7, **Pat's King of Steaks** (✉ 1237 E. Passyunk Ave., South Philadelphia ☎ 215/468–1546 ⊕ www.patskingofsteaks.com) hits the spot; get the cheese fries to

up to grease quotient. Expect a line of people, but the fast service makes up for it.

Generous portions of breakfast foods, including eggs, potatoes, and scrapple are available till late at **The Melrose Diner** (✉ 1501 Snyder Ave., South Philadelphia ☎ 215/467–6644).

NORTHERN LIBERTIES

You can grab meatloaf or cornmeal-crusted tofu at **Silk City** (✉ 435 Spring Garden St., Northern Liberties ☎ 215/592–8838 ⊕ www.silkci-typhilly.com) until 2 AM every night. During the warmer months you can take advantage of their wondrous beer garden to the side of the main building.

If you're looking for a traditional late-night haunt, try **Darling's** (✉ 1001 N. 2nd St., Northern Liberties ☎ 215/239-5775 ⊕ www.darling-scheesecake.com), one of the many new establishments sprouting around the Piazza across from Liberties Walk. There you can find the usual assortment of eggs, burgers, and salads, with a few more enterprising options such as peanut-butter pancakes with Nutella and their signature cheese-cake until 5 AM on weekends.

6

Wednesdays and a Sunday night reggae experience. Catering to a diverse crowd, they have both 21-and-over dance parties and all-ages shows. ✉ 951 Frankford Ave., Northern Liberties ☎ 215/634–7400 ⊕ www.myspace.com/thenewbarbary.

Shampoo. This giant, two-story space is teeming with revelry. The dance floors are generously spread out amid the eight bars. Be sure to visit the infamous outdoor groove garden—replete with hot tub. Friday brings in one of the city's best gay dance parties, Saturday usually involves visiting DJs spinning plenty of house and techno. ✉ 417 N. 8th St., Northern Liberties ☎ 215/922–7500 ⊕ www.shampooonline.com.

Fodor's Choice ★ **Silk City Diner Bar & Lounge.** Re-opened to great approval after a brief hiatus and change of ownership, Silk City has once again come to be a major player in Philly's club scene. Both a delicious diner and a dance club/live music venue, Silk offers the best of both worlds for downtown hipsters, hip-hoppers, and bohos looking to indulge their groove. ⊠ *435 Spring Garden St., Northern Liberties* ☎ *215/592–8838* ⊕ *www.silkcityphilly.com.*

JAZZ, BLUES, AND CABARET

Philadelphia has a rich jazz and blues heritage that includes such greats as the late, legendary jazz saxophonist John Coltrane and current players like Grover Washington Jr. That legacy continues today in clubs around town.

Chris' Jazz Café. This intimate hangout off the Avenue of the Arts showcases top local talent Monday through Saturday in a cigar- and pipe-friendly environment. ⊠ *1421 Sansom St., Center City West* ☎ *215/568–3131* ⊕ *www.chrisjazzcafe.com.*

★ **Ortlieb's Jazz Haus.** This century-old jazz club has music every night of the week; Tuesday and Sunday nights include a jam session for local musicians. ⊠ *847 N. 3rd St., Northern Liberties* ☎ *215/922–1035* ⊕ *www.ortliebsjazzhaus.com.*

Philadelphia Clef Club of Jazz & Performing Arts. Dedicated solely to jazz, including its history and instruction, the organization has a 200-seat cabaret-style theater for concerts. ⊠ *736–738 S. Broad St., Center City East* ☎ *215/893–9912* ⊕ *www.clefclub.org.*

★ **Warmdaddy's.** This rustic, down-home blues club and restaurant serves up live blues and Southern cuisine every night of the week. ⊠ *1400 Columbus Blvd., at Reed St., South Philly* ☎ *215/462–2000 reservations* ⊕ *www.warmdaddys.com.*

ROCK, POP, AND FOLK MUSIC

Despite Philly's baffling lack of a defining rock band to call its own, the city is still alive with the sounds of guttural growls and poignant six-strings. Though the vast majority of venues are owned by Live Nation, a good variety of touring bands is still represented on a nightly basis.

Electric Factory. Named in honor of the original Electric Factory, which opened in 1968 and hosted acts ranging from Jimi Hendrix to the Grateful Dead, this newer incarnation occupies a cavernous former warehouse just north of Center City and presents mainly alternative rock bands. It has a capacity of about 2,500, but that number mostly refers to standing room; the main concert area doesn't have seats, although you can sit down at a balcony bar and watch the proceedings from there. ⊠ *421 N. 7th St., Northern Liberties* ☎ *215/568–3222* ⊕ *www.livenation.com/venue/electric-factory-tickets.*

The Khyber. Small and loud, this Old City spot has lots of action. The music is all live, including alternative and rock performed by national and local talent. With more than 100 brands of beer, it has one of the best selections in town. The Khyber is open Monday to Saturday. ✉ *56 S. 2nd St., Old City* ☎ *215/238–5888* ⊕ *www.thekhyber.com.*

North Star Bar & Restaurant. Deceptively good-sized, the North Star lights up the Art Museum neighborhood with a diverse and satisfying line-up of local and nationally touring bands, tending toward the artistic and alternative side of the ledger; past gigs included Shonen Knife, The Libertines, and (back in the day) Luna. ✉ *2639 Poplar St., Art Museum* ☎ *215/787–0488* ⊕ *northstarbar.com.*

Theatre of Living Arts. The TLA, a former independent movie house, is a South Street institution that helped launch John Waters's film career; it was also the longtime home of the *Rocky Horror Picture Show.* Today the TLA presents concerts by a range of rock, blues, and adult alternative acts, including such diverse artists as Lucinda Williams and Toots and the Maytals. ✉ *334 South St., South Street* ☎ *215/922–1011.*

Tin Angel Acoustic Café. Local and national musicians hold forth at a 105-seat acoustic cabaret above the Serrano restaurant (patrons get preferred seating). You can sit at candlelight tables or at the bar and hear music from blues to folk. ✉ *20 S. 2nd St., Old City* ☎ *215/928–0770* ⊕ *www.tinangel.com.*

Trocadero. This spacious rock-and-roll club in Chinatown occupies a former burlesque house where W. C. Fields and Mae West performed. A lot of the old decor remains: mirrors, pillars, and balconies surround the dance floor. Most every up-and-coming band that's passing through Philly plays here to an under-30 crowd. On other nights local DJs play for dance parties. On Monday it hosts a popular movie series. ✉ *1003 Arch St., Center City East/Chinatown* ☎ *215/922–5483* ⊕ *www.the-troc.com.*

Fodor's Choice ★ **World Cafe Live.** A musical flagship in West Philly, the building also houses WXPN-FM, which features such acoustic and world-beat contemporary artists as Hothouse Flowers and Solas. The café also has two theaters—the largest of which, Downstairs Live, seats up to 500—and two restaurants. ✉ *3025 Walnut St., University City* ☎ *215/222–1400* ⊕ *www.worldcafelive.com.*

THE ARTS

Of all the performing arts, it's music for which Philadelphia is most renowned and the Philadelphia Orchestra of which its residents are most proud. The city also serves as a major stop for touring productions of shows from *A Chorus Line* to *Spring Awakening,* and the local theater scene, which supports more than two-dozen regional and local companies, is thriving.

INFORMATION AND TICKETS

For current performances and listings, the best guides to Philly's performing arts are the "Guide to the Lively Arts" in the daily *Philadelphia Inquirer,* the "Weekend" section of the Friday *Inquirer,* and the "Friday" section of the *Philadelphia Daily News.* Two free weekly papers, the *City Paper* and the *Philadelphia Weekly,* have extensive

FIVE GREAT ARTS EXPERIENCES

Kimmel Center: The crown jewel of the Avenue of the Arts, the massive and gorgeous Kimmel is home to the Philadelphia Orchestra.

Philly Fringe Festival: An annual affair that features more than two weeks of avant-garde theater, music, and performance art, it has quickly become indispensable.

Philadelphia Live Arts Festival: Concurrent with the Philly Fringe Festival, this fest offers a more curated approach to performance art.

Mann Center for the Performing Arts: An outdoor amphitheater in Philly's massive Fairmount Park, the Mann offers a wide variety of musical artists every week and is a summer staple.

Walnut Street Theatre: Over 200 years old, this classic drama house is one of the oldest theatrical venues in the country.

listings of concerts and clubs; they are available free in news boxes all over downtown.

The **Independence Visitor Center** (✉ *6th St. between Market and Arch, Independence Hall* ☎ *800/537–7676* ⊕ *www.independencevisitorcenter.com*) is open daily 8:30 to 5, and has information about performances.

TicketMaster (☎ *215/336–2000* ⊕ *www.ticketmaster.com*) sells tickets to rock concerts and other performing-arts events.

UpStages (✉ *1412 Chestnut St., Center City East* ☎ *215/569–9700* ⊕ *www.princemusictheater.org*) has tickets for many cultural events. Discount tickets, often reduced up to 50%, are offered on the day of the performance.

CLASSICAL MUSIC

Classical music in Philadelphia begins with the world-renowned Philadelphia Orchestra, which, under new music director Charles Dutoit, has kept its remarkable pedigree. But there is also the Chamber Orchestra, which is also housed in the glorious Kimmel Center; the venerable Philly Pops; and the very talented students of the Curtis Institute, to round out the bill.

Chamber Orchestra of Philadelphia. Directed by Ignat Solzhenitsyn, this prestigious group—formerly known as Concerto Soloists of Philadelphia—performs chamber music from September to June at the Perelman Theater at the Kimmel Center for the Performing Arts. ✉ *Broad and Spruce Sts., Center City West* ☎ *215/790–5800, 215/545–5451 concert information* ⊕ *www.chamberorchestra.org.*

Curtis Institute of Music. The gifted students at this world-renowned music conservatory give free recitals several times a week from October through May at 8 PM. All of its students are on full scholarships; its alumni include such luminaries as Leonard Bernstein, Samuel Barber, and Anna Moffo. The recital hotline lists events. The school also has an opera, alumni recital, and symphony orchestra series. ✉ *1726 Locust St., Rittenhouse Square* ☎ *215/893–5261 hotline, 215/893–7902 ticket office* ⊕ *www.curtis.edu/html/10000.shtml.*

★ **Peter Nero and the Philly Pops.** Grammy-winning pianist and conductor Peter Nero leads an orchestra of local musicians in programs that swing from Broadway to big band, or from ragtime to rock and roll, with ease. The six-concert series is presented at the Kimmel Center for the Performing Arts from October to May. ✉ *Broad and Spruce Sts., Center City West* ☎ *215/893–1900* ⊕ *www.phillypops.com.*

Philadelphia Chamber Music Society. From October to May, the society presents more than 60 concerts featuring nationally and internationally known musicians. The schedule is packed with a piano, vocal, and chamber music series, a special events and jazz series, and string recitals. Performances are held in the Perelman Theater at the Kimmel Center for the Performing Arts, at the Pennsylvania Convention Center, and at other locations in the city. ☎ *215/569–8587 information, 215/569–8080 box office* ⊕ *www.philadelphiachambermusic.org.*

★ **Philadelphia Orchestra.** Considered one of the world's best symphony orchestras, the Philadelphia Orchestra rose to fame under the batons of former conductors Leopold Stokowski, Eugene Ormandy, and Riccardo Muti. The musical reigns were taken over in 2008 by chief conductor and artistic advisor Charles Dutoit, who will continue his superlative efforts through the 2011–12 season. The orchestra's present home is the cello-shaped Verizon Hall at the Kimmel Center for the Performing Arts. The 2,500-seat hall is the centerpiece of the performing-arts center at Broad and Spruce streets—a dynamic complex housed under a glass-vaulted roof. Orchestra concerts during the September–May season are still among the city's premier social events. If you can get tickets, go. You'll see some of the city's finest performers in an opulent setting, with many Philadelphians dressed to match the occasion. In summer the orchestra stages a concert series at the Mann Center for the Performing Arts. ✉ *Broad and Spruce Sts., Center City West* ☎ *215/893–1999 box office, 215/893–1900 info* ⊕ *www.philorch.org.*

CONCERT HALLS

Since the opening of the Kimmel Center in 2001, Philadelphia has enjoyed an embarrassment of riches when it comes to performance space. The Academy of Music, the Philadelphia Orchestra's previous home, remains open in all its finery; the Annenberg and Painted Bride house everything from theater to performance art; and both the Mann Center and the Susquehanna Bank Center remain premier outdoor amphitheaters.

★ **Academy of Music.** Modeled after Milan's La Scala opera house and completed in 1857, the Academy of Music was the Philadelphia Orchestra's home for its first century. The Academy is now home to the Opera Company of Philadelphia and the Pennsylvania Ballet; the schedule is filled out with performances by major orchestras, theatrical and dance touring companies, and solo artists. It's worth the price of admission to experience the Academy's lavish, neo-baroque interior, with its red velvet seats, gilt, carvings, murals on the ceiling, and huge crystal chandelier. ☒ *Broad and Locust Sts., Center City West* ☎ *215/893–1999* ⊕ *www.academyofmusic.org.*

Annenberg Center. The performing-arts complex on the University of Pennsylvania campus has four stages, from the 120-seat Studio to the 962-seat Zellerbach Theater. Something's always going on—including productions of musical comedy, drama, dance, and children's theater. ☒ *3680 Walnut St., University City* ☎ *215/898–3900* ⊕ *www.pennpresents.org.*

Keswick Theatre. This 1,250-seat former vaudeville house with fine acoustics hosts rock, jazz, and country music concerts as well as musicals. ☒ *291 N. Keswick Ave., Glenside* ☎ *215/572–7650* ⊕ *www.keswicktheatre.com.*

FodorsChoice
★ **Kimmel Center for the Performing Arts.** This striking complex evokes Philadelphia's traditional redbrick structures, while making a contemporary design statement. The 450,000-square-foot facility by architect Rafael Viñoly includes the 2,500-seat cello-shaped Verizon Hall, the more intimate 650-seat Perelman Theater, a café and restaurant, a gift shop, rooftop terrace, and public plaza—all topped by a dramatic glass-vaulted roof. Along with its resident companies, such as the Philadelphia Orchestra, the Chamber Orchestra, and the American Theater Arts for Youth, the center presents touring orchestral, jazz, and dance performances. ☒ *Broad and Spruce Sts., Center City West* ☎ *215/893–1999* ⊕ *www.kimmelcenter.org.*

★ **Mann Center for the Performing Arts.** Pops, jazz, contemporary music, Broadway theater, opera, dance, and Shakespeare are presented in this open-air amphitheater in Fairmount Park from May through September. From late June through July, the Philadelphia Orchestra is in residence, along with noted soloists and guest conductors. International food booths and a tented buffet restaurant offer dinner before the show. ☒ *5201 Parkside Ave. in W. Fairmount Park, Fairmount* ☎ *215/893–1999* ⊕ *www.manncenter.org.*

Painted Bride Art Center. By day it's a contemporary art gallery showing bold, challenging works. By night it's a multidisciplinary, multicultural performance center, with performance art, prose and poetry readings, folk and new music, jazz, dance, and avant-garde theater. The gallery is open Tuesday–Saturday noon–6. ☒ *230 Vine St., Old City* ☎ *215/925–9914* ⊕ *www.paintedbride.org.*

Susquehanna Bank Center. Formerly known as the E-Centre, the Tweeter Center, across the Delaware River in Camden, New Jersey, programs everything from symphonies to rock and roll in an adaptable space. The indoor section ranges from 1,600 to 7,000 seats; the lawn seats 12,000. Shows include major rock and pop acts as well as touring musicals and children's theater. ☒ *1 Harbor Blvd., Camden, NJ* ☎ *856/365–1300 ticket information and directions* ⊕ *www.livenation.com/venue/susquehanna-bank-center-tickets.*

Wachovia Spectrum and Wachovia Center. Rock concerts are often staged in these enormous sports facilities on the south side of the city, each of which holds more than 16,000 fans. Recent headliners have included Bruce Springsteen, Beyoncé; monster truck competitions, wrestling matches, and circuses are also on the calendar. ✉ *S. Broad St. and Pattison Ave., off I–95, South Philadelphia* ☎ *215/336–3600* ⊕ *www.wachoviacenter.com.*

MUSIC FESTIVALS

Roots Picnic. A one-day free-for-all on Penn's Landing, the Roots Picnic is hosted by Philly's own hip-hop legends, The Roots, and includes a slew of hip-hop, indie, and DJ performances, including previous performers TV on the Radio, Public Enemy, and King Britt. ✉ *Columbus Blvd. and Spring Garden St., Northern Liberties* ☎ *215/569–9400 box office* ⊕ *www.okayplayer.com/rootspicnic* ✇ *$51.*

Fodor'sChoice **Philadelphia Folk Festival.** First held in 1962, the oldest continuously run-
★ ning folk festival in the country takes place each year for three days during the last week in August. Doc Watson, Taj Mahal, Joan Baez, and Judy Collins are just a few of the artists who have performed here. ✉ *Old Pool Farm, near Schwenksville* ☎ *215/242–0150 or 800/556–3655* ⊕ *www.pfs.org/PFF.php.*

DANCE

With everything from distinct ballet to hip-hop, the dance scene in Philly is well represented.

Dance Celebration/Next Move Series. Modern dance takes the stage at this Annenberg Center series, which presents works by local, national, and internationally known companies. Recent seasons have featured Dance-Brazil, Dance Theatre of Harlem, and Paul Taylor Dance Company, among others. ✉ *3680 Walnut St., University City* ☎ *215/898–3900* ⊕ *www.annenbergcenter.org.*

★ **Pennsylvania Ballet.** Artistic director Roy Kaiser leads the company through a season of classic favorites and new works; they dance on the stage of the Academy of Music. Their annual *Nutcracker* production is a holiday favorite. ✉ *Broad and Locust Sts., Center City* ☎ *215/551–7000* ⊕ *www.paballet.org.*

Philadelphia Dance Company. This modern dance troupe, also known as Philadanco, is recognized for its innovative performances that weld contemporary and classical forms with the traditions of other cultures. Its home is the Perelman Theater at the Kimmel Center for the Performing Arts. ✉ *Broad and Spruce Sts., Center City* ☎ *215/387–8200* ⊕ *www.philadanco.org.*

FILM

Philadelphians have a great love of film, which is evidenced by the many art house theaters, fabulously popular annual film fests, and hard-working film office, which toils to bring big-budget productions to the city.

CLOSE UP

Free Arts Festivals

One of the sizable perks of visiting a large metropolitan center is the proliferation of free cultural events throughout the year, and Philly is no exception.

In the 10 days leading up to Independence Day each summer, Philly puts on its biggest party of the year, the **Sunoco Welcome America! Festival** (✉ *26th St. and Ben Franklin Parkway, Art Museum* ☎ *215/683–2200* ⊕ *www.americasbirthday.com*). It takes place in various locations throughout the city with an assortment of family-friendly events, culminating each year in a huge, free public concert in front of the Art Museum, followed by a spectacular fireworks display. Past performers have included Boys II Men, John Legend, and Sheryl Crow.

Every spring the Main Branch of the Free Library hosts the two-day **Free Library Festival** (✉ *1901 Vine St., Art Museum* ☎ *215/686–5322* ⊕ *www.freelibrary.org*), which features readings and live music for children and adults of a literary bent.

The many festivals of the **PECO Multicultural Series** (✉ *Columbus Ave. and Chestnut St., Penn's Landing* ☎ *215/922–2386* ⊕ *www.pennslandingcorp.com*) held over summer weekends at the Great Plaza at Penn's Landing, are a welcome respite from the grueling dog days of the season.

The vivacious **Clark Park Summer Solstice Festival** (✉ *Baltimore Ave. and 43rd St., West Philadelphia* ☎ *215/552-8186* ⊕ *www.myspace.com/ clarkparkfest*) has a full line-up of live bands, performers, vendors, and the fabulous, multicultural energy of all West Philly has to offer.

Film Festivals

International Gay & Lesbian Film Festival. Organized by Theatre of Living Arts Video founder Raymond Murray, who has written several books on film, this festival is held annually in July in venues around the city. ☎ *267/765–9700* ⊕ *www.phillyfests.com.*

Philadelphia Festival of World Cinema. This 12-day event in May is filled with screenings, seminars, and events attended by critics, scholars, filmmakers, and cinema buffs. It's held at various venues around the city. ☎ *267/765–9700* ⊕ *www.phillyfests.com.*

OPERA

The Academy of Music, with its wonderful acoustics and exquisite appointments remains an excellent venue for viewing opera.

AVA Opera Theatre. The resident artists at the Academy of Vocal Arts, a four-year, tuition-free vocal training program, present four or five fully staged opera productions during their October to May season. They are accompanied by the Chamber Orchestra of Philadelphia and perform at various venues in and around the city. ✉ *1920 Spruce St., Rittenhouse Square* ☎ *215/735–1685* ⊕ *www.avaopera.org.*

Opera Company of Philadelphia. The company stages five or six productions a year between October and May at the Academy of Music; some operas have international stars. All performances are in the original language, with English supertitles above the stage. ⊠ *Broad and Locust Sts., Center City* ☎ *215/893–3600* ⊕ *www.operaphilly.com.*

Savoy Company. The oldest Gilbert and Sullivan company in the country stages one G&S operetta each May or June at the Academy of Music and at Longwood Gardens in Kennett Square. ☎ *215/735–7161* ⊕ *www.savoy.org.*

THEATER

The Walnut Street Theatre is one of oldest in the country; the Arden, Freedom, and Wilma often present serious and avant-garde dramas, and the Forrest and Merriam provide the thrills and chills of touring Broadway shows. For lovers of the more avant garde, the theater-heavy Philadelphia Live Arts Festival and Philly Fringe begin in early September and play in smaller theaters and venues throughout Old City.

The Adrienne. The main stage, once home to the prestigious Wilma Theater, now houses various up-and-coming theatrical groups, including **Flashpoint Theatre Company** (☎ *215/665–9720* ⊕ *www.flashpointtheatre.org*) and **InterAct Theatre** (☎ *215/568–8077* ⊕ *www.interacttheatre.org*). They offer improv comedy and host productions from visiting theater companies. ⊠ *2030 Sansom St., Rittenhouse Square* ☎ *215/569–9700.*

Arden Theatre Company. The Arden, formed in 1988, is known for premiering new works and offering a mix of classic drama, comedy, and musicals, with a special affinity for the works of Stephen Sondheim; the company has won many local Barrymore Awards. Recent productions have included *Something Intangible, Seafarer,* and *James and the Giant Peach.* Its home is in Old City. ⊠ *40 N. 2nd St., Old City* ☎ *215/922–1122* ⊕ *www.ardentheatre.org.*

Forrest Theatre. The Forrest is the place to catch Broadway blockbusters in Philadelphia. About eight high-profile shows are presented each season, including such Broadway smashes as *Spring Awakening, Avenue Q,* and *A Chorus Line.* ⊠ *1114 Walnut St., Center City East* ☎ *215/923–1515* ⊕ *www.forrest-theatre.com.*

Freedom Theatre. The oldest and most active African-American theater in Pennsylvania is nationally renowned. Performances are scheduled from September through June. ⊠ *1346 N. Broad St., North Philadelphia* ☎ *215/765–2793* ⊕ *www.freedomtheatre.org.*

Merriam Theater. Built in 1918 as the Shubert, the ornate 1,688-seat theater has showcased many stage greats, including Al Jolson, Helen Hayes, Katharine Hepburn, Sammy Davis Jr., Angela Lansbury, and Sir Laurence Olivier. Now owned by the University of the Arts and named after a local benefactor, the lavishly decorated Merriam hosts a full schedule of national tours of Broadway shows, modern dance companies, and solo performers, from the magicians Penn & Teller to tap dancer Savion Glover. ⊠ *250 S. Broad St., Center City West* ☎ *215/732–5446* ⊕ *www.merriam-theater.com*

Philadelphia Live Arts Festival & Philly Fringe. The Philadelphia Live Arts Festival and Philly Fringe are two performing arts festivals that take over the city for 16 days each September, starting around Labor Day.

6

The Live Arts portion is a curated festival of cutting-edge dance and theater from international and local groups. The Fringe is a free-for-all of longtime established companies to fly-by-night operations that produce their own shows. During the festival there are about 200 shows in 100 venues all over the city, with more than 1000 performances. ⊠ *Box office at the Hub: 626 North 5th St., SW corner of 5th and Fairmount Sts., Northern Liberties* ☎ *215/413–1318* ⊕ *www.livearts-fringe.org* 🗟 *$25–$30.*

Philadelphia Theatre Company. Philadelphia and world premieres of works by contemporary American playwrights are performed here. The company also produces Stages, a program showcasing new plays by American playwrights. In late 2007 they moved to their new permanent home, the 365-seat Suzanne Roberts theater on the Avenue of the Arts. ⊠ *480 S. Broad St., between Lombard and Pine Sts., Center City West* ☎ *215/985–0420* ⊕ *www.phillytheatreco.com.*

Prince Music Theater. Formerly known as the American Music Theater Festival, this organization has renovated an old movie theater and named it in honor of legendary Broadway director-producer Harold Prince. The theater presents original musicals and a cabaret series with national acts, including Andrea Marcovicci and Patti LuPone. ⊠ *1412 Chestnut St., Center City West* ☎ *215/569–9700* ⊕ *www.princemusictheater.org.*

Society Hill Playhouse. For more than 40 years, this small off-Broadway–style theater, just off South Street, has mounted original plays. Their *Lafferty's Wake,* a musical about a rowdy Irish funeral service, played for four years. The main stage is for contemporary works; the Second Space Cabaret Theater has musical comedies. ⊠ *507 S. 8th St., Society Hill* ☎ *215/923–0210* ⊕ *www.societyhillplayhouse.org.*

★ **Walnut Street Theatre.** Founded in 1809, this is the oldest English-language theater in continuous use in the United States. The schedule includes musicals, comedies, and dramas in a lovely 1,052-seat auditorium where almost every seat is a good one. Smaller stages showcase workshop productions of new plays, and are rented by other theater companies. ⊠ *825 Walnut St., Center City East* ☎ *215/574–3550* ⊕ *www.wstonline.org.*

Wilma Theater. Under artistic director Blanka Zizka, the Wilma has gained favorable critical notices for innovative presentations of American and European drama. Its season runs from September to June. ⊠ *265 S. Broad, at Spruce St., Center City East* ☎ *215/546–7824* ⊕ *www.wilmatheater.org.*

Sports and the Outdoors

By Bernard
Vaughan

Philadelphians are perhaps the most outrageous, most dedicated sports fans in the country. They deserve a notorious reputation for boorishness—booing Santa Claus, applauding opposing teams players' injuries—but this is merely a front for fragile hearts continually betrayed over the years by their beloved but faltering teams.

The Phillies World Series championship in 2008 reminded this city what winning feels like, and has only made fans hungrier for more. Years are not marked by the changing of the seasons for Philadelphia sports fans, but by the sports in season: the Eagles, 76ers, and Flyers keep them busy from fall through spring, when the Phillies step in for those long summer afternoons.

But Philadelphians don't just watch sports. The multitude of bikers, runners, and rollerbladers you can see on the streets and in parks attest to Philly's love of the outdoors.

On weekend mornings (7–noon) from April through October, the West River Drive is closed to car traffic, making this a prime spot for sports enthusiasts. In the afternoons, only the section from the Sweetbriar Cutoff to the East Falls Bridge is closed. Breathtaking trails for running, biking, and hiking thread through Fairmount Park. Walking along Forbidden Drive, a gravel trail along the Wissahickon Creek, you'll understand why artists from Thomas Eakins to Edgar Allan Poe felt inspired to immortalize the park in their work. Shafts of sunlight filter through the trees, while birdcalls complement the dense chorus of crickets bellowing from the mossy woods.

PARTICIPATION SPORTS

BIKING

Fodor'sChoice
★

One popular treat for cyclists is to ride the paved path along the east side of the **Schuylkill River**; cross East Falls Bridge, and return on the west side of the river. The path begins behind the Philadelphia Museum of Art and is parallel to Kelly Drive. This 8-mi loop is about an hour of casually paced biking. **Forbidden Drive**, a 5½-mi dirt-and-gravel bridle path along a stream in the Wissahickon, in the northwestern section of Fairmount Park, is a great ride.

The **Bicycle Club of Philadelphia** (⊕ *www.phillybikeclub.org*) organizes rides, from afternoon outings to weeklong events.

Bike Line (✉ *1028 Arch St., Art Museum* ☎ *215/923–1310* ⊕ *www.bikeline.com*) rents bikes for $25 to $35 per day for weekday rides. Prices go up to $45 to $60 per day on weekends.

FIVE GREAT OUTDOOR EXPERIENCES

Forbidden Drive: The winding gravel path along tree-lined Wissahickon Creek offers perhaps the most serene place in Philadelphia to bike, jog, or just take a relaxing walk. For a fun hike, ask around for Indian Rock, a majestic marble statue of the Indian chief Tedyescung that overlooks the creek.

Philadelphia Phillies: With its great views, reasonably priced tickets, and tasty food, Citizens Bank Park offers a great a place to spend an evening in spring, summer, or fall.

Imitate Rocky: Even if you can't bring yourself to raise your hands in triumph once you get to the top, it's fun to see if you can handle running up the Philadelphia Art Museum

steps. And, the top does offer a great view of the Benjamin Franklin Parkway and City Hall.

Horseback Riding: There are a number of stables that offer horseback riding for riders of all ages and skill levels in Fairmount Park and in the suburbs. Try Friends of the Wissahickon (⊕ www.fow.org/riding.php) or Ashford farm (⊕ www.ashford-farm.com).

Regattas: Even if you're not in town for the famed Dad Vail Regatta—the largest rowing even in the country—races on the Schuylkill River can be seen from dawn till dusk from February to October. It's a Philadelphia classic.

7

FISHING

On the banks of Wissahickon Creek and Pennypack Creek you can find good trout fishing; call **Fairmount Park** (☎ 215/683–0200 ⊕ www.fairmountpark.org) for information. Both creeks are stocked for the mid-April–December season. You'll need a license ($22.70 for Pennsylvania residents, up to $26.70 for a one-day tourist), available at local sporting-goods stores.

GOLF

Philadelphia has six 18-hole courses that are open to the public. Cobb's Creek is the most challenging; Roosevelt is the easiest.

Cobb's Creek Golf Club. For golfers who love lots of action, Cobbs Creek offers two adjacent courses: the Karakung and the Olde Course. Cobb's Creek plays in and around the creek itself, making for lovely vistas and challenging shots. Karakung has hilly fairways and smaller greens. Reservations are recommended, but not essential. ⊠ 7400 Lansdowne Ave., West Philadelphia ☎ 215/877–8707 ⊕ www.golfphilly.org ↟ 18 holes. 6,202 yds at Olde Course, 5,762 yds at Karakung. Par 71. Greens fee: $42/$47 at Olde course, $32 at Karakung ⚲ Facilities: driving range, putting green, pitching area, golf carts, rental clubs, pro shop, restaurant, bar.

Franklin D. Roosevelt Golf Club. A relatively flat course with wide fairways, the natural wetlands and a canal pose unique challenges. Reservations are recommended, but not essential. Greens fees fluctuate depending on whether you tee off in the morning or afternoon. ✉ *1954 Pattison Ave., South Philadelphia* ☎ *215/462–8997* ⊕ *www.golfphilly.org* ⚑ *18 holes. 6,004 yds. Par 69. Greens fee: $32–$37/$37–$42* ⚲ *Facilities: driving range, putting green, pitching area, golf carts, pull carts, rental clubs, pro shop, golf academy/lessons, bar.*

John F. Byrne. This is a short but challenging course with small greens, highlighted by Torresdale Creek, which comes into play on 10 holes. ✉ *9550 Leon St., Northeast Philadelphia* ☎ *215/632–8666* ⊕ *www.golfphilly.org* ⚑ *18 holes. 5,189 yds. Par 67. Greens fee: $17–$32/$22–$37* ⚲ *Facilities: putting green, pitching area, golf carts, rental clubs, pro shop, golf academy/lessons.*

Juniata. With Frankford Creek running through it, Juniata is an impressive par 66. The course doesn't have a driving range, but there is an unaffiliated range nearby. ✉ *1391 Cayuga St., Juniata* ☎ *215/743–4060* ⚑ *18 holes. 5,275 yds. Par 66. Greens fee: $22–$32/$27–$37* ⚲ *Facilities: putting green, pitching area, golf carts, rental clubs, pro shop, golf academy/lessons.*

Walnut Lane. Tree-lined fairways make Walnut Lane, a short (4,500 yards) course, into a fairly challenging par 62. Reservations are essential on weekends. ✉ *800 Walnut Lane, Roxborough* ☎ *215/482–3370* ⊕ *www.golfphilly.com* ⚱ *Reservations essential* ⚑ *18 holes. 4,500 yds. Par 62. Greens fee: $17–$32/$18–$38* ⚲ *Facilities: putting green, pitching area, golf carts, pull carts, rental clubs, pro shop, golf academy/lessons.*

SPAS

Philadelphia has no shortage of trendy day spas offering the latest and greatest in relaxation.

Adolf Biecker. In the Rittenhouse hotel, Adolf Biecker offers numerous treatments, including the "Day of Beauty," which includes a Caribbean body scrub, a steam and body massage, followed by a facial, manicure, and pedicure. The salon features a fitness club with top-notch exercise equipment and a glass-covered pool area filled with sunlight. ✉ *210 W. Rittenhouse Sq., Center City* ☎ *215/735–6404* ⊕ *www.adolfbiecker.com.*

Pileggi on the Square. Between Society Hill and Old City, this spa-salon is within walking distance of prime sightseeing and shopping areas. Duck into the renovated town house for the Elemis Exotic Lime and Ginger Salt Glow, a novel exfoliation treatment, or the Elemis Aroma Spa Ocean Wrap, a seaweed wrap detoxification treatment. ✉ *717 Walnut St., Society Hill* ☎ *215/627–0565* ⊕ *www.pileggisalon.com.*

The Spa at Four Seasons. The 80-minute Philadelphia Freedom Hot Towel Infusion combines deep massage with steaming hot towels steeped in aromatic herbs. Body treatments include a rosemary-citron sea-salt scrub and the signature massage—an 80-minute odyssey using a medley of massage techniques meant to symbolize the four seasons. ⊠ *1 Logan Sq., Benjamin Franklin Parkway/Museum Area* ☎ *215/963–1500* ⊕ *www.fourseasons.com/philadelphia/spa.*

Terme Di Aroma. Hanging vines of pothos and philodendron accompany you through the lobby into the dim, cozy interior lined with Syrian vases and antique Egyptian doors. Although the name nods to the ancient Mediterranean practices of meditation and healing offered here, you can also find Asian-influenced treatments, such as Shiatsu massage. Notable services include the prenatal massage, warm-stone therapy, and the Thai Yoga massage—a combination of stretches, acupressure, and inhalation work for health and well-being. ⊠ *32 N. 3rd St., Old City* ☎ *215/829–9769* ⊕ *www.termediaroma.com.*

★ **Toppers Spa.** Flowers and perfumes permeate this spotless, labyrinthine spa. In the Solarium, a greenhouse-like pagoda brimming with plants and natural light, you can enjoy a Lakota Indian–influenced Raindrop Therapy Massage in which essential oils are dripped onto the spine and followed up by a full spine massage. Other services include "The Grand Escape," a four-hour session featuring a hot-stone massage, hot-stone facial, and a hot-stone manicure and pedicure, as well as an aromatherapy neck warmer. ⊠ *117 S. 19th St., Rittenhouse Square* ☎ *215/496–9966* ⊕ *www.toppersspa.com.*

HIKING

There are 25 mi of fine solo walks or hikes in **Fairmount Park** (☎ *215/683–0200* ⊕ *www.fairmountpark.org*) and 54 mi in the unspoiled Wissahickon, a northern section of the park. Despite the bucolic quality of these areas, it's important to remember that you're in an urban setting and should take appropriate precautions. If you're alone, keep to the main paths along Kelly Drive and West River Drive, or consider joining a hiking group.

You can meet hikers at the **Batona Hiking Club** (☎ *215/233–0916* ⊕ *www.batonahikingclub.org*) on Sunday morning at a central Philadelphia location (such as Broad and Arch streets) and carpool to hiking areas within a two-hour drive of the city, including the Appalachian Trail, the Delaware Water Gap, and the New Jersey Pine Barrens. Batona is short for back to nature, and hikes range from 7 to 12 mi and tend to be more strenuous than those of other clubs. Visit the club's Web site for schedules, e-mail addresses, meeting places, and other announcements.

The Department of Recreation sponsors the **Wanderlust Hiking Club** (⊕ *www.phila.gov/recreation/parks/Wanderlust.html*). Relatively easy hikes of 5 to 8 mi, many through Fairmount Park and Pennypack Park, begin every Saturday afternoon at 1:30. Check the club's Web site for schedules.

7

HORSEBACK RIDING

☪ Of the numerous bridle paths coursing through Philadelphia, the most popular are the trails of the Wissahickon in the northwest, Pennypack Park in the northeast, and Cobb's Creek Park in the southwest. **Ashford Farm** (⊠ *River Rd., Lafayette Hill* ☎ *610/825–9838* ⊕ *www.ashford-farm.com*), just over the northwestern border of the city, has lessons for $50–$75 per hour.

ICE-SKATING

☪ You can skate outdoors—with the Delaware River and Benjamin Franklin Bridge as a backdrop—daily from November to March at the **Blue Cross RiverRink** (⊠ *Columbus Blvd. and Market St., Penn's Landing* ☎ *215/925–7465* ⊕ *www.riverrink.com*). Admission is $7–$8, skate rentals are $3. You can skate indoors at the **University of Pennsylvania Ice Rink at the Class of 1923 Arena** (⊠ *3130 Walnut St., University City* ☎ *215/898–1923* ⊕ *www.business-services.upenn.edu/icerink/contactUs.html*), which is open to the public from September through the first week of April. Admission is $5.50 weekdays, $6.50 weekends. Skate rentals are $2.50.

JOGGING

Joggers can be seen on streets all over the city, but probably no area is favored more than Kelly and West River drives, a scenic 8-mi route along the Schuylkill River. Then, of course, there are the steps of the art museum itself, host to Rocky-like runners who raise their arms in salute during early morning jaunts.

From dawn to dusk, the south walkway of the **Benjamin Franklin Bridge** provides a tough but rewarding 3½-mi round-trip run with a terrific view of the Delaware River waterfront. **Fairmount Park** (☎ *215/683–0200* ⊕ *www.fairmountpark.org*) —especially along the river drives and Wissahickon Creek—is a natural for joggers and runners. **Forbidden Drive** along the Wissahickon offers more than 5 mi of soft-surface trail along a picturesque creek in a secluded valley. Only runners, walkers, bikers, and horses can use the trail—motor vehicles aren't allowed.

If you're interested in the ultimate in running—through wide-open spaces on bike trails, horse trails, and grassy hills and dales—head outside Philadelphia to **Valley Forge National Historical Park.**

The **Northeast Roadrunners of Philadelphia** (⊕ *www.erols.com/runadvte*) has more information about jogging and running in the city.

SWIMMING

After doing laps in the 25-meter indoor pool at the **12th Street Gym** (⊠ *204 S. 12th St., Center City* ☎ *215/985–4092* ⊕ *www.12streetgym.com*), you can relax on a poolside lounge chair. The staffers pride themselves on keeping the pool spotless. Day passes are $20.

From Memorial Day weekend through September, **Philadelphia Sports Club** (⊠ *220–250 S. 5th St., Society Hill* ☎ *215/592–8900* ⊕ *www.*

philadelphiasports.com) opens a large outdoor pool for swimming laps or just cooling off. An extensive sundeck furnished with lounge chairs surrounds the L-shaped pool. Lifeguards are usually on duty. Day passes are $15 if you're with a member, $25 without a member.

> **PHILLY'S PROUD BASEBALL HISTORY**
>
> The Philadelphia Phillies are the oldest, continuous, single-name, one-city franchise in professional sports. The team played its first game in 1882, losing 4–3 to the Providence Grays and setting an unfortunate pattern of losing games. In 2008, however, the Phillies won their first World Series Championship since 1980.

TENNIS

Fairmount Park has more than 100 free public courts; courts are usually first-come, first-served. Call the **Department of Recreation** (☎ 215/683–3600 ⊕ *www.phila.gov/recreation*) or visit ⊕ *www.tennisphilly.com* for more information on tennis in Philadelphia.

Seger Park (⊠ *1000 Lombard St., near S. 10th St., Society Hill/Center City*) has two tennis courts. **FDR Park** (⊠ *S. Broad St. and Pattison Ave., South Philadelphia*), near the Wachovia Spectrum, has 15 tennis courts. **Mawkward Playground** (⊠ *26th St. and Pine St. Center City*) has two tennis courts.

SPECTATOR SPORTS

BASEBALL

Fodor'sChoice ★ Since 2004 the **Philadelphia Phillies** have played in **Citizens Bank Park** (⊠ *11th St. and Pattison Ave., South Philadelphia* ☎ *215/463–1000* ⊕ *www.philadelphiaphillies.com*), a beautiful stadium that makes for a great day or night outing in spring, summer, or fall. The season runs from April to October. Tickets range from $16 to $60.

The minor-league **Camden River Sharks,** a member of the independent Atlantic League, play late April through September at **Campbell's Field** (⊠ *401 N. Delaware Ave., Camden* ☎ *856/963–2600 or 866/742–7579* ⊕ *www.riversharks.com*) in New Jersey, across the Delaware River from Penn's Landing. Tickets are $6 to $12.

BASKETBALL

Philadelphia consistently produces first-rate basketball prospects, and vigorous, competitive pickup games can be found at hundreds of courts around the city.

The **Philadelphia 76ers** play at the **Wachovia Center** (⊠ *3601 S. Broad St., South Philadelphia* ☎ *215/339–7676* ⊕ *www.nba.com/sixers*) from November to April. Tickets are $15–$120.

Collegiate Big Five basketball (⊠ *Big Five Office, the Palestra, 235 S. 33rd St., University City* ☎ *215/898–6151* ⊕ *www.philadelphiabig5. org*) features teams from LaSalle, St. Joseph's, Temple, the University of Pennsylvania, and Villanova. The season runs from December to March.

BIKING

One of the world's top biking events, the **Philadelphia International Cycling Championship** (☎ 610/676–0390 ⊕ www.procyclingtour.com) is held each June. The 156-mi race starts and finishes at Benjamin Franklin Parkway. Highlights include the infamous Manayunk Wall, a steep hill in the Manayunk section of the city.

BOXING

★   The **Blue Horizon** (✉ 1314 N. Broad St., North Philadelphia ☎ 215/763–0500 ⊕ www.legendarybluehorizon.com) holds only 1,200 people—small in comparison to Madison Square Garden or Caesar's Palace—but every seat is close to the action. The club's reputation for being rather grungy has changed after a $3 million renovation. General admission seats are $45, and ringside views go for $47. VIP tickets are $65.

The Arena (✉ 7 W. Ritner St. ☎ 215/755–0611 ⊕ www.thearena.biz) hosts boxing matches, wrestling matches, martial-arts events, and other special events

FOOTBALL

Fodor's Choice   The **Philadelphia Eagles** can be seen in action at their state-of-the-art facil-
★   ity, **Lincoln Financial Field** (✉ 11th St. and Pattison Ave., South Philadelphia ☎ 267/570–4000 ⊕ www.philadelphiaeagles.com) from September through January. The stadium has a grass playing field and holds up to 68,000 fans. Many of the best seats go to season-ticket holders; individual tickets are $70 or $95.

Philadelphia Soul (✉ 3601 S. Broad St. ☎ 215/636–0421 ⊕ www.philadelphiasoul.com), one of arena football's top franchises, plays at the Wachovia Center from late January through May.

HOCKEY

The **Philadelphia Flyers** hit the ice at the **Wachovia Center** (✉ 3601 S. Broad St., South Philadelphia ☎ 215/952–7300 ⊕ flyers.nhl.com) from October to April. Tickets are $24–$105.

The **Philadelphia Phantoms**, the city's minor-league hockey team, are the Flyers' AHL affiliate. You can see them at the **Wachovia Spectrum** (✉ Broad St. and Pattison Ave., South Philadelphia ☎ 215/465–4522 ⊕ www.phantomshockey.com) from October through April. Tickets cost $9–$20.

ROWING

★   The placid Schuylkill River, the elegant Boathouse Row, the annual regattas, and a climate that allows an average of 360 rowing days a year all make Philadelphia the rowing capital of the world. From February

Philadelphia's Other Legacy: Boxing

Ask a lot of people what they know about Philadelphia, and after a brief mention of the Liberty Bell, they'll probably bring up the boxing epic *Rocky*. Indeed, Philadelphia has played a vital role in the history of boxing.

In the 1880s, saloons owned by ex-bare-knuckle fighters had unlicensed bouts in their back rooms; venues such as the Ariel Club were hosting regular matches by the 1890s. Prizefighting was illegal until 1884, so matches were deemed six-round exhibitions in which no decision was rendered. Gamblers outwitted the law by consulting newspaper verdicts the next day.

Outdoor boxing started in 1914 and continued for more than 40 years. Most memorable was the mythical 1926 battle between two "outsiders," or non-Philadelphians: heavyweight champion Jack Dempsey versus Gene Tunney at Sesquicentennial Stadium. Tunney upset the "Manassa Mauler" in a 10-round decision beneath a relentless rainstorm as 120,000 people watched.

The 1920s saw Philadelphia fighters rise to contention in nearly every weight class, and the onset of the Depression in the 1930s failed to hinder Philadelphia's boxing scene. Jewish brawler Lew Tendler, Strawberry Mansion's Harry Blitman, Tommy Loughran, and Big George Godfrey were feared throughout the boxing world. Midget Wolgast—at 5 feet, 3 inches and 108 pounds—was one of the all-time greats of the flyweight division, and there was the colorful "Two-Ton" Tony Galento, a 5-foot, 9-inch, 240-pounder whose diet and training were primarily focused on beer drinking. Convention Hall opened in 1932, and hosted such historic fights as Steve "Hurricane" Hamas's upset over Germany's legendary boxer Max Schmeling.

Camden's Jersey Joe Walcott was the region's first heavyweight champ, but he lost to Rocky Marciano in 1952 in what Herman Taylor, a Philly promoter and icon for nearly 70 years, called "the greatest heavyweight fight I ever looked at." Sonny Liston was based in North Philly from 1958 to 1962, and Joe Frazier—who would go on to beat Muhammad Ali—first put on his gloves in Philadelphia.

Although *Rocky* brought Philly boxing to the national consciousness, the city lost its standing for major boxing events in the 1980s, when casinos in Atlantic City, New Jersey, began to draw the big matches. But the culture of boxing continues in such venues as the Blue Horizon and the Arena, and storied gyms such as Joe Hand's continue to produce good, old-fashioned "Philadelphia fighters."

–Bernard Vaughan

7

to October you can watch single and team races out on the river, usually from 5 AM to dusk. Dozens of major meets are held here, including the largest college rowing event in the country, the **Dad Vail Regatta** (☎ 215/542–1443 ⊕ *www.dadvail.org*). This May event includes up to 500 sculls from more than 100 colleges from the U.S. and Canada. Free shuttle buses provide transportation for spectators from remote parking areas. More than 1,500 rowers compete in the **Independence Day Regatta** (☎ 302/479–9294), held around July 4. The May **Stotesbury**

CLOSE UP

The Legendary Boo Birds

Did Philly fans *really* boo Santa? The urban legend has come to exemplify the lengths Philadelphia's churlish fans will go to show their displeasure. Unfortunately, this is no myth. During halftime of the final regular season game in December 1968, an Eagles official asked Frank Olivo, a 20-year-old season-ticket holder wearing a Santa costume, to fill in for a hired Santa who was stranded by a snowstorm. A cold shower of snowballs and boos from a crowd of more than 54,000 greeted Olivo as he ran around the end zone while a band played "Here Comes Santa Claus." "When I hit the end zone, and the snowballs started, I was waving my finger at the crowd, saying 'You're not getting anything for Christmas,'" Olivo recalled to the Associated Press. Legendary television sports broadcaster Howard Cosell broadcast the event, and future Pennsylvania Governor Ed Rendell was in attendance. For years, rumors abounded that the fans were upset because Olivo was drunk and/ or because his costume was shabby. Olivo maintains that he was not drunk and most witnesses, including Rendell, believe the fans were venting their frustration at the lowly state of the Eagles, who went 2–12 that year.

Cup Regatta (☎ *302/479–9294*) includes more than 5,000 students from 180 schools.

SOCCER

Philadelphia Kixx, the city's first national professional soccer team, draws crowds of exuberant fans to the **Wachovia Spectrum** (✉ *Broad St. and Pattison Ave., South Philadelphia* ☎ *888/888–5499* ⊕ *www.kixxonline. com*). You can catch the team in action from November through April; tickets, which go on sale in late September, are $10–$25.

Shopping

Updated by
Caroline Tiger

Shop-a-holics love the City of Brotherly (and Sisterly) Love
for its style—funky artwork and highbrow housewares, fine
jewels, and haute couture.

Indeed, Philadelphia has spawned some influential fashion retailers. The
Urban Outfitters chain was born in a storefront in West Philadelphia.
Its sophisticated sister, Anthropologie, also has its roots in Philadelphia.
Lagos, the popular high-end jewelry line, was founded here, and all
items are still produced locally. High-fashion boutiques Joan Shepp,
Knit Wit, and Plage Tahiti, all in the Rittenhouse Square area, are well
regarded by locals for designer clothing and accessories.

Some of the most spirited shopping in town is also pleasing to the
palate. The indoor Reading Terminal Market and the outdoor Italian
Market are bustling with urban dwellers buying groceries and visitors
searching for the perfect Philadelphia cheesesteak. Equally welcoming is
the city's quaint, cobblestone Antiques Row, the three-block stretch of
Pine Street crammed with shops selling everything from estate jewelry to
stained glass and vintage furniture. Also worth a trip is the Third Street
Corridor in Old City, home to scads of independent, funky boutiques. In
Northern Liberties, the Piazza at Schmidt's is a giant mixed-use development inspired by Rome's Piazza Navona, which houses 100,000 square
feet of retail space bursting with creative entrepreneurs.

Neighborhoods in this chapter are presented clockwise starting from
the Old City, a commercial waterfront turned arts enclave on the Delaware River, moving south to South Philadelphia, then west to Center
City and Rittenhouse Square, across the Schuylkill River to University
City around the University of Pennsylvania campus, and ending in the
north with Northern Liberties.

⇨ *For information on shopping in Manayunk, Germantown, and
Chestnut Hill, see Chapter 3, Manayunk, Germantown, and Chestnut
Hill.*

HISTORIC AREA AND OLD CITY

Lofts, art galleries, furniture stores, and unique home-decor shops line
the streets of the Old City; there are also wonderful clothing stores with
work by local up-and-coming designers. After dark, young professionals
and students—many live in converted warehouses in the area—flock to
the neighborhood's bars and clubs. Some of Philadelphia's most innovative restaurants can also be found here. One of the best times to explore
Old City's gallery scene is during First Friday. As the name implies, on
the first Friday of each month, Old City galleries are open to the public from 5 to 9 at night. Many offer refreshments, and the street scene
becomes quite festive.

SHOPPING DISTRICTS AND MALLS

Across the street from the Liberty Bell is the **Bourse** (⊠ *21 S. 5th St.,
between Market and Chestnut Sts., Historic Area* ☎ *215/625–0300*), an
elegantly restored 1895 commodities exchange building. The six-story

FIVE GREAT SHOPPING EXPERIENCES

Reading Terminal Market: Sample Philly's many flavors under the roof of the world's largest single-arch train shed: cheesesteaks from D'Nic's, cupcakes from Flying Monkey, chocolate-chip cookies from Famous 4th Street, and exotic offerings from Downtown Cheese are just the beginning of what's in store at this famous indoor market.

Midtown Village: Thirteenth Street between Market and Walnut streets houses a bustling row of independent boutiques from locally made soaps and shampoos at Duross & Langell to tattoo-inspired apparel at Sailor Jerry's.

Fabric Row: In the early 1900s, this street was lined with pushcarts selling calico and notions. A few century-old fabric stores live on among the hip boutiques and coffee shops.

Rittenhouse Square boutiques: Searching for upscale shopping and grand architecture? Look no further.

Old City's Third Street Corridor: Fashion is fun again at the designer-owned boutiques that line 3rd Street, where the designers are up-and-coming and the knowledgeable staff is refreshingly attitude-free.

skylighted atrium contains a few fun shops catering to tourists, such as Best of Philadelphia, as well as a festive international food court.

Market Place East (⊠ *Market St. between 7th and 8th Sts., Historic Area* ☎ *215/592–8905*) is in a historic building saved from the wrecker's ball at the 11th hour. The century-old former Lit Brothers department store went through a $75 million renovation to emerge as an office building with a five-level atrium full of moderately priced stores and restaurants. It's more interesting for its historic facade—it's the only complete block of Victorian architecture in the city—than for the chain stores inside.

SPECIALTY STORES

ANTIQUES **Moderne Gallery.** Gallerist Bob Aibel is the world's foremost authority on furniture designer George Nakashima, who made his most famous work just north of Philadelphia, in New Hope. Aibel always has some Nakashima for sale as well as other pieces of furniture from the American Craft movement and Art Deco furniture, accessories, and lighting. ⊠ *111 N. 3rd St., Old City* ☎ *215/923–8536.*

ART AND CRAFT GALLERIES **Cereal Art.** This half-storefront half-gallery works with internationally known artists to design, produce, and sell multiples, or limited artist's editions, that are infinitely more affordable than the same artists' originals. The multiples are sold in museum and design shops around the world and are always three-dimensional objects that you wouldn't associate with high art, such as snow globes and ashtrays. ⊠ *149 N. 3rd St., Old City* ☎ *215/627–5060.*

Clay Studio. A nonprofit organization runs the gallery and conducts classes as well as an outreach program to inner-city schools. There are clay works and pottery by well-known artists; the gallery has juried shows and group exhibits. ⊠ *139 N. 2nd St., Old City* ☎ *215/925–3453.*

Locks Gallery. This gallery shows works by an impressive assortment of contemporary regional, national, and international painters, sculptors, and mixed-media artists, including David Hockney and Frank Stella. ⊠ *600 Washington Sq. S, Historic Area* ☎ *215/629–1000.*

Muse Gallery. Established in 1978 by the Muse Foundation for the Visual Arts, Muse Gallery is an artists' cooperative committed to increasing the visibility of local artwork and presenting experimental work in a variety of mediums. ⊠ *52 N. 2nd St., Old City* ☎ *215/627–5310.*

Snyderman-Works Gallery. One-of-a-kind handmade furniture pieces, glass objects, and craft-oriented fine art are displayed on the first floor of this venerable Old City gallery. ⊠ *303 Cherry St., Old City* ☎ *215/238–9576.*

Wexler Gallery. This gallery is known for specializing in historic and contemporary glass, but it always has an interesting mix of 20th- and 21st-century handcrafted furnishings and art. WALLS, on the gallery's second floor, carries more affordable paintings, prints, and photography. ⊠ *201 N. 3rd St., Old City* ☎ *215/923–7030.*

CLOTHING AND ACCESSORIES

Lele Design. Body-conscious styles and gorgeous fabrics are local designer Lele Tran's trademarks. Customers select samples from the racks, with alterations provided if needed. You can also make adaptations to existing styles for a custom design. ⊠ *30 S. 2nd St., Old City* ☎ *215/546–5975.*

Lost & Found. This laid-back shop has something for everyone with its well-curated mix of silk-screened tees, vintage dresses, and colorful wares by new designers. It also has a range of delightful accessories including vintage belt buckles, printed canvas totes, and cheeky jewelry. Prices here are lower than at many of the neighboring boutiques. ⊠ *133 N. 3rd St., Old City* ☎ *215/928–1311.*

Sugarcube. Some know Sugarcube as a vintage boutique; others go for its stock of hard-to-find designers like A.P.C., Hengst, Built by Wendy, and Saja. The stylish, friendly owner is usually on hand to advise how to match your Wranglers with your Prada. ⊠ *124 N. 3rd St., Old City* ☎ *215/238–0825.*

Vagabond. The two designing women/co-owners of nine-year-old Vagabond pioneered a formula—selling vintage wares alongside new, edgy labels and showcasing under-the-radar brands like their own (Stellapop and City of Brotherly Love). It's been imitated plenty ever since, but this boutique still does it best. ⊠ *37 N. 3rd St., Old City* ☎ *267/671–0737.*

Viv Pickle. This make-your-own-handbag boutique offers such a huge menu of shapes, sizes, fabrics for exteriors and linings, and handles, it's hard to walk away with just one. The wide fabric range means there's something for everyone from prep to hipster. ⊠ *21 N. 3rd St., Old City* ☎ *125/922–5904.*

GIFTS AND SOUVENIRS

Best of Philadelphia. A former commodities exchange office houses this fun spot for inexpensive souvenirs: on display are more than 100 different items, from Ben Franklin key chains to miniature Liberty Bells. ⊠ *Bourse Bldg., 111 S. Independence Mall E, Independence Hall* ☎ *215/629–0533.*

Scarlett Alley. Owned and operated by Mary Kay Scarlett and her daughter Liz, this delightful shop at the corner of 3rd and Race near the Betsy Ross House features an ever-changing assortment of unique jewelry, housewares, and stationery, as well as toys, soaps, and teas. Items are displayed on furniture designed and handcrafted by Richard Scarlett, Liz's father; it's also for sale or custom order. ⊠ *241 Race St., Old City* ☏ *215/592–7898.*

Xenos Candy and Gifts. Asher chocolates and Philly souvenirs from key chains to T-shirts are stocked here, near the sights of the historic district. ⊠ *231 Chestnut St., Old City* ☏ *215/922–1445.*

HOME DECOR AND HOUSEWARES

Bruges Home. A sophisticated, earthy store with two levels of furniture, art, and decorative accessories imported from around the globe. Everything is laid out in inviting vignettes that all seem well suited for the home of a wealthy, worldly aristocrat. ⊠ *323A Race St., Old City* ☏ *215/922–6041.*

Fodor's Choice ★

Foster's Urban Homewares. Quirky and useful home accessories, furniture, and table- and kitchenware are displayed in this spacious store with a cool, industrial-hip flavor. ⊠ *399 Market St., Old City* ☏ *267/925–0950.*

MUSIC

AKA Music. The largest independent record store in the city stands opposite a church where George and Martha Washington once worshipped. If CDs and vinyl had been invented, you can bet the First Couple would have shopped here. It's easy to become immersed in one section of this very long, very narrow store only to look up and realize you're out of time but you still have reggae, British psychedelic, jazz, experimental, and garage to look through. ⊠ *27 N. 2nd St., Old City* ☏ *215/922–3855.*

8

SOUTH PHILADELPHIA

South Philadelphia is made up of a few smaller neighborhoods, including Society Hill, South Street, Queen Village (home to Fabric Row), and the Italian Market, and the shopping here is as varied as these nabes. South Street's streetwear shops and hippie holdovers give way to indie boutiques and thrift shops in the satellite streets. The quirky Italian Market's specialty stores are a home cook's dream. A few excellent independent bookshops survive throughout South Philly.

SHOPPING DISTRICTS AND MALLS

For some of the most entertaining people-watching in the city, head to **South Street**, just south of Society Hill. Pierced and tattooed teens vie for space with moms wheeling strollers on this bustling strip from Front Street near the Delaware River to 9th Street. More than 300 unusual stores—high-fashion clothing, New Age books, music and health food, avant-garde art galleries, and 100 restaurants—line the area. Most shops are open in the evening. You can find a few of the national chains, but 95% of the stores are locally owned, selling things you won't find in the mall back home.

★ In the early 1900s, 4th Street, today's **Fabric Row,** was teeming with pushcarts selling calico, notions, and trimming, and was known as "der Ferder" or "the Fourth" in Yiddish. Today several century-old fabric stores still stand, but many of the storefronts are home to locals selling wares from European-label shoes to fair-trade coffee.

If you want local color, nothing compares with South Philadelphia's **Italian Market.** On both sides of 9th Street from Christian Street to Washington Avenue and spilling out onto the surrounding blocks, hundreds of outdoor stalls and indoor stores sell spices, cheeses, pastas, fruits, vegetables, and freshly slaughtered poultry and beef, not to mention household items, clothing, shoes, and other goods. It's crowded and filled with the aromas of everything from fresh garlic to imported salami. The vendors can be less than hospitable, but the food is fresh and the prices are reasonable. Food shops include the Spice Corner, Di Bruno Brothers House of Cheese, Claudio's, and Talluto's Authentic Italian Foods. Fante's is well known for cookware. The market's hours are Tuesday–Saturday 9–5:30; some vendors open earlier, and others close around 3:30. Some shops are open Sunday from 9:30 to 12:30.

SPECIALTY STORES

ANTIQUES **South Street Antiques Market.** This indoor market about half a block below South Street holds the stalls of 25 dealers who sell everything from furniture, paintings, and stained glass to jewelry and '50s collectibles. It's closed Monday and Tuesday. ⊠ *615 S. 6th St., South Street* ☎ *215/592–0256.*

BOOKSTORES **Brickbat Books.** The charming, worn-in feel of this store lined with wooden shelves befits the merchandise for sale: the focus is on rare, small-press used and new books, although it's not unheard-of to find a $4 Hardy Boys paperback next to a first-edition Edward Gorey. The store also acts as a venue for fringe musicians from near and far. ⊠ *709 S. 4th St., South Street* ☎ *215/592–1207.*

Garland of Letters. This is the original New Age bookstore that hails from the days when hippies arrived on South Street in 1969 and turned it into an arts enclave. Follow the smell of incense and step inside to find books on astrology, tarot, shamanism, and world religions and cultures, plus a large selection of jewelry, crystals, and candles. ⊠ *527 South St., South Street* ☎ *215/923–5946.*

Headhouse Books. Sunlight streams into the front windows of this well-curated indie bookshop. It's the kind of place that attracts regulars who sit sipping tea and reading for hours with a dog curled at their feet. This inviting shop has become a meeting place for the local literary community—both the readers and the writers. ⊠ *619 S. 2nd St., South Street* ☎ *215/923–9525.*

CLOTHING **Hats in the Belfry.** Pass by this bright corner shop and you'll be tempted to try on a hat from the huge window display. Go funky or fancy, casual or classic—you can find hats to suit each and every whim. ⊠ *245 South St., South Street* ☎ *215/922–6770.*

Kamikaze Kids. Unique designer fashions for infants to preteens are showcased in a child-friendly atmosphere, with cloud-painted walls and play areas. ⊠ *527 S. 4th St., South Street* ☎ *215/574–9800.*

Passional Boutique. Only the adventurous dare enter this shop where a blue-haired saleswoman will fit you for your very own luxurious handcrafted corset. The work on these custom steel-boned pieces is beautiful and unique. The high-end wares sold here are the real deal as compared to the many stores on nearby South Street that specialize in fishnets and Sexy Nurse costumes. You'll also find leather and bondage gear here. ✉ *704 S. 5th St., South Street* ☎ *215/829–4986.*

FOOD **Di Bruno Bros.** This is the original location of the famed cheese shop; the other is in Rittenhouse Square. The major difference between the two is size. The one uptown is enormous and covers two floors. This shop is tiny—long, narrow, and cave-like, with salamis hanging from the ceiling like stalactites. Still, it's jam-packed with all the specialties you expect from the Di Brunos—cheeses, olive oils, prepared foods—plus a sandwich counter and the usual über-knowledgeable staffers. ✉ *930 S. 9th St., South Philadelphia* ☎ *215/922–2876.*

House of Tea. This small shop feels timeless with its wood floors, wood counter, and built-in wood cubbies holding large brass tins of loose-leaf teas from around the world. It also stocks a good number of beautiful tea sets. ✉ *720 S. 4th St., South Street* ☎ *215/923–8327.*

GIFTS AND **Eyes Gallery.** The three floors of this unique store feel like a folk-art
SOUVENIRS museum with Peruvian alpaca sweaters, Day of the Dead art, and instruments, jewelry, and decorative items from all over Mexico and South America for sale. From basement to skylight, the store's interior is filled with mosaics by famed local artist Isaiah Zagar, who owns the shop with his wife. ✉ *402 South St., South Street* ☎ *215/925–0193.*

HOUSEWARES **Fante's Kitchen Wares Shop.** One of the nation's oldest gourmet supply stores has the largest selection of coffeemakers and cooking equipment in the United States. Family owned since 1906, Fante's is famous for oddball kitchen gadgets such as truffle shavers and pineapple peelers; restaurants and bakeries all over the country and overseas order from the store. It's in the Italian Market, so you can combine a visit here with other food shopping. ✉ *1006 S. 9th St., Italian Market* ☎ *215/922–5557.*

SHOES **Benjamin Lovell.** This small, locally based chain specializes in stylish comfort, e.g., Dansk, Naot, Clarks, Born, La Canadienne, Uggs, Pliner, and Birkenstocks. The prices are high, but this South Street location (there's another by Rittenhouse Square) takes the sting out with their large sale section in the back. ✉ *318 South St., South Street* ☎ *215/238–1969.*

Bus Stop Boutique. Owned by a British expat, this shop sells fashion-forward, cutting-edge shoes by European labels like Fornarina, Coclico, and Fly London that are hard to find on this side of the pond. ✉ *750 S. 4th St., South Street* ☎ *215/627–2357.*

CENTER CITY EAST

Center City East (meaning the blocks east of Broad Street) has a lot of great shopping up Pine Street (Antique Row) near Washington Square and also a few blocks west, along fun, colorful, bustling 13th Street corridor, also called Midtown Village. Antique Row has some holdovers that are traditional antiques shops, but some quirky housewares and gift shops make their home there, too. Street parking is possible by Antique Row but is harder to find near 13th Street. Nearby Macy's has a parking garage, but your best bet is to cab it, walk, or take the bus.

SHOPPING DISTRICTS AND MALLS

Macy's (⊠ *Surrounded by 13th, Juniper, Market, and Chestnut Sts., Center City East* ☎ *215/241–9000*) displays the chain's classic merchandise in the spacious former John Wanamaker department store, a Philadelphia landmark. Its focal point is the nine-story grand court with its 30,000-pipe organ—the largest ever built—and a 2,500-pound statue of an eagle, both remnants of the 1904 Louisiana Purchase Exposition in St. Louis. During Christmastime, the space is filled with families and office workers gazing (and listening) in awe at the store's legendary holiday sound-and-light show and organ performances.

A block north of Chestnut Street is Philadelphia's landmark effort at urban-renewal-cum-shopping, the **Gallery at Market East** (⊠ *Market St. between 8th and 11th Sts., Center City East* ☎ *215/925–7162*), America's first enclosed downtown shopping mall. The four-level glass-roof structure near the Pennsylvania Convention Center contains 150 low- to mid-price retailers. It includes 40 food outlets.

Fodor's Choice
★ The roots of the **Reading Terminal Market** (⊠ *12th and Arch Sts., Center City East* ☎ *215/922–2317*) date to 1892, when the Reading Railroad commissioned a food bazaar to be built in the train shed's cellar as part of its grand expansion plans. Stroll amid the bustling stalls and you can see and smell old and new culinary delights. Amish merchants sell baked goods and produce straight from the farm alongside vendors offering the latest gourmet vegetarian dishes, artisanal breads, and sushi. Vendors also sell exotic spices, flowers, crafts, jewelry, clothing, and cookbooks. Eighty-six merchants are represented here, but try not to miss Amish-owned Fisher's Soft Pretzels for piping hot, freshly rolled soft pretzels; Bassetts Ice Cream, America's oldest ice-cream makers; Metropolitan Bakery, for hearty breads and light pastries; and the Down Home Diner for affordable Southern-style fare. The market is open Monday through Saturday, 8–6, and Sunday, 9–5. The Amish vendors are open Wednesday through Saturday.

Pine Street from 9th Street to 12th Street has long been Philadelphia's **Antique Row.** The three-block area has a good number of antiques stores and curio shops, many specializing in expensive period furniture and Colonial heirlooms.

Jewelers' Row, centered on Sansom Street between 7th and 8th streets, is one of the world's oldest and largest markets of precious stones: more than 350 retailers, wholesalers, and craftspeople operate here. The 700 block of Sansom Street is a brick-paved enclave occupied almost exclusively by jewelers.

SPECIALTY STORES

ANTIQUES **Blendo.** More like an excellent flea market than an antiques shop, the truckload of finds at Blendo is so plentiful they overflow onto the sidewalk. There are new, retro-flavored items and plenty of vintage finds including clothing, lamps and small furniture, jewelry, prints, and linens. It has the magical, memorable effect of grandma's attic, assuming grandma had cultured and eclectic tastes. ⊠ *1002 Pine St., Center City East* ☎ *215/351–9260.*

★ **M. Finkel & Daughter.** Late-18th- and early-19th-century American furniture, needlework, samplers, and folk art make this an important outpost for lovers of Americana. They also publish the antiques journal *Samplings.* ⊠ *936 Pine St., Center City East* ☎ *215/627–7797.*

Vintage Instruments. Antique strings and woodwinds are displayed here; the store specializes in violins, and also carries American fretted instruments such as banjos, guitars, and mandolins. ⊠ *507 S. Broad St., Center City East* ☎ *215/545–1100* ✉ *1609 Pine St., Center City West* ☎ *215/545–1100.*

W. Graham Arader. This is the flagship store of a highly respected chain that stocks the world's largest selection of 16th- to 19th-century prints and maps, specializing in botanicals, birds, and the American West. ⊠ *1308 Walnut St., Center City East* ☎ *215/735–8811.*

NEED A BREAK?

An authentic Frenchman made the **Caribou Cafe** (⊠ *1126 Walnut St. , Center City East* ☎ *215/625–9535* ⊕ *cariboucafe.com*) into an authentic, unpretentious French bistro (complete with sometimes brusque service) when he took over this 20-year-old spot four years ago. Thanks to two floors full of seating, there's almost always a table, so it's a great place to rest and refuel. Choose from a long wine-by-the-glass list and a menu of solid bistro basics including salade niçoise, croque-monsieur (et madame), crepes, and steak frites.

ART AND CRAFTS GALLERIES

Fabric Workshop and Museum. A nonprofit arts organization runs this center and store dedicated to creating new work in fabric and other materials, working with emerging and nationally and internationally recognized artists. ⊠ *1214 Arch St., Center City East* ☎ *215/568–1111.*

★ **Show of Hands.** You'll find one-of-a-kind artisan crafts—exquisite jewelry, colorful vases, textiles, and unique lamps—in a wide range of price points here. The friendly owner is on hand to answer questions and encourages you to handle the fragile objects. ⊠ *1006 Pine St., Center City East* ☎ *215/592–4010.*

BOOKSTORES

★ **AIA Bookstore & Design Center.** Run by the Philadelphia chapter of the American Institute of Architects (AIA), this shop specializes in books on architectural theory, building construction, interior design, and furnishings. It also sells architectural drawings and watercolors, blueprint posters, international magazines, home furnishings, unusual gifts, and a great selection of unique cards. ⊠ *1218 Arch St., Center City East* ☎ *215/569–3188.*

Giovanni's Room. Focusing on books dealing with gay, lesbian, and feminist topics, this well-regarded store stocks an extensive inventory and sponsors many author appearances. ⊠ *345 S. 12th St., Center City East* ☎ *215/923–2960.*

CLOTHING

Sailor Jerry. This flagship shop of the local company sells tattoo-inspired apparel based on legendary "Sailor Jerry" Collins's designs. ⊠ *116–118 S. 13th St., Center City East* ☎ *215/531–6380.*

COSMETICS

Duross & Langell. The two co-owners for which this shop is named make most of the colorful wedges of soap and the organic scrubs, shampoos, and other skin- and hair-care products locally and infuse them with scents like ginger and mojito. Soap-making workshops are often offered on the weekends. ⊠ *117 S. 13th St., Center City East* ☎ *215/592–7627.*

FOOD
Fodor'sChoice
★

Capogiro Gelateria. Even in winter, people line up at this location and the one closer to Rittenhouse Square for the rich creamy gelati that come in exotic (rosemary-honey-goat-milk) and classic (stracciatella) flavors. New batches are made on-site each morning. ⊠ *119 S. 13th St., Center City East* ☎ *215/351–0900* ⊠ *117 S. 20th St., Rittenhouse Square* ☎ *215/636–9250.*

HOME DECOR

Hello Home. The outpost of the Rittenhouse Square shop Hello World focuses on the home and strikes a mid-century modern note with furniture and accessories that are either of the 1940s through '60s, look like they could be, or are contemporary designs that complement that clean, bright aesthetic. ⊠ *1201 Pine St., Center City East* ☎ *215/545–7060.*

Open House. This modern, hip, urban home boutique strikes the balance between *Domino* magazine and *Elle Décor.* The furniture, baby clothes, jewelry, candles, and soaps all manage to be clever and quirky. It's as fun to browse as it is to buy, as there's no pressure from the friendly sales staff. ⊠ *107 S. 13th St., Center City East* ☎ *215/922–1415.*

Ten Thousand Villages. Woven rugs, pottery, carvings, and other handcrafted gifts made by skilled artisans in 32 countries such as Kenya, Thailand, and India make this fair-trade store a favorite for innovative gifts with a social conscience. ⊠ *1122 Walnut St., Center City East* ☎ *215/574–2008.*

Twist. A former set designer for the international IKEA catalog turned interior designer is one of the owners of this sophisticated and fun home store. Its whitewashed floors are a striking backdrop for a proprietary line of furniture, called Algotform, which features pieces including a dusty blue, nubby slipper chair and a table with a riveted zinc top. Smaller, more affordable housewares and accessories are scattered about. ⊠ *1134 Pine St., Center City East* ☎ *215/925–1242.*

JEWELRY
★

Halloween. If the sheer quantity of baubles crammed into this tiny shop doesn't take your breath away, the gorgeous, one-of-a-kind designs will. The shelves, drawers, displays, and even the second-floor balcony overflow with rings, necklaces, earrings, bracelets, pins, and much more. The jewelry ranges from classic pearls to mystical amber. Owner Henri David (who designs some pieces) is well known for his lavish and outrageous Halloween fetes. He can do custom work, such as creating mates for single earrings. ⊠ *1329 Pine St., Center City East* ☎ *215/732–7711.*

J. E. Caldwell. A local landmark since 1839, the store is adorned with antique handblown crystal chandeliers by Baccarat, making it as elegant as the jewels it sells. Along with traditional and modern jewelry, Caldwell has one of the city's largest selections of gifts from Waterford and Reed & Barton. ⊠ *215 S. Broad St., Center City East* ☎ *215/864–7800.*

LUGGAGE

Robinson Luggage. This shop at Broad and Walnut carries moderate to expensive brands of luggage, leather, and travel accessories. The selection of briefcases and attaché cases is the largest in the Delaware Valley. ⊠ *201 S. Broad St., Center City East* ☎ *215/735–9859.*

SPORTING GOODS **I. Goldberg Army and Navy.** This store is hip and practical, with an emphasis on sporting apparel and camping gear. Goldberg's is crammed with government-surplus, military-style clothing; jeans and work clothes; unusual footwear; and exclusive foreign imports. Rummaging here is a sport in itself. ⊠ *1300 Chestnut St., Center City East* ☎ *215/925–9393.*

CENTER CITY WEST AND RITTENHOUSE SQUARE

You'll find many upscale chains in Center City West, especially along Walnut Street between Broad and 18th streets, including Kenneth Cole, Banana Republic, Burberry, and Barneys Co-Op. Plenty of other chains, including Express and J. Crew, hold court at the Shops at Liberty Place. There is more local flavor off the beaten path, down numbered streets and smaller streets around Rittenhouse Square such as Sansom and Rittenhouse Square streets. Parking is tough in this area, and you'll pay a pretty penny for a meter or a lot. You'll have more fun and see much more if you walk these lively streets and let yourself get a little lost.

SHOPPING DISTRICTS AND MALLS

At 16th and Chestnut streets is the upscale **Shops at Liberty Place** (⊠ *1625 Chestnut St., Center City West* ☎ *215/851–9055*). The complex features a food court and popular stores, including Ann Taylor Loft, Aveda, Victoria's Secret, Express, J. Crew, and the Body Shop. More than 60 stores and restaurants are arranged in two circular levels within a strikingly handsome 90-foot glass-roof atrium.

The elegant **Shops at the Bellevue** (⊠ *Broad and Walnut Sts., Center City West*) include Polo–Ralph Lauren, with the designer's classic styles; the chic clothes of Nicole Miller; Tiffany & Co.; Origins bath and body products; and a Williams-Sonoma cookware store. A downstairs food court is bustling at lunchtime; several upscale restaurants in the historic building, which also houses an elegant hotel, are popular in the evening.

Fodor's Choice ★ Shop-'til-you-droppers make a beeline for **Rittenhouse Row,** the area between Broad and 21st streets and Spruce and Market streets. Lately the chains have been taking over Walnut Street between Rittenhouse Square and Broad Street, but this is still the greatest concentration of swanky stores and tony boutiques, art galleries, and jewelers you'll find in the city.

SPECIALTY STORES

ANTIQUES **Calderwood Gallery.** Art Nouveau and Art Deco furniture, glass, and bronze tempt discerning collectors at this fine establishment housed in a beautifully renovated town house. ⊠ *1622 Spruce St., Rittenhouse Square* ☎ *215/546–5357* ⊕ *www.calderwoodgallery.com.*

★ **Freeman's.** Founded in 1805 this is the city's most prominent auction house and America's oldest. Specialty departments include fine paintings, American and European furniture and decorative arts, 20th-century design, and rare books and prints. They're known for their Pennsylvania Impressionists, Colonial-period Pennsylvania furniture, and lately for a growing presence in modern and contemporary furniture and art.

8

Antiques Shopping Walk

Philadelphia makes the old new again with its plethora of antiques shops. Take a stroll through Center City and Rittenhouse Square for a good selection of shops. For further information about these stores, refer to the individual listings.

Begin your shopping in the high-end shops on Pine Street between 9th and 12th streets, long known as Antique Row. **M. Finkel & Daughter** (⊠ *936 Pine St., Center City East*) is known for furniture and needlework from the late 18th and early 19th centuries. **Freeman's** (⊠ *1808 Chestnut St., Rittenhouse Square*), an auction house one block from the upscale Shops at Liberty Place, is in the oldest building designed specifically for an auction house, and spans six floors. Explore the store's specialty departments,

which include fine American and European art and rare books and prints. Nearby you can find plenty of places to stop for a quick bite. Walk a block south on 19th Street to Rittenhouse Square and stroll through the park for a taste of the good life in the city. A number of antiques shops can be found in the elegant area surrounding the park. **Lisa M. Reisman et Cie** (⊠ *1714 Rittenhouse Sq., Rittenhouse Square*) has been a secret source for decorators and collectors for years. Her Art Nouveau furniture and accessories and large collection of fin de siècle posters are now available to everyone at this elegant two-story shop. **Niederkorn Silver** (⊠ *2005 Locust St., Rittenhouse Square*) specializes in decorative items such as antique silver picture frames.

Freeman's auctioned one of the original fliers on which the Declaration of Independence was printed and posted throughout the city. It sold for $404,000 in 1968. Check out their Web site for info on upcoming auctions. ⊠ *1808 Chestnut St., Rittenhouse Square* ☎ *215/563–9275* ⊕ *www.freemansauction.com.*

Niederkorn Silver. A fine selection of silver items, including jewelry, pieces for the desk and dresser, and a nice selection of baby silver, makes this a worthwhile stop. ⊠ *2005 Locust St., Rittenhouse Square* ☎ *215/567–2606.*

David David Gallery. American and European paintings, drawings, and watercolors from the 16th to the 20th century are on display. ⊠ *260 S. 18th St., Rittenhouse Square* ☎ *215/735–2922.*

Fleisher Ollman Gallery. You can find fine works by 20th-century self-taught American artists here, such as Martin Ramirez, Bruce Pollack, and Ray Yoshida. ⊠ *1616 Walnut St., Suite 100, Rittenhouse Square* ☎ *215/545–7562.*

Gross McCleaf Gallery. This is a good place to see works by both prominent and emerging artists, with an emphasis on Philadelphia painters. ⊠ *127 S. 16th St., Rittenhouse Square* ☎ *215/665–8138.*

Helen Drutt. This gallery presents contemporary American and European artists, with a focus on ceramics and jewelry. ⊠ *2220 Rittenhouse Square., Rittenhouse Square* ☎ *215/735–1625.*

I. Brewster. The specialty here is contemporary paintings and prints by such artists as Salvador Dalí, Peter Max, Marc Chagall, Louis Icart,

CLOSE UP

Art and Crafts Galleries Walk

Philadelphia is an excellent hunting ground for arts and crafts, particularly in Rittenhouse Square. Begin downtown, with Chestnut and Walnut, two major shopping streets. Between 16th and 18th streets you can find some wonderful galleries specializing in contemporary art, such as **Schmidt/Dean Gallery** (⊠ *1710 Sansom St., Rittenhouse Square*), which presents paintings by local artists. **Works on Paper** (⊠ *1611 Walnut St., Ritten-*

house Square) is well regarded for its selection of modern prints.

You can find contemporary art in trendy Old City as well, by venturing down Chestnut Street on foot or by bus to 3rd Street. For a great selection of craft-oriented fine art in mediums including glass, ceramics, fiber, and jewelry, head to **Works Gallery** (⊠ *303 Cherry St., Old City*). **Snyderman Gallery,** at the same address, sells fine art, studio furniture, and beautiful glass pieces.

Erté, Andy Warhol, Pablo Picasso, and Roy Lichtenstein. ⊠ *2200 Market St., Rittenhouse Square* ☎ *215/731–9200.*

Newman Galleries. The city's oldest gallery dates back to 1865, and displays work that range from 19th-century paintings to contemporary lithographs and sculpture. Many of the most notable 20th-century painters from the Bucks County area are showcased here. ⊠ *1625 Walnut St., Rittenhouse Square* ☎ *215/563–1779.*

Schmidt/Dean Gallery. Contemporary paintings, sculpture, prints, and photographs are shown; the specialty is work by Philadelphia artists. ⊠ *1710 Sansom St., Rittenhouse Square* ☎ *215/569–9433.*

Schwarz Gallery. American and European paintings of the 18th to 20th century are the focus, with an emphasis on Philadelphia artists. ⊠ *1806 Chestnut St., Rittenhouse Square* ☎ *215/563–4887.*

Works on Paper. The contemporary prints here by American Masters like Chuck Close and Robert Rauschenberg and by artists represented by the gallery have won Works on Paper a reputation as one of the city's best. ⊠ *1611 Walnut St., Rittenhouse Square* ☎ *215/988–9999.*

BOOKSTORES **Fat Jack's Comicrypt.** For more than 30 years, Fat Jack's has been a mecca for local comic devotees with fresh-off-the-presses copies from major and independent publishers, including Japanese mangas plus 3-D posters, action figures, and the obligatory Dungeons & Dragons supplies. ⊠ *2006 Sansom St., Rittenhouse Square* ☎ *215/963–0788.*

Joseph Fox. Quaint and cozy, this small bookstore specializes in art, architecture, and design—all well organized in diminutive quarters. ⊠ *1724 Sansom St., Rittenhouse Square* ☎ *215/563–4184.*

Whodunit. The city's only store specializing in mysteries, spy stories, and adventure books also stocks out-of-print mysteries and general-interest books. Co-owner Art Bourgeau has published six mysteries and a nonfiction book on mystery writing. ⊠ *1931 Chestnut St., Rittenhouse Square* ☎ *215/567–1478.*

8

NEED A BREAK?

At Tria (✉ *18th and Sansom Sts., Rittenhouse Square* ☎ *215/972–TRIA* ⊕ *triacafe.com*), you'll learn the three things denoted by the name "tria" are all fermented: beer, cheese, and wine. With extensive menus for each plus tasty sandwiches and salads, this popular beer, wine, and tapas bar does not disappoint. The only drawback is the clamor of the young-professional crowd that crams in post-work. It's better to catch Tria during its off-hours.

CLOTHING FOR CHILDREN

Born Yesterday. This shop is filled with unique clothing and toys for haute tots. Specialties include handmade goods, imported fashions, and styles not available elsewhere. ✉ *1901 Walnut St., Rittenhouse Square* ☎ *215/568–6556.*

Children's Boutique. The store carries a look between conservative and classic in infant to preteen clothes and shoes. You can buy complete wardrobes, specialty gifts, and handmade items. An extensive toy department carries the latest in kiddie crazes. ✉ *1702 Walnut St., Rittenhouse Square* ☎ *215/732–2661.*

CLOTHING FOR MEN AND WOMEN

Adrese. Simple, spare, and smashing, this award-winning boutique has been regaled by *Philadelphia* magazine for its high-style selection of exquisite silk dresses, luxurious cashmere, and designer handbags. ✉ *1706 Locust St., Center City West* ☎ *215/985–3161.*

Anthropologie. The flagship shop of the locally based national chain takes up three floors of an elegant Rittenhouse Square building (once someone's mansion, of course). The sales floors that encircle the grand stone staircase are brimming with lush colors, floral patterns, and vintage and ethnic-inspired styles that offer a departure from the ordinary. Pretty jewelry, stylish shoes and handbags, and other accessories add an enchanting femininity to fashion. Head downstairs for an array of home decor, including glassware, pottery, pillows, and mirrors. Be sure to check out the lower level for racks of bargain-priced sale items, and don't forget to look up at the towering first-floor ceiling of the one-time front parlor. ✉ *1801 Walnut St., Rittenhouse Square* ☎ *215/568–2114.*

★ **Boyds.** Beneath the burgundy canopy and white-marble entrance, you can find the largest single-store men's clothier in the country, with nine shops that present the traditional English look, avant-garde Italian imports, and dozens of other styles and designers, from Armani to Zegna. The store has departments for extra tall, large, and short men; formal wear; and shoes; and there's an excellent café for lunch, free valet parking, and 60 tailors on the premises. Women can find a small selection of high-quality designer clothes, too. An excellent sushi café on the mezzanine level is a peaceful place for a quick bite. ✉ *1818 Chestnut St., Rittenhouse Square* ☎ *215/564–9000.*

Echo Chic. This haute boutique manages to somehow be both cutting-edge and accessible; maybe it's the bubbly shopgirls who are enthusiastic about whatever's new in stock, from party dresses by Aussie label Sass & Bide to denim from L.A.M.B. The shelves that rim the tiny shop are always filled with vintage and new accessories—handbags, shoes, earrings—to complete the look. ✉ *1700 Sansom St., Rittenhouse Square* ☎ *215/569–9555.*

Jacques Ferber. Since 1879, this famed furrier has been offering high-style furs in sable, mink, and more, as well as shearlings, outerwear, and accessories that make a fashion statement. ✉ *1708 Walnut St., Rittenhouse Square* ☎ *215/735–4173.*

★ **Joan Shepp.** Cutting-edge fashion is displayed in a setting reminiscent of a New York loft. Notable designers include Chloe, Ivan Grundahl, Rich Owens, Eskander, Marni, Morgane LeFay, Jean-Paul Gaultier, and shoes by Prada. ✉ *1616 Walnut St., Rittenhouse Square* ☎ *215/735–2666.*

Kiki Hughes. This funky, luxe boutique on the corner of a residential street stocks unusual garments that stand out for their unexpected twists—a wide-leg pant in black velvet, a white oxford embroidered with flowers—as well as outright showstoppers like Asian tunics with mandarin collars and shimmering silk tafetta skirts. The owner designed the store interior herself, down to the hand-carved vines in the wood-work and the draped-fabric ceiling. ✉ *259 S. 21st St., Rittenhouse Square* ☎ *215/546–1534.*

★ **Knit Wit.** High-fashion clothes and accessories from sportswear to cock-tail dresses are the focus here. Blumarine, Vera Wang, Norma Kamali, Ella Moss, and Paul Smith are among the designs you can find here, with a few unique vintage shoes. ✉ *1718 Walnut St., Rittenhouse Square* ☎ *215/564–4760.*

Nicole Miller. You can find loads of this successful designer's quirky scarves, boxer shorts, and ties at eponymous boutiques in Center City and Manayunk. Women's collections include simple and elegant sports-wear, evening wear, and handbags in beautiful colors. ✉ *Shops at the Bellevue, Broad and Walnut Sts., Center City West* ☎ *215/546–5007.*

Petulia's Folly. This uncluttered, upscale shop sells everything to outfit the picky fashionista's life, from designer duds by Philip Lim, Catherine Malandrino, and Rebecca Taylor to John Derian decoupage platters and Moroccan poufs (round ottomans) for those extra dinner guests. ✉ *1710 Sansom St., Rittenhouse Square* ☎ *215/569–1344.*

Philadelphia Vintage. Shopping here is like combing through the closet of a funky heiress: It's stocked with ermine stoles and fur capelets, Berg-dorf dresses, Bakelite bangles, Gucci bags, and costume jewelry from the 1930s through '80s, much of it at prices a non-blueblood can afford. ✉ *2052 Locust St., Rittenhouse Square* ☎ *215/834–3733.*

Plage Tahiti. This leading showcase for promising young high-fashion designers carries a wide selection of chic and charming swimwear and designs by Theory, Diane Von Furstenberg, Ghost, Garfield, and Marks and Seven. Hot styles by top designers like Betsey Johnson have been known to show up at this trendy boutique. ✉ *128 S. 17th St., Center City West* ☎ *215/569–9139.*

Sophy Curson. Don't expect to find fashions in this shop that dates back to 1929 to be displayed in the usual way. Instead, the staff will show you the latest designer styles that are totally you, such as Lacroix dresses and Blumarine blouses with a mid-20th-century approach. ✉ *19th St. and Sansom St., Rittenhouse Square* ☎ *215/567–6442.*

Urban Outfitters. What started out as a storefront selling used jeans to students in West Philadelphia is now a trendsetting chain on campuses across the country. Three floors showcase an eclectic array of hip clothing, unusual books, and funky housewares that can go from the dorm room to the family room. ⊠ *1627 Walnut St., Rittenhouse Square* ☎ *215/569–3131.*

Wayne Edwards. Stylish without being intimidating, the store carries exclusive lines of classic contemporary clothing from Italy, Japan, France, and the United States. Designers include Postman, Vestimenta, and Armani. ⊠ *1525 Walnut St., Center City West* ☎ *215/731–0120.*

FOOD   **Di Bruno Bros.** There are two locations to tempt the palate—the original
★   one in the Italian Market and the hipper one in Rittenhouse Square. Di Bruno's is a mecca for cheese lovers—the store carries more than 300 different varieties from around the world, as well as some housemade kinds. You can also find barrels of olives, imported olive oils, Abbruzze sausage, and balsamic vinegar that's been aged for 75 years. The staff is very knowledgeable and will provide friendly advice on storage, preparation, and serving ideas. Ask for recipes and samples. ⊠ *1730 Chestnut St., Rittenhouse Square* ☎ *215/665–9220.*

Maron Fine Chocolates and Scoop de Ville. America's oldest independent retail candy store, opened by Swiss candy maker Conrad Maron in 1850, is thriving in its location near Rittenhouse Square. This family-run confectionery's specialties include chocolate-dipped fruits, truffles, sugar-free treats, and molded chocolates. Sweet tooth still not satisfied? Maron operates in the same space as a much-loved ice-cream parlor, Scoop de Ville. Choose from an extensive list of decadent toppings to create a custom-blended treat. ⊠ *1734 Chestnut St., Rittenhouse Square* ☎ *215/988–9992.*

Fodor'sChoice   **Naked Chocolate Cafe.** The local company's first location was so jam-
★   packed all the time that the owner soon opened two outposts, including this one and one in University City. All the confections are made locally by the owner, whose passion for sweets is infectious should you happen to see him at work in the open kitchen of the original midtown location (at 1317 Walnut Street). The dessert café features coffee drinks and a sinfully thick, European-style hot chocolate. ⊠ *30 S. 17th St., Rittenhouse Square* ☎ *215/564–3856;* ⊠ *1317 Walnut St., Rittenhouse Square* ☎ *215/735–7310* ⊠ *3401 Walnut St., University City* ☎ *215/222–3710.*

Premium Steap. This tiny tea-lover's paradise stocks a bevy of rare loose-leaf teas (Papaya Wild Pineapple Green Tea; Earl Gray Rose) in brass canisters that line the walls. Try a variety or two at the little bar in the back where the intense yet extremely knowledgeable owner is often brewing a cuppa. There's a great, if limited, selection of teaware. ⊠ *111 S. 18th St., Rittenhouse Square* ☎ *215/568–2920.*

GIFTS AND   **Details.** A 20th-century town house has been transformed into a jewel
SOUVENIRS   box of a gift shop, with details like picture frames, shimmering glassware, cards, and fine stationery. ⊠ *103 S. 18th St., Rittenhouse Square* ☎ *215/977–9559.*

Holt's Cigar Company. Stogie aficionados make a point of stopping by this cigar emporium, whose Philadelphia roots date back more than 100 years. The shop features a comfortable smoking lounge and one of the nation's largest walk-in humidors. Find private-label Ashton cigars, a wide array of smoking accessories and humidors, and writing instruments from Mont Blanc, Waterman, and Cross. ☒ *1522 Walnut St., Center City West* ☎ *215/732–8500.*

HOME DECOR AND HOUSEWARES

Kitchen Kapers. From one store in South Jersey, this family business has grown to be one of the largest independent kitchenware stores in the United States. This is a good source for fine cookware, French copper, cutlery, coffees, and teas. ☒ *213 S. 17th St., Center City West* ☎ *215/546–8059.*

Lisa Reisman et Cie. This exceptional shop in an elegant town house on a tiny street off of the Square is a treasure waiting to be found. Fin de siècle posters, Art Nouveau furniture and objets d'arts, Baccarat jewelry, engraved writing paper, and scented candles from Paris make you feel as if you've traveled back in time to the 19th century and stepped into a store off the Champs Elysées. ☒ *1714 Rittenhouse Sq., Rittenhouse Square* ☎ *215/735–2781.*

Usona. Furniture and accessories are what the owner calls "global modern," reflecting a fusion of different styles, periods, and materials. Accent pieces, like picture frames and mirrors, are interesting and affordable. ☒ *113 S. 16th St., Center City West* ☎ *215/496–0440.*

JEWELRY

Egan Day. This low-key, stripped down boutique set in a beautiful town house specializes in fine jewelry by contemporary designers like Ted Muehling and Maria Beaulieu, who craft refined, restrained pieces that highlight the materials and the wearer. ☒ *260 S. 16th St., Rittenhouse Square* ☎ *267/773–8833.*

★ **Lagos–The Store.** Lagos jewelry, sold in upscale department stores, gets top billing here. All pieces are handcrafted and designed in Philadelphia by Ann and Steven Lagos. Aficionados are thrilled by the selection, including the Diamond and Caviar, Glacier Deco, and Delta Pearl designs with gorgeous stones and museum-like settings. ☒ *1735 Walnut St., Rittenhouse Square* ☎ *215/567–0770.*

Richard Kenneth. Jewelry from the late-Georgian, Victorian, Art Nouveau, Art Deco, and '40s-retro periods are what you can find at this shop near Rittenhouse Square. Kenneth specializes in repairs and appraisals. ☒ *202 S. 17th St., Rittenhouse Square* ☎ *215/545–3355.*

Scriven. Designer Keith Scriven started selling handmade jewelry from a corner of his art gallery. When customers were wowed by the designs, Scriven knew it was time to open a separate store. His spare, elegant shop showcases his signature bold designs, formed from precious metals and precious and semiprecious stones. The intricate "Angela" link necklace is exquisite. ☒ *1602 Spruce St., Center City West* ☎ *215/545–8820.*

Tiffany & Co. This is the local branch of the store, famous for its exquisite gems, fine crystal, and china, and, of course, its signature blue gift box. ☒ *Shops at the Bellevue, 1414 Walnut St., Center City West* ☎ *215/735–1919.*

MUSIC

Theodor Presser. The best selection of sheet music in Center City draws musicians from far and wide. The store specializes in classical but also carries pop and will special order anything. ☒ *1718 Chestnut St., Rittenhouse Square* ☎ *215/568–0964.*

PERFUME AND **Bluemercury.** Makeup and skin-care junkies can get their fix at this sleek
COSMETICS shop featuring products from Aqua di Parma, Bliss, Bumble & Bumble,
Fresh, Trish McEvoy, Nars, Laura Mercier, and many others. Sweetly
scented candles and fragrances in intoxicating blends of fruits and spices
fill the shop. In the back of the store, spa services are offered in a serene
setting. ⊠ *1707 Walnut St., Rittenhouse Square* ☏ *215/569–3100.*

Kiehl's Since 1851. Step inside this store and you can feel like you're
in an Old World apothecary—with a sleek, modern twist. The staff
is friendly and helpful and knows everything about the extensive line
of natural lotions, balms, and cosmetics. This chain is known for giving away generous samples. ⊠ *1737 Walnut St., Rittenhouse Square*
☏ *215/636–9936.*

Sephora. Locals rejoiced when the national cosmetic chain finally landed
in Center City. It stocks lots of must-have make-up, skincare, hair-
care, and perfume brands, including Bare Essentials, Nars, Benefit,
Laura Mercier, and Stila. ⊠ *1714 Chestnut St., Rittenhouse Square*
☏ *215/563–6112.*

SHOES **Aerosoles.** You can find all looks from sporty to dressy at this store, whose
stylish, comfortable line comes in a rainbow of colors from lavender to
marigold. ⊠ *1700 Walnut St., Rittenhouse Square* ☏ *215/546–5407.*

Head Start Shoes. Floor-to-ceiling windows showcasing a huge selection
of Italian shoes and boots beckon to shoppers passing by this hip shop.
Inside you can find women's, men's, and children's footwear in the trendiest styles. ⊠ *126 S. 17th St., Rittenhouse Square* ☏ *215/567–3247.*

Sherman Brothers Shoes. This discount retailer of men's shoes has name-
brand merchandise and excellent service. The store stocks extra-wide
and extra-narrow widths, as well as sizes up to 16. Look for classic
comfort shoes by Cole Haan, Clarks, and Rockport. ⊠ *1520 Sansom
St., Center City West* ☏ *215/561–4550.*

Stiletto. Seeking comfortable flats? You won't find them here. Instead,
you'll find sexy, sky-high styles that give the store its name. An abundance of stilettos and high-heeled boots give this shop its own "Sex
and the City" take on style. ⊠ *124 S. 18th St., Center City West*
☏ *215/972–0920.*

UNIVERSITY CITY

Most of the action in University City revolves around the universities,
specifically the University of Pennsylvania and Drexel University. An
active retail scene has sprouted around the U. of Penn's campus to serve
that huge population of students. A pocket of interesting, eclectic shops
and restaurants has also sprung up farther west, in a residential area
that's home to mostly grad students and professors on the other side
of Clark Park.

SPECIALTY STORES

BOOKSTORES **House of Our Own.** Despite its location in a brownstone flanked by University of Pennsylvania fraternity houses, there's nothing fratty about
this erudite bookstore. Its two floors of rambling rooms with shelves
reaching up to the soaring ceilings boast an enormous amount of literature mixed in with course books for Penn students and used books.

Part of the appeal is to spend a frivolous hour perusing books in a place that makes you feel like you're back in college. ✉ *3920 Spruce St., University City* ☎ *215/222–1576.*

Penn Bookstore. The 60,000-square-foot store, operated by Barnes & Noble, is the largest academic bookstore in the United States. Highlights include tomes from the University of Pennsylvania faculty, loads of Penn-insignia clothing and memorabilia, a multimedia section, and a children's reading room. You can also find a Starbucks and the requisite best sellers. ✉ *3601 Walnut St., University City* ☎ *215/898–7597.*

ART AND CRAFTS GALLERIES
VIX Emporium. This collective of mostly local designers—ceramicists, jewelers, clothing designers—is located in a former millinery with the original built-in cabinetry and beveled-glass windowpanes. The couple that owns the shop have a background in retail and are artisans themselves—she's a jeweler and he's a graphic designer. That's typical of the creative entrepreneurs popping up in the section of West Philadelphia. ✉ *5009 Baltimore Ave., University City* ☎ *215/471–7700.*

GIFTS AND SOUVENIRS
Avril 50. This narrow shop fulfills several functions: an international newsstand—if you're looking for a particularly obscure foreign periodical, you'll find it here; excellent coffee and espresso shots; unusual postcards; high-end chocolate; and specialty cigarettes and tobacco. The patio seating is an added bonus—enjoy your newspaper and coffee while people-watching. ✉ *3406 Sansom St., University City* ☎ *215/222–6108.*

NORTHERN LIBERTIES

Northern Liberties is a taxi or bus ride from Old City, but it's worth checking out, especially since the Piazza at Schmidt's, a new retail space on the former site of Schmidt's Brewery, opened in 2009. Its more than 100,000 square feet of independent shops, galleries, and restaurants have strengthened the pulse of this already lively neighborhood with an industrial heritage and an artsy vibe.

SHOPPING DISTRICTS AND MALLS

The **Piazza at Schmidt's** (✉ *2nd and Hancock Sts., Northern Liberties* ⊕ *atthepiazza.com*), a local developer's mixed-use interpretation of Rome's Piazza Navona, was a long time coming, and was the cause of so much controversy over the years that locals were almost shocked to see it finally open in summer 2009. A "curator" handpicks the independent retailers and gallerists who fill nearly 40 ground-floor commercial spaces. (Condos occupy the floors above.) They ring a giant plaza with pavement scalloped in the same pattern as in Rome and featuring a giant stage and screen. Especially during warm-weather months, there's usually some kind of event or live entertainment going on at the piazza.

SPECIALTY STORES

ANTIQUES
Architectural Antiques Exchange. Victorian embellishments from saloons and apothecary shops, stained and beveled glass, gargoyles, and advertising memorabilia entice shoppers here. ✉ *715 N. 2nd St., Northern Liberties* ☎ *215/922–3669.*

ART AND CRAFTS GALLERIES

Art Star. Two grads of the local Tyler School of Art run this retail shop and gallery that carries independent designers and artists with a crafty bent. You'll find everything from necklaces made with recycled bottle caps and silk-screened T-shirts to original art.⊠ *623 N. 2nd St., Northern Liberties* ☎ *215/238–1557.*

Bambi Gallery and Boutique. Bartender-turned-curator Candace Karch shows emerging local and nonlocal artists in her soaring space in the Piazza at Schmidt's. Her shows change monthly, but she always carries some pieces by local designers, such as lamps made from old skateboard decks by Victor Navez. ⊠ *1001–13 N. 2nd St., Northern Liberties* ☎ *215/423–2668.*

Nexus Foundation for Today's Art. A group of artists started this nonprofit organization in 1975. The emphasis is on experimental art as well as new directions in traditional mediums. ⊠ *Crane Arts LLC, 1400 N. American St., Fishtown* ☎ *215/629–1103.*

CLOTHING

Arcadia Boutique. This open and airy clothing store is all-green, all-the-time: the tees are made from bamboo fibers and shelves are fashioned from reclaimed timber. ⊠ *819 N. 2nd St., Northern Liberties* ☎ *215/667–8099.*

Maison du Very Bad Horse. This shop showcases local designer Kim Montenegro, whose signature hip-hugging, laced-and-studded custom denim jackets and jeans are a favorite with rock stars and those who want to look like rock stars. The store has been known to open for very late-night fittings for acts that are on tour and playing a venue in town. ⊠ *1050 N. Hancock St., Northern Liberties* ☎ *267/455–0449.*

FOOD

Brown Betty. One of many women-owned businesses endemic to the nabe, Brown Betty is revered for its pineapple pound cake and for its long menu of cupcakes. The overall favorite might be Jean's Road Trip (a cupcake with red velvet cake and chocolate icing), but it's a toss-up. Enjoy a treat on the cozy bakery's curvaceous antique couch. ⊠ *1000 N. 2nd St., Northern Liberties* ☎ *215/629–0999.*

Side Trips from Philadelphia

THE BRANDYWINE VALLEY AND VALLEY FORGE

WORD OF MOUTH

"I think Longwood Gardens is worth a visit any time of year but during the Christmas season it is even more special."

—AnnMarie_C

"We had very limited time, but Winterthur is an amazing place. I would like to return and explore it at length. We did a quick garden tour with a docent and the general overview tour of the house with a docent. Du Pont was an amazing man and his collections are beautiful and vast."

—Centralparkgirl

Updated by Robert DiGiacomo

It's easy to expand your view of the Philadelphia area by taking one or more day trips to destinations that are within an hour's drive of the city. Head southwest, and in 30 minutes you can be immersed in a whole new world—or make that "worlds."

First you can see the verdant hills and ancient barns of the Brandywine Valley, home to three generations of Wyeths and other artists inspired by the rural landscapes outside their windows. Then you can visit the extravagant realm of du Pont country, including Pierre S. du Pont's resplendent Longwood Gardens, whose summer fountain displays are world-renowned, and Winterthur, an important repository of American decorative furnishings, over the border in Delaware. Or you can explore the Revolutionary War battlefield of Brandywine at Chadds Ford. These attractions are year-round favorites of Philadelphians, and area bed-and-breakfasts and inns make the Brandywine appealing as an overnight or weekend trip and as a day excursion.

The historical park at Valley Forge adds another dimension to the revolutionary story that began in Independence Hall. Not far away, the town called King of Prussia dates to that period, but is now primarily synonymous with shopping, thanks to its huge upscale mall. It's a half-hour from Philadelphia and easily accessible by public transportation.

ORIENTATION AND PLANNING

GETTING ORIENTED

The Brandywine Valley's major attractions are less than an hour's drive from each other, so you can cover a fair amount of ground. In just a few days' time you can explore quiet country roads, admire the art collections and gardens of some of the region's best-known families, visit key sites from the Revolutionary War, taste a little wine, and hike, walk, or bike along some of the area's most lovely byways.

The Brandywine Valley. Ruled by two families, the Wyeths and the du Ponts, there are many reasons to stay awhile here, whether it's to take in the quintessential Brandywine vistas or explore other top attractions like Winterthur and Longwood Gardens.

Valley Forge. The two main draws of Valley Forge are at odds with one another—George Washington's Revolutionary War encampment at Valley Forge National Historical Park on the one hand and the King of Prussia mall on the other.

TOP REASONS TO GO

Brandywine River Museum: The work of iconic American painter Andrew Wyeth, as well as that of his illustrator father, N. C. Wyeth, and son, Jamie, is celebrated at this museum.

Longwood Gardens: The internationally renowned gardens and conservatories are worth a visit any time of the year.

From farm to table: Enjoy a gourmet lunch in the homey Talula's Table in Kennett Square or stock up

on provisions for a picnic lunch or supper.

American History lesson: Valley Forge, the site of the American revolutionary force's difficult encampment in the winter of 1777, is now a lovely park with miles of walking and jogging trails.

One man's treasure: The collection of American furniture and objects amassed by Henry Francis du Pont at Winterthur offers a window on the nation's past through design.

PLANNING

WHEN TO GO

Each season provides plenty of reasons to visit this area, which is about 45 minutes' to an hour's drive from Center City Philadelphia. Spring and summer bring a Technicolor display of flowers at Longwood and verdant green to the Brandywine Valley countryside and Valley Forge National Park. The chance to witness some spectacular fall foliage and crisper weather is a compelling case for an autumnal visit, although the spectacular holiday light show at Longwood and the chance to relax by a cozy fire at a charming inn are reason enough to come during the cold-weather months. You can easily make day trips here from the city, but be sure to avoid traveling west on Interstate 76, and to a lesser extent, south on Interstate 95, during rush hour. Weekends, spring through fall, tend to be the busiest season for visitors.

GETTING HERE AND AROUND

BUS TRAVEL

To get to Valley Forge, you can take SEPTA Bus 125 from 13th and Market streets (it leaves twice an hour starting at 5:15 AM) for King of Prussia (including the Plaza and the Court) and continue on to Valley Forge National Historical Park.

Bus Contacts **SEPTA** (☎ 215/580–7800 ⊕ www.septa.com).

CAR TRAVEL

For the Brandywine Valley, take U.S. 1 south from Philadelphia; it is about 25 mi away, and many attractions are on U.S. 1. To reach Wilmington, pick up U.S. 202 south just past Concordville or take I–95 south from Philadelphia.

For Valley Forge, take the Schuylkill Expressway (I–76) west from Philadelphia to Exit 327 (Mall Boulevard). Make a right onto Mall Boulevard and a right onto North Gulph Road. Follow the road 1½ mi to Valley Forge National Historical Park. Mall Boulevard also provides easy access to the Plaza and the Court shopping complex.

TRAIN TRAVEL

Amtrak has frequent service from Philadelphia's 30th Street Station to Wilmington's station at Martin Luther King Jr. Boulevard and French Street on the edge of downtown. It's a 25-minute ride.

SEPTA's R2 commuter train has hourly departures to Wilmington from Philadelphia's Suburban, 30th Street, and Market East train stations. The trip takes one hour.

Train Contacts **Amtrak** (☎ 800/872–7245 ⊕ www.amtrak.com). **SEPTA** (☎ 215/580–7800 ⊕ www.septa.com).

TOURS

Colonial Pathways organizes full-day bus tours through the Brandywine Valley. Brandywine Outfitters rents out canoes and kayaks and offers a range of scenic trips on the Brandywine River April through September.

Tour Contacts **Brandywine Outfitters** (✉ 2096 Strasburg Rd., Coatesville ☎ 610/486–6141 or 800/226–6378 ⊕ www.canoepa.net). **Colonial Pathways** (✉ Box 879, Chadds Ford 19317 ☎ 610/388–2654 or 800/421–2654 ⊕ www. colonialpathways.com).

RESTAURANTS

It seems that most restaurants in the Brandywine Valley serve American cuisine, with creative contemporary touches at the better establishments. Most also present local specialties—fresh seafood from the Chesapeake Bay and dishes made with Kennett Square mushrooms. As an added pleasure, some of the region's best restaurants are in restored Colonial and Victorian homes.

HOTELS

Many of the region's accommodations may be considered bed-and-breakfasts because of their intimate atmosphere, but they're far from the typical B&B—which is usually a room in a private home—and are more accurately characterized as inns or small hotels.

WHAT IT COSTS				
	¢	$	$$	$$$	$$$$
Restaurant	under $10	$10–$14	$15–$19	$20–$24	over $24
Hotel	under $100	$100–$150	$151–$200	$201–$250	over $250

Restaurant prices are for one main course at dinner. Hotel prices are for two people in a standard double room.

VISITOR INFORMATION

The visitor center at the entrance to Longwood Gardens is operated by the Chester Country Conference and Visitors Bureau. It's open daily 10–6.

Visitor Information **Chester Country Conference and Visitors Bureau** (✉ 300 Greenwood Rd., Kennett Square ☎ 800/228–9933)

THE BRANDYWINE VALLEY

You'll probably experience a strong sense of déjà vu during a journey to the Brandywine Valley. While creating some of the most beloved works in 20th-century American art, Andrew Wyeth made the valley's vistas instantly recognizable. Using colors quintessentially Brandywine—the earthen brown of its hills, the slate gray of its stone farmhouses, and the dark green of its spruce trees—the famous American realist captured its unostentatiously beautiful personality. He also inspired many people to flock to this valley and fall in love with its peaceful byways. The Philadelphia suburbs are encroaching: new housing developments continuously crop up, and the main highways, U.S. 1 and Route 202, bring with them traffic snarls. Yet, traveling down country roads, particularly those that intersect Route 52, makes you feel you have discovered a remote treasure.

The Brandywine Valley actually incorporates parts of three counties in two states: Chester and Delaware counties in Pennsylvania and New Castle County in Delaware. Winding through this scenic region (about 25 mi southwest of Philadelphia), the Brandywine River flows lazily from West Chester, Pennsylvania, to Wilmington, Delaware. Although in spots it's more a creek than a river, it has nourished many of the valley's economic and artistic endeavors.

The valley is also the site of one of the more dramatic turns in the American Revolution, the Battle of Brandywine, and a fascinating museum dedicated to helicopters. Antiques shops, fine restaurants, and cozy country inns dot the region. Your best bet is to rent a car and explore on your own.

If you start early enough, and limit your time at each stop, you can tour the valley's top three attractions—the Brandywine River Museum, Longwood Gardens, and Winterthur—in one day. If you have more time to spend in the valley, you can visit additional sites in Pennsylvania and then move on to Wilmington.

KINGDOM OF THE DU PONTS

Although paintings of the Wyeth family distilled the region's mystery, it was the regal du Pont family that provided more than a bit of its magnificence, adding grand gardens, mansions, and mills. Their kingdom was established by the family patriarch, Pierre-Samuel du Pont, who had escaped with his family from post-Revolutionary France and settled in northern Delaware. The Du Pont company was founded in 1802 by his son Éleuthère Irénée (E.I.), who made the family fortune, first in gunpowder and iron and later in chemicals and textiles.

E.I. and five generations of du Ponts lived in Eleutherian Mills, the stately family home on the grounds of a black-powder mill that has been transformed into the Hagley Museum. The home, from which Mrs. Henry du Pont was driven after accidental blasts at the powder works, was closed in 1921. Louise du Pont Crowninshield, a great-granddaughter of E.I., restored the house fully before opening it to the public. Louise's relatives were busy, too. Henry Francis du Pont was filling his country estate, Winterthur, with furniture by Duncan Phyfe, silver by

Paul Revere, splendid decorative objects, and entire interior woodwork fittings salvaged from homes built between 1640 and 1860.

Pierre S. du Pont (cousin of Henry Francis) devoted his life to horticulture. He bought a 1,000-acre 19th-century arboretum and created Longwood Gardens, where he entertained his many friends and relatives. Today 350 acres of the meticulously landscaped gardens are open to the public. Displays range from a tropical rain forest to a desert; acres of heated conservatories, where flowers are in bloom year-round, create eternal summer. Pierre also built the grand Hotel du Pont, adjacent to the company's headquarters in downtown Wilmington. No expense was spared; more than 18 French and Italian craftspeople labored for two years, carving, gilding, and painting. Alfred I. du Pont's country estate, Nemours, was named after the family's ancestral home in north-central France. It encompasses 300 acres of French gardens and a mansion in Louis XVI style.

WEST CHESTER

30 mi west of Philadelphia via I–95.

The county seat since 1786, this historic mile-square city holds distinctive 18th- and 19th-century architecture, with fine examples of Greek Revival and Victorian styles. A small but vital downtown has shopping possibilities as well as restaurants and bars serving everything from classic American fare to the latest microbrews. Fine examples of classical architecture, including the Chester County Courthouse and Market Street Station, can be found near the intersection of High and Gay streets. The town is also home to one of the area's most-visited attractions, the QVC Studios, in an industrial park off U.S. 202.

GETTING HERE AND AROUND

From Philadelphia, West Chester is a 45-minute drive via I–95 and U.S. Route 322 West and U.S. Route 202 South. The town itself is highly walkable, but you will need a car to access QVC Studios and other nearby attractions.

ESSENTIALS

Visitor Information **Chester County Conference and Visitors Bureau** (⊠ *17 Wilmont Mews, Suite 400, West Chester 19382* ☎ *610/719–1730 or 800/228–9933* ⊕ *www.brandywinevalley.com*).

EXPLORING

ℭ   **American Helicopter Museum & Education Center.** Ever since Philadelphian
★   Harold Pitcairn made the first rotorcraft flight in 1928, the Southeastern Pennsylvania area has been considered the birthplace of the helicopter industry. In fact, two of the three major U.S. helicopter manufacturers trace their roots to this region. This heritage is showcased here, and you can learn about and climb aboard nearly three dozen vintage and modern aircraft that reflect the copter's historic roles in war and rescue missions, in agriculture, and in police surveillance. ⊠ *1220 American Blvd.* ☎ *610/436–9600* ⊕ *www.helicoptermuseum.org* ⌂ *$6* ☉ *Wed.– Sat. 10–5, Sun. noon–5.*

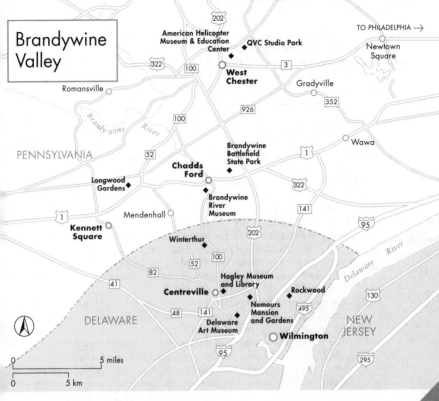

Chester County Historical Society. The society's architectural complex, known as the History Center, includes a former opera house where Buffalo Bill once performed. Galleries tell about the region's settlers and the decorative furniture they crafted. A hands-on history lab lets you churn butter and dress up in a hoop skirt. The society's collection of American cross-stitch samplers is extensive; in the museum shop you can get everything you need to start stitching yourself. ✉ *225 N. High St.* ☎ *610/692–4800* ⊕ *www.chestercohistorical.org* 🎫 *$5* ☺ *Wed.– Sat. 10–5*

★ **QVC Studio Park.** This is the world's largest electronic retailer, which in one year alone answered more than 180 million phone calls, shipped more than 165 million packages, and recorded more than $7 billion in sales. On a one-hour guided tour of the company headquarters you can catch a glimpse of its round-the-clock live broadcast from five studio views and see how QVC products make the route from testing to television. The tour is designed for ages 6 and up. If you want free tickets to be part of a studio audience for a live broadcast, call ahead or visit the Web site to reserve a seat. The studio is wheelchair accessible. ✉ *1200 Wilson Dr.* ☎ *800/600–9900* ⊕ *www.qvctours.com* 🎫 *Tours $7.50* ☺ *Daily tours offered at 10:30, noon, 1, 2:30, and 4.*

WHERE TO EAT

$$$$
AMERICAN
Fodor's Choice
★

✕**Dilworthtown Inn.** Fresh seafood from the Chesapeake Bay, Australian lamb, and chateaubriand are among the entrées at this longtime favorite for romantic dining. The 15 dining rooms of the elegant 1754 country inn are carefully restored and decorated with antiques and Oriental rugs. The wine cellar, one of the region's best, stocks more than 800 vintages, including a merlot and a chardonnay bottled exclusively for the inn. Jackets are suggested for men. The restaurant also offers cooking and wine classes at its Inn Keeper's Kitchen. ⊠ *1390 Old Wilmington Pike, West Chester* ✛ *5 mi south of downtown West Chester* ☎ *610/399–1390* ⊕ *www.dilworthtown.com* ▤ *AE, D, DC, MC, V* ⊗ *No lunch.*

$$$$
FRENCH
★

✕**Gilmore's French Cuisine.** Owned by Peter Gilmore, a former *chef de cuisine* at Philadelphia's well-regarded Le Bec-Fin, this intimate restaurant serves classic French cuisine with a modern American update. The menu includes novel items such as a "haute dog" consisting of shellfish encased in a lobster mousse and coated with Panko bread, as well as more traditional favorites from Gilmore's Le Bec-Fin days, such as a crab cake in a lemon beurre-blanc sauce. ⊠ *133 E. Gay St., West Chester* ☎ *610/431–2800* ⊕ *www.gilmoresrestaurant.com* ▤ *MC, V* ⊗ *Closed Sun.–Mon. No lunch.*

$$$
SOUTHERN
★

✕**High Street Caffe.** Massive mirrors and silver beaded lighting fixtures create a fun and sexy vibe at this small café. Everything here is done up in the color purple—walls, tablecloths, and even the coffee mugs. The staff in the kitchen and dining room is attentive to details. Louisiana smoked alligator sausage and crawfish tails in a spicy barbecue sauce are popular starters. Jambalaya, étouffée, and other favorites from the French Quarter predominate, but you can also find seared ahi tuna and Jamaican-seasoned pork with pineapple mint salsa on the menu. There's live jazz Friday to Sunday night. ⊠ *322 S. High St.* ☎ *610/696–7435* ⊕ *www.highstreetcaffe.com* ▤ *AE, MC, V* ⊗ *Closed Mon. No lunch weekends.*

SHOPPING

Baldwin's Book Barn (⊠ *865 Lenape Rd.* ☎ *610/696–0816* ⊕ *www.book-barn.com*) is a book lover's dream. This off-the-beaten-path bookstore in a converted barn has nooks and crannies filled with more than 300,000 used and rare books on almost every subject, along with historic maps and prints.

The Brandywine Valley workshop of the renowned Irish glassblower **Simon Pearce** (⊠ *1333 Lenape Rd., Rte. 52* ☎ *610/793–0949* ⊕ *www.simonpearce.com*) is stocked with original glass and pottery. You can watch the glassblowers at work, or stop for lunch or dinner at the adjacent restaurant overlooking the Brandywine River. The food—served on Simon Pearce china, of course—is American with global influences, and emphasizes locally sourced produce, meats, and other products.

CHADDS FORD

11 mi south of West Chester, 30 mi southwest of Philadelphia via I–95 and U.S. 322.

Immortalized in Andrew Wyeth's serene landscapes, Chadds Ford was less bucolic in the 18th century, when one of the bloodiest battles of the Revolutionary War was fought here along Brandywine Creek. A

battlefield park and a fine art museum celebrating American masters, including Brandywine Valley natives, make this historic town appealing. There are some pretty side roads to explore as well.

GETTING HERE AND AROUND

From Philadelphia, take Interstate 95 South to U.S. Route 322 toward West Chester and follow signs to U.S. Route 1. The latter is the major thoroughfare to visit the various attractions in Chadds Ford, and can get congested on weekends, so be prepared for lots of stop-and-go traffic.

ESSENTIALS

Visitor Information **Delaware County's Brandywine Conference and Visitors Bureau** (✉ *1 Beaver Valley Rd., Chadds Ford* ☎ *610/565–3679 or 800/343–3983* ⊕ *www.brandywinecvb.org*).

EXPLORING

Brandywine Battlefield State Park is near the site of the Battle of Brandywine, where British general William Howe and his troops defeated George Washington on September 11, 1777. The Continental Army then fled to Chester, leaving Philadelphia vulnerable to British troops. The visitor center has displays about the battle that are a good introduction to the area's history. On the site are two restored Quaker farmhouses that once sheltered Washington and General Lafayette. The 50-acre park is a fine place for a picnic. ✉ *U.S. 1* ☎ *610/459–3342* ⊕ *www.brandywinebattlefield.org* ✏ *Park free, house tours $6* ☉ *Park: Mar.–Nov., Tues.–Sat. 9–5, Sun. noon–5; Dec.–Feb., Thurs.–Sat. 9–5, Sun. noon–5.*

Fodor'sChoice ★ In a converted Civil War–era gristmill, the **Brandywine River Museum** showcases the art of Chadds Ford native Andrew Wyeth, a major American realist painter, as well as his father, N. C. Wyeth, illustrator of many children's classics; and his son, Jamie. The collection also emphasizes still lifes, landscape paintings, and American illustration, with works by such artists as Howard Pyle and Maxfield Parrish. The glass-wall lobby overlooks the river and countryside that inspired the Brandywine School. The museum uses a system of filters, baffles, and blinds to direct natural light. Outside the museum, you can visit a garden with regional wildflowers and follow a 1-mi nature trail along the river.

The N. C. Wyeth House and Studio, where N. C. painted and raised his children, is open part of the year. The 1911 home, set on a hill, holds many of the props N. C. used in creating his illustrations. His daughter, Carolyn, lived and painted here until 1994. You can also tour the

9

Kuerner Farm, a mile away. Andrew discovered it on a walk when he was 15; he used the farm's landscape, buildings, and animals as the subjects of many of his best-known paintings. A shuttle takes you from the museum to the house or to the farm for an hour-long guided tour. Reservations can be made two weeks in advance. ⊠ *U.S. 1 and Rte. 100* ☎ *610/388–2700* ⊕ *www.brandywinemuseum.org* ⊜ *$10 museum, $5 house, $5 farm* ⊗ *Museum daily 9:30–4:30; house, Apr.–Nov., Tues.– Sun. 10–3:15; farm Apr.–Nov., Thurs.–Sun. 10–3:15.*

In a restored barn, the **Chaddsford Winery** (⊠ *632 Baltimore Pike, U.S. 1* ☎ *610/388–6221* ⊕ *www.chaddsford.com*) offers tastings and tours of its wine-making facilities. On Friday nights in July and August, pack a picnic and settle in for live music under the stars.

WHERE TO EAT AND STAY

¢
AMERICAN

✕ **Hank's Place.** Locals flock to this wood-panel outpost for hearty breakfast specials, such as shiitake mushroom omelets and eggs Benedict topped with chipped beef. Hank's is also open for home-style lunches and dinners (come early, as it closes at 7 PM). The Irish-style chili with mashed potatoes, fresh fish, and "Steerburger" with fresh sautéed Kennett Square mushrooms beckon. The strawberry pie and apple dumplings are specialties. ⊠ *U.S. 1 and Rte. 100* ☎ *610/388–7061* ⊕ *www. hanks-place.net* ⊟ *No credit cards* ⊗ *No dinner Sun. and Mon.*

$

☷ **Brandywine River Hotel.** Near the Brandywine River Museum, this two-story hotel has tasteful Queen Anne–style furnishings, classic English chintz, and floral fabrics that create a homey B&B feel. Suites have fireplaces and whirlpool baths. Afternoon tea with homemade cookies and a plentiful continental breakfast with fresh fruit and homemade muffins are included; wine and beer are available in the lobby's cash bar. Request a room that overlooks the surrounding pasture. **Pros:** convenient to attractions; good value for money; afternoon snacks. **Cons:** inconsistent service; some rooms could use updating; not as charming as a B&B. ⊠ *U.S. 1 and Rte. 100* ☎ *610/388–1200* ⊕ *www.brandywineriverhotel.com* ⇥ *29 rooms, 10 suites* ⚑ *In-room: refrigerator (some), Internet. In-hotel: bar, gym, some pets allowed, no-smoking rooms* ⊟ *AE, D, DC, MC, V* ⧀ *CP.*

$$–$$$

☷ **Fairville Inn.** This B&B, halfway between Longwood Gardens and Winterthur, has bright, airy rooms furnished with Queen Anne and Hepplewhite reproductions and dramatic white-draped canopy beds. The main house, built in 1857, has a striking living room with a fireplace. Rooms in the carriage house and springhouse have decks; those in the latter have a sweeping view down to the pond. The Fairville serves a complimentary breakfast, which includes a choice of three entrées, such as an egg dish, homemade pancakes, or Belgian waffles, and an afternoon tea with home-baked cookies, fruit, and cheese. **Pros:** gracious hosts; central location. **Cons:** some rooms have squeaky floors; some rooms need updating; grounds could be nicer. ⊠ *506 Kennett Pike, Rte. 52* ☎ *610/388–5900* ⊕ *www.fairvilleinn.com* ⇥ *13 rooms, 2 suites* ⚑ *In-room: VCR (some), Wi-Fi. In-hotel: no elevator, laundry service, no kids under 12, no-smoking rooms* ⊟ *AE, D, MC, V* ⧀ *BP.*

$$–$$$
Fodor'sChoice
★

Sweetwater Farm. This historic property—part of William Penn's land grant to the Hemphill family—carves out a tranquil 50 acres of Brandywine Valley countryside. Rooms in the 1734 Quaker farmhouse include the Dormer, once a hospital for the Underground Railroad. Rooms in the 1815 Georgian addition have four-poster beds and fireplaces. Among the seven cottages are a former greenhouse and the thoroughly modern Hemphill and Brandywine units, with gas fireplaces and flat-screen TVs. Both fun and nature are bountiful here, thanks to a billiards room, massage services, and hiking trails. The three-course breakfast is served in the dining room or on the outdoor patio, which overlooks the pond and the resident horses and goats. **Pros:** elegant decor; well-maintained grounds; accommodating staff. **Cons:** some guest rooms are small; some may not like presence of pets; late breakfast not available. ⊠ *50 Sweetwater Rd., Glen Mills* ☎ *610/459–4711 or 800/793–3892* ⊕ *www.sweetwaterfarmbb.com* ↪ *7 rooms, 7 cottages* ⟨ *In-room: kitchen (some), DVD (some), VCR (some), Wi-Fi. In-hotel: golf course, pool, gym, no elevator, public Internet, public Wi-Fi, some pets allowed, no-smoking rooms* ⊟ *MC, V* ⊧ *BP.*

CENTREVILLE, DELAWARE

5 mi south of Chadds Ford via U.S. Route 1 and PA Route 52 (Kennett Pike).

The village is aptly named: Centreville, Delaware, founded in 1750 and listed in the National Register of Historic Places, was a midway point between the farms of Kennett Square and the markets of Wilmington. The tiny village, with a historic tavern and some art and antiques shops, is in the middle of the Brandywine Valley's attractions. Longwood Gardens, Winterthur, and the Brandywine River Museum are all less than 5 mi away. Kennett Pike (Route 52) runs through the village; the surrounding two-lane roads take you through some of the still-bucolic parts of the valley.

9

GETTING HERE AND AROUND

Traffic on both Kennett Pike and Route 1 picks up on weekends, especially in the spring and fall.

EXPLORING

⟳
★

A restored mid-19th-century mill community on 235 landscaped acres along the Brandywine River, the **Hagley Museum and Library** provides an enlightening look at the development of early industrial America. This is the site of the first of the du Pont family's black-powder mills. Live demonstrations depict the dangerous work of the early explosives industry. "Du Pont Science and Discovery" traces the company's evolution and displays a NASCAR car and a space suit. Admission includes a narrated bus tour through the powder yards with stops at Eleutherian Mills, the 1803 Georgian-style home furnished by five generations of du Ponts; Workers' Hill, where costumed interpreters describe the life of a typical mill worker; and a French Renaissance–style garden. Allow about two hours for your visit. The coffee shop is open for lunch except in winter. ⊠ *Rte. 141 between Rte. 100 and U.S. 202* ☎ *302/658–2400* ⊕ *www. hagley.org* ⟐ *$11* ☉ *Mid-Mar.–Dec., daily 9:30–4:30; Jan.–mid-Mar.,* *weekends 9:30–4:30; winter tours, weekdays at 1:30.*

Henry Francis du Pont (1880–1969) housed his 85,000 objects of American decorative art in a sprawling nine-story country estate called **Winterthur.** The collection, displayed in 175 rooms, is recognized as one of the nation's finest. Its objects, made or used in America between 1640 and 1860, include Chippendale furniture, silver tankards by Paul Revere, and Chinese porcelain made for George Washington. To sample the collection, you can choose between an hour-long introductory tour, different one-hour theme tours (like "Elegant Entertaining"), and two-hour tours that delve into ceramics, textiles, or furniture. The museum also has galleries with permanent displays and changing exhibitions of antiques and crafts that you can study at your own pace. No children under 8 are allowed except on the daily family tour, which is open to all but geared to kids ages 4 to 12. Surrounding the estate are 982 acres of landscaped lawns and naturalistic gardens, which you can visit on a 30-minute narrated tram ride or on your own. The Enchanted Woods is a fantasy-theme 3-acre children's garden with an 8-foot-wide bird's nest, a faerie cottage with a thatch roof, and a troll bridge. A gift shop and cafeteria, which serves Sunday brunch, are also on the grounds. ⊠ *5105 Kennett Pike, Rte. 52, 5 mi south of U.S. 1, Winterthur, Delaware* ☎ *302/888–4600* ⊕ *www.winterthur.org* 🎫 *$18 for house, garden, and introductory tour; ticket good for two consecutive days; $30 for house, garden, and one-hour specialty tour; $40 for house, garden, and two-hour specialty tour* ☉ *Tues.–Sun. 10–5; introductory tours offered 10:30–3:30*

Fodor'sChoice
★

WHERE TO EAT AND STAY

$$

AMERICAN

✕ **Buckley's Tavern.** Though this 1817 roadside tavern serves your typical burgers and beers (local microbrews are on tap), the menu surprises you with wild-mushroom calzones, Asian-style shrimp salad, and roasted beet and goat cheese salad. The shoestring sweet-potato fries and the crab and artichoke dip are favorites. There's a sunny porch and a dining room with a fireplace. You can pick from the wine list or buy a bottle from the shop next door. ■ TIP→ **If you wear your pajamas to the Sunday brunch, your entrée will be half off. You won't be alone, either, about a third of brunch diners eat in their PJs.** ⊠ *5812 Kennett Pike* ☎ *302/656–9776* ⊕ *www.buckleystavern.org* ⊟ *AE, MC, V.*

$$–$$$
★

🛏 **Inn at Montchanin Village.** This luxurious lodging includes 11 painstakingly restored 19th-century cottages that once housed workers from the nearby Du Pont powder mills. Each elegant room is decorated with oil paintings, reproductions of antique furniture, and four-poster or canopy beds covered with Frette linens. All have kitchenettes and luxurious marble baths; some have porches with wicker rockers. The great room, where evening hors d'oeuvres are served, has overstuffed chairs, game tables, and a stone hearth that stretches from floor to ceiling. The inn is nestled in a series of peaceful gardens intersected with landscaped walkways. **Pros:** good mix of new amenities and period charm; luxurious bathrooms; beautiful gardens. **Cons:** sprawling property; inconsistent service; some rooms need updating. ⊠ *Rte. 100 and Kirk Rd., Montchanin, Delaware* ☎ *302/888–2133 or 800/269–2473* ⊕ *www.montchanin.com* ⇲ *12 rooms, 16 suites* ⚖ *In-room: safe, kitchen, complimentary soft drinks, DVD, dial-up (some), Wi-Fi (some). In-hotel: restaurant, room service, bar, gym, spa, laundry service, concierge, no-smoking rooms* ⊟ *AE, D, DC, MC, V.*

KENNETT SQUARE

8 mi northwest of Centreville via PA Route 52 and U.S. Route 1.

Kennett Square is where mushroom cultivation began in the United States. By the mid-1920s, 90 percent of the nation's mushrooms were grown in southeastern Pennsylvania. The town celebrates its heritage with its annual Mushroom Festival in September. Most visitors come to visit Longwood Gardens, a lovely spot about 3 mi northeast of Kennett Square. The town itself, with its Victorian-era homes lining the tree-lined streets, is also worth a visit; there are shops, galleries, and restaurants along East State Street between Broad and Union.

EXPLORING

Fodor'sChoice ★ ♻ **Longwood Gardens** has established an international reputation for its immaculate, colorful gardens full of flowers and blossoming shrubs. In 1906 Pierre S. du Pont (1870–1945) bought a simple Quaker farm and turned it into the ultimate early-20th-century estate garden. Attractions include magnolias and azaleas in spring; roses and water lilies in summer; chrysanthemums in fall; and camellias, orchids, and palms in winter. You can stroll in the Italian water garden or explore a meadow full of wildflowers on the garden's 350 acres. Bad weather is no problem, as 4 acres of cacti, ferns, and bonsai plants are housed in heated conservatories. Outdoors is the Bee-aMazed Children's Garden, with a honeycomb maze, queen bee throne, and small splashing fountains. The Indoor Children's Garden has a bamboo maze, a grottolike cave, and a drooling dragon. There is a regular summer concert series, as well as special fireworks and fountain events. The cafeteria (open year-round) and dining room (closed January–March) serve reasonably priced meals. ⊠ *1001 Longwood Rd., 3 mi northeast of Kennett Square along U.S. 1* ☎ *610/388–1000* ⊕ *www.longwoodgardens.org* ▦ *$16* ⊙ *Apr.–May, daily 9–6; June–Aug., Sun.–Wed. 9–6, Thurs.–Sat. 9–9; Sept.–late-Nov., daily 9–5; late-Nov.–early Jan., daily 9–9; early Jan.–Mar., daily 9–5.*

WHERE TO EAT

$$$$ ITALIAN ★ ✕ **Sovana Bistro.** Chef Nicholas Farrell transforms local and organic ingredients into satisfying meals at this popular rustic restaurant, which is part French bistro and part Italian trattoria. Hand-cut pasta in a wild-boar sauce, grass-fed New York strip steak in a Burgundy crema, and strawberry shortcake with lemon chiffon using local berries are highlights of the seasonal menu. Though a lunch of a grilled ham-and-cheese sandwich and tomato soup might sound mundane, it's anything but: the ham is imported, the mozzarella and bread are made in-house, and the

9

tomato soup is roasted and drizzled with basil-infused oil. The wood-oven pizzas, breads, and pastries are sold in an adjacent café, which also has breakfast items. ⊠ *696 Unionville Rd.* ☎ *610/444–5600* ⊕ *www.sovanabistro.com* ☴ *AE, MC, V* ⊘ *No lunch Sun; closed Mon.* ☖ *BYOB is allowed ($5 corkage fee), although restaurant has full wine list.*

$–$$ ✕ **Talula's Table.** A couple of Philadelphia restaurateurs moved to Ches-
AMERICAN ter County and put their considerable talents into this gourmet market. Talula's has its own artisan cheeses, house-cured meats, and handmade breads and pastas, along with a coffee bar and prepared meals for take-out. The menu, which changes daily, includes treats like lobster potpie, eggplant and goat-cheese sandwiches, and ham and cheddar scones. You can pick up the makings for a picnic or eat at the farmhouse table. ⊠ *102 W. State St.* ☎ *610/444–8255* ⊕ *www.talulastable.com* ☴ *AE, D, DC, MC, V.*

WILMINGTON, DELAWARE

15 mi southeast of Kennett Square via PA Route 52.

Delaware's commercial hub and largest city has handsome architecture—with good examples of styles such as Federal, Greek Revival, Queen Anne, and Art Deco—and abundant cultural attractions. Wilmington began in 1638 as a Swedish settlement and later was populated by employees of various du Pont family businesses and nearby poultry ranches. The four-block Market Street Mall marks the city center and is distinguished by the Grand Opera House. The four-story theater, built by the Masonic Order in 1871, has a white cast-iron facade in French Second Empire style to mimic the old Paris Opera. The adjoining Giacco Building houses a smaller theater and art galleries. Outside Wilmington's compact city center are several outstanding museums, including some that are legacies of the du Ponts.

GETTING HERE AND AROUND

The city of Wilmington is less than 45 minutes by car via I–95 South from Philadelphia and is easily accessible by AMTRAK. But since you won't want to miss visiting Longwood Gardens, Winterthur, or some of the other stately mansions in the area, you'll want to have a car. Typically, those driving south from Philadelphia to Wilmington during rush hours will encounter some traffic, but not gridlock, because the commute mostly runs the opposite way. Downtown Wilmington is compact and walkable, but it tends to shut down after business hours.

ESSENTIALS

Visitor Information **Greater Wilmington Convention and Visitors Bureau**
(⊠ *100 W. 10th St., Wilmington, DE* ☎ *302/652–4088 or 800/489–6664* ⊕ *www.visitwilmingtonde.com*).

EXPLORING

A treat for art lovers, the **Delaware Art Museum** is housed in a splendid 85,000-square-foot building. The lighted roofline changes colors according to the celestial calendar, and Dale Chihuly's Persian Window installation draws attention to the entrance. The museum's holdings include a good collection of paintings by Howard Pyle (1853–1911), a Wilmington native known as the "father of American illustration," as well as works by his students N. C. Wyeth, Frank Schoonover, and Maxfield Parrish. Other American artists represented are Benjamin West, John Sloan, Winslow Homer, Edward Glackens, and Edward Hopper. The museum also has the largest American collection of 19th-century English pre-Raphaelite paintings and decorative arts and a children's interactive gallery. *The Crying Giant,* by Tom Otterness, is one of the highlights of the 9-acre Sculpture Park. ⊠ *2301 Kentmere Pkwy.* ☎ *302/571–9590* ⊕ *www.delart.org* ☑ *$12, free Sun. and first Fri. of month, 4–8* ⊗ *Wed.–Sat. 10–4, Sun. noon–4; first Fri. of month, extended hours from 4–8.*

For a look at how the very wealthy lived, visit **Nemours Mansion and Gardens,** a 300-acre country estate built for Alfred I. du Pont in 1910. This modified Louis XVI château, which underwent a $39 million restoration that was completed in 2008, showcases 102 rooms of European and American furnishings, rare rugs, tapestries, and art dating to the 15th century. The gardens, reminiscent of those at Versailles, are landscaped with fountains, pools, and statuary. The estate can be seen only on guided two-hour tours. Visitors must be at least 12 years old. ⊠ *1600 Rockland Rd., between Rte. 141 and U.S. 202* ☎ *302/651–6912* ⊕ *www.nemoursmansion.org* ☑ *$15* ⊗ *May–Dec., Tues.–Sat. tours at 9, 11, 1 and 3; Sun. 11, 1, 3; closed Jan.–Apr.*

WHERE TO EAT AND STAY

$$$–$$$$
AMERICAN

✕ **Domaine Hudson Wine Bar & Eatery.** Wine enthusiast Tom Hudson oversees this sophisticated bistro that makes wine tasting approachable. He offers 40 to 50 wines by the glass—served in high-end German crystal—so you can try several varieties in an evening. Recipes, such as duck and exotic mushroom croquette, coffee and spice-rubbed buffalo fillet, and she-crab soup with Old Bay croutons, were chosen to complement the wines, and many are available in half-size versions, leaving room for a cheese course. The handsome dining room, with faux leather walls and dark woods, has a clubby feel. ⊠ *1314 N. Washington St.* ☎ *302/655–9463* ⊕ *www.domainehudson.com* ☰ *AE, D, MC, V* ⊗ *No lunch.*

$$$–$$$$

▥ **Hotel du Pont.** Built in 1913 by Pierre S. du Pont, this luxury hotel in downtown Wilmington has hosted everyone from Charles Lindbergh to John F. Kennedy. The elegant 12-story building radiates an Old World feel. The lobby has a spectacular carved, gilded, and painted ceiling, polished marble walls, and Queen Anne and Chippendale furnishings. The walls display more than 700 original works of art, including Wyeths and Schoonovers. The spacious guest rooms have a contemporary flair, with soothing Tuscan yellow color schemes and earthy textures. The Green Room is known for its marvelous Sunday brunches. **Pros:** fine dining, luxe ambience, responsive service. **Cons:** small elevators, staff can be too formal, few restaurants or shops in immediate vicinity. ⊠ *11th and Market Sts.,* ☎ *302/594–3100 or 800/441–9019* ⊕ *www.hoteldupont. com* ⇨ *206 rooms, 11 suites* ♿ *In-room: safe, refrigerator, Wi-Fi. In-hotel: restaurant, room service, bar, gym, laundry service, concierge, public Wi-Fi, airport shuttle, parking (fee), no-smoking rooms* ☰ *AE, D, DC, MC, V.*

VALLEY FORGE

20 mi northeast of downtown Philadelphia via I–76.

A major site of the Revolutionary War is near the suburban village of Valley Forge. The town was named for an iron forge built in the 1740s.

The monuments, markers, huts, and headquarters in Valley Forge National Historical Park illuminate a decisive period in U.S. history. The park, with its quiet beauty that seems to whisper of the past, preserves the area where George Washington's Continental Army endured the bitter winter of 1777–78.

GETTING HERE AND AROUND

When traffic is flowing on Interstate 76, the major east–west highway between Philadelphia and Valley Forge, the trip can take just 35 to 40 minutes. But frequent gridlock, especially during rush hour, can stretch the trip to 90 minutes, so try to time your visit accordingly. Once you're at the park, you can access the major sites via a free shuttle bus. Other area attractions will require a car for access, however.

TOURS   The self-driven Valley Forge National Historical Auto-Tour can be purchased from the Welcome Center ($10 tape, $12 CD). A narrated trolley tour of the park is available from June through October for $15 per person.

ESSENTIALS

Bus Information SEPTA (☎ 215/580–7800 ⊕ www.septa.com).

Visitor Information Valley Forge Convention and Visitors Bureau (✉ 600 W. Germantown Pike, Suite 130, Plymouth Meeting ☎ 610/834–1550 or 800/441–3549 ⊕ www.valleyforge.org). **Valley Forge Welcome Center** (✉ Rte. 23 and N. Gulph Rd. ☎ 610/783–1077 ⊕ www.nps.gov/vafo).

EXPLORING

Chanticleer, the onetime estate of the owner of a local pharmaceutical company, is now a 30-acre pleasure garden that bursts with color in the spring when 10,000 bulbs bloom. The grounds offer a range of settings, including lush woodlands with rare Asian specimens, a formal house garden, and a serpentine-shaped "avenue" lined with young junipers, wheat and barley, and gingko trees. ✉ *786 Church Rd., Wayne* ☎ *610/687–4163* ⊕ *www.chanticleergarden.org* 💲 *$5* 🕙 *Apr.–Oct., Wed.–Sun. 10–5; May–Aug., Fri. 10–8.*

The **Mill Grove Audubon Center** was the first American home of Haitian-born artist and naturalist John James Audubon (1785–1851). Built in 1762, the house is now a museum displaying the major works of this renowned American naturalist, including his paintings of birds and wildlife, and an original copy of his massive *Birds of America.* The attic has been restored to a studio and taxidermy room. The National Audubon Society, which runs the museum, has restored these treasures and added others. Mill Grove, 2 mi north of Valley Forge National Historical Park is within the 175-acre Audubon Wildlife Sanctuary, which has 5 mi of marked walking trails with scenic views of Perkiomen Creek that were once trod by Audubon himself. ✉ *Audubon and Pawlings*

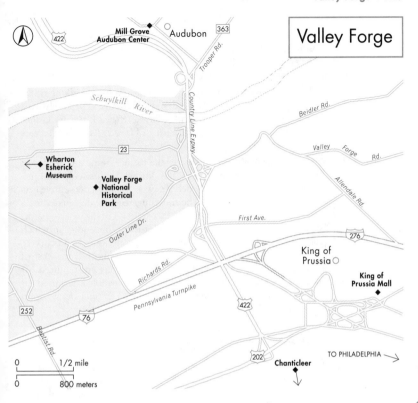

Valley Forge

Rds. ☎ 610/666-5593 ⊕ *pa.audubon.org* ✉ *Museum $4, grounds free* ☉ *Museum Tues.–Sat. 10–4, Sun. 1–4; grounds Tues.–Sun. 7–dusk.*

★ **Valley Forge National Historical Park,** administered by the National Park Service, is the location of the 1777–78 winter encampment of General George Washington and the Continental Army. Stop first at the Valley Forge Welcome Center to see the 18-minute orientation film (shown every 30 minutes) and view exhibits. In summer you can take a narrated trolley tour for $16 person and a free shuttle that makes a continuous loop around the park. Stops include reconstructed log huts of the Muhlenberg Brigade and the National Memorial Arch, which pays tribute to the soldiers who suffered through the brutal winter. Other sites are the bronze equestrian statue of General Anthony Wayne, in the area where his Pennsylvania troops were encamped; Artillery Park, where the soldiers stored their cannons; and the Isaac Potts House, which served as Washington's headquarters.

The park is quiet today, but in 1777 the army had just lost the nearby battles of Brandywine, White Horse, and Germantown. While the British occupied Philadelphia, Washington's soldiers were forced to endure horrid conditions here—blizzards, inadequate food and clothing, damp quarters, and disease. Although no battle was fought at Valley Forge, 2,000 soldiers died here.

The troops did win one victory that winter—a war of will. The forces slowly regained strength and confidence under the leadership of Prussian drillmaster Friedrich von Steuben. In June 1778 Washington led his troops away from Valley Forge in search of the British. Fortified, the Continental Army was able to carry on the fight for five years more.

The park contains 6 mi of jogging and bicycling paths and hiking trails, and you can picnic at any of three designated areas. A leisurely visit to the park takes no more than half a day. ⊠ *Rte. 23 and N. Gulph Rd.* ☎ *610/783–1077* ⊕ *www.nps.gov/vafo* ⊠ *Free* ☉ *Park daily dawn–dusk; welcome center daily 9–5.*

The **Wharton Esherick Museum** preserves the former home and studio of the "Dean of American Craftsmen." Best known for his sculptural furniture, Esherick (1887–1970) shaped a new aesthetic in decorative arts by bridging art with furniture. The museum, recently designated as a National Historic Landmark, houses 200 examples of his work—paintings, woodcuts, furniture, and wood sculptures. The studio, in which everything from the light switches to the spiral staircase is hand-carved, is one of his monumental achievements. The museum is 2 mi west of Valley Forge National Historical Park. Reservations are required for the hourly tours. On weekdays a minimum of five people is required for a tour. ⊠ *1520 Horseshoe Trail* ☎ *610/644–5822* ⊕ *www.levins.com/esherick.html* ⊠ *$10* ☉ *Mar.–Dec., Sat. 10–5, Sun. 1–5.*

SHOPPING

The **Chapel Cabin Shop** (⊠ *Alongside Washington Memorial Chapel on Rte. 23* ☎ *610/783–0576*) is staffed primarily by volunteers from the parish, who make the cakes, candies, and jams that are sold here. Proceeds help keep the privately owned chapel afloat. You can also find fine pewter, Colonial art, and souvenirs related to the American Revolution. The shop includes a tiny luncheonette—and outdoor picnic tables—where you can enjoy daily specials, such as Martha's 16-Bean Soup.

Fodor's Choice ★ The **King of Prussia Mall** (⊠ *U.S. 202 at Schuylkill Expressway, 160 N. Gulph Rd.* ☎ *610/265–5727* ⊕ *www.kingofprussiamall.com*), one of the nation's largest shopping complexes, is a tourist destination in itself. Comprising two main buildings—the Plaza and the Court—the mall contains more than 40 restaurants, 365 shops and boutiques, and seven major department stores, including Bloomingdale's, Nordstrom, and Neiman Marcus. Dining options include Morton's of Chicago, Legal Sea Foods, the Cheesecake Factory, and three food courts.

Bucks County

"[Bucks County] was just voted one of the most romantic places in the country and many of its towns (New Hope, for example) are great for walking, shopping, eating, relaxing, and history. It's north of Philly and I'm pretty sure you could get there in 2 hours."

—KeyGal

"I have lived in Lambertville for 2 years now & find that I never get sick of strolling thru both towns [Lambertville and New Hope], dining in the wide variety of restaurants, checking out the art galleries & boutiques. One thing I have observed over the years is that Lambertville is much more of a residential community than New Hope."

—NJriverchick

By Andrea
Lehman

Bucks County, about an hour's drive northeast of Philadelphia, could have remained 625 square mi of sleepy countryside full of old stone farmhouses, lush hills, and covered
bridges if it hadn't been "discovered." First, New York artists and intelligentsia bought country homes here in the
'30s. More recently, suburbanites and exurbanites bought
or built year-round houses, eager to live in an area of rela-
tive peace and quiet within a long commute of New York
and Philly.

Over the years Bucks County has been known for art colonies and
antiques, summer theater, and country inns. Cookie-cutter housing
developments are now planted where grain once grew, however. It's
not unusual to find suburban sprawl and hyper-development adjacent
to an old clapboard farmhouse or ancient stone barn. Yet many areas
of Central and Upper Bucks County remain as bucolic as ever—a feast
of lyrical landscapes, with canal and river vistas, rolling hills, and fertile
fields. Driving back roads is one of the county's pleasures, and making
your way through quiet little towns, stopping at historic sites, checking
out antiques shops, and staying overnight in an appealing inn make for
a classic weekend getaway.

That a river runs through it—or, more accurately, alongside it—has long
left its imprint on the county. The Delaware has provided its share of
challenges, from the ice-choked seeming impassibility that made General Washington's nighttime crossing such a surprise to recent floods
that have forced some businesses to close and some buildings to be
raised. But the river also provides outdoor opportunities. Canals carved
into both its banks are now popular recreation arteries, and the river
itself is great for fishing, floating, or gazing at as it rolls along.

ORIENTATION AND PLANNING

GETTING ORIENTED

Many Bucks County sights are along two perpendicular corridors: U.S.
202, which runs northeast from Doylestown to New Hope, and Route
32, also known as River Road, which runs northwest parallel to the
Delaware River and Canal. The former connects the county's leading
destination towns: Doylestown, the county seat and home to several
interesting museums; New Hope, a bustling tourist mecca of shops and
restaurants; and Lambertville, a tamer version of New Hope that feels
Bucks-like even though it's actually in Hunterdon County, New Jersey.
The latter connects a number of historical sites as it winds from the re-
created 17th-century Pennsbury Manor past the important 18th-century

TOP REASONS TO GO

Country drives: Bring your GPS and sense of adventure on the winding back roads of Central and Upper Bucks. Getting a little lost is part of the experience as you pass old farms, new estates, and perhaps even a covered bridge.

The towpath: Biking, strolling, jogging, or even cross-country skiing along the relatively flat Delaware Canal towpath are safe, scenic, and soothing ways to get a little exercise.

R&R at B&Bs: As if rural settings, 18th- and 19th-century buildings, indulgent breakfasts, and whirlpool tubs in tasteful, antiques-filled rooms weren't enough, local inns have been adding massage and other spa treatments to their reasons to unwind here.

Contemporary and vintage shopping: The corridor between Lahaska and Lambertville is peppered with enough flea markets and antiques shops as well as stores and galleries selling new art and crafts, clothing, jewelry, housewares, tchotchkes, and outlet "bargains" to fill your car and empty your wallet.

Tour the wineries: The eight wineries of the Bucks County Wine Trail offer tastings of the local vintages.

events of Washington Crossing and on through New Hope and small, quaint river towns farther north.

Lower Bucks County. Bordering Philadelphia, Lower Bucks consists of older, more densely populated suburbs dotted with really old settlements. It's not unusual to see the vestiges of 18th- and 19th-century hamlets, little more than a farmhouse or a few buildings at a crossroads, surrounded by big-box stores, malls, and post-war housing, including the well-known Levittown. A handful of tourist gems can be mined in Lower Bucks County, in Colonial corners and malls alike.

Central Bucks County. A little farther from Philadelphia, Central Bucks offers more elbow room than its southern neighbor. In general, there are bigger gaps between the towns and housing developments. Though not home to as many residents as Lower Bucks, this area is home to the majority of the county's sightseeing and specialty shopping, in such towns as New Hope and Doylestown.

10

PLANNING

WHEN TO GO

There truly is no bad time to visit Bucks County, though most visitors come April through December, bringing with them higher lodging prices and potentially harder-to-get restaurant reservations. On warm, sunny weekends, New Hope's sidewalks and parking spaces fill up. If you're averse to crowds or groups of motorcyclists, come on a weekday or rainy day. In summer, splashing around at Sesame Place or taking a cooling float down the Delaware are great antidotes to the heat. In autumn, a drive through rolling hills painted in fall colors followed by a glass of wine next to a stone fireplace makes for a romantic day. Before and around the holidays, you'll find festivals, the annual reenactment of Washington crossing the Delaware, and, of course, plentiful shopping.

GETTING HERE AND AROUND

CAR TRAVEL

From Philadelphia the most direct route to Bucks County is I–95 north, which takes you near sights in the southern part of the county. From the last exit before you cross into New Jersey, you can turn left (north) on Taylorsville Road and then right (east) on Woodside Road to head directly to Route 32, which runs along the Delaware River past Washington Crossing Historic Park. New Hope is about 40 mi northeast of Philadelphia.

Bucks County is a large area—40 mi long and up to 20 mi wide—and is almost impossible to tour without a car. Main roads are River Road (Route 32), U.S. 202, and Route 611. One great pleasure of a visit here can be exploring country back roads.

TRAIN TRAVEL

The Southeastern Pennsylvania Transportation Authority (SEPTA) provides frequent service from Philadelphia's Market Street East, Suburban, and 30th Street stations to Doylestown on the R5 line. The trip takes up to 90 minutes, depending on the number of local stops.

Train Contacts **SEPTA** (☎ 215/580–7800 ⊕ www.septa.org).

RESTAURANTS

Bucks County has no regional specialties to call its own, but you can discover some sophisticated restaurants as well as casual country spots. What makes dining here special are the enchanting settings, ranging from a French-style auberge to Colonial-era manor. Fine meals of French or American fare are served in restored mills, pre-Revolutionary taverns, stagecoach stops, small cafés, and elegant Victorian mansions. In summer and fall it's best to make reservations for weekend dining.

HOTELS

Bucks County has relatively limited lodging options for families; larger inns, hotels and motels, and campgrounds are the best bets. There are numerous choices for couples: accommodations ranging from modest to elegant can be found in historic inns, small hotels, and B&Bs. Most hostelries include breakfast in their rates. Reserve early—as much as three months ahead for summer and fall weekends. Many accommodations require a two-night minimum stay on weekends and a three-night minimum on holiday weekends. Many inns prohibit or restrict smoking. Because some inns are historic homes furnished with fine antiques, the owners may not allow children or may have age restrictions.

Bucks County Bed & Breakfast Association of Pennsylvania (⊕ *www.visitbucks.com*) represents more than 30 inns within Bucks County and Hunterdon County, New Jersey.

WHAT IT COSTS					
	¢	$	$$	$$$	$$$$
Restaurant	under $10	$10–$14	$15–$19	$20–$24	over $24
Hotel	under $100	$100–$150	$151–$200	$201–$250	over $250

Restaurant prices are for main course at dinner. Hotel prices are for two people in a standard double room in high season.

VISITOR INFORMATION

The Bucks County Conference & Visitors Bureau provides a wealth of information, including a useful visitor's guide. The Central Bucks Chamber of Commerce provides lists of hotels and restaurants and other information.

Visitor Information **Bucks County Conference & Visitors Bureau** (⊠ 3207 Street Rd., Bensalem ☎ 215/639–0300 or 800/836–2825 ⊕ www.visitbuckscounty.com). **Central Bucks Chamber of Commerce** (⊠ 252 W. Swamp Rd., Doylestown ☎ 215/348–3913 ⊕ www.centralbuckschamber.com).

LOWER BUCKS COUNTY

Lower Bucks is the densest section of Bucks County with the oldest development. The northern end of Lower Bucks is generally more upscale. This area is great for families and history buffs to explore, with everything from Sesame Place to the spot where George Washington crossed the Delaware.

SESAME PLACE

25 mi northeast of Philadelphia via I-95.

EXPLORING

☺ **Sesame Place.** Next to the Oxford Valley Mall, this water and theme park based on the popular children's show, *Sesame Street,* is mostly for kids 2 to 10 and their families. Here children crawl, climb, and jump; float, slide, and splash; and meet, greet, and perhaps hug the ageless Big Bird and his friends. Though there are plenty of dry-land activities, the highlights of the park—especially on a hot summer day—are the water rides, including the popular Rambling River and Sky Splash, and the new interactive Count's Splash Castle. As befits a park for preteens, the three "thrill" rides in Elmo's World and the roller coaster—Vapor Trail—are modest by theme-park standards, but they've got more than enough excitement for young riders. Other kid favorites are the daily parades and shows and Sesame Neighborhood, a replica of the beloved TV street. ⊠ 100 Sesame Rd., off Oxford Valley Rd. near U.S. 1 at I–95, Langhorne ☎ 215/752–7070 or 866/464–3566 ⊕ www.sesameplace. com 🎟 $50.95 ⊙ Late May–early Sept., daily; early May and early Sept.–late Oct., weekends; hrs vary.

10

FALLSINGTON

4 mi east of Sesame Place via U.S. 1.

The pre-Revolutionary village of Fallsington displays more than 300 years of American architecture, from a simple 17th-century log cabin to the Victorian excesses of the late 1800s. Ninety period homes are found in the village, which is listed on the National Register of Historic Places.

Historic Fallsington. Three historic buildings—a 17th-century log cabin and a turn-of-the-19th-century tavern and house—have been restored and opened for guided tours by Historic Fallsington. ⊠ *4 Yardley Ave., off Tyburn Rd.* W ☎ *215/295–6567* ⊕ *www.historicfallsington.org* ▭ *$6* ☉ *Mid-May–mid-Oct., Tues.–Sat. 10:30–3:30; Mid-Oct.–mid-May, Tues.–Fri. by appt.*

PENNSBURY MANOR

6 mi southeast of Fallsington.

GETTING HERE AND AROUND

Pennsbury Manor is about 15 minutes away from the town of Morrisville. From Philadelphia, take I–95 to Exit 46A (Route 1 North, Morrisville). Travel Route 1 North to the Route 13 South (Bristol) Exit. Exit at Tyburn Road East. Take a right at first traffic light onto New Ford Mill Road. Take a right at end of road onto Bordentown Road. Take the first left onto Pennsbury Memorial Road. The manor is located at the end of the road.

EXPLORING

Pennsbury Manor. On a gentle rise 150 yards from the Delaware River, Pennsbury Manor is a 1939 reconstruction of the Georgian-style mansion William Penn built in the 1680s. Living-history demonstrations on 43 of the estate's original 8,400 acres provide a glimpse of everyday life in 17th-century America. The property, including formal gardens, orchards, an icehouse, a smokehouse, and a bake-and-brew house, helps paint a picture of the life of an English gentleman 300 years ago. The plantation also shows that although history portrays Penn as a dour Quaker, as governor of the colony he enjoyed the good life by importing the finest provisions and keeping a vast retinue of servants. These extravagances led to financial difficulties that resulted in Penn's spending nine months in a debtor's prison. Though you can wander about the grounds on your own, the house can be seen only on a tour. One Sunday a month in the warmer months there are special programs devoted to historic trades, such as open-hearth cooking or beer brewing. To get here, follow the blue-and-yellow historical markers. ⊠ *400 Pennsbury Memorial Rd., between Morrisville and Bristol* ☎ *215/946–0400* ⊕ *www.pennsburymanor.org* ▭ *$7* ☉ *Grounds Tues.–Sat. 9–5, Sun. noon–5. Tours Apr.–Nov., Tues.–Fri. at 10, 11:30, 1:30, and 3:30, Sat. at 11, 12:30, 2, and 3:30, Sun. at 12:30, 1:30, 2:30, and 3:30; Dec.–Mar., less frequent.*

NEED A
BREAK?

Not far from the river in a nondescript corner of town is a delightful Asian fusion restaurant, **Concerto Fusion Cuisine** (✉ *2 S. Delmorr Ave.* ☎ *215/428–2899* ⊕ *www.concertofusion.com* ▤ *AE, MC, V*). Past the wall of water is a modern bar and dining room, where you can order from an ample menu that merges a host of Asian (and some non-Asian) cuisines. Start with crab Rangoon or phyllo-crusted prawns before moving on to wok-seared ginger duck, Thai red snapper, or a large selection of sushi and sashimi. Lunch specials are a good deal.

BRYN ATHYN

18 mi west of Fallsington via US-1.

Bryn Athyn was founded in the late 1800s as a community for New Church members, who follow the religious writings of Emanuel Swedenborg (1688–1772). About a 20-mi drive north of the city, the community is still very much intact with a boys' school, a girls' school, and a college. The two reasons to visit are the spectacular cathedral and Glencairn, the house turned antiquities museum. The Pitcairns, the family who footed the bill for almost everything, had another house, Cairnwood, which can be toured. The sights constitute a National Historic Landmark, and even though they are on the same large, grassy hill, they are run separately. While technically located in neighboring Montgomery County, not Bucks County, Bryn Athyn is a short drive from the other sights nearby.

EXPLORING

★ **Bryn Athyn Cathedral.** Construction began in 1913, but Raymond Pitcairn, who provided the vision and the funds, insisted that the cathedral be built the old way—he wanted a medieval cathedral and he wanted the medieval techniques of stone cutting and stained glass making used as well. Also, the cathedral was built from models, not blue prints, and these models became adaptable over the course of construction. While the cathedral is impressive from the outside, the most interesting architectural discoveries are in the inside, where the cathedral becomes more than a copy of medieval motifs, and where many New Church beliefs are melded into the architecture. Throughout the interior is optical refinement, meaning there are no hard angles, and no two things are the same—every archway, door, and window, is slightly different: even every lock has its own special key, and no two carving details are alike. The walls are all slightly curved and it is not something you notice until it is pointed out to you, and then you go about the tour marveling over the subtle changes. Known for its stained glass, which was all made on site, the actual cathedral is a wash of red and blue, a stunning glow that changes throughout the day, depending on the sun. From Center City, go north on Broad Street to Route 611, right on County Line Road, and south on Route 232 to the second traffic light; the cathedral will be on your right. ✉ *1001 Cathedral Rd.* ✛ *15 mi north of Center City* ☎ *215/947–0266* ⊕ *www.brynathyncathedral.org* ▧ *Free* ☉ *Tues.–Sun. 1–4; services Sun. 9:30 and 11.*

10

Glencairn Museum. Built after the cathedral between 1928 and 1939, this neo-Romanesque 90-room former home of Raymond and Mildred Pitcairn, now houses the family's collection of antiques that were gathered by John and his son Raymond. The house has some fantastic details, but the best part is walking into old bedrooms that now serve as galleries for ancient Greek, Roman, Egyptian, African, Native American, and Sumerian artworks as well as a fantastic basement gallery full of 13th-century European stained glass and sculpture. Part of the New Church teaching is that god has always been present in all ancient religions. Try to come during the week when you can customize your tour to your interest—the general weekend tour doesn't really allow you the opportunity to enjoy one gallery in particularly and the family story is told sounds more like hagiography than history. The view from the observation deck, 149 feet up, is worth the tight elevator ride up there. ⊠ *1001 Cathedral Rd.* ☎ *267/502–2993* ⊕ *www.glencairnmuseum.org* ☲ *$7* ☉ *Weekdays 9–5; Sat. 75-min highlights tour at 11, 11:30, 12:30, and 1.*

WASHINGTON CROSSING

12 mi north of Fallsington via I-95.

The small village of Washington Crossing is home to a smattering of basic services and residential areas as well as Washington Crossing Historic Park. Upriver from its central crossroads is a research library dedicated to the American Revolution, while just to the west, where Route 532 crosses the canal, you'll find access to the towpath with parking.

GETTING HERE AND AROUND
Washington Crossing Historic Park stretches along River Road (Rte. 32). The Lower Park, at the intersection with Route 532, is the site of both the actual crossing and the visitor center. There is a narrow bridge here, which makes crossing to New Jersey somewhat easier today. The Upper Park and wildflower preserve are 5–6 mi north of the visitor center.

Washington Crossing Historic Park. It was from the site of what is now Washington Crossing Historic Park that on Christmas night in 1776 General Washington and 2,400 of his men crossed the Delaware River, attacked the Hessian stronghold at Trenton, and secured a much-needed victory for the Continental army. Today park attractions, including historic houses and memorials, are divided between the Lower Park and Upper Park.

In the Lower Park, the visitor center screens a free 15-minute introductory movie and displays a reproduction of Emanuel Leutze's famous 1851 painting of the crossing (the original hangs in the Metropolitan Museum of Art in New York). Here you can purchase tickets for guided tours of the Lower Park. You can tour the McConkey Ferry Inn, where tradition has it that Washington and his staff had Christmas dinner while waiting to cross the river. You can also see replicas of the Durham boats used in that fateful crossing, and visit some of the early-19th-

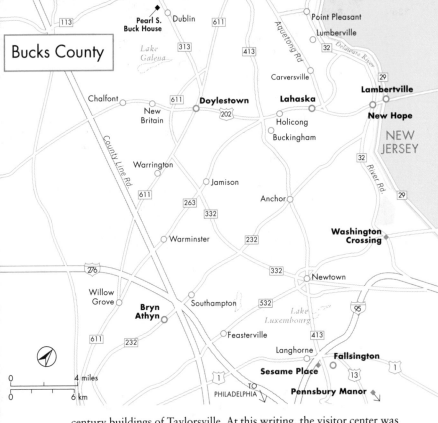

Bucks County

century buildings of Taylorsville. At this writing, the visitor center was slated to close for renovations.

In the Upper Park, 125-foot-tall Bowman's Hill Tower offers a commanding view of the Delaware River. An elevator takes you up the 1931 tower, which is open seasonally. A half-mile farther north, the Thompson-Neely House, an 18th-century miller's house, and the Thompson-Neely gristmill offer tours that tell of life in Bucks County during and after the American Revolution. The house was used as a hospital during the 1776–77 encampment of Washington's army. Some Revolutionary soldiers are buried near the home.

The park holds special events throughout the year, including a reenactment of the crossing in December. ⊠ *Rte. 32* ☎ *215/493–4076* ⊕ *www. ushistory.org/washingtoncrossing* ▣ *Grounds free, tour and tower $7* ⊙ *Park Tues.–Sat. 9–5, Sun. noon–5; tours Tues.–Sat. at 10, 11, 1, 2, 3, and 4; Sun. at noon, 1, 2, 3, and 4.*

Bowman's Hill Wildflower Preserve. The 134-acre preserve showcases hundreds of species of wildflowers, trees, shrubs, and ferns native to Pennsylvania. Take the guided tour (included in the cost of admission) or follow any of the short well-marked trails. ⊠ *1635 River Rd.* ☎ *215/862–2924* ⊕ *www.bhwp.org* ▣ *$5* ⊙ *Grounds daily dawn–dusk; visitor center daily 9–5; tours Apr.–Oct., daily at 2.*

Crossing Vineyards. On a 200-year-old estate near where Washington crossed the Delaware, the family-run vineyard mixes vintage charm with modern wine-making techniques. Despite a nod to the rustic (a beam ceiling in the tasting room and gift shop), the old gambrel-roofed barn feels fresh and upscale. In a 15- to 20-minute tasting, the staff lets you know what to expect from the different types of wines. Ask to see Lucy and Ethel, the computerized press and crusher-destemmer, respectively. Concerts are offered in summer. ⊠ *1853 Wrightstown Rd., off Rte. 532* ☎ *215/493–6500* ⊕ *www.crossingvineyards.com* ⊑ *$8* ⊙ *Daily noon–6.*

WHERE TO EAT

$$$

ITALIAN

✕ **Francisco's on the River.** Cozy rooms, including an enclosed front porch, beamed ceiling, white tablecloths, and windows all around, give a refined but undeniably country feel to this river-view, BYOB restaurant. Chef Francisco Argueta, who also owns Florentino's in Newtown, breathes new life into old favorites like lobster ravioli, eggplant *parmigiano*, linguine *al frutti di mare fradiavolo,* and lasagna with a hint of smoked bacon. Though the specials, which lean heavily to seafood, are standard size, pasta portions are enormous. If you don't have access to a fridge for your leftovers, consider sharing. ⊠ *1251 River Rd.* ☎ *215/321–8789* ⊕ *www.franciscosontheriver.com* ⊟ *AE, D, MC, V* ⌓ *BYOB* ⊙ *Closed Mon. No lunch.*

CENTRAL BUCKS COUNTY

This part of Bucks Country tends to be more rural, with a growing number of new developments sprouting on old farmland. New Hope and Lambertville have cute downtowns to explore and make a great base for seeing all that the area has to offer.

NEW HOPE

8 mi north of Washington Crossing via Rte. 32, 40 mi northeast of Philadelphia via I-95.

The cosmopolitan village of New Hope, a hodgepodge of old homes, narrow streets and alleys, courtyards, and busy restaurants, attracts artists, shoppers, hordes of day-trippers and motorcyclists, who clog both streets and boutiques on summer weekends. It's also one of the East Coast's most popular weekend getaways among gays and lesbians. The town, listed on the National Register of Historic Places, is easy to explore on foot; the most interesting sights and stores are clustered along four blocks of Main Street and on the cross streets—Mechanic, Ferry, and Bridge streets—which lead to the river. Some parts of town are older than others. As you might guess from their names, Ferry Street dates back to colonial times; Bridge Street is Victorian.

GETTING HERE AND AROUND

Getting to New Hope is easy. Both U.S. 202 and Route 32 run through it. Getting around New Hope on a busy weekend is harder. If you see cars backed up along Main Street, drive around the periphery instead, as it can take a fair amount of time to inch your way through town.

Bucks County History

Named after England's Buckinghamshire, Bucks County was opened to European settlement by William Penn in 1681 under a land grant from Charles II. The county's most celebrated town, New Hope, was settled in the early 1700s and, together with its neighbor across the river, Lambertville, New Jersey, was called Coryell's Ferry. (One of the original gristmills is now the home of the Bucks County Playhouse.) The town was the Pennsylvania terminal for stagecoach traffic and Delaware River ferry traffic. Barges hauled coal along the 60-mi Delaware Canal until 1931.

Commerce built up New Hope, but art helped sustain it. An art colony took root in the late 19th century, and the area was revitalized beginning in the 1930s by theater and literary folk, such as lyricist Oscar Hammerstein II and playwright George S. Kaufman and more recently with the arrival of galleries and artists from around the country. Writers James Michener (winner of the Pulitzer Prize) and Pearl Buck (winner of the Pulitzer and Nobel prizes) also left their marks on Bucks County, which the latter called, "a region where the landscapes were varied, where farm and industry lived side by side, where the sea was near at hand, mountains not far away, and city and countryside were not enemies."

Grab a parking spot when you find one—either on the street or in a municipal lot (bring change for the meter or metered ticket)—and walk where you want to go.

ESSENTIALS
New Hope Visitors Center (⊠ *1 W. Mechanic St., at Main St., New Hope* ☎ *215/862–5030* ⊕ *www.newhopevisitorscenter.org*).

EXPLORING

↻ **New Hope & Ivyland Rail Road.** The passenger train, pulled by an authentic steam locomotive or vintage diesel, makes a 9-mi, 45-minute scenic round-trip between New Hope and Lahaska. The route crosses a trestle used in the rescue scenes in silent films like *The Perils of Pauline*. The New Hope depot is an 1891 Victorian gem. Special events, which require reservations, include dinner trips on Saturday evenings and holiday excursions in December. ⊠ *W. Bridge and Stockton Sts.* ☎ *215/862– 2332* ⊕ *www.newhoperailroad.com* ⊠ *$16.50* ⊙ *Jan.–Mar., weekends; Apr.–late May and Nov., Fri.–Sun.; late May–Oct. and late Dec., daily; early Dec., Thurs.–Sun.; daily departure times vary.*

NEED A BREAK?

Grab a cup of coffee and a yummy pastry or light meal at **C'est la Vie** (⊠ *20 S. Main St.* ☎ *215/862–1956*), where you can eat at tables overlooking the river. It's down a little alley off Main Street. **The Last Temptation** (⊠ *115 S. Main St.* ☎ *215/862–3219*) dishes up delicious Thomas Sweet ice cream, a local favorite. You can blend in M&Ms and other decadent delights.

Parry Mansion. Built in 1784, this stone house is notable because the furnishings reflect decorative changes from 1775 to the Victorian

10

era—including candles, white-washed walls, oil lamps, and wall-paper. Wealthy lumber-mill owner Benjamin Parry built the house, which was occupied by five generations of his family. ⊠ *S. Main and Ferry Sts.* ☎ *215/862–5652* ⊕ *www.newhopehs.org* ⊠ *$5 donation requested* ☉ *Tours May–Oct., weekends 1 and 3.*

WHERE TO EAT

$$$$　✕ **La Bonne Auberge.** One of Bucks
FRENCH　County's most elite and expensive
★　restaurants, La Bonne Auberge, serves classic French cuisine in a pre-Revolutionary farmhouse. The Terrace Room has a modern French country ambience. Some specialties are sautéed Dover sole with capers and rack of lamb. The three-course table d'hôte menu, available Thursday evenings in addition to the regular menu, is a bargain. The restaurant is in a residential development called Village 2. ⊠ *1 Rittenhouse Cir.* ☎ *215/862–2462* ⊕ *www.bonneauberge.com* ⊟ *AE, D, MC, V* ☉ *Closed Mon.–Wed. No lunch.*

$$$$　✕ **Martine's River House.** In a renovated circa 1717 post-and-beam barn
AMERICAN　on the site of an old ferry landing, Martine's offers a dining room with a view. Those who wish to get even closer to the river can eat on the two-level deck. Salads, sandwiches, and small plates compose the lunch menu, while dinner is split between land and sea: filet mignon wrapped in bacon with a red-onion jam and Gorgonzola mousse or grilled striped bass over cilantro and lime-scented vegetables. ⊠ *14 E. Ferry St.* ☎ *215/862–2966* ⊕ *www.martinesriverhouserestaurant.com* ⊟ *AE, MC, V.*

$$　✕ **Triumph Brewing Company.** Shiny vats glistening through the windows
AMERICAN　alert you to the focus of this restaurant. Brick walls and exposed beams and ductwork add to the industrial feel, while outside dining has a view of the New Hope Rail Road. Salads, sandwiches, and entrées are available at lunch and dinner, with slightly more limited offerings late at night. Not surprisingly, the fish-and-chips are beer battered, and the brewhouse burger and braised short ribs come with an India pale ale barbecue sauce. Wash everything down with the seven-beer sampler. There's live music Friday, Saturday, and some Wednesday nights; Texas Hold 'Em on Monday and Thursday, get there by 6:30 to sign up for the 7:30 game; and a ceremonial barrel tapping the first Friday of the month at 6. ⊠ *400 Union Sq.* ☎ *215/862–8300* ⊕ *www.triumphbrewing.com* ⊟ *AE, D, MC, V.*

WHERE TO STAY

$–$$　🏨 **Logan Inn.** Established in 1727 as an extension of the Ferry Tavern, this inn once accommodated passengers riding the ferry to Lambertville. George Washington is said to have stayed here at least five times—and one can only imagine what he would think of the crowds of shoppers who stroll past the inn, which is now smack dab in the busiest part of town. Rooms have original and reproduction Colonial and Victorian furnishings and canopy beds; some have river views. The friendly restaurant ($$$$) serves breakfast on weekends, lunch, dinner, and a popular all-day tavern menu featuring such favorites as burgers and buffalo wings. The Magnolia Terrace is a seasonal outdoor bar. **Pros:** tidy rooms—and free parking!—in the thick of New Hope. **Cons:** if you're looking for a good-size breakfast, the coffee, juice, and muffins available Saturday and Sunday may not do the trick, and it's only coffee and juice on weekdays. ☒ *10 W. Ferry St.* ☏ *215/862–2300* ⊕ *www.loganinn.com* ⤴ *16 rooms* ⚮ *In-room: Wi-Fi. In-hotel: restaurant, bar, laundry service, no-smoking rooms* ☰ *AE, D, MC, V.*

$-$$ ⊞ **Wedgwood Inn.** The accommodations at this B&B include two 1870 Victorians (including a blue "painted lady" with a gabled roof, porch, and a porte cochere) and a Federal-style 1840 stone manor house. A few blocks from Main Street, the inn has 2 acres of parklike grounds with colorful gardens. Every room is decorated with the namesake china, and many have two-person whirlpool tubs, wood-burning stoves, fireplaces, and private porches. A hearty continental breakfast (dietary restrictions accommodated) is served in the breakfast room, on the porch or in the gazebo, or in your room. At night, sip the hosts' homemade almond liqueur. For a fee you can arrange tennis and pool privileges at a nearby club. **Pros:** lovely grounds near to, but set apart from, the middle of town, welcomes children and dogs. **Cons:** rooms are tasteful, but if you don't like Victoriana, wall stencils, and Wedgwood blue, this may not be for you. ☒ *111 W. Bridge St.* ☏ *215/862–2570* ⊕ *www.wedgwood-inn.com* ⤴ *14 rooms, 5 suites* ⚮ *In-room: refrigerator (some), DVD (some), Wi-Fi. In-hotel: some pets allowed, no-smoking rooms* ☰ *AE, MC, V* ⍾ *CP.*

NIGHTLIFE AND THE ARTS

The **Bucks County Playhouse** (☒ *70 S. Main St.* ☏ *215/862–2041* ⊕ *www.buckscountyplayhouse.com*), housed in a historic mill, stages Broadway musical revivals. Shows range from *My Fair Lady* to *Rent*. The season runs from April to December.

Havana (☒ *105 S. Main St.* ☏ *215/862–9897* ⊕ *www.havananewhope.com*) has karaoke Mondays, open mike Tuesdays, and jazz, blues, R&B, singer-songwriter, Latin, reggae, funk, and rock, including cover and dance bands the rest of the week.

Since 1972, **John & Peter's** (☒ *96 S. Main St.* ☏ *215/862–5981* ⊕ *www.johnandpeters.com*) has featured live, original music seven nights a week. Jazz musicians, singer-songwriters, and plenty of rockers all take the stage, as do the not-yet-famous on Monday's open mike night.

SPORTS AND THE OUTDOORS

New Hope Cyclery (☒ *404 York Rd.* ☏ *215/862–6888*) rents mountain bikes for $24 for five hours. The staff can direct you to scenic bike routes.

Join the more than 100,000 people a year who take to the water in inner tubes every summer. **Bucks County River Country** (☒ *2 Walters La., Point Pleasant* ☏ *215/297–5000* ⊕ *www.rivercountry.net*) rents rafts, canoes, and kayaks. Even when the Delaware River is a mass of yellow and green tubes, it's still peaceful.

10

SHOPPING

New Hope's streets are lined with shops selling a touristy mix of upscale and lowdown. Very nice arts and crafts and handmade accessories, clothing, antiques, and jewelry are juxtaposed with campy vintage items, kinky adult paraphernalia, doggie treats, tarot readers, and gargoyle-related gifts.

BOOKS The crowded shelves at **Farley's Bookshop** (⊠ *44 S. Main St.* ☎ *215/862–2452* ⊕ *www.farleysbookshop.com*), a New Hope institution, hold plenty of choices, including books about the region.

CRAFTS A branch of the Lambertville store of the same name, **A Mano Gallery** (⊠ *128 S. Main St.* ☎ *215/862–5122* ⊕ *www.amanogalleries.com*), stocks jewelry, clay, wood, glass, and other decorative items.

You can find art glass and jewelry at **Topeo** (⊠ *35 N. Main St.* ☎ *215/862–2750* ⊕ *www.topeo.com*).

There are contemporary crafts in a mixture of mediums at **Topeo South** (⊠ *15 N. Main St.* ☎ *215/862–4949*).

FOOD For chocolate, including yummy truffles and chocolate-covered pretzels, you'll have to head a little outside the main business district to the delectable **Pierre's Chocolates** (⊠ *360 W. Bridge St.* ☎ *215/862–0602* ⊕ *www.pierreschocolates.com*).

A typically unusual shop, **Suzie Hot Sauce** (⊠ *19A W. Bridge St.* ☎ *215/862–1334* ⊕ *www.suziehotsauce.com*) sells spicy sauces, snacks, and "hot" chocolate year-round. To buy one of the truly fiery products, you'll be asked to sign a release.

LAMBERTVILLE, NEW JERSEY

Across the Delaware River from New Hope, 40 mi from Philadelphia via I–95 and Rte. 29.

If you're interested in New Hope's refrain but prefer it in a lower key, head directly across the Delaware River. You can find more charm and even better antiques in this New Jersey village. In fact, you can't swing a cabriole leg without hitting an antiques shop, as there are some 30 dealers in the small town, as well as a delightfully chic assemblage of boutiques, art galleries, and fine restaurants. One of Lambertville's chief pleasures doesn't involve commerce at all: the towpath along the Delaware Canal is a retreat for strolling, running, or biking. Heading south takes you to the popular Washington Crossing State Park, directly across from the similarly named Pennsylvania park; the less busy northern route leads past other appealing river hamlets.

WHERE TO EAT

¢ ✕ **Full Moon.** Decorated with stained glass and neon lights, this popular
AMERICAN breakfast and lunch spot is filled with the sounds of happy customers. Egg dishes, including assorted omelets and benedicts, figure prominently on the breakfast menu. Among the sandwiches, salads, and burgers that make up the lunch options are a smoked-turkey wrap with cucumber, mango, and curried mayonnaise; pink salad, with pears, apples, raspberries, and candied walnuts; and portobello mushrooms sautéed with onions and peppers topped with provolone and pesto and served on

French bread. Dinner, served only during the full moon, is a special treat. ✉ *23 Bridge St.* ☎ *609/397–1096* 🖃 *MC, V* ☺ *Closed Tues.*

$$$$
MEDITERRANEAN
★

✕ **Hamilton's Grill Room.** Calling this place a "hidden gem" is an understatement. It's not visible from the street, but fans of the changing menu of simply prepared Mediterranean-inspired dishes know where to go. As the name suggests, an open grill—the centerpiece of the Grill Room, one of five dining rooms—figures in the kitchen's preparations. Starters might include grilled shrimp with anchovy butter or iced North Atlantic oysters. Typical entrées are a grilled whole dorade with cherry tomatoes and capers and aged rib-eye steak with a bordelaise sauce and crisp leeks. In summer the doors of the Garden Room open to catch the breeze, or

> **MAD ABOUT SHAD**
>
> Not quite the running of the bulls, the running of the shad—when these members of the herring family swim upstream to their freshwater spawning ground—is the inspiration for Lambertville's biggest annual event: Shad Fest. This late April festival dates to the early 1980s, when the oily, bony, strong-tasting fish—a local food source for both Native Americans and colonists—returned to the Delaware after years of absence due to pollution. The weekend celebration includes arts and crafts, entertainment, demonstrations of the seine technique of catching shad, and lots of food, including the fish of honor.

you can dine in the courtyard garden to the sound of the fountain. After years of serving only dinner, lunch has been added on weekends. ✉ *8 Coryell St.* ☎ *609/397–4343* ⊕ *www.hamiltonsgrillroom.com* 🖃 *AE, D, DC, MC, V* 🍴 *BYOB* ☺ *No lunch weekdays.*

$$$$
FRENCH

✕ **Manon.** The mural of Van Gogh's *Starry Night* on the ceiling transports you to a whimsical corner of Provence at this farmhouse-cozy bistro. Start with the warm goat-cheese salad or country pâté, and follow it up with the bouillabaisse or rack of lamb with a mustard and thyme crust. ✉ *19 N. Union St.* ☎ *609/397–2596* 🖃 *No credit cards* 🍴 *BYOB* ☺ *Closed Mon. and Tues. No lunch.*

$$$$
AMERICAN

✕ **No. 9 Restaurant.** This simple, unpretentious dining room is noisy on weekends, thanks to the many diners who flock here for the creative American cuisine created by Matthew and Colleen Kane. The menu changes seasonally, leaning heavily on local and organic ingredients, but there are some dishes you can count on. The signature entrées include the braised beef short ribs and the porterhouse pork chop, but you can also find fresh fish, generally with an Asian-style preparation. ✉ *9 Klines Ct.* ☎ *609/397–6380* 🖃 *AE, MC, V* 🍴 *BYOB* ☺ *Closed Mon. and Tues. No lunch.*

$
THAI

✕ **Siam.** You don't come here for fancy decor or polished service; both are as plain and straightforward as they come. You come for the delicious Thai food. You could easily make a meal of the tasty appetizers: crispy panfried wontons, rich chicken-and-coconut soup, and vermicelli salad with shrimp and ground pork. But it would be a shame not to save room for the flaky fried whole fish in three-flavor sauce, the spicy curries, and the stir-fried pork with spicy peanut sauce on a bed

10

of watercress. ✉ *61 N. Main St.* ☎ *609/397–8128* ▭ *No credit cards* ⌸ *BYOB* ⊘ *Closed Mon. No lunch Tues.–Wed.*

$ ╳ **Tortuga's Cocina.** In this out-of-the-way rustic eatery with orange walls,
MEXICAN   brick, and hewn wood, it's easy to fill up on the chips and chunky, cilan-
★   tro-redolent salsa. You should save room, however, for your equally
yummy entrée. The regular menu has familiar Tex-Mex fare, including grilled chicken and steak, create-your-own combination plates,
and house specialties like chipotle shrimp and chicken mole. Among
the vegetarian options, the enchiladas *supremas* are made with refried
beans, guacamole, and a deliciously decadent cream sauce. Nightly
specials add more authentic Mexican dishes to the mix. ✉ *11½ Church
St.* ☎ *609/397–7272* ⊕ *www.tortugascocina.com* ▭ *No credit cards*
⊘ *Closed Mon. No lunch weekdays.*

WHERE TO STAY

$$$ 🏨 **Inn at Lambertville Station.** The "station" in the hotel's name refers to
the restaurant ($$–$$$), an 1867 stone building designed by Thomas
Ustick Walter, architect of the dome on the U.S. Capitol, as the head-
quarters of the Belvidere-Delaware Railroad. The hotel itself is a more
modern building, but the lobby's soaring wood ceiling and wall of
antique portraits sets a timeless tone. Guest rooms are decorated slightly
differently from one another, with antiques and reproduction furnish-
ings in styles that hint at the city each room is named for. The pricier
rooms have sitting areas and gas fireplaces, but every room has a river
view because the inn is set at right angles to the Delaware. Complimen-
tary continental breakfast is delivered to rooms. The restaurant serves
American fare, including rack of lamb, filet mignon, and maple-mustard
salmon, but it's the train touches, such as the kitchen-in-a-boxcar and
outdoor canal-side dining on the platform, that make it unusual. **Pros:**
on the waterfront; watching the sun set over the river can be especially
pretty; weekday prices are a bargain. **Cons:** restaurant's food and ser-
vice can be spotty. ✉ *11 Bridge St.* ☎ *609/397–4400 or 800/524–1091*
⊕ *www.lambertvillestation.com* ⤲ *45 rooms* ♿ *In-room: refrigerator
(some), Wi-Fi. In-hotel: restaurant, room service, bar, laundry service,
no-smoking rooms* ▭ *AE, DC, MC, V* ⫶◯⫶ *CP.*

$$$ – $$$$ 🏨 **Lambertville House.** This handsome stone building, a former stage-
★   coach stop dating to 1812, stands on Lambertville's main drag, steps
away from shops and the bridge to New Hope. Rooms, all with jetted
tubs and most with gas fireplaces, are furnished with period reproduc-
tions. Three have a two-sided fireplace that can be enjoyed from bed-
room and tub. Several rooms have balconies overlooking a courtyard
where guests gather for drinks, and two have porches where you can sit
and watch the activity on Bridge Street. A continental breakfast buffet is
served in the breakfast room, or you can have breakfast brought to your
room. Left Bank Libations is a cozy spot for cocktails with an inviting
outdoor porch that's open seasonally. Privileges at a local fitness center
are included. **Pros:** the little details like robes and refreshment trays in
rooms and coffee/tea/hot chocolate service on each floor make all the
difference. **Cons:** bar can be taken over by corporate groups, as business
travelers make up about half of guests. ✉ *32 Bridge St.* ☎ *609/397–
0200 or 888/867–8859* ⊕ *www.lambertvillehouse.com* ⤲ *20 rooms, 6*

suites ☆ In-room: refrigerator (some), Wi-Fi. In-hotel: bar, room service, laundry service, no-smoking rooms ☰ AE, D, MC, V ▣ CP.

SHOPPING

Antiques shops, furniture stores, and galleries line Union Street, heading north from Bridge Street, and the intersecting cross streets. This is where the serious antiques collectors shop, as well as those seeking contemporary crafts and furniture.

ANTIQUES **Broadmoor Antiques** (✉ 6 N. Union St. ☎ 609/397–8802) packs in 10 rooms of paintings, antiques, and decorative items.

You can discover Art Deco treasures, toy trains, porcelain, and memorabilia from the '60s and '70s in the dozens of antiques shops at the **Golden Nugget Antique Market** (✉ 1850 River Rd. ☎ 609/397–0811 ⊕ www.gnmarket.com), open Wednesday and weekends 6–4. Sunday is the biggest day, with more than 200 outdoor vendors also competing for your business. A green market, selling locally grown produce, flowers and plants, and locally produced goods, operates on weekends in season.

Teak-furniture lovers will enjoy perusing the **Orchard Hill Collection** (✉ 22 N. Union St. ☎ 609/397–1188), which carries some Dutch-Colonial antiques and plenty of handcrafted reproductions from Indonesia.

HOUSE-
WARES AND
FURNITURE

A Mano Gallery (✉ 42 N. Union St. ☎ 609/397–0063) stocks jewelry, glass, kaleidoscopes, and wearable art, as well as contemporary furniture.

Bucks County Dry Goods (✉ 5 Klines Ct. ☎ 609/397–1288) has got the goods—a varied assortment or jewelry, mid-century furniture, housewares, design books, gifts, and hip clothing.

Greene & Greene Gallery (✉ 32 Bridge St. ☎ 609/397–7774) refers to contemporary furniture designer Jeffrey Greene and his wife. The store carries Greene's lovely hardwood furniture as well as fine jewelry, ceramics, textiles, and other art for the home.

NEED A
BREAK?

Lambertville has several places to grab a sweet or caffeinated pick-me-up. Part bakery, part café, **Baker's Treat** (✉ 9B Church St. ☎ 609/397–2272) sells scones, cookies, cakes by the slice (including the popular coconut), and other pastries as well as soups, sandwiches, and other light savories. Profits are all donated to benefit women recovering from alcohol and substance abuse. Stop by **Lambertville Trading Company** (✉ 43 Bridge St. ☎ 609/397–2232) for a cappuccino and some homemade goodies or to pick up gourmet treats to take home. **Rojo's Roastery** (✉ 243 N. Union St. ☎ 609/397–0040) roasts its artful Fair Trade blends on the premises.

10

LAHASKA

4½ mi west of New Hope via Rte. 202.

Shopping packs in the crowds here, primarily because of the boutiques at Peddler's Village. If bargains are your goal, you can also find outlet stores. Antiques shops line U.S. 202 between New Hope and Lahaska.

WHERE TO EAT

$$
AMERICAN
☾

✗ **Sweet Lorraine's.** Artisans' touches such as colorful blown-glass pendant lights and chandeliers, etched-glass room dividers, an acid-washed copper bar, and funky painted-wood peppermills adorn this fresh café, which also offers Peddler's Village's first outdoor dining. The eclectic menu matches the funky decor, from such comfort-food options as down-home pot roast and Aunt Bea's mac and cheese with meatballs to more modern, ethnically influenced creations like Zen garden pasta with Pennsylvania mushrooms and seasonal vegetables sautéed in sesame oil with ginger-soy glaze and Asian noodles, and the lunchtime Bahama burger, topped with an avocado crab cake. The restaurant serves all three meals and is family-friendly. ⊠ *U.S. 202 and Street Rd.* ☎ *215/794–4040* ⊕ *peddlersvillage.com/dining/sweet_lorraines.htm* ▤ *AE, D, DC, MC, V.*

WHERE TO STAY

$–$$
★

☲ **Ash Mill Farm.** Past a pasture of grazing and bleating sheep and goats, this handsome taupe manor house dating to 1790 is now a country B&B. Indefatigable innkeeper David Topel and Beau, his golden retriever, provide a warm welcome. Ornate moldings and four-poster beds satisfy those who love vintage, while flat-screen TVs and wireless Internet access attract those who can't leave modern life behind. Fun details include window sashes transformed into mirrors. In addition to the main house, you can stay in the charming Bo Peep's Hideaway, which was converted from feed storage, or Shepherd's Cottage, with pale wood paneling, a potbellied stove, kitchenette, whirlpool tub, and a glass door that the sheep press their noses to. David's buffet breakfasts—with healthy and decadent options, such as challah French toast with grilled maple mango—can be enjoyed outdoors on the deck or in the breakfast room. Guests here on Saturday mornings are invited to join the Zumba Latin-inspired fitness class held in the bright, airy converted barn, and an on-site masseur is available. **Pros:** farm charm with modern conveniences; attention to details: French sheep soap, gym membership, use of guest fridge for leftovers, welcome snacks. **Cons:** not for those averse to barn animals or their aroma when the wind blows just right. ⊠ *5358 York Rd., Holicong* ☎ *215/794–5373* ⊕ *www. ashmillfarm.com* ⇩ *5 rooms, 2 suites* ⚹ *In-room: no phone, kitchen (some), DVD (some), Wi-Fi. In-hotel: no kids under 14, no-smoking rooms* ▤ *AE, MC, V* �🍽 *BP.*

$$$$
Fodor's Choice
★

☲ **Barley Sheaf Farm Estate & Spa.** Once the home of playwright George S. Kaufman, this remarkable country retreat has a staff that takes a devilish delight in the details. Suites, all named for Kaufman works, are exquisitely furnished with pieces like the ornate carved East Asian canopy bed in the Seven Lively Arts Suite. The 19th-century barn has original touches like wood beams and ladders, while the Manor House, whose original section dates to 1740, features exposed stone walls. Tastefully chosen art and crafts—Mercer tiles, stained glass, luscious textiles, and hand-painted murals—are sprinkled throughout. Pleasing the senses doesn't stop with the eye, however. Wine and cheese are delivered to your door when you arrive, gas fireplaces and whirlpool tubs keep you feeling toasty warm, and the on-site spa (which uses all-natural, organic products) lets you pamper yourself. A delicious breakfast is served in the glass-walled dining room, where you can also enjoy a seven-course tasting menu with wine pairings on Friday and Saturday night. **Pros:** spot-on artistic touches; charm of faithful historic restoration with modern amenities; Chef Tom's tasty meals. **Cons:** you won't have enough room to eat all the breakfast goodies; dinner is offered only two nights a week. ⊠ *5281 Old York Rd., Box 10, Holicong* ☎ *215/794–5104* ⊕ *www.barleysheaf.com* ⊅ *16 suites* ♿ *In-room: safe, kitchen (some), refrigerator, DVD (some), Internet, Wi-Fi (some). In-hotel: restaurant, room service, pool, gym, spa, laundry service, some pets allowed, no-smoking rooms* ⊟ *AE, D, DC, MC, V* ⊚ *BP.*

$$–$$$ ☷ **Golden Plough Inn.** Nestled within Peddler's Village, this hotel has 22 spacious guest rooms in the main building, with the rest scattered about the village—in an 18th-century farmhouse, a historic carriage house, and Merchant's Row. Many rooms are decorated in a classic country style, with four-poster or canopy beds, lace and ruffles, floral prints and plaids, and cozy window seats. Others feel more like a modern hotel, some with Murphy beds. Vouchers good for a bottle of local wine from a nearby wine shop and toward breakfast at Sweet Lorraine's are included. **Pros:** in the thick of Peddler's Village with many shopping opportunities. **Cons:** in the thick of Peddler's Village crowds; voucher doesn't cover full cost of breakfast. ⊠ *Peddler's Village, U.S. 202 and Street Rd.* ☎ *215/794–4004* ⊕ *www.goldenploughinn.com* ⊅ *70 rooms* ♿ *In-room: kitchen (some), refrigerator, DVD (some), Wi-Fi. In-hotel: restaurant, bar, gym, spa, laundry service, no-smoking rooms* ⊟ *AE, D, DC, MC, V.*

$$ ☷ **Mill Creek Farm.** Like most old Bucks County farmhouses (the oldest part of the house dates to 1730), this one has been expanded over the years. Curl up by the Mercer-tile fireplace in the library, pay a visit to the Thoroughbreds who gallop nearby (there are even facilities to board your horse), or gaze at the creek and pond from the glass-walled dining room. Guest rooms are named for presidents. In the George Washington Suite, the master bedroom has stone walls and a beam ceiling. The second bedroom, which is great for children, has a bed tucked in an alcove, which is painted to look like a four-poster bed. **Pros:** tranquil farmlike setting with plenty to do: tennis, swimming, fishing, and massage. **Cons:** if you want to be where the action is, this may be too quiet and out of the way. ⊠ *2348 Quarry Rd., Buckingham* ☎ *215/794–3121* ⊕ *www.millcreekfarmbb.com* ⊅ *4 rooms, 1 suite* ♿ *In-room: no phone, Wi-Fi. In-hotel: tennis court, pool, some pets allowed, no-smoking rooms* ⊟ *AE, D, MC, V* ⊚ *BP.*

SHOPPING

Peddler's Village (⊠ *U.S. 202 and Rte. 263* ☎ *215/794–4000* ⊕ *www.peddlersvillage.com*) began in the early 1960s, when the late Earl Jamison bought a 6-acre chicken farm, moved local 18th-century houses to the site, and opened a collection of specialty shops and restaurants. The 70 shops in the village peddle books, toys, clothing, jewelry, candles, cookware, and housewares, crafts, and other items. The Grand Carousel, a restored 1922 merry-go-round, still works, and Giggleberry Fair offers a bonanza of games for its loud little visitors. Crowd-drawing seasonal events include May's Strawberry Festival and September's Scarecrow Festival.

Penn's Purchase Factory Outlet Stores (✉ *U.S. 202* ☎ *215/794–0300* ⊕ *www.pennspurchase.com*) include two-dozen shops selling name-brand merchandise at discount prices. You can find Brooks Brothers, Coach, Easy Spirit, Izod, Jones New York, Nine West, and Orvis. All 15 buildings in this complex have been designed in an Early American country style that harmonizes with the look of Peddler's Village, across the road.

Near Peddler's Village, **Rice's Market** (✉ *6326 Greenhill Rd., Solebury* ☎ *215/297–5993* ⊕ *www.ricesmarket.com*) is an open-air market with bargains on new and used items, including clothing, toys, produce, meats, and baked goods. There are some antiques and collectibles, too. It's open Tuesday (year-round) and Saturday (March–December) 7–1.

DOYLESTOWN

6 mi west of Lahaska via Rte. 202.

The county seat, this charming small town was an important coach stop during the 18th century and today showcases Early American architecture. You can find Federal-style brick buildings on Lawyers' Row and gracious Queen Anne, Second Empire, and Italianate homes scattered about the nearby streets. The historic district, nearly 1,200 buildings, is listed on the National Register of Historic Places. Here you can find the locally owned shops and restaurants (Starbucks notwithstanding) that are fast disappearing elsewhere in the county. Some of Doylestown's most unusual buildings, however, are those built by the eccentric Henry Mercer on what is now known as Mercer Mile. His influence is also seen in the Mercer tiles found throughout the area.

GETTING HERE AND AROUND

Like most thoroughfares in Bucks County, the two roads that intersect, almost at right angles, in Doylestown are both marked as north–south routes. U.S. 202 connects Doylestown to Lahaska, New Hope, and Lambertville, while Route 611 comes up from the Philadelphia area and the Pennsylvania Turnpike. Metered street and lot parking is available, if not always plentiful, though some of the museums have their own free parking. Walking around town is hilly but easy, and one of the pleasures of Doylestown.

EXPLORING

Fonthill Museum. You almost expect to see a dragon puffing smoke outside Fonthill, Henry Mercer's storybook home. Don't be at all surprised if you see one inside. Mercer began building the house in 1908, modeling it after a 13th-century castle. Outside, it bristles with turrets and balconies. Inside, the multilevel structure is truly mazelike. The concrete castle is built from the inside out—without using blueprints—resulting in a jumble of differently shaped rooms (44 in all) and stairways (following close behind with 32). Gothic doorways, dead-end passages, and inglenooks add to the fairy-tale effect. Ancient tiles that Mercer found around the world as well as Arts and Crafts tiles from his own kilns

CLOSE UP

Henry Mercer: A Most Unusual Man

An expert in prehistoric archaeology, University of Pennsylvania Museum curator, homespun architect, master potter, Harvard-educated millionaire, and writer of Gothic tales, Henry Chapman Mercer was a renaissance man who looked back as much as forward. Living at the turn of the 20th century, Mercer was a proponent of the Arts and Crafts movement, extolling the authenticity of material and craft over the industrialization that was altering American life. He founded a pottery that still produces Mercer-inspired tiles, collected and preserved evidence of pre-industrial America, and constructed three

brilliantly bizarre structures using reinforced concrete (following a technique he perfected), a handful of laborers, and his beloved horse, Lucy.

The tiles are classic Arts and Crafts with earthy tones of brown, blue, and terra-cotta with a handmade look to them. Much of the imagery used in the tiles is nature-, history-, or Bible-inspired. Several B&Bs and local homeowners use the tiles in kitchen or bathroom backsplashes, on their floors, or hung on walls. In Doylestown there are even some tiles in the sidewalk. You can purchase your own at the Moravian Pottery and Tile Works.

(depicting scenes from the Bible to *Bluebeard*) seem to cover every surface—floors, walls, columns, and ceilings. To see this amazing incrustation, however, you must take an hour-long tour (reservations suggested). If you come the first Saturday of the month, opt for the Tower Tour. ⊠ *E. Court St. and Swamp Rd., Rte. 313* ☎ *215/348–9461* ⊕ *www. fonthillmuseum.org* ⊠ *$9.50, $14 includes Mercer Museum* ☉ *Mon.– Sat. 10–5, Sun. noon–5.*

James A. Michener Art Museum. Named for the late best-selling novelist and Doylestown native, this museum, across the street from the Mercer Museum, has a permanent collection and changing exhibitions that focus on 19th- and 20th-century American art, especially those by Bucks County artists. It's known for its collection of early-20th-century Pennsylvania impressionists, representing such artists as Edward Redfield and Daniel Garber. The museum occupies the buildings and grounds of the former Bucks County jail, which dates from 1884. A 23-foot-high fieldstone wall surrounds seven galleries, an outdoor sculpture garden, and a Gothic-style warden's house. There's also a re-creation of Michener's Doylestown study. A new gallery accommodates larger traveling exhibits, and admission is included in the price. ⊠ *138 S. Pine St.* ☎ *215/340–9800* ⊕ *www.MichenerArtMuseum.org* ⊠ *$10* ☉ *Tues.–Fri. 10–4:30, Sat. 10–5, Sun. noon–5.*

♨ **Mercer Museum.** In the center of town, the Mercer Museum, opened in 1916, displays Mercer's collection of tools, including more than 50,000 objects from before the steam age. An archaeologist, Mercer worried that the rapid advance of industrialization would wipe out evidence of preindustrial America. Consequently, from 1895 to 1915 he scoured the back roads of eastern Pennsylvania, buying folk art, tools, and articles of everyday life to display in another of his concrete castles. In what

10

amounts to a six-story attic, log sleds, cheese presses, fire engines, boats, and bean hullers are suspended from walls and ceilings and crammed into rooms organized by trade or purpose. Interactive activities, like the "Animals on the Loose" exhibit, and a special audio-guide channel keep children amused. A museum expansion, planned for 2010, will include galleries for traveling exhibits as well as items in the collection not currently on display. ⊠ *84 S. Pine St.* ☎ *215/345–0210* ⊕ *www. mercermuseum.org* ⊠ *$9, free 1st Tues. of month after 5, $14 includes Fonthill* ⊙ *Mon. and Wed.–Sat. 10–5, Tues. 10–9, Sun. noon–5.*

Moravian Pottery and Tile Works. On the grounds of the Fonthill estate, the tile works still produces Arts and Crafts–style tiles from Mercer's designs. These tiles adorn such well-known structures as Grauman's Chinese Theater in Hollywood, as well as many of the homes and sidewalks of Doylestown. The late author and Bucks County resident James Michener described them as follows: "Using scenes from the Bible, mythology, and history, Henry Chapman Mercer produced wonderfully archaic tiles about 12 or 14 inches square in powerful earth colors that glowed with intensity and unforgettable imagery." You can watch a 17-minute video and take a self-guided tour past artisans at work in the 1912 factory, which resembles a Spanish mission. ■ TIP→ **You can purchase tiles at the works, which range in price from $3.25 for a 2" x 2" tile to $500 and up for a mosaic.** ⊠ *130 Swamp Rd., Rte. 313* ☎ *215/345–6722* ⊕ *www.buckscounty.org/government/departments/ tileworks* ⊠ *$4.50* ⊙ *Daily 10–4:45.*

NEED A BREAK? If you're early enough, you can get a yummy croissant or melt-in-your-mouth sticky bun before they sell out from **La Maison Cheese** (⊠ *51 W. State St.* ☎ *215/348–7543*) to fortify you for your day of sightseeing.

National Shrine of Our Lady of Czestochowa. Driving up to the shrine, you can't help but realize that you're not in Kansas anymore. This enormous Polish spiritual center has drawn millions of pilgrims, including Pope John Paul II, since its opening in 1966. The complex includes a modern church with huge stained-glass panels depicting the history of Christianity in Poland and the United States. The gift shop and bookstore sell religious gifts, many imported from Poland, and the cafeteria serves hot Polish and American food on Sunday. ⊠ *Ferry Rd., off Rte. 313* ☎ *215/345–0600* ⊕ *www.czestochowa.us* ⊠ *Free* ⊙ *Daily 9–4:30.*

OFF THE BEATEN PATH

Pearl S. Buck House. Writer Pearl S. Buck, best known for her novel *The Good Earth,* lived at Green Hills Farm, a country house not too far from Doylestown. Here she wrote nearly 100 novels, children's books, and works of nonfiction while raising seven adopted children and caring for many others. The house, now a National Historic Landmark, still bears the imprint of the girl who grew up in China and became the first American woman to win both the Nobel and Pulitzer prizes. The house also contains the writer's collection of Asian and American antiques and personal belongings. ⊠ *520 Dublin Rd., off Rte. 313, Perkasie* ☎ *215/249–0100 or 800/220–2825* ⊠ *$7* ⊙ *Tours Mar.–Dec., Tues.–Sat. 11, 1, and 2, Sun. 1 and 2.*

WHERE TO EAT

$$$$
AMERICAN
★

✕ **Honey.** If you come to this sweet D-town spot expecting familiar flavors, you'll be delightfully disappointed. Hip Honey is refreshingly different. The eating experience is all about sampling by way of a seasonally changing menu of small plates meant to be shared. Meanwhile, the food is all about contrasts: hot and cold, crunchy and creamy, savory and, yes, sweet. Black tea–glazed spare ribs dusted with toasted sesame and salted pine nuts come with a small scoop of spicy ginger ice cream. It all melts in your mouth and then gives you a hot little kick for good measure. The appetizer-size portions might range from a $4 exotic olive plate to $28 foie-gras sliders, with a few larger and more expensive options available. Diners typically order two plates per person and then see if they want more. Drinks include all-Pennsylvania beers, all-American wines, and all-unexpected specialty cocktails. Even the desserts can be hot and spicy. ⊠ *42 Shewell Ave.* ☎ *215/489–4200* ⊕ *www.honeyrestaurant.com* ⊟ *AE, D, DC, MC, V* ⊗ *Closed Sun. No lunch.*

¢
PIZZA

✕ **Jules Thin Crust Pizza.** Jules pizza combines the bounty from local farms and dairies with a killer thin crust. The menu comprises 28 interesting pizza varieties made with local organic ingredients. Meat #8 (black beans, ground beef, jalapeno, cilantro, mozzarella, fresh tomato) and veggie #1 (feta, kalamata olives, chopped tomato, red onion, romaine, and tomato sauce) reflect international inspiration, while veggie #4 (Brie, sliced pears, toasted almonds, and rosemary) and meat #7 (fig jam, Gorgonzola, prosciutto, and rosemary) must have sprung from the mind of founder John Ordway. The oblong pizzas are sold by the pie or the inch, with each slice a few inches wide. ▪TIP➔ **Gluten-free crust is available.** ⊠ *78 S. Main St.* ☎ *215/345–8565* ⊕ *www.julesthincrust. com* ⊟ *AE, D, MC, V.*

¢
LATIN-AMERICAN

✕ **Lilly's Café America.** The colorful metal cactus standing guard over the sidewalk seating is a tip-off that the name of this place refers to Latin America. Run by the same folks who own the adjoining Lilly's Gourmet, Café America has the same casual feel. Unlike its neighbor, this place also has a bar. Sip some sangria or a pomegranate mojito while you choose from among the *platos grandes* (which translates as "big dishes"). Chimichurri steak; grilled blackened salmon; Cuban pressed sandwich; Latina Caesar salad with Mexican cheese, avocado, and blackened shrimp; chicken tamale; and taco pizza are some of the options. ⊠ *1 W. Court St.* ☎ *215/348–7838* ⊕ *www.lillysgourmet.com/ cafe.html* ⊟ *AE, MC, V* ⊗ *Closed Sun. No dinner Mon. and Tues.*

¢
AMERICAN

✕ **Lilly's Gourmet.** From the whisk-shaped door handles to the colander lamps to the sandwiches named after musicians, Lilly's is full of fun. This busy downtown counter-service lunch spot also serves inventive salads and soups, which you can eat in the small, lively dining room or take with you. Try the Red Hot Chile Peppers (peppered turkey breast, cheddar, romaine, tomato, and Cajun mayo on sourdough) or Ol' Blue Eyes (grilled marinated steak, barbecue onions, tomato, mixed greens, and blue cheese on marble rye). Make sure you read the blackboards, which list the specials. A light breakfast of muffins, bagels, and fresh fruit is also available. ⊠ *1 W. Court St.* ☎ *215/230–7883* ⊕

10

www.lillysgourmet.com/gourmet.html ▭ *AE, MC, V* ⊗ *Closed Sun. No dinner.*

WHERE TO STAY

$$–$$$ 🏨 **Doylestown Inn.** Guests have been flocking to this hotel in the middle of town since 1902. Through the neat, clean, and professional lobby and past two levels of office and retail space, the inn's guest rooms, on the third floor, are individually decorated with dark woods and traditional furnishings. Some rooms have whirlpool tubs and fireplaces. Rates include a certificate good for a continental breakfast at Starbucks. **Pros:** in the heart of town; good for vacationers, visiting families, special events, and business travelers. **Cons:** free parking pass for borough lot provided, but lot is sometimes full. ⊠ *18 W. State St., at Main St.* ☎ *215/345–6610* ⊕ *www.doylestowninn.com* 📲 *11 rooms* ♿ *In-room: refrigerator, Wi-Fi. In-hotel: bar, no-smoking rooms* ▭ *AE, MC, V* ⑩ *CP.*

$$ 🏨 **Hargrave House.** The spirited British innkeeper, Lorna, watches over Hargrave House like someone who helped re-create it, because she did. Formerly the 1814 House Inn, this B&B—Doylestown's only true bed-and-breakfast—has been completely spruced up and refurnished. The inn's previous name came from the era the oldest section was constructed, its new name is courtesy of Thomas Hargrave, the stonemason who built it. The Nest, a cozy room tucked under a beamed ceiling, is the only room in the original part of the house. The other rooms, which are larger, are in a new annex; most have fireplaces and whirlpool tubs. Feather beds and 600-thread-count linens show the innkeeper's attention to detail, as do her cooked-to-order full breakfasts, prepared at a time of each guest's choosing (and accommodating dietary constraints). Don't be surprised if she offers you a glass of sherry in winter to go with some afternoon nibbles. **Pros:** attentive and flexible innkeeper; free on-site parking; central location. **Cons:** only one room in historic part of house. ⊠ *50 S. Main St.* ☎ *215/348–3334* ⊕ *www.hargravehouse. net* 📲 *7 rooms* ♿ *In-room: refrigerator (some), Wi-Fi. In-hotel: laundry service, no-smoking rooms* ▭ *AE, D, MC, V* ⑩ *BP.*

NIGHTLIFE AND THE ARTS

One of those independent throwbacks of which Doylestown residents are so proud, the nonprofit, community-based **County Theater** (⊠ *20 E. State St.* ☎ *215/345–6789* ⊕ *www.countytheater.org*) is an Art Deco movie house that screens foreign and independent films.

Puck (⊠ *Printers Alley* ☎ *215/348–9000* ⊕ *www.pucklive.com*) is a bar and music venue, with bands playing indoors and occasionally out on the patio.

SHOPPING

Doylestown is filled with the kind of specialty shops that are just plain fun to browse through. They carry housewares and women's wear, gifts and antiques, and whatever you need for your favorite hobby (there are several knitting shops, for example).

Pennsylvania Dutch Country

WITH HERSHEY AND GETTYSBURG

WORD OF MOUTH

"New Holland, Bird In Hand, and Intercourse are great areas for pictures. Go south on Rte. 896 through Strasburg and there's some great shots along that route."

—Jgroff2506

"I also found downtown Lancaster an intriguing town to walk around and see the architecture; also enjoyed visiting its Central Market, Lancaster Quilt and Textile Museum, and Lancaster Cultural History Museum. Also had a belly busting meal at Good and Plenty."

—bachslunch

Updated
by Robert
DiGiacomo

Neatly painted farmhouses dot the countryside of Lancaster County, nearly 65 mi west of Philadelphia. Whitewashed fences outline pastures, and the landscape looks like a patchwork quilt of squares and rectangles. On the back roads the Amish travel in horse-drawn buggies and lead a lifestyle that has been carried on for generations.

Here the plain and fancy live side by side. You can glimpse what rural life was like 100 years ago, because whole communities of the "Plain" people—as members of the Old Order Amish are called—shun telephones, electricity, and the entire world of American gadgetry. Clinging to a centuries-old way of life, the Amish, one of the most conservative of the Pennsylvania Dutch sects, eschew the amenities of modern civilization, using kerosene or gas lamps instead of electric lighting, and horse-drawn buggies instead of automobiles. Ironically, in turning their backs on the modern world, the Amish have attracted its attention.

Today the county's main roads are lined with souvenir shops and sometimes crowded with busloads of tourists. The area's proximity to Philadelphia and Harrisburg has brought development as non-Amish farmers sell land. In fact, the National Trust for Historic Preservation has put Lancaster County on its list of the nation's most endangered historic places because of rapid suburbanization. But beyond the commercialism and development, general stores, one-room schoolhouses, country lanes, and tidy farms remain. You can find instructive places to learn about the Amish way of life, pretzel factories to tour, quilts to buy, and a host of railroad museums to explore.

ORIENTATION AND PLANNING

GETTING ORIENTED

The city of Lancaster, located at the heart of Pennsylvania Dutch Country, is an appealing city of row houses with a thriving arts and cultural scene that's worth exploring in its own right. Dating to 1710, it's one of the nation's oldest inland cities and makes for a fitting gateway to historic sites, such as Wheatland, the home of U.S. president James Buchanan, the Landis Valley Museum, which focuses on rural life before 1900, and the many hamlets and small towns where locals still follow a more traditional way of life.

Around Lancaster. Less than a half-hour outside the city limits, you can get a taste of the country in the small towns of Intercourse and Bird-in-Hand, with their markets, outlet shops, and sights that interpret Amish life. Nearby is Strasburg, where you can learn all about the history of

11

TOP REASONS TO GO

Amish country life: Experience a traditional way of life that continues despite the intrusion of the modern world.

Lancaster's Central Market: Visit the nation's oldest continuously operating farmers' market, which dates to the 1730s.

Plenty in store: Shop till you drop in Adamstown, a small town with three major markets—Renninger's, Stoudt's Black Angus, and Shupp's Grove—selling all manner of antiques, collectibles, and coins.

Gettysburg Battlefield: This sacred ground offers a stirring history lesson about the U.S. Civil War. The new Gettysburg Museum and Visitor Center is worth a visit in itself, with state-of-the-art exhibits and the Gettysburg Cyclorama, an 1884 painting of Pickett's Charge, which if unfurled would be longer than a football field.

Sweet times: You can't go wrong with a visit to a place inspired and built by chocolate—Hershey—site of a grand hotel, famed amusement park, and other attractions.

railroads and go for a scenic ride on a restored train. Also in the vicinity are the historic villages of Ephrata, site of a religious community dating to the 18th century, and Lititz, where you can still twist your own at one of the region's best-known pretzel makers.

Western Lancaster County. Western Lancaster County is a quieter part of the county, where you can bicycle down winding lanes, sample local wines and authentic Mennonite cooking, and explore uncrowded villages. Its history is rooted in the Colonial period, the residents are of Scottish and German descent, and architecture varies from log cabins to Victorian homes.

Hershey and Gettysburg. If you've brought your children as far as Lancaster, you may want to continue northwest to Hershey, the "Chocolate Town" founded in 1903 by Milton S. Hershey. Here the number-one attraction is Hersheypark, a theme park with kiddie and thrill rides, theaters, and live shows. Or you may wish to journey southwest to the Civil War battlefields and museums of Gettysburg, also within driving distance.

PLANNING

WHEN TO GO

Lancaster County can be hectic, especially on summer weekends and in autumn when the fall foliage attracts crowds. Farmers' markets and family-style restaurants overflow with people. The trick is to visit the top sights and then get off the beaten path. If possible, plan your trip for early spring, September, or Christmas season, when the area is less crowded. You should note that although many restaurants, shops, and farmers' markets close Sunday, commercial attractions remain open.

GETTING HERE AND AROUND

CAR TRAVEL

From Philadelphia, take the Schuylkill Expressway (I–76) west to the Pennsylvania Turnpike. Lancaster County sights are accessible from exits 20, 21, and 22. Another option is to follow U.S. 30 west from Philadelphia, but be prepared for a lot of traffic. It's about 65 mi to the Pennsylvania Dutch Country.

A car is the easiest way to explore the many sights in the area; it also lets you get off the main roads and into the countryside. Lancaster County's main arteries are U.S. 30 (also known as the Lincoln Highway) and Route 340 (also called Old Philadelphia Pike). Some pleasant back roads can be found between routes 23 and 340. Vintage Road is a country road running north over U.S. 30 and then along Route 772 west to Intercourse. You get a look at some of the farms in the area and also see Amish schoolhouses, stores, and the Amish themselves. ⚠ **Remember that you must slow down for horse-drawn buggies when you're driving on country roads.**

TOURS

At Plain & Fancy Farm, Amish Country Tours has large bus or minivan excursions. Most popular is the two-hour Amish farmlands trip, with a visit to a farmhouse, a wine tasting, and shopping for crafts; tours to Hershey are available on Tuesday. Brunswick Tours has private guides who accompany you in your car. The company also has a self-guided audio tour with 28 stops that begins at the Pennsylvania Dutch Convention & Visitors Bureau and takes three to four hours. The Mennonite Information Center has local Mennonite guides who join you in your car. These knowledgeable escorts lead you to country roads, produce stands, and Amish crafts shops and also acquaint you with their religion.

Glick Aviation, at Smoketown Airport, offers 18-minute flights in a four-seater plane (pilot plus three) that gives you a splendid aerial view of rolling farmlands.

Tour Contacts **Amish Country Tours** (✉ 3121 Old Philadelphia Pike, Rte. 340, Bird-in-Hand ☎ 717/768–3600 ⊕ www.amishexperience.com). **Brunswick Tours** (✉ 2102 Lincoln Hwy., Lancaster ☎ 717/397–7541 or 800/979–8687 ⊕ www. brunswicktours.com). **Glick Aviation** (✉ 311 Airport Dr., off Rte. 340, Smoketown ☎ 717/394–6476). **Mennonite Information Center** (✉ 2209 Millstream Rd., Lancaster ☎ 717/299–0954 ⊕ www.mennoniteinfoctr.com).

TRAIN TRAVEL

Amtrak has regular service from Philadelphia's 30th Street Station to the Lancaster Amtrak station. The trip takes 80 minutes.

Train Contacts **Amtrak** (✉ 53 McGovern Ave. ☎ 215/824–1600 or 800/872–7245 ⊕ www.amtrak.com).

PLANNING YOUR TIME

Lancaster County, with its working farms, offers a window on a traditional way of life. The city of Lancaster, with its rich arts and cultural scene, can be used as a hub while visiting the surrounding countryside, or as a jumping-off point, before moving on to explore the area's more rural scenery. Try to spend at least one night at a bed-and-breakfast. Families will want to allocate at least a day or two for Hersheypark's rides and attractions, while history buffs should schedule one or two days to explore Gettysburg, site of one of the most important battles of the Civil War.

RESTAURANTS

Like the German cuisine that influenced it, Pennsylvania Dutch cooking is hearty and uses ingredients from local farms. Though their numbers are dwindling, there are still a few traditional Pennsylvania Dutch restaurants where you can dine family style. Lancaster County has numerous reasonably priced family restaurants, along with a number of eateries offering more exotic fare. The cuisine is changing and expanding to include many flavors beyond traditional Amish. Unless otherwise noted, liquor is served.

HOTELS

Lancaster County lodgings are much like the people themselves—plain or fancy. You can rough it in one of the many campgrounds in the area, stay at a historic inn, or indulge yourself at a luxurious resort. A good selection of moderately priced motels caters to families. Although hotels welcome guests year-round, rates are highest in summer. Some inns and bed-and-breakfasts have minimum stays in high season.

Many working Amish and non-Amish farms throughout Lancaster County welcome guests to stay for a few days to observe and even participate in farm life. Operated as bed-and-breakfast establishments with a twist, the farms invite you to help milk the cows and feed the chickens, and afterward share a hearty breakfast with the farmer and his family or help with other farm chores. Reservations must be made weeks in advance, as most farms are heavily booked in summer. The Pennsylvania Dutch Convention & Visitors Bureau has a listing of all area B&Bs and farms that welcome guests. Lancaster County Bed-and-Breakfast Association has information on 15 area B&Bs.

Contacts **Lancaster County Bed-and-Breakfast Inns Association** (⊠ 62 W. Main St, Adamstown ☎ 717/464–5588 or 800/848–2994 ⊕ www.padutchinns.com).

WHAT IT COSTS				
¢	$	$$	$$$	$$$$
Restaurant	under $10	$10–$14	$15–$19	$20–$24	over $24
Hotel	under $100	$100–$150	$151–$200	$201–$250	over $250

Restaurant prices are for one main course at dinner. Hotel prices are for two people in a standard double room in high season.

VISITOR INFORMATION

The Pennsylvania Dutch Convention & Visitors Bureau is the welcome center for Pennsylvania Dutch Country, with a wide selection of brochures, maps, and other materials, as well as direct connections to hotels. There's also a multi-image presentation, "Lancaster County: People, Places & Passions," which serves as a good introduction to the area. It's open Monday–Saturday 8:30–5 and Sunday 9–5 in summer.

Eating Well in Pennsylvania Dutch Country

Traditional Pennsylvania Dutch cooking isn't for those watching calories. Family-style meals are multi-dish affairs, with fried chicken, ham, and roast beef, often accompanied by dried corn, buttered noodles, mashed potatoes, pepper cabbage, and "chow-chow" (pickle relish). There are always traditional "sweet and sours," vegetable dishes made with a vinegar-and-sugar dressing. This is the way the Amish, who hate to throw things out, preserve leftover vegetables.

Make sure you save room for dessert, which is sure to include shoofly pie (made with molasses and brown sugar), *snitz* (dried apple) pie, and other kinds of pies, even for breakfast. Bake shops proudly point out that this region invented the hole in the doughnut by cutting out the center of *fastnacht* (a deep-fried potato pastry); in fact, the English word "dunk" comes from the Pennsylvania Dutch *dunke*. Other treats include buttery soft pretzels hot from the oven, fresh ice cream, and locally made birch beer.

The Mennonite Information Center serves mainly to "interpret the faith and practice of the Mennonites and Amish to all who inquire." It has information on local inns and Mennonite guest homes as well as a 20-minute video about the Amish and Mennonite people. It's open Monday through Saturday 8–5.

Visitor Information **Mennonite Information Center** (✉ 2209 Millstream Rd., Lancaster ☎ 717/299–0954 or 800/858–8320 ⊕ www.mennoniteinfoctr.com). **Pennsylvania Dutch Convention & Visitors Bureau** (✉ 501 Greenfield Rd., Lancaster ☎ 717/299–8901 or 800/735–2629 ⊕ www.padutchcountry.com).

AROUND LANCASTER

The city of Lancaster has plenty to see, and makes a good base for exploring the surrounding countryside. East of the city, between routes 340 and 23 in towns with names such as Intercourse, Blue Ball, Paradise, and Bird-in-Hand, lives most of Lancaster County's Amish community. Strasburg, to the southeast, has sights for train buffs. No more than 12 mi north of Lancaster, Ephrata, and Lititz are lovely historic towns.

LANCASTER

75 mi west of Philadelphia via I-76.

Near the heart of Pennsylvania Dutch Country, Lancaster is a colorful small city that combines Colonial and Pennsylvania Dutch influences. During the French and Indian War and the American Revolution its craftsmen turned out fine guns, building the city's reputation as the arsenal of the colonies. On September 27, 1777, Lancaster became the nation's capital for a day, as Congress fled the British in Philadelphia. Today markets and museums preserve the area's history. East of town on U.S. 30 are some of the area's more commercial attractions, such as miniature golf and fast-food eateries.

GETTING HERE AND AROUND

The most direct route from Philadelphia is to take Interstate 76 to the Pennsylvania Turnpike. But you should try to depart before or after the morning or afternoon rush hour to avoid getting stuck in commuter traffic. Once in Lancaster, if you're staying near Penn Square, you can walk to the Central Market, the major museums, and cultural attractions. But you'll need a car to access certain sites within the city, including Wheatland, as well as the surrounding countryside. For lovely views of farms and unspoiled land, take a spin along the smaller roads between routes 23 and 340.

ESSENTIALS

Visitor Information **Downtown Visitor Center** (✉ *13 W. King St., Lancaster* ☎ *717/735–0823* ⊕ *www.padutchcountry.com*).

EXPLORING
TOP ATTRACTIONS

Fodor'sChoice
★ A must-see in Lancaster City is the Romanesque **Central Market,** constructed in 1889. The market began as open-air stalls in 1742. Here local people shop for fresh fruits and vegetables, meats (try the Lebanon bologna), fresh flowers, and baked goods such as sticky buns and shoofly pie. Central Market has the distinction of being the oldest continuously operating farmers' market in the country. ✉ *Penn Sq.* ☎ *717/291–4723* ⊙ *Tues. and Fri. 6–4, Sat. 6–2.*

★ The **Hans Herr House,** the oldest in Lancaster County, is considered the best example of medieval-style German architecture in North America. The subject of several paintings by Andrew Wyeth, it was the Colonial home of the Herr family, to whom the Wyeths were related. Today the house is owned by the Lancaster Mennonite Historical Society, which educates the public about the Mennonite religion. The 45-minute tour covers the grounds and the 1719 sandstone house, a former Mennonite meeting place. It's 5 mi south of Lancaster off U.S. 222. ✉ *1849 Hans Herr Dr.* ☎ *717/464–4438* ⊕ *www.hansherr.org* ✍ *$5* ⊙ *Apr.–Nov., Mon.–Sat. 9–4.*

The **Historic Lancaster Walking Tour** is a 90-minute stroll through the heart of this old city by costumed guides who impart anecdotes about notable points of interest. There are also theme tours. Tours of the six-square-block area depart from the downtown visitor center. ✉ *100 S. Queen St.* ☎ *717/392–1776* ✍ *$7* ⊙ *Apr.–Oct., Tues., Fri., and Sat. at 10 and 1, Sun., Mon., Wed., and Thurs. at 1; Nov.–Mar., by reservation.*

Fodor'sChoice
★ The **Landis Valley Museum** is an open-air museum of Pennsylvania German rural life and folk culture before 1900. Started by brothers Henry and George Landis, the farm and village are now operated by the Pennsylvania Historical and Museum Commission. You can visit more than

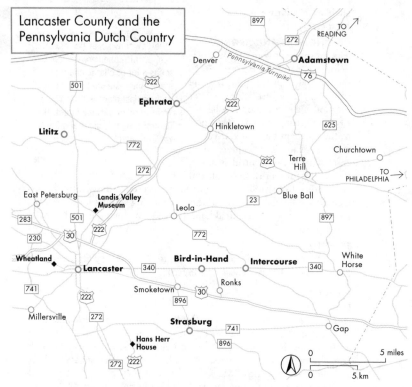

Lancaster County and the Pennsylvania Dutch Country

15 historical buildings, from a farmstead to a country store, with costumed guides providing interesting bits of history. There are demonstrations of skills such as spinning and weaving, pottery making, and tinsmithing. Many of the crafts are for sale in the Weathervane Shop. ✉ *2451 Kissel Hill Rd., off Oregon Pike, Rte. 272* ☎ *717/569–0401* ⊕ *www.landisvalleymuseum.org* 💲 *$12* ⊙ *Mar.–Dec., Mon.–Sat. 9–5, Sun. noon–5.*

WORTH NOTING

The **Demuth Foundation** includes the restored 18th-century home, studio, and garden of Charles Demuth (1883–1935), one of America's first modernist artists. A watercolorist, Demuth found inspiration in the geometric shapes of machines and modern technology, as well as the flowers in his mother's garden. Several of his works are on display. The gallery also features a changing exhibit of regional and national artists. The complex includes the oldest operating tobacco shop in the country, which dates back to 1770. ✉ *120 E. King St.* ☎ *717/299–9940* ⊕ *www.demuth.org* 💲 *Donation requested* ⊙ *Feb.–Dec., Tues.–Sat. 10–4, Sun. 1–4.*

☺ Now owned by Hersheypark, the 44-acre **Dutch Wonderland** features rides and activities. Designed by and for kids, this amusement park is especially suited for families with younger children. Most rides, such as the roller coaster, merry-go-round, and giant slide, are quite tame. ✉ *2249 U.S. 30, east of Lancaster* ☎ *717/291–1888* ⊕ *www. dutchwonderland.com* 🖘 *$30.95* ⊙ *Memorial Day–Labor Day, daily 10–8; Labor Day–Oct. and Easter–Memorial Day, weekends 10–6.*

The Old City Hall, reborn as the **Heritage Center Museum,** documents the Colonial history of the region and the culture of the Pennsylvania German settlers. The museum fea-

tures timeless work of Lancaster County artisans and craftspeople— clocks, furniture, homemade toys, rifles, and *Fraktur* (documents in a style of calligraphy with folk-art decorations). ✉ *King and Queen Sts. on Penn Sq.* ☎ *717/299–6440* ⊕ *www.lancasterheritage.com* 🖘 *Free* ⊙ *Tues.–Sat. 10–5; first Friday of each month, 5–9* ⊙ *Closed Sun.*

The **Historic Rock Ford Plantation** is the restored home of General Edward Hand, Revolutionary War commander, George Washington's confidant, and member of the Continental Congress. Eighteenth-century antiques and folk art are displayed in the 1794 Georgian-style mansion. There are changing exhibits in the Kauffman Barn. ✉ *881 Rock Ford Rd.* ☎ *717/392–7223* ⊕ *www.rockfordplantation.org* 🖘 *$6* ⊙ *Wed.– Sun. 11–3.*

Not far from Central Market, the **Lancaster Quilt & Textile Museum** has a breathtaking display of Amish quilts and other textiles. The quilts were collected in the 1970s by the Esprit Company, where they were displayed in its San Francisco headquarters. Now the quilts have come home to their roots, dramatically displayed with their rich colors and bold designs. This is the place to see authentic Amish quilts, as well as changing exhibits of other crafts. The museum was recently expanded by 4,500 square feet to display special textile exhibits. ✉ *37 Market St.* ☎ *717/299–6440* ⊕ *www.lancasterheritage.com* 🖘 *$6* ⊙ *Mon.–Sat. 9–5; first Friday of each month, 5–9* ⊙ *Closed Sun.*

★ **Wheatland** was the home of the only U.S. president from Pennsylvania, James Buchanan, who served from 1857 to 1861. The restored 1828 Federal-style mansion and outbuildings display the 15th president's furniture just as it was during his lifetime. A one-hour tour includes a profile of the only bachelor to occupy the White House. There are holiday candlelight tours with costumed guides. It's off Route 23, 1½ mi west of Lancaster. ✉ *1120 Marietta Ave.* ☎ *717/392–8721* ⊕ *www. wheatland.org* 🖘 *$8* ⊙ *Apr.–Oct., Tues.–Sat. 10–4; Nov.–Dec., Fri.– Sat. 10–4.*

WHERE TO EAT

$$ ✕ **Annie Bailey's Irish Pub.** A bit o' Ireland in downtown Lancaster, this
AMERICAN popular newcomer is in the former Sayers, Scheid & Sweeton Men's Store. The native Irish owners have decorated the pub with artifacts from Ireland, and the words "Cead mile Failte" ("A Hundred Thousand

Welcomes") are inscribed in the stone inlaid doorway. The menu includes fish-and-chips, Irish stew, and plenty of Guinness and Irish whiskeys. ✉ *28–30 E. King St.* ☎ *717/393–4000* ⊕ *www.anniebailey-sirishpub.com* ▭ *AE, MC, V.*

$$$$ ✗ **Carr's Restaurant.** This refreshingly simple and appealing restaurant
AMERICAN has the feel of a French café and an extensive wine list. Fresh meats, fowl, vegetables, and fruits are featured. Signature dishes are the organic grilled chicken or the jumbo lump crab sauté with puff pastry and asparagus. There's also a take-out food store and a stall at nearby Central Market. ✉ *Market and Grant Sts., across from Central Market* ☎ *717/299–7090* ⊕ *www.carrsrestaurant.com* ▭ *AE, D, DC, MC, V* ☉ *Closed Mon.*

$$$–$$$$ ✗ **Gibraltar.** The Mediterranean flair of this seafood restaurant decorated
SEAFOOD in sunny yellows accented by cobalt blue makes it especially appealing.
Fodor's Choice The freshly baked bread served with olive oil accompanies a changing
★ menu. Selections might include a hearty fisherman's chowder, seared diver scallops with wild mushroom risotto, and potato gnocchi with mushroom ragout. The trendy Aqua Bar is a popular weekend spot with an extensive wine selection. ✉ *931 Harrisburg Pike* ☎ *717/397–2790* ⊕ *www.gibraltargrille.com* ▭ *AE, MC, V.*

$ ✗ **Lancaster Dispensing Co.** Relaxed, fun, and casual, this eatery is next
AMERICAN to Central Market and on the site of the Grape Tavern of 1893. Fajitas, salads, sandwiches, and pita pizzas are served until midnight in a stylish, boisterous, Victorian-style pub. As the name implies, the selection of imported beers is extensive. There's live music on weekends. ✉ *33–35 N. Market St.* ☎ *717/299–4602* ⊕ *www.dispensingco.com* ▭ *AE, D, MC, V.*

$$$$ ✗ **Mazzi.** This sophisticated restaurant offers a blend of Mediterranean,
AMERICAN Asian, and American fare in a lush setting with golden stucco walls, heavy oak furnishings, lots of greenery, and fine artwork. Among the many favorites are Chilean sea bass, fillet of beef with truffled scented potato puree, and poached salmon with spinach mascarpone ravioli. The eatery is 7 mi northeast of Lancaster. ✉ *46 Deborah Dr., off Rte. 23, Leola* ☎ *717/656–8983* ⊕ *www.restaurantmazzi.com* ▭ *AE, D, DC, MC, V.*

$$$$ ✗ **The Pressroom.** The menus look like newspapers at this casual bistro in an old warehouse. The classic mahogany bar adds to the atmosphere. The open kitchen has an exposed baking hearth. There's a nice selection of crab cakes, burgers, salads, and pasta dishes. In summer the brick patio is a pleasant outdoor dining spot. ✉ *26–28 W. King St.* ☎ *717/399–5400* ⊕ *www.pressroomrestaurant.com* ▭ *AE, MC, V.*

$$$$ ✗ **Stockyard Inn.** The Stockyard Inn, a longtime Lancaster tradition with a refined elegance, serves well-prepared and -presented steaks and seafood. The restaurant's best-known dishes include lump crab cakes with mustard sauce, hand-cut steaks, and rack of lamb. ✉ *26–1147 Lititz Pike* ☎ *717/394–7975* ⊕ *www.stockyardinn.com* ▭ *AE, MC, V.*

WHERE TO STAY

$$–$$$ ▦ **Arts Hotel.** This downtown boutique hotel occupies what was once a tobacco warehouse in the 1800s. The sleek rooms have executive desks, flat-screen TVs, iPod docking stations, and free Wi-Fi. There

are also whirlpool tubs in the suites. Local artists' work adorns the walls of rooms, which are decorated with exposed brick, stone, wood floors, and chestnut beams that create a rustic yet sophisticated feel. The adjoining restaurant and bar, John J. Jeffries, offers impeccably prepared organic dishes, such as aged bison steak in a merlot reduction with chimichurri. **Pros:** hip rooms; great restaurant; personalized service. **Cons:** located away from downtown attractions; on a busy street; no pool. ☒ *300 Harrisburg Ave.,* ☎ *717/299–3000 or 866/720–2787* ⊕ *www.lancasterartshotel.com* ➟ *63 rooms, 3 suites* ⟷ *In-room: Wi-Fi. In-hotel: restaurant, gym, bicycles, Wi-Fi, parking (free), no-smoking rooms* ▭ *AE, DC, MC, V* ⦿ *CP.*

$$ 🛏 **King's Cottage.** An elegant 1913 Spanish-style mansion on the ★ National Register of Historic Places has been transformed into this B&B. The blend of architectural elements includes an Art Deco fireplace and stained-glass windows. Several rooms have whirlpools and fireplaces, including two first-floor bedroom chambers. An outdoor hot tub accented by a soothing goldfish pond and patio is pleasant in warm weather. The price includes full breakfast and afternoon tea. **Pros:** gourmet breakfast and afternoon tea; personal service; homey ambience. **Cons:** some rooms on small side; fireplaces are electric; not in a country setting. ☒ *1049 E. King St.* ☎ *717/397–1017 or 800/747–8717* ⊕ *www.kingscottagebb.com* ➟ *7 rooms, 1 cottage* ⟷ *In-room: DVD, Wi-Fi. In-hotel: Wi-Fi, parking (no fee), no kids under 16.* ▭ *D, MC, V* ⦿ *BP.*

$–$$ 🛏 **Lancaster Host Resort and Conference Center.** This sprawling family resort is in the heart of the busy Pennsylvania Dutch tourist area and features cherrywood furnishings. You can jog or rent a bike and ride around the beautifully landscaped golf course and grounds. **Pros:** knowledgeable staff; indoor pool; plenty of activities. **Cons:** some dingy hallways; gym needs upgrading; smell of manure from nearby fields. ☒ *2300 Lincoln Hwy. E, U.S. 30* ☎ *717/299–5500 or 800/233–0121* ⊕ *www.lancasterhost.com* ➟ *330 rooms, 8 suites* ⟷ *In-room: Internet. In-hotel: 2 restaurants, room service, bar, golf course, tennis courts, pools, bicycles* ▭ *AE, DC, MC, V.*

$$–$$$ 🛏 **Lancaster Marriott at Penn Square.** In the heart of the city, this 19-story upscale hotel incorporates the Beaux–Arts–style facade of the former Watt & Shand department store with a 15-story tower completed in 2009. The contemporary interior boasts a sprawling lobby with cathedral ceilings, marble floors, mahogany paneling, and free Wi-Fi access. The sleekly furnished guest rooms offer a "plug and play" system to link laptops with TVs. The hotel is part of a new convention center facility that offers 90,000 square feet of meeting space. **Pros:** downtown location; newly opened in 2009; upscale amenities. **Cons:** business-oriented focus; no period charm; urban setting. ☒ *25 S. Queen St.* ☎ *717/239–1600* ⊕ *www.marriott.com* ➟ *299 rooms* ⟷ *In-room: safe, Wi-Fi. In-hotel: restaurant, room service, pool, gym, spa, Wi-Fi, parking (fee).* ▭ *AE, DC, MC, V.*

$$–$$$ 🛏 **Willow Valley Family Resort and Conference Center.** Smorgasbord meals, ☾ large rooms, a duck pond, and indoor pools make this large, stylish resort a great family place. Rooms are spread out over three buildings;

those in the Atrium Building surround a striking skylighted lobby. The extensive Sunday brunch in the Palm Court is a favored feast. Since the resort is Mennonite-owned, liquor is not permitted on the premises. **Pros:** indoor pools; fresh baked goods; central location. **Cons:** restaurant gets mixed reviews; no alcohol served. ⊠ *2416 Willow St. Pike* ☎ *717/464–2711 or 800/444–1714* ⊕ *www.willowvalley.com* ⇥ *342 rooms, 50 suites* ♿ *In-hotel: 2 restaurants, golf course, tennis courts, pools, gym* ⊟ *AE, D, DC, MC, V.*

NIGHTLIFE AND THE ARTS

The 1,600-seat **American Music Theatre** (⊠ *2425 Lincoln Hwy. E* ☎ *717/397–7700 or 800/648–4102* ⊕ *www.americanmusictheatre. com*) presents full-scale original musical productions and an annual Christmas show. There are late-morning, afternoon, and evening shows. Each season there are 40–50 celebrity concerts, with performers such as Bill Cosby, Hall & Oates, and the Beach Boys.

The draws at the 400-seat **Dutch Apple Dinner Theater** (⊠ *510 Centerville Rd., at U.S. 30* ☎ *717/898–1900* ⊕ *www.dutchapple.com*) are the candlelight buffet and Broadway musicals, such as *Rent, Singin' in the Rain,* and *The King and I!* Call for reservations.

A National Historic Landmark, the 1853 **Fulton Opera House** (⊠ *12 N. Prince St.* ☎ *717/397–7425* ⊕ *www.fultontheatre.org*) has been sumptuously renovated. It's home to the Fulton Theater Company, the Actors Company of Pennsylvania, the Lancaster Symphony Orchestra, and the Lancaster Opera. Recent shows have included *Les Miserables* and *Annie.*

SHOPPING

CRAFTS   Although craftspeople in the Lancaster County area produce fine quilts and needlework, much of the best work is sold to galleries around the country and never shows up in local shops. Still, there are some good craft shops to check out.

The **Olde Mill House Shoppes** (⊠ *105 Strasburg Pike* ☎ *717/299–0678*), one of the area's oldest country stores, stocks a fine selection of pottery, folk art, and country-style furniture. Among the few places that carry fine local crafts is the **Weathervane Shop** (⊠ *2451 Kissel Hill Rd.* ☎ *717/569–9312*) at the Landis Valley Museum. Many of the items are made on the premises, and they include everything from braided rugs to cane chairs.

OUTLETS   U.S. 30 is lined with outlet malls. With more than 120 stores, from Bass to Nike, **Rockvale Square Outlets** (⊠ *U.S. 30 and Rte. 896* ☎ *717/293–9595*) is the largest outlet center in Lancaster. The **Tanger Outlet Center** (⊠ *311 Outlet Dr., U.S. 30 E* ☎ *717/392–7260* ⊕ *www.tangeroutlet. com*) is a collection of 60 upscale outlets, including Banana Republic, Ralph Lauren, and J. Crew.

INTERCOURSE

10 mi east of Lancaster via Rte. 340.

The town's odd name came from the Colonial term for intersection. At the intersection of Routes 340 and 772, this town is a center of Amish

11

life. Between Intercourse and Bird-in-Hand up the road, the Amish way of life can be explored by observing their farms, crafts, quilts, and various educational experiences.

GETTING HERE AND AROUND

From downtown Lancaster, the drive to Intercourse is a straight shot east along Route 340 to Route 772, the center of this small town.

EXPLORING

The **People's Place** is a "people-to-people interpretation center," providing an excellent introduction to the Amish, Mennonite, and Hutterite communities. There's a gallery showcasing the paintings of local communities by P. Buckley Moss and an extensive bookshop with cookbooks and other titles. Across the street you can find the People's Place Quilt Museum and the Olde Country Store, with handcrafted furniture, quilts, folk art, and other items. ⊠ *3513 Old Philadelphia Pike, Rte. 340* ☎ *717/768–7171 or 800/390–8436* ⊕ *www.thepeoplesplace.com* 🎫 *Free* ☉ *Memorial Day–Labor Day, Mon.–Sat. 9:30–8; Labor Day–Memorial Day, Mon.–Sat. 9:30–5.*

WHERE TO EAT AND STAY

¢–$ ✕ **Kling House.** This family home has been converted into a pleasant, casual restaurant serving innovative breakfast and lunch selections. Favorites include the Peach Melba pancakes for breakfast and the cranberry chicken salad sandwich for lunch. The complimentary appetizer of crackers with cream cheese and red-pepper jam is a treat, as are the homemade soups and desserts, such as luscious shoofly pie and extra fluffy coconut cream pie. A children's menu is available. It's open for breakfast and lunch throughout the year, but open for dinner only Thursday to Saturday evenings from April to November. ⊠ *Kitchen Kettle Village, Rtes. 340 and 772* ☎ *717/768–8261* ⊕ *www.kitchenkettle.com/klinghouse.html* ⊟ *D, MC, V* ☉ *Closed Sun.*

AMERICAN

$$ ✕ **Stoltzfus Farm Restaurant.** Homemade Pennsylvania Dutch foods are served family style (or à la carte at lunch) in this small country farmhouse. Many of the ingredients are grown on the farm. Most dishes, such as the ham loaf with vinegar and brown sugar, are so tasty that you'll likely want the recipes—and the owners happily supply them. The price is $16.75 for adults. ⊠ *Rte. 772 E, ½ mi east of Rte. 340* ☎ *717/768–8156* ⊕ *www.stoltfusfarmrestaurant.com* ⊟ *AE, D, MC, V* ☉ *Closed Sun. and Dec.–Mar.*

AMERICAN

¢–$ △ **Spring Gulch Resort Campground.** Glorious farmland and forest are the setting for the pleasantly shaded campsites ($29–$62) and a limited number of rental cottages ($62–$172). A full schedule of weekend activities includes country dances and chicken barbecues. Campsites range from bare-bones tent sites to fully equipped RV sites with electric, water, sewer, and cable hook-ups. Ask for a spacious and quiet "mountain" site. **Pros:** clean public bathrooms; activities for families; friendly staff. **Cons:** some campsites are crowded; cabins need updating; no lifeguard at pool. ⊠ *Rte. 897 between Rtes. 340 and 322, New Holland* ☎ *717/354–3100 or 800/255–5744* ⊕ *www.springgulch.com* 🛏 *500 sites, 4 cottages* ♿ *Flush toilets, full hookups, dump station, drinking* *water, guest laundry, showers, fire pits, picnic tables, electricity, public telephone, general store, play area, swimming (lake and pool), Wi-Fi.*

SHOPPING

CRAFTS   **Amishland Prints** (✉ *3504 Old Philadelphia Pike* ☎ *717/768–7273*) sells prints depicting the Amish in rural daily life as well as landscapes by well-known artist and folklorist Xtian Newswanger. Other local artists like Freiman Stoltzfus, Susie Riehl, and Liz Hess also show their work here.

Fodor's Choice ★   The 39 shops of **Kitchen Kettle Village** (✉ *Rte. 340* ☎ *717/768–8261 or 800/732–3538*) showcase local crafts ranging from leather goods to music boxes. There's also an abundance of relishes, jams, and jellies that you can sample before you buy. Kling House serves local dishes, and stands sell ice cream, fudge, and other goodies. The shops are closed on Sunday.

The **Old Road Furniture Company** (✉ *3457 Old Philadelphia Pike* ☎ *717/768–0478 or 800/760–7171*) has lovely furniture handcrafted by Amish and Mennonite craftspeople. You can find harvest and farm tables, chairs, chests, cupboards, storage cabinets, and desks. The company specializes in custom orders. The store is closed on Sunday.

BIRD-IN-HAND

3 mi west of Intercourse via Rte. 340.

This village, which dates to 1734, remains a center for the Pennsylvania Dutch farming community. Its name, according to local lore, is attributed to two road surveyors, who had to decide whether to remain where they were or travel to Lancaster. They decided to stay, the story goes, when one said, "A bird in the hand is worth two in the bush." An early tavern began to be known as the Bird-in-Hand Inn and the name stuck.

GETTING HERE AND AROUND

Bird-in-Hand is situated just a few minutes drive from Intercourse. Its attractions are clustered on Route 340 or nearby on Route 30.

EXPLORING

☺   **Aaron & Jessica's Buggy Rides** offers four tours of the Amish countryside, each about 3½ mi and a half-hour long, taking passengers through a covered bridge in an authentic Amish carriage. The rides depart from Plain & Fancy Farm. ✉ *3121 Old Philadelphia Pike, Rte. 340, between Bird-in-Hand and Intercourse* ☎ *717/768–8828* ⊕ *www.amishbuggy-rides.com* 🎫 *$10* ⊘ *Mon.–Sat. 8 AM–dusk.*

☺   **Abe's Buggy Rides** is a 2-mi spin down country roads in an Amish buggy with a real Amish driver, who provides a friendly chat about the customs of the Pennsylvania Dutch and the sights along the way. ✉ *2596 Old Philadelphia Pike, Rte. 340* ☎ *717/392–1794* ⊕ *www.abesbug-gyrides.com* 🎫 *$10* ⊘ *Mon.–Sat. 9 AM–dusk.*

The **Amish Country Homestead,** a re-creation of a nine-room Old Order Amish house, is the fictional home of the characters in the Amish Experience film *Jacob's Choice.* On a guided tour of nine furnished rooms, you can learn about the culture and clothing of the Amish and how they live without electricity. The house is part of Plain & Fancy Farm. ✉ *3121 Old Philadelphia Pike, Rte. 340, between Bird-in-Hand and Intercourse* ☎ *717/768–3600* ⊕ *www.amishexperience.com* ✍ *$8.95, $15.95 includes Amish Experience* ⊘ *July–Oct., Mon.–Sat. 9:45–6:45; Apr.–June and Nov., Mon.–Sat. 9:45–4:15; Dec.–Mar., weekends 9:45–4:15.*

At Plain & Fancy Farm, the **Amish Experience** is a multimedia theatrical presentation about the history of the Amish, using multiple screens, three-dimensional sets, and special effects. In *Jacob's Choice*, the teenage main character struggles between traditional ways and the temptations of the modern world. A $28.95 package includes the show, the Amish Country Homestead, and Amish Country Tours, a bus tour of the farmlands. ✉ *3121 Old Philadelphia Pike, Rte. 340, between Bird-in-Hand and Intercourse* ☎ *717/768–8400* ⊕ *www.amishexperience. com* ✍ *$8.95 homestead, $9.95 show, $29.95 bus tour, $39.95 includes all three* ⊘ *Apr.–June, Mon.–Sat. 8:30–5, Sun. 10–5; July–Oct., Mon.–Sat. 8:30–8, Sun. 10:30–5; Nov.–Mar., daily 10–5; shows on the hr.*

The **Amish Farm and House** has 40-minute tours through a 10-room circa-1805 house furnished in the Old Order Amish style. A map guides you to a waterwheel, lime kiln, and even a traditional covered bridge. One of the older attractions in the area, it dates back to 1955. ✉ *2395 Lincoln Hwy. E, Smoketown* ☎ *717/394–6185* ⊕ *www.amishfarmandhouse. com* ✍ *$7.95* ⊘ *Apr., May, Sept., and Oct., daily 8:30–5; June–Aug., daily 8:30–6; Nov.–Mar., daily 8:30–4.*

The **Folk Craft Center** includes a museum, shops, and a bed-and-breakfast, housed in 18th- and 19th-century buildings. The museum presents an authentic overview of the lifestyles and culture of the Pennsylvania Germans, with displays of pottery, glassware, toys, and household implements. An antique loom is on exhibit in the main building. Woodworking and print-shop demonstrations show early techniques. In spring and summer the ornamental and herb gardens come alive with color. Amish quilts and pillows, hooked rugs, punched tinware, and other crafts are for sale in the shops. The B&B, in an 1851 farmhouse, has three rooms filled with handmade furnishings and crafts. ✉ *441 Mt. Sidney Rd., ½ mi west of Bird-in-Hand, Witmer* ☎ *717/397–3609* ⊕ *www.folkcraftcenter.com* ✍ *Donation requested* ⊘ *Apr.–Nov., Mon.–Sat. 10–5; Dec., Feb., and Mar., Sat. 10–5.*

WHERE TO EAT

¢–$ ✕ **Amish Barn.** Pennsylvania Dutch cuisine—generous helpings of meat,
AMERICAN   potatoes, and vegetables, plus breads and pies—is served in this family-style eatery. You can also choose from an à la carte menu. Apple dumplings and shoofly pie are specialties. Breakfast is available, too. No liquor is served. ✉ *3029 Old Philadelphia Pike, Rte. 340* ☎ *717/768–8886* ▭ *AE, D, MC, V.*

$–$$ ✕ **Bird-in-Hand Family Restaurant.** This family-owned diner has a good
AMERICAN   reputation for hearty Pennsylvania Dutch home cooking. The big attrac-
★   tions are the huge weekday lunch and dinner buffets with selections that often include chicken potpie, fried chicken, pork and sauerkraut, and

oyster pie. No liquor is served. ⊠ *2760 Old Philadelphia Pike, Rte. 340* ☎ *717/768–8266* ▭ *MC, V* ⊘ *Closed Sun.*

$$$ ✕ **Good 'N Plenty.** If you don't mind sharing the table with a dozen or so
AMERICAN   others, you'll be treated to a family-style meal of hearty regional fare like baked country ham, crispy fried chicken, chowchow, mashed potatoes, and traditional sweets and sours. More than 650 can be served at a time in this bustling family-style restaurant, set within a remodeled Amish farmhouse. The all-you-can-eat meal is $20. ⊠ *Rte. 896, ½ mi north of U.S. 30* ☎ *717/394–7111* ⊕ *www.goodnplenty.com* ▭ *MC, V* ⊘ *Closed Sun. and Jan.*

$$$ ✕ **Miller's Smorgasbord.** The spread here is lavish, with a good selection
AMERICAN   of Pennsylvania Dutch foods at the daily smorgasbord from noon to
★   7 PM. The Sunday breakfast buffet features omelets, pancakes, eggs cooked to order, fresh fruits, pastries, bacon, sausage, potatoes, and much more. ⊠ *2811 Lincoln Hwy. E, U.S. 30, Ronks* ☎ *717/687–6621* ⊕ *www.millerssmorgasbord.com* ▭ *AE, D, MC, V.*

$$ ✕ **Plain & Fancy Farm.** You can get heaping helpings of stick-to-your-ribs
AMERICAN   Pennsylvania Dutch food at this family-style restaurant. The rustic, county feeling is accented by the pine paneling in the dining room. Selections include fried chicken, roast beef, and chicken potpie. Also on the grounds are specialty shops selling everything from quilts to baked goods, and attractions like the Amish Experience. ⊠ *3121 Old Philadelphia Pike, Rte. 340, between Bird-in-Hand and Intercourse* ☎ *717/768–4400* ⊕ *www.plainandfancyfarm.com* ▭ *AE, MC, V.*

WHERE TO STAY

$ ▦ **Bird-in-Hand Family Inn.** The rooms are simple, clean, and comfortable, and the staff is friendly at this family-run motel. The property offers a host of recreational opportunities. **Pros:** free tour of Amish farm; indoor pools; convenient to farmers' market. **Cons:** small bathrooms; some rooms need updating; no alcohol permitted. ⊠ *2740 Old Philadelphia Pike, Rte. 340* ☎ *717/768–8271 or 800/537–2535* ⊕ *www.bird-in-hand. com/familyinn* ⊅ *125 rooms, 4 suites* ⌂ *In-room: refrigerator. In-hotel: restaurant, tennis court, pools, gym, bicycles* ▭ *AE, D, DC, MC, V.*

¢   ⚠ **Historic Mill Bridge Village and Camp Resort.** This campground is adjacent to a restored 18th-century village that was home to Herr's Grist Mill. Campers get free admission to the village, which has a farm, gristmill, and one of the longest covered bridges in the area. There's a general store, café, and snack bar on the premises. **Pros:** convenient location; cabins have conveniences of home; quiet farm setting. **Cons:** bathroom facilities need updating; sites are close together; some sites are paved. ⊠ *S. Ronks Rd., ½ mi south of U.S. 30, Ronks* ☎ *717/687–8181 or 800/645–2744* ⊕ *www.millbridge.com* ⊅ *101 sites, 2 resort cabins* ⌂ *Flush toilets, full hookups, dump station, drinking water, guest laundry, showers, fire pits, picnic tables, food service, electricity, public telephone, general store, play area, swimming (pool), Wi-Fi.*

SHOPPING

Bird-in-Hand Farmers' Market (⊠ *2710 Old Philadelphia Pike* ☎ *717/393–9674*) consists of produce stands, gift shops, and a snack counter. It's open weekends all year, as well as Thursday, July to October, and Wednesday, April to June and November.

STRASBURG

5 mi south of Bird-in-Hand via U.S. 30.

Although settled by French Hugue-nots, the village of Strasburg is today a community of Pennsylvania Dutch. It's best known as the rail-road center of eastern Pennsylva-nia; railroad buffs can easily spend a day here. You can also visit the Amish Village, which has buildings typical of the area.

GETTING HERE AND AROUND

Strasburg is about a 15-minute drive from Bird-in-Hand and is a compact destination with many of the railroad exhibits and other attractions located within walking distance or short drive from the center of town.

EXPLORING

The **Amish Village** offers guided tours through an authentically furnished Amish house. Afterward you can wander around the village, which includes a barn, one-room schoolhouse, a blacksmith shop, village store, and an operating smokehouse built by Amish craftsmen. From December to February, only the house is open. ✉ *Rte. 896 between U.S. 30 and Rte. 741* ☎ *717/687–8511* ⊕ *www.800padutch.com/avillage. html* ✇ *$7.75* ⊙ *Mar.–Nov., Mon.–Sat. 9–5, Sun. 10–5.*

↻ What started as a family hobby in 1945 with a single train chugging around the Groff family Christmas tree is now the **Choo-Choo Barn, Traintown, USA.** This 1,700-square-foot display of Lancaster County in miniature has 20 trains, mainly in O-gauge, with 150 animated scenes, including an authentic Amish barn raising, a huge three-ring circus with animals and acrobats, and a blazing house fire with fire engines rushing to the disaster. Periodically, the overhead lights dim and the scene turns to night, with streetlights and locomotive headlights glowing in the darkness. ✉ *Rte. 741 E, near Fairview Rd.* ☎ *717/687–7911* ⊕ *www. choochoobarn.com* ✇ *$6* ⊙ *Mar.–Dec., daily 10–5.*

↻ The **National Toy Train Museum,** the showplace of the Train Collectors Association, displays antique and modern toy trains. The museum has five huge operating layouts, with toy trains from the 1800s to the pres-ent, plus nostalgic films and hundreds of locomotives and cars in display cases. ✉ *Paradise La., north of Rte. 741* ☎ *717/687–8976* ⊕ *www.ntt-museum.org* ✇ *$6* ⊙ *May–Oct., Fri.–Mon. 10–5, and Christmas wk, daily 10–5; Apr. and Nov.–mid-Dec., weekends 10–5.*

↻ The **Railroad Museum of Pennsylvania and the Railway Education Center,**
★ across the road from the Strasburg Rail Road, holds 75 pieces of train history, including 13 colossal engines built between 1888 and 1930; 12 railroad cars, including a Pullman sleeper; and memorabilia

documenting the history of Pennsylvania railroading. Newly remodeled and updated, the museum features a railroad town, a gift shop, and a learning center. The "Moveable Feast" exhibit chronicles railroad dining and food shipment across the United States. ⊠ *300 Paradise La., off Rte. 741* ☎ *717/687–8628* ⊕ *www.rrmuseumpa.org* ☜ *$10* ⊙ *May–Oct., Mon.–Sat. 9–5, Sun. noon–5; Nov.–Apr., Tues.–Sat. 9–5, Sun. noon–5.*

ℭ The **Strasburg Rail Road** marks more than 175 years of history, and visitors can step back in time to travel the rails on a scenic 45-minute round-trip excursion through Amish farm country from Strasburg to Paradise on a rolling antique chartered in 1832 to carry milk, mail, and coal. Called America's oldest short line, the Strasburg run has wooden coaches pulled by an iron steam locomotive. Eat lunch in the dining car or buy a box lunch in the restaurant at the station and have a picnic at Groff's Grove along the line. Visit the Reading Car No. 10, a restored business car that carried the top brass of the Philadelphia and Reading Railroad back in the early 1900s. Kids are crazy for the Thomas the Tank Engine shop and special events. Trains usually depart hourly. Dinner trains, which board at 6:30, run April to November. ⊠ *Rte. 741, ½ mi east of Strasburg* ☎ *717/687–7522* ⊕ *www.strasburgrailroad. com* ☜ *$13–$20* ⊙ *Mid-Feb.–mid-Apr. and Nov.–mid-Dec., weekends noon–2; mid-Apr.–Oct., weekdays 11–4, weekends 11–5.*

WHERE TO EAT AND STAY

$$$–$$$$
AMERICAN
✕ **Iron Horse Inn.** Owners Richard and Denise Waller (of the nearby Limestone Inn) continue the tradition of this rustic candlelight pub with a menu that features steaks, seafood, salads, and home-style desserts like warm apple pie. The bar features a number of microbrews. Housed in the original 1780s Hotel Strasburg, the restaurant and pub are open throughout the year. ⊠ *135 E. Main St.* ☎ *717/687–6362* ⊕ *www.iron-horsepa.com* ☰ *AE, D, DC, MC, V.*

$
ℭ
🏨 **Hershey Farm Restaurant and Motor Inn.** This motel just south of Bird-in-Hand overlooks flower and vegetable gardens, a picture-perfect pond, and a farm. It's especially geared to families. Simply furnished rooms are available in three buildings: Country Meadows, Carriage House, and Farm House. The restaurant serves a complimentary breakfast smorgasbord and reasonably priced buffet and à la carte meals featuring homegrown produce. Walking trails lace the grounds. **Pros:** helpful staff; lovely grounds; tasty free breakfast buffet. **Cons:** location a little too close to highway; rooms in carriage house need updating; thin walls between guest rooms. ⊠ *Rte. 896, Ronks* ☎ *717/687–8635 or 800/827–8635* ⊕ *www.hersheyfarm.com* ⇗ *60 rooms, 2 family suites* ⌂ *In-hotel: restaurant, pool, no-smoking rooms* ☰ *AE, D, MC, V* ⌖❙ *BP.*

$–$$
🏨 **Limestone Inn Bed and Breakfast.** Richard and Denise Waller are the gracious hosts at this 1786 Georgian-style home listed on the National Register of Historic Places. The formal living room, library, and sitting room with a fireplace are nice places to relax, as is the fishpond in the small garden. The guest rooms feature Amish quilts and four-poster beds; each has a private bath, and some have old-fashioned claw-foot tubs. The hearty breakfast might include cinnamon-raisin French toast, eggs with country sausage, or creamed chipped beef with Parmesan

cheese. The B&B is in the center of the village, within walking distance of many attractions. **Pros:** Old World charm; fireplaces and stoves in rooms; home-style breakfasts. **Cons:** some guest rooms on small side; lack of privacy. ⊠ *33 E. Main St.* ☏ *717/687–8392 or 800/278–8392* ⊕ *www.thelimestoneinn.com* ⤳ *6 rooms* ⊟ *AE, D, MC, V* ⏀ *BP.*

¢–$ 🏨 **Mill Stream Country Inn and Restaurant.** This country-style motel overlooking a pretty stream has long been a popular choice for affordable accommodations. It's close to Bird-in-Hand Restaurant, where you can enjoy hearty Pennsylvania Dutch fare. **Pros:** friendly staff; clean rooms; complimentary tour of local farms. **Cons:** no elevator to reach third-floor rooms; rooms a little out-of-date; noise from tour buses. ⊠ *170 Eastbrook Rd., Ronks* ☏ *717/299–0931* ⤳ *52 rooms, 2 suites* ⚬ *In-hotel: restaurant, pool, no-smoking rooms* ⊟ *AE, D, MC, V* ⏀ *BP.*

$ 🏨 **Historic Strasburg Inn.** On 16 acres overlooking adjacent farms and woodlands, this hotel offers comfortable, but basic quarters geared toward families and those traveling with pets. The Fireside Tavern ($$–$$$) features burgers, shepherd's pie, and other hearty fare. The luxurious Spa Orange provides massages, foot and nail treatments, body wraps, and aromatherapy with 21 different scents. **Pros:** clean rooms; near attractions; scenic grounds. **Cons:** some rooms need updating; rough towels. ⊠ *1400 Historic Dr., off Rte. 896* ☏ *717/687–7691 or 800/872–0201* ⊕ *www.historicinnofstrasburg.com* ⤳ *102 rooms, 9 suites* ⚬ *In-hotel: 2 restaurants, pool, gym, spa, bicycles, Wi-Fi, parking (free), some pets allowed* ⊟ *AE, D, DC, MC, V.*

EPHRATA

22 mi north of Strasburg via U.S. 222, 15 mi northeast of Lancaster via U.S. 222.

This is a classic American town, with a wide Main Street, a variety of shops selling locally made crafts, and an entertaining farmers' market. Except for the Ephrata Cloister, there's little to remind you of the town's austere beginning as a religious commune.

EXPLORING

★ The **Ephrata Cloister** preserves the remains of a religious communal society founded in 1728 by German immigrant Conrad Beissel. The monastic society of brothers and sisters lived an austere life of work, study, and prayer. They ate one meal a day of grains, fruits, and vegetables, and encouraged celibacy. They even slept on wooden benches with wooden "pillows." Known for its a cappella singing and publishing, the society lived and worked in a cluster of striking buildings with steep-roofed medieval-style architecture. The last sister died in 1813. Guides lead 45-minute tours of three restored buildings, after which you can browse through the stable, print shop, and crafts shop. There's also on-site archaeological research. ⊠ *Rtes. 272 and 322* ☏ *717/733–6600* ⊕ *www. ephratacloister.org* 🎟 *$9* ⏱ *Mon.–Sat. 9–5, Sun. noon–5.*

Fodor's Choice Friday is bustling at the **Green Dragon Farmers Market and Auction,** one
★ of the state's largest farmers' markets, occupying 30 acres. The 400 indoor and outdoor stands run by Amish and Mennonite farmers sell meats, cheeses, fruits, vegetables, baked goods, flowers, and crafts. It's

a traditional agricultural market with a country-carnival atmosphere. There's also a flea market and an evening auction of small animals. ⊠ *955 N. State St., off Rte. 272* ☎ *717/738–1117* ⊕ *www.greendragonmarket.com* ☯ *Fri. 9–9.*

WHERE TO EAT AND STAY

$$$

AMERICAN

Fodor'sChoice

★

✕ **Lily's on Main.** The food is artistically presented in a stylish Art Deco setting; tables are draped with crisp white linens and topped with a single lily. Chef and owner Steve Brown welcomes guests with regional American fare that's known for its "flair," such as Santa Fe chicken with peppers, lobster macaroni and cheese, and grilled meat loaf with roasted onion gravy. You can also dine on lighter fare, such as the crab and avocado salad. The gorgeous view overlooking town is another plus. ⊠ *124 E. Main St., in Brossman Business Complex* ☎ *717/738–2711* ⊕ *www.lilysonmain.com* ☰ *AE, D, DC, MC, V.*

¢–$

ECLECTIC

★

✕ **Nav Jiwan Tea Room.** This delightful café in Ten Thousand Villages takes you to destinations far and near. On any given week the menu may feature foods from India, Mexico, Laos, Haiti, Ethiopia, Nepal, the Philippines, Tanzania, Indonesia, or Thailand. The bountiful Friday evening buffet offers a sampling of foods from the featured country. The lunch entrées are prepared and served in an authentic style. ⊠ *240 N. Reading Rd.* ☎ *717/721–8400* ☰ *D, MC, V* ☯ *Closed Sun. No dinner Mon.–Thurs.*

¢–$

Fodor'sChoice

★

▦ **Smithton Inn.** This B&B, a stagecoach inn built in 1763, has been authentically restored and filled with hand-tooled furniture that is true to the period. Some rooms have fireplaces and canopy beds; the third-floor suite has a skylight, cathedral ceiling, and Franklin stove. Pleasant luxuries include oversize pillows, feather beds, and bouquets of flowers. A huge dahlia garden is the outdoor centerpiece, accented by a lily pond and fountain. Full breakfast is included. **Pros:** authentic period decor; spotlessly clean rooms; charming country setting. **Cons:** location is near busy intersection; some rooms and public areas need upgrading; guest rooms can't be locked from outside. ⊠ *900 W. Main St., at Academy Dr.* ☎ *717/733–6094 or 877/755–4590* ⊕ *www.historicsmithtoninn.com* ⬫*7 rooms, 1 suite* ⚬ *In-room: Wi-Fi. In-hotel: some pets allowed, no kids under 8.* ☰ *AE, MC, V* ⦿*BP.*

SHOPPING

CRAFTS

Ten Thousand Villages (⊠ *Rte. 272, north of Ephrata Cloister* ☎ *717/721–8400* ⊕ *www.tenthousandvillages.com*) lets you shop with a social conscience. Run by the Mennonite Central Committee, it's designed to benefit artisans in low-income countries. The vast store stocks more than 3,000 items—including jewelry, needlework, baskets, toys, rugs, and clothing—from more than 30 countries. The Oriental Rug Room has hand-knotted Persians, Bokharas, Kilims, Dhurries, and Afghani tribal rugs crafted by fairly paid adult labor. Sales in January and July offer excellent bargains. Sample a different country's cuisine each week in the Nav Jiwan Tea Room.

ADAMSTOWN

11

21 mi northeast of Lancaster via Rte. 222 and Rte. 272.

Known as "Antiques Capital USA," Adamstown has dozens of shops, galleries, and markets selling goods from bygone eras. The bigger markets, such as Renninger's Antique Market and Stoudt's Black Angus Antiques Mall, have aisles and aisles of collectibles, including furniture, toys, jewelry, crystal, china, glassware, linens, and coins. For outdoor antiquing, there's nothing like Shupp's Grove, with acres of shady woods filled with an array of antiques and collectibles. There are many other smaller markets and galleries as well.

GETTING HERE AND AROUND

There's no real downtown in this small community, so you'll have to navigate the various markets and shopping areas by car.

WHERE TO EAT AND STAY

$$$ ✕ **Black Horse Restaurant.** With a growing reputation for fine seafood, this
STEAK   restaurant and tavern is just off the Pennsylvania Turnpike. Long setting the standard for certified Angus beef, the Black Horse has expanded creatively, with dishes such as salmon stew with lemongrass and ginger broth and ahi tuna with jalapeño emulsion. There are also 74 rooms and suites in the adjacent Black Lodge. ⊠ *Route 272 N* ☎ *717/336–6555* ⊕ *www.blackhorselodge.com* ▤ *AE, DC, MC, V.*

$$$$ ✕ **Stoudt's Black Angus.** Prime rib from certified Angus beef is the specialty of this Victorian-style restaurant, adjacent to the Black Angus Antiques Mall. The menu also features updated takes on classic dishes, such as seared breast of duckling with a dried cherry balsamic drizzle and local rainbow trout in a lemon beurre blanc. Stoudt's beer, brewed right next door, is on tap. On weekends from August to October, a Bavarian-style festival with bands and a pig roast takes over Brewery Hall. Stop at Eddie's Breads for old-fashioned favorites like walnut-raisin bread. ⊠ *Reading Rd., Rte. 272* ☎ *717/484–4385* ⊕ *www.stoudtsbeer.com/restaurant-pub.html* ▤ *AE, DC, MC, V* ⊙ *No lunch Mon.–Thurs.*

$$–$$$ 🏠 **Adamstown Inns and Cottages.** These two elegant Victorian inns are
★   less than a half-block from each other. Both the Adamstown Inn and the Amethyst Inn have spacious rooms with private baths, handmade quilts, fresh flowers, and lace curtains. A number of the rooms have whirlpools, fireplaces, and European-style steam showers. Set high on a hill, the Amethyst Inn is a true Painted Lady, with an exterior clad in deep eggplant, forest green, amethyst, and gold. New to the inns are two cozy cottages for guests. And there's even an old English sheepdog to greet you. A hearty continental breakfast is served each morning in the Adamstown Inn's dining room. **Pros:** romantic atmosphere; nice bathrooms; friendly innkeepers. **Cons:** buildings are a little creaky; full breakfast not available. ⊠ *62 W. Main St.* ☎ *717/484–0800 or 800/594–4808* ⊕ *www.adamstown.com* ➔ *10 rooms, 2 cottages* ⚴ *In-hotel: no kids under 12, no-smoking rooms* ▤ *AE, MC, V* ⏣ *CP.*

SHOPPING

The huge **Renninger's Antique and Collector's Market** (⊠ *Rte. 272, ½ mi north of Pennsylvania Tpke., Exit 21* ☎ *717/336–2177* ⊕ *www.renningers.com*) draws thousands of collectors and dealers on Sunday from 7:30 to 5. Nearly 400 indoor stalls, open year-round, overflow with every conceivable type of antique; on good-weather days the outdoor flea market adds to the selection. There are food stands, too.

★ **Shupp's Grove** (✉ *Off Rte. 897, south of Adamstown* ☎ *717/484–4115* ⊕ *www.shuppsgrove.com*), the oldest of the Adamstown antiques markets, has acres of dealers in a tree-shaded grove. Tables are piled with antiques, art, and collectibles. The market is open weekends, 7–5, from April through October. Extravaganzas offer fascinating displays of antiques and collectibles.

At **Stoudt's Black Angus Antiques Mall** (✉ *Rte. 272* ☎ *717/484–4385*) more than 500 dealers display old books and prints, estate jewelry, linens, china and glassware, coins, and plenty of furniture, inside and outside. There's also a restaurant. The mall is open Sunday, 7:30–5.

LITITZ

10 mi southwest of Ephrata via Rothsville Rd., 20 mi southwest of Adamstown via U.S. 222.

Lititz was founded in 1756 by Moravians who settled in Pennsylvania and created their own private community. Lititz's historic character remains, with tree-shaded streets lined with 18th-century houses and shops selling antiques, crafts, clothing, and gifts. This is a great town for walking; be sure to see the beautiful Moravian church, which dates back to 1787 and served as a hospital to treat the wounded during the Revolutionary War.

GETTING HERE AND AROUND

Park the car and take a stroll around this quaint town that still retains much of its 18th-century charm.

EXPLORING

☺ At the **Julius Sturgis Pretzel House,** the oldest pretzel bakery in the United States, the dough is knotted by hand and baked in brick ovens the same way Julius Sturgis did it in 1861. It's worth checking out if you want to learn the art of pretzel twisting. ✉ *219 E. Main St.* ☎ *717/626–4354* ⊕ *www.juliussturgis.com* ☒ *$3* ⊙ *Jan.–mid-Mar., Mon.–Fri. 10–4, Sat. 9–5; mid-Mar.–Dec., Mon.–Sat. 9–5.*

☺ The first thing you notice in Lititz is the smell of chocolate emanating from the **Wilbur Chocolate Company.** Their Candy Americana Museum and Factory Candy Outlet is a small museum of candy-related memorabilia with a large retail store filled with brand-name chocolates made with Wilbur Chocolate and signature Wilbur Buds. ✉ *48 N. Broad St.* ☎ *717/626–3249* ⊕ *www.wilburbuds.com* ☒ *Free* ⊙ *Mon.–Sat. 10–5.*

WHERE TO STAY

$ **General Sutter Inn.** Built in 1764, this is the oldest continuously run inn
★ in Pennsylvania. It was named after the man who founded Sacramento in 1839, only to lose his home during the frenzy of the gold rush. He retired in Lititz while seeking to be reimbursed by Washington. The inn is on the main square of Lititz, within easy walking distance of the historic district. The 1764 Restaurant ($$–$$$) offers fine dining with an artistic flourish; favorite selections include crab cakes, rack of

lamb, and Pennsylvania trout. In warm weather the brick patio is a favorite dining spot. **Pros:** great on-site dining options; central location; accommodating staff. **Cons:** some rooms need updating; climate control issues; no elevator. ⊠ *14 E. Main St., corner of Rtes. 501 and 772,* ☎ *717/626–2115* ⊕ *www.generalsutterinn.com* ⇌ *12 rooms, 3 suites* ♻ *In-hotel: restaurants, bar, no-smoking rooms* ⊟ *AE, D, MC, V.*

$–$$ ⬚ **Swiss Woods.** Innkeepers Werner and Debrah Mosimann designed
★ this chalet while they were still living in Switzerland. They planted it on 30 acres, creating an open and airy, European-style B&B with light pine furnishings, contemporary country decor, and goose-down comforters in bold checks and patterns. Nestled on the edge of the woods overlooking Speedwell Forge Lake, the chalet is surrounded by extensive flower gardens. Each room has its own patio or balcony. The full country breakfast is a highlight and features a changing rotation of dishes like vegetable quiche and blueberry-orange French toast. **Pros:** delicious breakfast; picture-perfect setting; great hospitality. **Cons:** small guest rooms; no restaurants within walking distance. ⊠ *500 Blantz Rd.* ☎ *717/627–3358 or 800/594–8018* ⊕ *www.swisswoods.com* ⇌ *6 rooms, 1 suite* ♻ *In-room: refrigerator (some), Wi-Fi. In-hotel: Wi-Fi, parking (no fee).* ⊟ *AE, D, MC, V* ⦿ *BP.*

WESTERN LANCASTER COUNTY

You can avoid the crowds and commercialism of parts of eastern Lancaster County by staying in the peaceful towns along or near the Susquehanna River, including Columbia, Marietta, and Mount Joy. There's plenty of scenery and Colonial history to explore, and you can sample good Mennonite food as well.

COLUMBIA

10 mi west of Lancaster via Rte. 462.

They're quiet towns now, but Columbia and other river communities were bustling in the days when boats were one of the easiest methods of transporting goods. Eighteenth-century Quaker missionary John Wright worked in this area, and two of his sons set up a ferry that became an important destination for settlers moving west. Today there are several museums and the tranquil countryside to explore.

ESSENTIALS

Visitor Information Susquehanna Valley Chamber of Commerce and Visitor Center (⊠ *445 Linden St., Box 510, Columbia* ☎ *717/684–5249* ⊕ *www. parivertowns.com*).

EXPLORING

Built in 1869, the **Market House and Dungeon** is one of the oldest farmers' market sites in the state. The basement really was a dungeon; you can still see the ground-level windows through which prisoners were shoved down a chute into the darkness. ⊠ *308 Locust St., off Rte. 441* ☎ *717/684–5249* ⊕ *www.columbiamarkethouse.com.*

★ The **National Watch and Clock Museum** exhibits more than 12,000 time-pieces and time-related items, including early sundials and water clocks; a 19th-century Tiffany globe clock; a German Black Forest organ clock with 94 pipes; moon-phase wristwatches; and the showstopper, the Engle Clock, an 1878 timepiece intended to resemble the famous astronomical cathedral clock of Strasbourg, France. You can also see what a century-old clock shop and a modern watch factory look like. ⊠ *514 Poplar St.* ☎ *717/684–8261* ⊕ *www.nawcc.org/index.php/museum-library* ⊡ *$8* ⊙ *Apr., May., Sept.–Nov., Tues.–Sat. 10–5, Sun. noon–4; June–Aug., Mon.–Sat. 10–5, Sun. noon–4.*

Wright's Ferry Mansion was the residence of English Quaker Susanna Wright, a silkworm breeder whose family helped open the area west of the Susquehanna. The 1738 stone house showcases period furniture in the William & Mary and Queen Anne styles and a great collection of English needlework, ceramics, and glass, all predating 1750. ⊠ *38 S. 2nd St.* ☎ *717/684–4325* ⊡ *$5* ⊙ *May–Oct., Tues., Wed., Fri. and Sat. 10–3.*

WHERE TO EAT AND STAY

$$ ✕ **Prudhomme's Lost Cajun Kitchen.** Owned by David and Sharon Prud-
CAJUN homme, relatives of the famous Paul Prudhomme of New Orleans, this Cajun-style restaurant attracts visitors from as far away as Philadelphia and Baltimore. You can dine on authentic Louisiana fare, such as crawfish étouffée, blackened catfish, gumbo, jambalaya, and fried alligator. The dishes are prepared as hot as you like, or more mild mannered with reduced spices. ⊠ *Rte. 462 and Cherry St.* ☎ *717/684–1706* ⊕ *www.lostcajunkitchen.com* ▭ *AE, D, MC, V.*

$ ▦ **The Columbian.** This Victorian mansion in the heart of the village has a tiered staircase that leads to rooms filled with antiques. Several rooms have fireplaces. The rate includes a country breakfast with such favorites as a German apple pancake or cheese and egg casserole seasoned with herbs from the garden. **Pros:** central location; gracious atmosphere; well-prepared breakfast. **Cons:** busy street; neighborhood lacks charm; staff polite but not especially warm. ⊠ *360 Chestnut St.* ☎ *717/684–5869 or 800/422–5869* ⊕ *www.columbianinn.com* ⟿ *4 rooms, 1 suite* ⚭ *In-hotel: no-smoking rooms* ▭ *MC, V* ⏣ *BP.*

MARIETTA

5 mi northwest of Columbia via Rte. 441.

Almost half of the buildings in Marietta are listed on the National Register of Historic Places; the architecture ranges from rustic log cabins to elegant Federal and Victorian homes. This restored river town, now seeing new life as an artists' community, is perfect for a stroll past the well-preserved facades of art galleries and antiques shops.

EXPLORING

At the 52-acre **Nissley Vineyards and Winery Estate,** you can review the grape-growing process on a self-guided tour. This scenic winery, which produces award-winning vintages, has tastings and a shop with bottles for sale. You can picnic on the grounds. In summer there's a concert

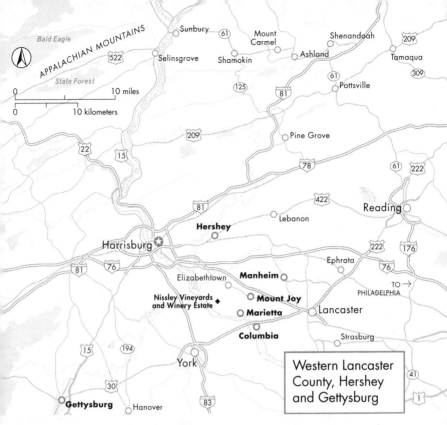

series with jazz, big band, and folk music. The winery is northwest of Marietta near Bainbridge. ⊠ *140 Vintage Dr., 1½ mi off Rte. 441* ☎ *717/426–3514* ⊕ *www.nissleywine.com* 🎟 *Free* ◷ *Mon.–Sat. 10–5, Sun. 1–4.*

WHERE TO STAY

¢–$ 🏨 **Olde Fogie Farm Bed and Breakfast.** Even grown-ups get to act like kids
☺ at this old-fashioned farm inn that gets a "four-pig" rating. Guests can
★ milk the goats and bottle-feed the calves. The accommodations have
names like the Hayloft Suite and the Pig Pen Room. The old frame home
has an Amish cookstove; the property has a creek, a playhouse, and a
stable for pony rides. The swimming pool has waterfalls and a sitting
area. A hearty breakfast is included if you stay in one of the rooms;
guests in the apartments are given ingredients to make their own. **Pros:**
welcoming hosts; great for children; lovely gardens; swimming pond.
Cons: basic guest rooms; few amenities; early hours of a working farm.
⊠ *106 Stackstown Rd.* ☎ *717/426–3992 or 877/653–3644* ⊕ *www.*
oldefogiefarm.com 🛏 *2 rooms, 2 apartments* 🛎 *In-room: no phone,*
kitchen (some), refrigerator (some). In-hotel: children's programs (all
ages), parking (no fee). ▤ *MC, V* ❙◯❙ *BP.*

SHOPPING

George's Woodcrafts (✉ *9 Reichs Church Rd.17547* ☎ *717/426–1004 or 800/799–1685* ⊕ *www.georgeswood.com*) sells handcrafted furniture for every room in the house in walnut, oak, maple, and cherry. You can watch pieces being made and then place an order. The store is closed Sunday.

MOUNT JOY

5 mi northeast of Marietta via Rte. 772.

A historic brewery and some good restaurants are the highlights of this little town.

EXPLORING

Dating from before the Civil War, **Bube's Brewery** is the only brewery in the United States that has remained intact since the mid-19th century. A guided tour takes you 43 feet below the street into the brewery's vaults and passages, which were built in a cave; these passages also served as part of the Underground Railroad. Three different restaurants are found on the grounds of this old brewery as well. ✉ *102 N. Market St.* ☎ *717/653–2056* ⊕ *www.bubesbrewery.com* 🎫 *Free* ☉ *Tours Memorial Day–Labor Day, daily 10–5.*

WHERE TO STAY

$–$$ ▦ **Rocky Acre Farm.** The ideal family getaway, this 200-year-old stone
☺ farmhouse was once a stop on the Underground Railroad. This is a dairy farm with calves to feed and cows to milk. Children love the abundance of kittens, roosters, and sheep, as well as the fishing and boating in the creek. There are also free pony, barrel train, and tractor rides. **Pros:** fun atmosphere for kids; filling breakfast; great value. **Cons:** communal breakfast not for everyone; must book far in advance; smell of animals. ✉ *1020 Pinkerton Rd.* ☎ *717/653–4449* ⊕ *www.rocky-acre.com* 🛏 *8 rooms, 2 efficiency units* ⚘ *In-room: no phone, kitchen (some), refrigerator (some), Wi-Fi. In-hotel: children's programs (all ages), Wi-Fi, parking (no fee).* ▭ *No credit cards* �|⚭| *BP.*

HERSHEY AND GETTYSBURG

It's easy to combine a trip to Lancaster County with two popular sights not more than an hour's drive from Lancaster. Hershey, to the northwest, has an amusement park and some chocolate-theme attractions. Gettysburg, to the southwest, is the county seat of Adams County and the site of Gettysburg National Military Park and museums that examine the significance of the Civil War battle.

HERSHEY

30 mi northwest of Lancaster.

Hershey is Chocolate Town, a community built around a chocolate factory and now home to a huge amusement park, the Hershey Museum, and other diversions for children and adults. Founded in 1903 by

11

confectioner Milton S. Hershey, a Mennonite descendant, it celebrates chocolate without guilt, from streetlights shaped like foil-wrapped candies to avenues named Chocolate and Cocoa. Hershey is also known as a fine golf center.

GETTING HERE AND AROUND

From Philadelphia, take I–76, the Pennsylvania Turnpike, west to the Lebanon-Lancaster exit. Proceed north on PA Route 72 to U.S. Route 322 to Hershey. Once there, you will need your car for some attractions. If you're staying at the Hotel Hershey or Hershey Lodge, a free shuttle bus is available to take you to Hersheypark.

EXPLORING

At **Hersheypark** you can enjoy thrilling rides and socialize with 6-foot-tall Hershey Bars and Reese's Peanut Butter Cups. Advertised as "the Sweetest Place on Earth," the park has more than 100 landscaped acres, with 60 rides, five theaters, a "Boardwalk" section with a lazy river and wave pool, and ZooAmerica, an 11-acre wildlife park with more than 200 animals. Begun in 1907, Hersheypark is prized as one of America's cleanest and greenest theme parks. Among its historical rides are the Comet, a 1946-vintage wooden roller coaster, and a carousel built in 1919 that has 66 hand-carved wooden horses. For thrill seekers, some of the newer rides include the exciting Lightning Racer double-track wooden racing coaster, the Great Bear steel inverted coaster, and the Roller Soaker—half roller coaster, half water ride. There are also big name concerts and sporting events at Hersheypark Stadium, the Pavilion, and the Giant Center. ⊠ *Hersheypark Dr., Rte. 743 and U.S. 422* ☎ *717/534–3090* ⊕ *www.hersheypa.com* ☜ *$43.95* ☉ *Memorial Day–Labor Day, daily 10–10, some earlier closings; May and Sept., weekends only, call for hrs.*

At **Hershey's Chocolate World** a free 10-minute automated ride takes you through the steps of producing chocolate, from picking the cocoa beans to making candy bars in Hershey's kitchens. The Chocolate Tasting Adventure (separate admission) offers a multimedia overview of chocolate history and other trivia, as well as samples of Hershey's chocolate. This is the town's official visitor center, so you can get information while tasting your favorite Hershey confections and buying gifts in a spacious conservatory filled with tropical plants. ⊠ *Park Blvd.* ☎ *717/534–4900* ⊕ *www.hersheypa.com* ☜ *Free; $9.95 for Chocolate Adventure tasting tour* ☉ *June–Aug., daily 10 AM–11 PM, Sept.–May, daily 9–5.*

Hershey Gardens began with a single 3½-acre plot of 7,000 rosebushes and has grown to include 10 theme gardens on 23 landscaped acres, along with 1,200 varieties of roses and 22,000 tulips. The gardens come to life in spring as thousands of bulbs burst into bloom. Flowering displays last until fall, when late roses open. Kid-theme areas include a butterfly house and a children's garden. ⊠ *170 Hotel Rd. near Hotel Hershey* ☎ *717/534–3492* ⊕ *www.hersheygardens.org* ☜ *$10* ☉ *Apr.–May and Sept.–Oct., daily 9–5; June–Aug., daily 9–8; Nov.–Dec., daily 10–4; Jan.–Feb., weekends 10–4.*

★ The **HersheyStory**, which replaced the Hershey Museum, is an highly interactive facility that tells all about the life and work of Milton S.

Hershey, who founded the town bearing his name and just about everything in it. On display are a working Hershey Kisses wrapping machine and other memorabilia from the company's long history. A highlight is the Chocolate Lab, where you can take classes on grinding cocoa beans by hand, and tempering, molding, and dipping chocolate. Café Zooka offers a range of light meals, snacks, desserts, and a sampler of hot chocolates from around the world. ⊠ *111 W. Chocolate Ave.* ☎ *717/534–3439* ⊕ *www.hersheystory.org* ☜ *$10 for museum only; $17.50 for museum and chocolate lab class* ☉ *Jan.–mid-June, daily 10–5; mid-June–early Sept. daily 9–8; mid-Sept.–Dec., daily 9:30–5.*

> ## WORD OF MOUTH
>
> "When you're in Hershey, be sure to check out Chocolate World. It's a free ride through the making of Hershey's products.... You get a free sample of their latest product at the end of the ride."
> —Spivonious

WHERE TO EAT AND STAY

¢–$
AMERICAN

✕ **Hershey Pantry.** The decor is warm and homey in this family-friendly restaurant that serves generous portions of simple food made with fresh ingredients. The menu includes sandwiches, salads, and homemade desserts; the hearty breakfasts are notable. ⊠ *801 E. Chocolate Ave.* ☎ *717/533–7505* ⊕ *www.hersheypantry.com* ⊟ *No credit cards* ☉ *Closed Sun.*

$$–$$$

▦ **Hershey Lodge and Convention Center.** This bustling expansive modern resort caters to both families and business travelers. There are four restaurants, including the upscale Forebay. The hotel hosts groups of up to 1,300 in its Chocolate Ballroom, and it can be hectic during conventions. Ask for a room in the Guest Tower. **Pros:** free shuttle to Hersheypark; amenities for kids; choice of restaurants. **Cons:** ordinary guest rooms; sprawling layout not ideal for families with young children; staff could be more responsive. ⊠ *W. Chocolate Ave. and University Dr.* ☎ *717/533–3311 or 800/533–3131* ⊕ *www.hersheylodge.com* ☜ *665 rooms, 28 suites* ⚷ *In-hotel: 3 restaurants, room service, bars, tennis courts, pools, gym, laundry service* ⊟ *AE, D, DC, MC, V.*

$$$$
Fodor'sChoice
★

▦ **Hotel Hershey.** The grande dame of Hershey, this gracious Mediterranean villa–style hotel is a sophisticated resort with plenty of options for recreation, starting with the golf course that wraps around the hotel. Inspired by the fine European hotels Milton S. Hershey encountered in his travels, elegant touches abound, from the mosaic-tile lobby to rooms with maple armoires, paintings by local artists, and tile baths. The Spa at the Hotel Hershey has body treatments that include chocolate bean polish, cocoa butter scrub, chocolate fondue wrap, and a whipped cocoa bath. Outdoor activities include carriage rides, a ropes course, and nature trails, while newer amenities include an ice-skating rink and wing of boutique-style shops. **Pros:** gourmet dining; swimming pool and lush grounds; attentive service. **Cons:** some guest rooms are small; front desk not helpful; overcrowded spa. ⊠ *100 Hotel Rd.* ☎ *717/533–2171 or 800/533–3131* ⊕ *www.thehotelhershey.com* ☜ *234 rooms, 20 suites* ⚷ *In-hotel: 3 restaurants, room service, bar, golf courses, tennis courts, pools, gym, spa, bicycles, laundry service* ⊟ *AE, D, DC, MC, V.*

SPORTS AND THE OUTDOORS

The **Country Club of Hershey** (✉ *1000 E. Derry Rd.* ☎ *717/533–2464* ⊕ *www.hersheycountryclub.com*) maintains two private 18-hole courses, which are available to guests of the Hotel Hershey, and a third course that is also open to the public. Greens fees are $100–$140. **Spring Creek Golf** (✉ *450 E. Chocolate Ave.* ☎ *717/533–2847* ⊕ *www.spring-creekhershey.com*), a 9-hole course, was originally built by Milton Hershey for youngsters to hone their strokes. Green fees start at $13.

SHOPPING

ANTIQUES **Crossroads Antique Mall** (✉ *825 Cocoa Ave.* ☎ *717/520–1600* ⊕ *www.crossroadsantiques.com*) has more than 90 dealers and an assortment of antiques and collectibles. It's housed in Hershey's largest circular barn. The mall is open January–May and September–December, Thursday to Monday, 10–5:30; June–August, daily 10–5:30

Ziegler's in the Country (✉ *2975 Elizabethtown Rd.* ☎ *717/533–1662* ⊕ *www.zieglersantiques.com*) is on a restored 1850s homestead, with several buildings from that era. An air-conditioned barn has space for 92 antiques dealers and an herb and body products shop (open on weekends). Hours are Thursday to Monday, 9–5.

GETTYSBURG

53 mi west of Lancaster on U.S. 30.

"The world will little note, nor long remember, what we say here, but it can never forget what they did here." These words from Abraham Lincoln's famous address were delivered in Gettysburg to mark the dedication of its national cemetery in November 1863. Four months earlier, from July 1 to 3, 51,000 Americans were killed, wounded, or counted as missing in the bloodiest battle of the Civil War. The events that took place in Gettysburg during those few days marked the turning point in the war. Although the struggle raged on for almost two more years, the Confederate forces never recovered from their losses.

At the national military park and at 20 museums in Gettysburg, you can recapture the power of those momentous days. You can see battlefields such as Little Round Top, Big Round Top, and Devil's Den.

GETTING HERE AND AROUND

The most direct route from Philadelphia to Gettysburg from Lancaster is to take the I–76, the Pennsylvania Turnpike, west to U.S. Route 15 South to U.S. Route 30, which takes you into the downtown. From Lancaster, take PA Route 462 West to U.S. Route 30. Once in Gettysburg, you can park your car in town and walk to restaurants, shops, and some attractions, including the David Wills House and the Shriver House. But you will need to use your car to access the battlefield and visitor center.

The Gettysburg Convention and Visitors Bureau, in the former Western Maryland Railroad Passenger Depot, has free brochures and maps of area attractions. Be sure to pick up a self-guided walking-tour map of the town's historic district, centered on Baltimore Street. You can find a number of museums along the route, as well as markers that point out homes and sites significant to the history of the town and to the battle.

PLANNING YOUR TIME

The state-of-the-art visitor's center at the Gettysburg National Military Park is an essential stop to fully comprehend the significance of the battlefield and its impact on the outcome of the Civil War. Plan on spending at least three to four hours at the museum; the admission includes a documentary film and the "Battle of Gettysburg" cyclorama painting. Families with younger children who are concerned about short attention spans may wish to spend less time at the museum and opt instead for a free ranger talk. Rather than attempting to drive around the sprawling battlefield, you're better off hiring a certified guide for a two-hour tour. The guide not only will explain the events in compelling detail, but also drive your vehicle, so you don't have to worry about navigating the sprawling battlefield.

WORD OF MOUTH

"[T]here are wonderful battle-walks, which are free of charge given by the park ranger program. The park rangers are historians (many have written books) and if you love American History, you will love this. You will walk in the footsteps of the soldiers as the ranger tells the story. You can also have a personal guide. He will drive your car, and the tour will be what you want—either a view of the 3 day battle or will go into more detail—all based on what you want to learn about. I highly recommend this too, we do this all the time and learn so much and meet very interesting people."
—Annabel

ESSENTIALS

Visitor Information Gettysburg Convention and Visitors Bureau (✉ 35 Carlisle St. ☎ 717/334–6274 ⊕ www.gettysburg.com).

EXPLORING

TOP ATTRACTIONS

★ There are few landmarks as touching as the **Gettysburg National Military Park,** where General Robert E. Lee and his Confederate troops encountered the Union forces of General George Meade. There are more than 1,300 markers and monuments honoring the casualties of the battle in the 6,000-acre park. More than 30 mi of marked roads lead through the park, highlighting key battle sites. In the first week of July, Civil War reenactors dress in period uniforms and costumes to commemorate the three-day battle. ✉ 97 Taneytown Rd. ☎ 717/334–1124 ⊕ www.nps. gov/gett 🎟 Free ☉ Park roads Apr.–Oct., daily 6 AM–10 PM; Nov.–Mar., daily 6 AM–7 PM.

Fodor's Choice In 2008 the **Gettysburg National Military Park Museum and Visitor Center** ★ moved to a $103 million facility, which makes for an excellent starting point to understand the events leading up to the battle, its significance to the Civil War, and its impact on the town. The center includes a dozen interactive galleries, which feature a compelling mix of artifacts such as a wooden desk believed to have been used by General Robert E. Lee, paired with the latest in interactive video and audio displays. Each section takes its name from a phrase used in Lincoln's Gettysburg Address.

It is also home to the 377-foot **"Battle of Gettysburg" cyclorama paint-ing** from 1884, which has been completely restored including a 3-D foreground. The painting, a must-see in its colorful, life-like depiction of Pickett's Charge, along with a documentary film, "A New Birth of Freedom," are packaged together as a 45-minute ticketed experience. There is a restaurant and a bookstore on site. The Park Service also provides a free map with an 18-mi driving tour through the battlefield, walking-tour guides, and schedules of free ranger-conducted programs which range from walks and talks about the battle to the aftermath and the Civil War experience. Private, licensed guides may also be hired at the center. ■TIP➔ Value package information and online purchase spe-cials are available on the Web site. ✉ *1195 Baltimore Pike* ☎ *717/334–1124* ⊕ *www.gettysburgfoundation.org* ✉ *Free for visitor information; $10.50 for museum, film, cyclorama; $6 for museum only; $55 for two-hour guided auto tour for one to six people* ⊙ *Apr.–May, Sept.–Oct., daily 8–6; June–Aug., daily 8–7; Nov.–Mar., daily 8–5.*

The **Gettysburg Tour Center** is the departure point for two-hour nar-rated tours of the battlefield. Open-air double-decker buses depart every 15–45 minutes. ✉ *778 Baltimore St.* ☎ *717/334–6296* ✉ *$24.95* ⊙ *Jan.–May and Sept.–Dec., daily 8–5; June–Aug., daily 8–7.*

The **Soldiers' National Cemetery,** dedicated by President Abraham Lin-coln in his Gettysburg Address on November 19, 1863, is now the final resting place of more than 7,000 servicemen and their depen-dents. ✉ *Off Baltimore Pike, across from visitor center* ✉ *Free* ⊙ *Daily dawn–dusk.*

WORTH NOTING

The **David Wills House** is where Abraham Lincoln stayed and completed his Gettysburg Address on November 18, 1863. The restored building features seven galleries, including the bedroom where Lincoln slept and worked on the final versions of his speech, as well as the office of Wills, a prominent lawyer who helped direct the city's clean-up after the battle and was a leading force behind the creation of the national cemetery. ✉ *12 Lincoln Sq.17325* ☎ *717/334–8188* ⊕ *www.gettysburgpa.com/willshouse.html* ✉ *$6.50* ⊙ *Mar.–May, Sept.–Nov., Tues.–Sun. 10–5; June–Aug., daily 10–6; Dec.–Feb., Wed.–Sun. 10–5.*

★   The **Eisenhower National Historic Site** was the country-estate residence of President Dwight D. Eisenhower, who bought it in 1950. He and his wife used it as a weekend retreat and a meeting place for world leaders. From 1961 until his death in 1969 it was the Eisenhowers' full-time residence. The brick-and-stone farmhouse is preserved in 1950s style. The farm adjoins the battlefield and is administered by the Park Ser-vice, which sells daily ticketed tours only on a first-come, first-served basis at the Gettysburg National Military Park Visitor Center. ✉ *250 Eisenhower Rd.* ☎ *717/338–9114* ⊕ *www.nps.gov/eise* ✉ *$7.50* ⊙ *Daily 9–4.*

General Lee's Headquarters. General Robert E. Lee established his per-sonal headquarters in this old stone house, which dates from the 1700s. On July 1, 1863, Lee made plans for the Battle of Gettysburg in this house. The home now holds a collection of Civil War artifacts and has a museum store. ⊠ *401 Buford Ave.* ☎ *717/334–3141* ⊕ *www.civil warheadquarters.com* ⊠ *$3* ⊙ *Mar.–Nov., daily 9–6.*

The **Lincoln Train Museum** reenacts the president's journey from Washington to Gettysburg in November 1863. A 12-minute ride simulates the sights and sounds, and features actors portraying the reporters and officials on the train. You can also see the 1890 caboose, model train display, and military rail collection. ⊠ *425 Steinwehr Ave.* ☎ *717/334–5678* ⊠ *$7.25* ⊙ *Mid-Mar.–Apr., Sept.–Nov., daily 9–5; May–Aug., daily 9–7.*

The **National Civil War Wax Museum** presents the story of the Civil War era and the Battle of Gettysburg through more than 200 life-size figures in 30 scenes, including a reenactment of the Battle of Gettysburg and an animated Abraham Lincoln delivering his Gettysburg Address. ⊠ *297 Steinwehr Ave.* ☎ *717/334–6245* ⊕ *www.gettysburgmuseum. com* ⊠ *$5.50* ⊙ *Mar.–Dec., daily 9–5, with extended seasonal hrs. and additional hrs. on weekends in Jan. and Feb.*

The **Shriver House** was the home of George and Henrietta Shriver and their two children, and shows what civilian life was like during the war. After George joined the Union troops and his family fled to safety, the home was taken over by Confederate sharpshooters, two of whom were killed in its garret during the battle. The restored home is a recipient of the Pennsylvania State Historic Preservation Award. ⊠ *309 Baltimore St.* ☎ *717/337–2800* ⊕ *www.shriverhouse.org* ⊠ *$7.50* ⊙ *Apr.–late Nov., Mon.–Sat. 10–5, Sun. noon–5; Dec. and Mar., Sat. 10–5, Sun. 10–2.*

WHERE TO EAT

$$ ✕ **Blue Parrot Bistro.** This bustling bar and restaurant is within walking
AMERICAN distance of many attractions. The Blue Parrot serves an eclectic selection of creatively prepared dishes, including salads, soups, and sandwiches. Innovative entrées include seafood stew and meat-loaf stack. ⊠ *35 Chambersburg St.* ☎ *717/337–3739* ⊕ *www.blueparrotbistro.com* ▤ *MC, V* ⊙ *Closed Mon.*

$ ✕ **The Ragged Edge Coffee House.** This homey café is a great spot to start
AMERICAN your day with an egg sandwich or breakfast wrap, or take a history break with a coffee drink or fresh-squeezed juice. Also on offer are a changing menu of soups, sandwiches, and salads served all day. ⊠ *110 Chambersburg St.,* ☎ *717/334–4464* ⊕ *www.raggededgecoffeehs.com* ▤ *AE, MC, V.*

WHERE TO STAY

¢ ⛺ **Artillery Ridge Campground.** You can pitch a tent or park an RV a mile south of the Gettysburg National Military Park Visitor Center. Horse owners can even bring their steeds. Families may enjoy the fishing pond. The sprawling property includes shaded and sun-drenched sites for tents and RVs, as well as rental cabins with room for up to six people. The campground also offers two-hour guided horseback tours of the battlefield. **Pros:** fishing pond; horseback riding; variety of camping options. **Cons:** crowded in summer; sites are not secluded. ⊠ *610 Taneytown Rd.* ☎ *717/334–1288* ⊕ *www.artilleryridge.com* ⇨ *45 tent sites, 105 camper or RV sites* ⚹ *Flush toilets, full hookups,* dump station, drinking water, guest laundry, showers, bear boxes, fire grates, fire pits, grills, picnic tables, food service, electricity, public telephone, general store, ranger station, play area, fishing pond, swimming pool, Wi-Fi ⊟ D, MC.

$ 🏨 **Baladerry Inn.** During the Battle of Gettysburg, this 1812 home on the edge of the battlefield served as a field hospital. Today it serves breakfast to the guests who overnight here, in the main house or in the carriage house. The carefully restored rooms are filled with antiques; many have fireplaces. Those on the ground floor of the carriage house have their own patios. **Pros:** homey atmosphere; convenient to park visitor center; tasty breakfast. **Cons:** children under 12 not allowed; no Internet connection or TV in guest rooms. ⊠ 40 Hospital Rd. ☎ 717/337–1342 ⊕ www.baladerryinn.com ➷ 10 rooms ⚓ In-hotel: tennis court, no kids under 12 ⊟ AE, D, MC, V �託 BP.

WORD OF MOUTH

"I'm a Civil War nut so I've been to Gettysburg about 7 times. The best time to go is during a reenactment.... The Dobbin house is a renovated 18th century tavern and restaurant. The bar and eating area downstairs will take you back in time and they've got some of the best ribs ever! This place was also a stop on the Underground RR and you can see where the runaways were hidden by the Dobbin family. Don't miss the cyclorama and an organized tour will help a lot considering the size and scope of the battlefields."
—utrenchtman

$ 🏨 **Historic 1776 Dobbin House Tavern and Gettystown Inn.** Overlooking the spot where Lincoln gave his Gettysburg Address, this inn has period furnishings and four-poster beds. There are also guest rooms in two adjacent buildings. The Dobbin House Tavern ($$–$$$) was built in 1776, making it the oldest building in town. American and Colonial fare such as baked king's onion soup and duckling roasted with local apples are served in the tavern's six rooms with fireplaces and antiques. You can dine in wing chairs in the parlor, take your meal in the spinning room, or have dinner in your room. There's also the more casual Springhouse Tavern, with sandwiches and other light fare. **Pros:** convenient to shopping and attractions; period ambience; on-site dining. **Cons:** some street noise; window-unit air-conditioners; limited grounds. ⊠ 89 Steinwehr Ave. ☎ 717/334–2100 ⊕ www.dobbinhouse.com ➷ 4 rooms, 4 suites ⚓ In-hotel: 2 restaurants, no kids under 5 ⊟ AE, MC, V ⍓ BP.

$–$$ 🏨 **Historic Best Western Gettysburg Hotel 1797.** Built before the Civil War, this hotel is in the heart of the downtown historic district. Prominent guests have included Carl Sandburg, Henry Ford, and General Ulysses S. Grant. During the Cold War the hotel served as President Eisenhower's national operations center while he was recuperating at his nearby home. Rooms are furnished in traditional style, and suites have fireplaces and whirlpool baths. There's a cannonball from the battle that's still embedded in the brick wall across the street. **Pros:** great location in center of town; good housekeeping; helpful staff. **Cons:** some street noise; some rooms need updating; parking not included. ⊠ 1 Lincoln Sq., ☎ 717/337–2000 or 800/528–1234 ⊕ www.hotelgettysburg.com ➷ 67 rooms, 27 suites

⚲ *In-room: refrigerator, Internet. In-hotel: restaurant, room service, bar, pool, parking (free), no-smoking rooms* ⊟ *AE, D, DC, MC, V.*

$-$$ 🎥 **Historic Farnsworth House Restaurant & Inn.** Civil War–era dishes such
★ as game pie, peanut soup, pumpkin fritters, and spoon bread are the
specialty at this historic dining room ($$–$$$). The 1810 building has
more than 100 bullet holes from the battle. The tranquil outdoor garden
has sculptures and fountains. Each guest room is lushly and individu-
ally decorated with lace canopy beds, period sewing machines, Victro-
las, and antique clothing. The inn conducts ghost tours of Gettysburg
($9–$16) that begin with dramatizations and stories in the basement's
Mourning Theater. There's an art and book gallery, as well as a Civil
War memorabilia shop. **Pros:** friendly staff; period atmosphere; ghost
tour experience. **Cons:** some rooms need updating; housekeeping could
be better; some noise from other guest rooms. ✉ *401 Baltimore St.*
☎ *717/334–8838* ⊕ *www.farnsworthhouseinn.com* ⤸ *11 rooms* ⚲ *In-
hotel: restaurant* ⊟ *AE, D, MC, V* ¦◎¦ *BP.*

$-$$ 🎥 **James Gettys Hotel.** It flourished in the 1920s, and is now an afford-
ably priced, attractively furnished suites-only hotel. Each suite has a
sitting room with a kitchenette including a refrigerator, microwave
oven, and small dining table. A continental breakfast is brought to each
room. At the neighboring Thistlefields Tea Room you can relax with
full English afternoon tea. **Pros:** convenient to downtown restaurants
and shops; continental breakfast; kitchenettes. **Cons:** some street noise;
desk clerk not on duty 24/7; farther from battlefield than some hotels.
✉ *27 Chambersburg St.* ☎ *717/337–1334 or 888/900–5275* ⊕ *www.
jamesgettyshotel.com* ⤸ *11 suites* ⚲ *In-room: kitchen, refrigerator. In-
hotel: laundry service* ⊟ *AE, D, MC, V* ¦◎¦ *CP.*

SHOPPING

Gallon Historical Art (✉ *9 Steinwehr Ave.* ☎ *717/334–8666*) exhibits original paintings and prints of Gettysburg battle scenes by Dale Gallon, the
town's artist-in-residence.

The Horse Soldier (✉ *777 Baltimore St.* ☎ *717/334–0347*) carries one of
the country's largest collections of military antiques—everything from
bullets to discharge papers. Its **Soldier Genealogical Research Service**
can help you find your ancestors' war records prior to 1910. The store
is closed Wednesday.

Travel Smart
Philadelphia

GETTING HERE & AROUND

Philadelphia is a city of distinct neighborhoods, and some named streets (as opposed to numbered streets) repeat in more than one neighborhood. You can find several streets coming to an end at the Schuylkill River or Fairmount Park, only to resume on the other side. It's important therefore to phone ahead for driving directions—or make good use of your GPS—if you're traveling to destinations in neighborhoods beyond Center City. In Center City the numbered streets generally run north and south, while the named streets run east and west. If you're heading from Old City (on the eastern edge of Center City) to Rittenhouse Square (western edge), you can easily grab a cab, or, if you have about 20 minutes, you can walk the distance. Center City is divided from the Eastern side and the Western Side by Broad Street, which neatly bisects the city and leads directly into City Hall. In recent years a lot of time and money has been put into making the section of Broad Street roughly from Fitzwater Street to Cherry Street into the Avenue of the Arts—a strip that includes the Kimmel Center, the Academy of Music, the University of the Arts, and the Wilma Theater.

Navigating Center City is relatively easy, as the streets run in a grid, but when you leave the perimeter, the orderly grid dissolves, and navigating becomes more difficult. West and South Philly still use the numbered streets, but they are far more winding and complicated.

Within Center City the numbered streets start on the eastern side, from the Delaware River, beginning with Front Street (consider it "1st Street"), all the way west to 25th Street on the banks of the Schuylkill (pronounced "SKOO-kull") River. In between Lombard and Market streets, most of the east–west streets have tree names (from north to south, Chestnut, Walnut, Locust, Spruce, and Pine). Center City has four roughly equal-size city squares, one in each quadrangle. In the northwest quadrangle there's Logan Square; in the southwest is Rittenhouse; in the northeast there's Franklin Square, recently renovated as a child-friendly destination, with a vibrant playground, mini-golf course, and working carousel; and in the southeast is Washington Square. Running along the banks of the Delaware River is Columbus Boulevard/Delaware Avenue. From Spring Garden Street, Delaware Avenue is to the north and Columbus Boulevard is to the south.

▌ AIR TRAVEL

Flying time from Boston is one hour; from Chicago, 2¼ hours; from Miami, 2½ hours; from Los Angeles, six hours.

Airlines & Airports Airline and Airport Links.com (⊕ www.airlineandairportlinks.com).

Airline Security Issues Transportation Security Administration (⊕ www.tsa.gov).

Air Travel Resources in Philadelphia Pennsylvania Attorney General's Office (⊕ www.attorneygeneral.gov). Dept. of Transportation (⊕ airconsumer@dot.gov).

AIRPORTS

The major gateway to Philadelphia is Philadelphia International Airport (PHL), 8 mi from downtown in the southwest part of the city. Renovations in the past few years have made the terminals more appealing; shops and more eating options are welcome additions. For $5.50 you can take the SEPTA Regional Rail R1 line directly into Center City from each of the four main airport terminals.

The Philadelphia Airport has various shops and eateries. If you have the time, you can shop at stores like the Body Shop, Swarovski Crystal, and Brookstone; and choose to eat from a variety of options, including standard fast food (Burger King, Sbarro, Mrs. Field's), sit-down dinner (Cibo Bistro, Jack Duggan's Pub), and some local, more regional cuisine (Philly Steak & Gyro, Philly Soft Pretzels, Chickie's, and Pete's).

As an alternative, you could consider Newark Liberty International Airport (EWR), about 85 mi to the northeast in New Jersey. From there you can take an AIRTRAIN shuttle to the Newark Airport station, then take a NJ Transit train to Trenton, and from Trenton take SEPTA down into Philly. Expect a cost of about $21 per person and a minimum of an additional two hours to your travel time.

Airport Information **Philadelphia International Airport** (PHL ⊠ 8000 Essington Ave., off I–95 ☎ 215/937–6937 or 800/745–4283 ⊕ www.phl.org). **Newark Liberty Airport** (EWR ⊠ Pulaski Skyway, between Rt. 1 and I–95 ☎ 973/961-6000 ⊕ www.panynj.gov).

GROUND TRANSPORTATION

Allow at least a half-hour, more during rush hour, for the 8-mi trip between the airport and Center City. By car the airport is accessible via I–95 south or I–76 east.

Taxis at the airport are plentiful but expensive—a flat fee of $28.50 plus tip— or, if you're heading to a location south of South Street, you can ask to use the meter for a slightly reduced fare. Follow the signs in the airport and wait in line for a taxi. Limousine service and shuttle buses are also available. Shuttle buses cost $10 and up per person and will make most requested stops downtown as well as the suburbs. You can make shuttle arrangements at the centralized ground transportation counter in the baggage claim areas.

The Southeastern Pennsylvania Transportation Authority (SEPTA) runs the Airport Rail line R1, which leaves the airport every 30 minutes from 5:09 AM to 12:09 AM. The trip to Center City takes about 20 minutes and costs $7.00. Trains serve the 30th Street, Suburban (Center City), Market East, and University City stations.

Limousines **Carey Limousine Philadelphia** (☎ 610/667–1576). **London Limousine &**

Town Car Service (☎ 215/745–8519 ⊕ www. londonlimousine.net).

Shuttles **Priority Shuttle** (☎ 215/632–2885 ⊕ www.priorityshuttle.com). **Suvana Philadelphia Airport Shuttle** (☎ 267/390-4122 ⊕ www.suvana.com/philadelphia-airport-shuttle.html).

Train **Airport Information Desk** (☎ 800/745–4283). **SEPTA** (☎ 215/580-7800 ⊕ www.septa.org).

FLIGHTS

All major airlines offer service to and from Philadelphia. It's a hub for USAirways, which offers the most nonstop domestic flights. You can find discounted airfares on Southwest Airlines and smaller carriers like Air Tran. Both USAirways and British Airways offer daily nonstop service from London, and Air France frequently offers discounted fares from London with a stop in Paris. American, United, and Virgin Atlantic are also popular.

Airline Contacts **American Airlines** (☎ 800/433–7300 ⊕ www.aa.com). **Southwest Airlines** (☎ 800/435–9792 ⊕ www.southwest. com). **USAirways** (☎ 800/428–4322 ⊕ www. usairways.com).

▌ BOAT TRAVEL

The RiverLink Ferry, a seasonal (May-September) passenger ferry, offers service between Philadelphia and Camden, site of the Adventure Aquarium, the Susquehanna Bank Center, the battleship *New Jersey*, and Campbell's Field. Ferries depart every hour from Penn's Landing daily between 10 and 5 and from Camden's waterfront on the half-hour, daily from 9:30-4:30, with extended hours and continuous service for Penn's Landing and Susquehanna Bank Center concerts, and Camden Riversharks baseball games. The cost is $6 round-trip, the ride takes 12 minutes, and the ferry is wheelchair-accessible.

RiverLink Ferry tickets must be purchased at the terminal at Penn's Landing (Walnut

Street and Columbus Avenue), outside the Independence Seaport Museum or at the Camden terminal. ■TIP➜ **Payment can be made by cash only.**

Boat Information RiverLink Ferry (⊠ *Penn's Landing near Walnut St.* ☎ *215/925–5465* ⊕ *www.riverlinkferry.org*).

▌ BUS TRAVEL

SEPTA BUSES

Buses make up the bulk of the SEPTA system, with more than 110 routes extending throughout the city and into the suburbs. Although the buses are comfortable and reliable, they should be used only when you're not in a hurry, as traffic on the city's major thoroughfares can add some time to your trip.The distinctive purple minibuses you see around Center City are SEPTA's convenience line for visitors, the PHLASH. The 21 stops run from the Philadelphia Museum of Art on the Benjamin Franklin Parkway through Center City to Penn's Landing. Since a ride on the PHLASH costs $2 for a one-way ticket (seniors and children under five ride free), consider the handy all-day, unlimited-ride pass available for $5 per passenger or $10 for the family (two adults and two children, ages 6–17). These buses run daily from 10 AM to 6 PM from May 1 to October 31. There's service every 12 minutes.

The base fare for subways, trolleys, and buses is $2, paid with exact change or a token. Transfers cost 75¢. Senior citizens (with valid ID) ride free during off-peak hours and holidays. Up to two children (less than 42 inches tall) ride free with each paying adult. Tokens sell for $1.45 and can be purchased in packages of 2, 5, or 10 from cashiers along the Broad Street subway and Market-Frankford lines and in many downtown stores (including some Rite Aid pharmacies). You can also purchase them online at ⊕ *shop.septa.org.*

If you plan to travel extensively within Center City, it's a good idea to get a SEPTA pass. The Day Pass costs $6 and is good for 24 hours of unlimited use on all SEPTA vehicles within the city, plus one trip on any regional rail line, including the Airport Express train. A weekly transit pass costs $20.75. Tokens and transit passes are good on buses and subways but not on commuter rail lines.

You can purchase tokens and transit passes in the SEPTA sales offices in the concourse below the northwest corner of 15th and Market streets; in the Market East station (8th and Market Sts.); and in 30th Street Station (30th and Market Sts.).

Bus Information PHLASH (☎ *215/599-0776* ⊕ *www.gophila.com/phlash*). **SEPTA** (☎ *215/580–7800* ⊕ *www.septa.org*).

▌ CAR TRAVEL

Getting to and around Philadelphia by car can be difficult—at rush hour it can be a nightmare. The main east–west freeway through the city, the Schuylkill Expressway (I–76), is often tied up for miles.

The main north–south highway through Philadelphia is the Delaware Expressway (I–95). To reach Center City heading southbound on I–95, take the Vine Street exit.

From the west the Pennsylvania Turnpike begins at the Ohio border and intersects the Schuylkill Expressway (I–76) at Valley Forge. The Schuylkill Expressway has several exits in Center City. The Northeast Extension of the turnpike, renamed I–476, runs from Scranton to Plymouth Meeting, north of Philadelphia. From the east the New Jersey Turnpike and I–295 access U.S. 30, which enters the city via the Benjamin Franklin Bridge, or New Jersey Route 42 and the Walt Whitman Bridge into South Philadelphia.

With the exception of a few wide streets (notably the Benjamin Franklin Parkway, Broad Street, Vine Street, and part of Market Street), streets in Center City are narrow and one-way. Philadelphia's compact 5-square-mi downtown is laid out in a grid. The traditional heart of the city is Broad and Market streets, where City Hall stands. Market Street divides the city north and south; 130 South 15th Street, for example, is in the second block south of Market Street. North–south streets are numbered, starting with Front (1st) Street, at the Delaware River, and increasing to the west. Broad Street, recently renamed the Avenue of the Arts, is the equivalent of 14th Street. The diagonal Benjamin Franklin Parkway breaks the grid pattern by leading from City Hall out of Center City into Fairmount Park. One final car travel note, the South Street Bridge, which connects West Philly to Center City has been closed for renovations, and promises to be under construction for at least a couple of years. In order to bypass the resultant logjam at the Walnut Street Bridge, you might want to consider going the southern route and taking the South 34th Street Bridge to get into West Philly.

GASOLINE

Most downtown gas stations can be found on Broad Street or Delaware Avenue. Most gas stations in the area stay open late (24 hours in some locations), except in rural areas, where Sunday hours are limited and where you may drive long stretches without a refueling opportunity.

PARKING

Parking in Center City can be tough. A spot at a parking meter, if you're lucky enough to find one, costs between 50¢ and $1 per hour. Parking garages are plentiful, especially around Independence Hall, City Hall, and the Pennsylvania Convention Center, but can charge up to $7 per 15 minutes and up to $40 or more for the day. Police officers are vigilant about ticketing illegally parked cars, and fines begin at $26. Fortunately, the city is compact, and you can easily get around downtown on foot or by bus after you park your car. If you plan to stay in a hotel in Center City, you should call ahead to find out whether they have their own parking facility or will send you to a nearby parking garage for a reduced rate, as it can add significant cost to your total bill.

ROAD CONDITIONS

Traffic flows relatively freely through the main thoroughfares of the city. You will often see Philly natives employing both the "rolling stop" at stop signs (found plentifully in South Philly) and the "red light jump" when drivers sitting at a red light will drive through it just as (or just before) it turns green. When possible, try to avoid driving through the central-most streets in Center City, including Walnut and Chestnut—you'll have much better luck driving down one of the perimeter streets (Bainbridge to the south, Arch to the north) before turning to cut across the city. Chinatown is always jammed with traffic, so you should try to park outside of its perimeter (roughly from 9th to 13th Street and Race and Vine) rather than drive into it. Road (and house) construction is a way of life for residents of South Philly, so be prepared to change roads more than once if you plan on driving through it.

Use extra caution when maneuvering the narrow one-way streets of Center City. Drivers on the Philadelphia stretch of the Schuylkill Expressway (I–76) routinely drive well over the speed limit (and the many accidents on this highway attest to this). If you can, choose gentler routes to your destination, such as Kelly Drive or West River Drive.

RULES OF THE ROAD

Pennsylvania law requires all children under age four to be strapped into approved child-safety seats, and children ages five to eight to ride in toddler booster seats. All passengers must wear seat belts. In Pennsylvania, unless otherwise indicated, you may turn right at a red light after stopping if there's no oncoming traffic. When in doubt, wait for the green. Speed limits in Philadelphia are generally 35–40 mph on side streets, 55 mph on the surrounding highways.

CAR RENTAL

If you plan on spending the majority of your time within the immediate city confines, especially in Center City, you don't need to rent a car. You can take the R1 Regional Rail line from the airport into the city and then use a combination of walking, taxis, and SEPTA buses and trains to get around. From river to river, Center City is about 25 blocks, which takes approximately an hour to traverse. For rental cars, rates in Philadelphia begin around $60 a day and $240 a week for an economy car with air-conditioning, an automatic transmission, and unlimited mileage. This does not include airport surcharges and the various taxes on car rentals, which equal 11%.

In Philadelphia and the surrounding areas you must be 21 to rent a car, and rates may be higher if you're under 25. Child seats are compulsory for children under eight. Non-U.S. residents need a reservation voucher (for prepaid reservations that were made in the traveler's home country), a passport, a driver's license, and a travel policy that covers each driver, when picking up a car.

Major Rental Agencies Avis (☏ 800/331–1212 ⊕ www.avis.com). **Budget** (☏ 800/527–0700 ⊕ www.budget.com). **Hertz** (☏ 800/654–3131 ⊕ www.hertz.com). **National Car Rental** (☏ 877/222-9058 ⊕ www.nationalcar.com).

▌ SUBWAY TRAVEL

The Broad Street Subway runs from Fern Rock station in the northern part of the city to Pattison Avenue and the sports complex (First Union Center and Veterans Stadium) in South Philadelphia. The Market-Frankford line runs across the city from the western suburb of Upper Darby to Frankford in Northeast Philadelphia. Both lines shut down from midnight to 5 AM, during which time "Night Owl" buses operate along the same routes. Tickets may be purchased at all subway stations. The one-way fare within the city is $2, with transfers costing 75¢. There's an extra $2 charge for buying tickets on the train while riding Regional Rail lines

if the station you're leaving has a working ticket machine.

While the subway does have its limitations, it can still be a good way to maneuver around the city and avoid having to park a car, which, during business hours, can be a frustrating experience.

Subway Information SEPTA (☏ 215/580–7800 ⊕ www.septa.org).

▌ TAXI TRAVEL

Cabs cost $2.70, plus 23¢ per 0.10 mi thereafter. They're plentiful downtown and throughout Center City—especially along Broad and Market streets and near major hotels and train stations. At night, during primetime hours, your best bet is to go to a hotel and have the doorman hail a taxi for you. Or, you can call for a cab, but they frequently show up late and occasionally never arrive. Be persistent: calling back if the cab is late will often yield results. Recently, each cab in Center City has been outfitted with a credit-card machine, so you can pay your fare using a major credit card, just tell the driver to put the meter in "time off" mode when you are ready to pay. The standard tip for cabdrivers is about 20% of the total fare.

Taxi Companies Olde City Taxi (☏ 215/338–0838 ⊕ www.215airport.com). **Quaker City Cab** (☏ 215/728-8000). **Yellow Cab** (☏ 267/672-7391).

▌ TRAIN TRAVEL

Philadelphia's beautifully restored 30th Street Station, at 30th and Market streets, is a major stop on Amtrak's Northeast Corridor line. The 90-minute Philadelphia to New York trip is about $45 each way. Amtrak's high-speed *Acela* trains run frequently between Washington and Boston, always stopping in Philadelphia. You can shave 20 minutes off the Philadelphia–New York trip, but it'll cost you about $130 each way. The trains cater to business travelers and are equipped with conference tables and electrical outlets at every seat.

You can travel by train between Philadelphia and New York City on the cheap by taking the SEPTA commuter line R7 to Trenton, New Jersey, and transferring to a NJ Transit commuter line to Manhattan. Ask for the excursion rate. The trip takes an extra 30 minutes, but costs $20.50 one-way.

Amtrak also serves Philadelphia from points west, including Harrisburg, Pittsburgh, and Chicago.

Philadelphia's fine network of commuter trains, operated by SEPTA, serves both the city and the suburbs. The famous Main Line, a cluster of affluent suburbs, got its start—and its name—from the Pennsylvania Railroad route that ran westward from Center City. All SEPTA commuter trains stop at 30th Street Station and connect to Suburban Station (16th Street and John F. Kennedy Boulevard, near major hotels), and Market East Station (10th and Market streets), near the historic section and beneath the Gallery at Market East shopping complex. Fares, which vary according to route and time of travel, range from $3 to $7 each way. These trains are your best bet for reaching Germantown, Chestnut Hill, Merion (site of the Barnes Foundation), and other suburbs.

PATCO (Port Authority Transit Corporation) High Speed Line trains run underground from 16th and Locust streets to Lindenwold, New Jersey. Trains stop at 13th and Locust, 9th and Locust, and 8th and Market streets, then continue across the Benjamin Franklin Bridge to Camden. It's one way to get to the Adventure Aquarium or the Susquehanna Bank Center; New Jersey Transit has a shuttle bus from the Broadway stop to the aquarium on weekends and to the center during concerts. Fares run from $1.25 to $2.70. Sit in the very front seat for a great view going across the bridge.

You can get train schedules and purchase tickets at the 30th Street, Market East, and Suburban stations or online from the SEPTA Web site. Several smaller stations are open for ticket sales in the morning. You may also purchase tickets on the train, but will pay a surcharge if you're departing from a station that sells tickets. PATCO schedules can be obtained from their station at 16th and Locust streets. Tickets for both SEPTA and PATCO train travel may be purchased with cash or a major credit card.

Although reservations are not always necessary, it's a good idea to purchase Amtrak tickets in advance, particularly for travel during peak holiday times. SEPTA and PATCO reservations are not necessary.

Train Information Amtrak (☎ *800/872–7245* ⊕ *www.amtrak.com*). **New Jersey Transit** (☎ *973/275-5555* ⊕ *www.njtransit. com*). **PATCO** (☎ *215/922–4600* ⊕ *www.ride-patco.org*). **SEPTA** (☎ *215/580–7800* ⊕ *www. septa.org*).

▌ TROLLEY TRAVEL

Philadelphia once had an extensive trolley network, and a few good trolley lines are still in service and run by SEPTA. Route 10 begins west and north of Center City and ends on Market Street; routes 11, 13, 34 and 36 each come from the west and south of Center City and also end on Market.

ESSENTIALS

▮ COMMUNICATIONS

INTERNET

Philadelphia has many Internet cafés, located throughout the city (start with any local coffee shop), but the city also has been one of the first in the country to offer inexpensive Wi-Fi to all its citizens. Currently, the citywide initiative is being tested in a zone north of Chinatown and up through North Philly, but there are still free high-speed hot spots available in Love Park (next to City Hall), Benjamin Franklin Parkway, Penn's Landing, FDR Park, Belmont Parkway, and several other locations. Cybercafes.com lists more than 4,000 Internet cafes worldwide.

Contacts **Cybercafes** (⊕ *www.cybercafes.com*).

▮ HOURS OF OPERATION

Banks are open weekdays 9–3; a few are open Saturday and Sunday, with limited hours. The main post office is open 24 hours daily; some branches are open 9 to 5 weekdays and Saturday 9 to noon. All banks and post offices are closed on national holidays.

Many museums and sights are open 10–5; a few stay open late one or two evenings a week, and a number are closed on Monday. Historic area sights are open daily, with longer hours in summer, but it's wise to check ahead.

Most downtown pharmacies are open 9–6. Hours vary in the outlying neighborhoods and suburbs.

Bars and nightclubs close at 2 AM, but there are several after-hours clubs for the serious night owls.

Downtown shopping hours are generally 9:30 or 10 to 5 or 6. Many stores are open until 9 PM on Wednesday. Most downtown stores are closed on Sunday, but the Gallery, the Shops at Liberty Place, and some stores in the Bellevue are open noon–5 or 6. The Bourse is open Sunday 11–5 from spring to fall. Antiques stores and art galleries may be closed some mornings or weekdays; it's wise to call ahead for hours.

▮ MONEY

Philadelphia can be expensive, although it's less so than New York. A cup of coffee will cost $1 at a food cart but $2–$3 at an upscale restaurant; a sandwich will set you back $4–$8. Taxi rides begin at $2.70 and can quickly add up to $6 or more for a ride across Center City. Most sites in Independence National Historical Park are free; museums in the city cost $3–$16.

Prices throughout this guide are given for adults. Substantially reduced fees are almost always available for children, students, and senior citizens.

ATMS AND BANKS

Automatic teller machines are available in the lobbies or on the outside walls of most banks. They can also be found at branches of the local convenience store chain Wawa, and in larger grocery stores.

ATM Locations **Cirrus** (☎ *800/424–7787*). **Visa** (⊕ *www.visa.com/mobileatm*).

CREDIT CARDS

Throughout this guide, the following abbreviations are used: **AE**, American Express; **D**, Discover; **DC**, Diners Club; **MC**, MasterCard; and **V**, Visa.

▮ PACKING

Portage and luggage trolleys are hard to find, so pack light. Philadelphia is a fairly casual city, although men will need a jacket and tie in some of the better restaurants. Jeans and sneakers or other casual clothing is fine for sightseeing. You'll need a heavy coat and boots for winter, which can be cold and snowy. Summers are hot and humid, but you'll need a shawl or jacket for air-conditioned restaurants.

Many areas are best explored on foot, so bring good walking shoes.

RESTROOMS

Public rest rooms are near Independence Mall on the west side of 5th Street and in the Independence Visitor Center on 6th Street between Market and Arch streets.

Find a Loo The Bathroom Diaries (⊕ *www. thebathroomdiaries.com*).

SAFETY

Center City and the major tourist destinations are generally safe, but it's wise to take certain precautions, depending on where you go and how late you plan on staying out. You should always be aware of your surroundings, and take care not to count change on the street or regularly flash an extremely expensive camera or iPod. Keep your handbag on your lap—not on the floor or dangling on the back of your chair—in restaurants and theaters. Exercise caution, particularly after dark, in the areas north of Center City and west of University City; avoid deserted streets. You can ask hotel personnel or guides at the Independence Visitor Center about the safety of places you're interested in visiting. As you would in any city, keep your car locked and watch your possessions carefully. Remember to remove items from your car, especially GPS systems and iPods.

Subway crime has diminished in recent years. During the day cars are crowded and safe. However, platforms and cars can be relatively empty in the late evening hours. Instead of waiting for a subway or train in off-hours, take a cab late at night.

Although crime is low in the Rittenhouse Square section of town at all times, other hot spots can be a bit trickier. South Street and Old City attract a young crowd that can get rowdy, though the areas are well patrolled by police both on foot and by bike. Northern Liberties, while not as young and testosterone-fueled as the other two neighborhoods, still sits in an area that is rather hit and miss. It's best to take a cab directly to the bar or club, rather than park a distance away and walk, especially late at night.

TAXES

The main sales tax in Philadelphia and the surrounding areas is 7%. This tax also applies to restaurant meals. Various other taxes—including a 10% liquor tax—may apply. There's no sales tax on clothing. Hotel taxes are 14% in Philadelphia, 8% in Bucks County, and 6% in Lancaster County.

TIME

Philadelphia and the surrounding areas are in the eastern time zone. Daylight saving time is in effect from mid-March through late October; Eastern standard time, the rest of the year. Clocks are set ahead one hour when daylight saving time begins, back one hour when it ends. Philadelphia is three hours ahead of Los Angeles and one hour ahead of Chicago.

Time Zones Timeanddate.com (⊕ *www.time-anddate.com/worldclock*).

TIPPING

TIPPING GUIDELINES FOR PHILADELPHIA	
Bartender	$1 to $5 per round of drinks, depending on the number of drinks
Bellhop	$1 to $5 per bag, depending on the level of the hotel
Hotel Concierge	$5 or more, if he or she performs a service for you
Hotel Doorman	$1–$2 if he helps you get a cab
Hotel Maid	$1–$3 a day (either daily or at the end of your stay, in cash)
Hotel Room-Service Waiter	$1 to $2 per delivery, even if a service charge has been added

TIPPING GUIDELINES FOR PHILADELPHIA	
Porter at Airport or Train Station	$1 per bag
Skycap at Airport	$1 to $3 per bag checked
Taxi Driver	15%–20%, but round up the fare to the next dollar amount
Tour Guide	10% of the cost of the tour
Valet Parking Attendant	$1–$2, but only when you get your car
Waiter	15%–20%, with 20% being the norm at high-end restaurants; nothing additional if a service charge is added to the bill
Restroom and Coat-Check Attendant	Restroom attendants in more expensive restaurants expect some small change or $1. Tip coat-check personnel at least $1–$2 per item checked unless there is a fee, then nothing.

▌ TOURS

With a fine assortment of Colonial architecture, many museums, and some of the country's most significant historical artifacts and edifices, the city is perfect for a tour. In a relatively small area, Philadelphia offers history buffs, artisans, and architecture aficionados a wealth of fascinating material. Certainly, the most common tourist destination remains Independence Mall, encompassing Independence Hall, the Liberty Bell, and the National Constitution Center among other highlights; but there are many other historic and architectural tours to enjoy throughout the city. The mode of transportation largely dictates the type of tour, be it boat, bus, on foot, or horse and buggy, but you can explore everything from the cuisine of the city to the vast number of gorgeous giant art murals on the city's buildings.

BICYCLE TOURS

Biking in the city can be a bit of a challenge, but bike tours are a great way to see a wide expanse of Philadelphia in a short period of time. Philadelphia Bike Tours offers both guided tours (generally beginning at the Atwater Kent Museum rear garden, at Ranstead Street between 6th and 7th streets) and bike and moped rentals.

Contacts **Philadelphia Bike Tours** (☎ 215/334-0790 or 866/211-3808 ⊕ www.philadelphiabiketour.com).

BOAT TOURS

Liberty Belle Cruises, aboard a 600-passenger Mississippi paddle-wheel riverboat, offers lunch, dinner, and Sunday brunch cruises with a banjo player, sing-alongs, and a buffet. Board at Penn's Landing (Columbus Blvd. at Lombard Circle).

The *Spirit of Philadelphia* runs lunch and dinner cruises along the Delaware River. This three-deck ship leaves Penn's Landing at Lombard Circle and Columbus Boulevard for lunch, dinner, and starlight cruises. Dinner cruises include a live musical revue and dance music.

Contacts **Liberty Belle** Cruises (☎ 215/757-0800 ⊕ www.libertybelle.com). **Spirit of Philadelphia** (☎ 866/455-3866 ⊕ www.spiritcruises.com).

BUS AND TROLLEY TOURS

Philadelphia Trolley Works offers narrated tours in buses designed to resemble Victorian-style trolleys. The fare is an all-day pass, allowing unlimited stops. Board at any stop, including the Pennsylvania Convention Center and the Liberty Bell. The tour takes about 90 minutes and costs $27 ($25 if you buy your ticket online). It makes 20 stops on a route covering the Historic Area, the Benjamin Franklin Parkway, the Avenue of the Arts (South Broad Street), Fairmount Park, the Philadelphia Zoo, Eastern State Penitentiary, and Penn's Landing. For a different kind of Philly experience, you can also try the Philadelphia Mural Arts Tour, a trolley ride that visits some of the more than

2,000 public murals the city has to offer; or the Philly By Night Tour, which gives patrons a chance to see the city under the stars in the comfort of a double-decker open top bus.

Contacts Philadelphia Trolley Works
(☎ 215/389-8687 ⊕ www.phillytour.com).
Mural Arts Tour (☎ 215/389-8687 ⊕ www.
phillytour.com). **Philly By Night Tour**
(☎ 215/389-8687 ⊕ www.phillytour.com).

CARRIAGE RIDES
Numerous horse-drawn carriages wind their way through the narrow streets of the Historic Area. Tours last anywhere from 20 minutes to an hour and cost from $30 to $80 for up to four people. Carriages line up on Chestnut and 6th streets near Independence Hall between 10 AM and 6 PM and at South Street and 2nd Street between 7 PM and midnight. You can reserve a carriage and be picked up anywhere downtown. Carriages operate year-round, except when the temperature is below 20°F or above 92°F.

Contacts '76 Carriage Company
(☎ 215/923-8516 ⊕ www.phillytour.com).

DUCK TOURS
Ride the Ducks offers 80-minute surf-and-turf tours of Philadelphia's historic district, Penn's Landing, and the Delaware River using military-designed land-sea vehicles. The "ducks" are circa-1945 Army DUKW trucks with watertight hulls converted into 38-passenger open-air vehicles. Tours run from mid-March through November and start at $25.

Contacts Ride the Ducks (☎ 877/887–8225 ⊕ www.phillyducks.com).

SEGWAY TOURS
Tours on Segways, high-tech motorized scooters, are available at the Art Museum, allowing patrons to zip along the museum corridor area of the city and along gorgeous Kelly Drive. The 2.5- to 3-hour tour includes a 20 to 30-minute hands-on training session to become acquainted with the machines and costs from $49.00–$69.00 depending on the time of day.

Contacts IGlide Segway Tours (☎ 877/454-3381 ⊕ www.iglidetours.com/philadelphia).

WALKING TOURS
Centipede Tours offers tours of Independence Park led by guides in Colonial dress. Tours of the city's ethnic heritage and of its circles and squares are also available, as are multilingual guides. Walk Philadelphia's 50 different tours of the city and the region focusing on architecture and history. One of the most popular historic tours remains the Constitutional, which hits most of the major highlights along Independence Mall ($17.50 adults, $12.50 children, with a special $55.00 family pack of four). For food buffs, the Taste of Philadelphia: Market Tour of Reading Terminal Market offers a fascinating look behind some of Philly's most well-loved edibles, including soft pretzels and cheesesteaks. The tour is offered at 10 AM every Wednesday and Saturday morning ($14.95 adults. $8.95 children). The more gourmand-minded might appreciate the Center City Food Lovers Adventure, which leads you through various Center City shops to meet with chefs and owners of some of Philly's most esteemed gourmet establishments, tasting farmstead cheeses, hand-made chocolates, and either loose-leaf tea or gelato ($29 adults). For families, one of the more exciting tours is the evening light-and-sound spectacular Lights of Liberty Tour, an interactive experience using the historic landmarks of the city as its backdrop ($19.50 adults, $13.00 children). Finally, mild spookiness can be found during the Spirits of '76 Ghost Tour ($17.50 adult, $12.50 children), which begins at 4th and Chestnut streets and guides its patrons through some of the ancient architecture of Old City, including famous film locations from spooky Philly-based films like *The Sixth Sense*.

Contacts Centipede Tours (☎ 215/735–3123 ⊕ centipedeinc.com). **Center City Food Lovers Adventure** (☎ 212/209-3370 ⊕ www.zerve.com/CityFoods/Philly). **Constitutional Walking Tour** (☎ 215/525–1776

⊕ www.theconstitutional.com). **Landmark Tours** (☎ 215/925-2251 ⊕ www.philalandmarks.org/landmarks.aspx). **Lights of Liberty** (☎ 877/462-1776 ⊕ www.historicphiladelphia. org/night/lights-of-liberty). **Spirits of '76 Ghost Tour** (☎ 215/525-1776 ⊕ www.spiritsof76.com). **Taste of Philadelphia: Walking Tour** (☎ 215/545-8007 ⊕ www.readingterminalmarket.org/events/tours).

▌ VISITOR INFORMATION

For general information before you go, call or check the Web sites of the Greater Philadelphia Tourism Marketing Corporation and the Pennsylvania Office of Travel and Tourism. When you arrive, stop by the Independence Visitor Center on 6th Street between Market and Arch streets.

⇨ *If you're planning to make side trips from Philadelphia or are traveling on to Bucks County or Lancaster County, you should also see Visitor Information in Chapters 9, 10, and 11.*

Contacts Greater Philadelphia Tourism Marketing Corporation (☎ 215/599-0776 ⊕ www.gophila.com). **Independence Visitor Center** (✉ 6th St. between Market and Arch Sts. ☎ 800/537-7676 ⊕ www.independencevisitorcenter.com). **Pennsylvania Office of Travel and Tourism** (☎ 800/847-4872 ⊕ www.visitpa.com). **Philadelphia Convention and Visitors Bureau** (✉ 1700 Market St., Suite 3000 ☎ 215/636-3300 🖶 215/636-3327 ⊕ www.philadelphiausa.travel). In the U.K.: **Pennsylvania Tourism Office** (✉ Destination Marketing, Power Road Studios, 114 Power Rd., Chiswick, London ☎ 020/8994-0978 🖶 020/8994-0962).

ONLINE TRAVEL TOOLS

Philly Fun Guide (⊕ *www.phillyfunguide. com*), **Gophila** (⊕ *www.gophila.com*) and **CitySearch Philadelphia** (⊕ *www.philadelphia.citysearch.com*) each have reviews and events listings for families and adult travelers. The home page for the *Philadelphia Inquirer* (⊕ *www.philly.com*) has hundreds of articles on the region. The Web

site for *Philadelphia* magazine (⊕ *www. phillymag.com*) has information on arts, nightlife, shopping, and dining. For those more historically inspired, **Independence National Historical Park** (⊕ *www.nps.gov/ inde*) offers planning tools in addition to visitor information, and the Web site for the **National Constitution Center** (⊕ *www. constitutioncenter.org*) includes extensive educational resources. For a decidedly different take on the city, **Philly Blog** (⊕ *www. phillyblog.com*) has an often interesting cross section of residents, natives, and travelers opining about the city; **uwishunu** (⊕ *www.uwishunu.com*), an offshoot of the city's marketing department, serves up interesting dish on the dining and nightlife scene; and **Philebrity** (⊕ *www.philebrity.com*) gives city-related gossip and cultural commentary with a healthy dose of sardonic wit.

INDEX